The Translators and Editors

ROBERT M. ADAMS was Professor of English (Emeritus) at the University of California at Los Angeles. He was the author of many books, including *Ikon: John Milton and the Modern Critics; Strains of Discord: Studies in Literary Openness; Proteus, His Lies, His Truth: Discussions of Literary Translation; The Land and Literature of England;* and *Shakespeare—The Four Romances.* In addition to the Norton Critical Edition of *Utopia* (he was translator and editor of the First and Second Editions), Professor Adams was editor of five other Norton Critical Editions including *The Prince* by Machiavelli, *Candide* by Voltaire, and *The Praise of Folly and Other Writings* by Erasmus, the texts of which he also translated. He was a founding editor of *The Norton Anthology of English Literature.*

GEORGE M. LOGAN is James Cappon Professor of English Language and Literature (Emeritus) at Queen's University, Canada, and a Senior Fellow of Massey College in the University of Toronto. He is the author of *The Meaning of More's "Utopia"* and principal editor of the current standard Latin-English edition of *Utopia* (Cambridge University Press), editor of More's *History of King Richard the Third* and of *The Cambridge Companion to Thomas More,* and senior editor of the sixteenth-century section of *The Norton Anthology of English Literature.* At Queen's, he was Head of the Department of English for nine years and an award-winning teacher.

NORTON CRITICAL EDITIONS IN THE
HISTORY OF IDEAS

FOR A COMPLETE LIST OF NORTON CRITICAL EDITIONS, VISIT
www.norton.com/college/English/nce_home.htm

A NORTON CRITICAL EDITION

Thomas More
UTOPIA

A REVISED TRANSLATION

BACKGROUNDS

CRITICISM

THIRD EDITION

Edited and with a Revised Translation by

GEORGE M. LOGAN
QUEEN'S UNIVERSITY

First and Second Editions Translated and Edited by

ROBERT M. ADAMS
LATE OF THE UNIVERSITY OF CALIFORNIA AT LOS ANGELES

W · W · NORTON & COMPANY · *New York* · *London*

W. W. Norton & Company has been independent since its founding in 1923, when William Warder Norton and Mary D. Herter Norton first published lectures delivered at the People's Institute, the adult education division of New York City's Cooper Union. The firm soon expanded its program beyond the Institute, publishing books by celebrated academics from America and abroad. By midcentury, the two major pillars of Norton's publishing program—trade books and college texts—were firmly established. In the 1950s, the Norton family transferred control of the company to its employees, and today—with a staff of four hundred and a comparable number of trade, college, and professional titles published each year—W. W. Norton & Company stands as the largest and oldest publishing house owned wholly by its employees.

Composition by Westchester Book Group
Manufacturing by Maple Vail
Production manager: Eric Pier-Hocking

Library of Congress Cataloging-in-Publication Data

More, Thomas, Sir, Saint, 1478–1535.
  [Utopia. English]
  Utopia : a revised translation, backgrounds, criticism / Thomas More ;
edited and with a revised translation by George M. Logan ; based on the
Robert M. Adams translation.—3rd ed.
      p. cm.—(A Norton critical edition)
  Includes bibliographical references and index.
  ISBN 978-0-393-93246-1 (pbk.)
  1. Utopias—Early works to 1800.   I. Logan, George M., 1941–   II. Title.
  HX810.5.E54   2011
  335'.02—dc22

                                                          2010010623

W. W. Norton & Company, Inc., 500 Fifth Avenue, New York, N.Y. 10110
www.wwnorton.com

W W. Norton & Company Ltd., Castle House, 75/76 Wells Street, London
W1T 3QT

   7   8   9   0

For Nick Adams
and
for Massey College
in the University of Toronto

Contents

Preface

Utopia is one of those mercurial, jocoserious writings that turn a new profile to every advancing generation, and respond in a different way to every set of questions addressed to them. Though small in size and sometimes flippant in tone, it is in fact two very heavy books. The first part propounds a set of riddles such as every thoughtful person who enters public life is bound to ponder, whether living in early-capitalist England, late-capitalist America, or any other society dominated by the money-mad and the authority-intoxicated. He or she must think, What good can I do as an honorable person in a society of power-hungry individuals? What evil will I have to condone as the price of the good I accomplish? And how can I tell when the harm I am doing, by acting as window-dressing for evil, outweighs my potential for good? The second part of *Utopia* offers a set of no less difficult and disturbing questions. For example, Can a community be organized for the benefit of all, and not to satisfy the greed, lust, and appetite for domination of a few? How much repression is a good society justified in exercising in order to retain its goodness? And finally, When we give some persons power in our society (as we must), and appoint others to watch them (as we'd better), who is going to watch the watchers? Can we really stand a society in which everybody watches everybody?

Almost everyone has seen that these are some of the major questions *Utopia* raises; they include many of the classical questions of political theory and social organization. As for what answers the author of *Utopia* meant it to suggest, we are still in dispute; he was a complex man who understood very well that it is not always safe or politic to speak one's entire mind—even supposing it were ever possible to do so. Most of the authorities whose essays are assembled in the "Criticism" section of this edition try to calculate the answers More gave to his questions by studying the way in which they are framed or the contexts, social or intellectual (sampled in the "Backgrounds" section), in which they occurred to him. Some see him as a man modern far beyond his era, proposing prophetic remedies for the problems of an outworn social system; others see him as a conservative, medieval-minded man whose ideal community was patterned on that of the monastery. One denies that he had a serious intention at all, preferring to describe his book as a joke. Some feel that the book can be understood in terms of its literary form or genre, in terms of its predecessors among the imaginary commonwealths, or in terms of the ideals prevalent among More's literary friends on the Continent. One finds the key to its equivocal patterns of meaning in an equivocal pattern of syntax.

But whatever the book "really" meant when it was written, an aspect of it that contextual and critical materials cannot properly convey is the enormous influence it has had on human thought and life. This influence is most obvious in the thriving tradition of utopian (and dystopian) fiction that was launched—and given its name—by More's book. But to grasp the influence of *Utopia* in its broadest terms, we must start from the realization that Columbus's first voyage to the Americas was fewer than twenty-five years in the past when the book first appeared in print. Europeans knew very little about the lands beyond the ocean, and what information they got from the first explorers was sparse, ill-written, and, worst of all, not very interesting, especially when it was accurate. Just at this moment, More appeared with a finished and elegant literary production describing some intriguing people who, in addition to all the "natural" virtues like innocence, simplicity, and native honor, had some very sophisticated institutions perfectly suited to comment on the most notorious abuses of contemporary Europe. No wonder the book took European readers by storm. Naive folk of the early sixteenth century swallowed More's account of Utopia as a fair description of the New World; tougher and more practical ones still tended, when they came to America, to see the natives as potential Utopians or ex-Utopians. In Mexico and South America the best and most generous of the explorers tried to form the tribes and pueblos they discovered into communities modeled on More's account of the principal Utopian city, Amaurot. These, of course, disintegrated; but throughout the centuries and across most of the American latitudes, there have rarely failed to be found little groups of true believers whose social ideals owed something to the inspiration of More's *Utopia*. The book is thus of special interest to inhabitants of the Americas, North and South; it helped make us what we are today by determining, not our immediate institutions, but the nature and level of our expectations. And in the long run that may be the most important, though the least formal, of our institutions.

The power of the book's idealism is a real ingredient of its structure; that fact has been demonstrated, not merely in scholarship but in the testimony of history. We may interpret it as we will, but the way a book like *Utopia* has been read and lived across the centuries is an authentic part of its nature. However we choose to read it, we cannot deprive it of qualities it has proved on the pulses of humankind. On these terms it cannot be other than a compassionate and generous book—that is, one interested in living people and the way they live, not just in verbal phantoms and personae.

Addendum: The Third Edition

I am grateful to Carol Bemis for recruiting me to update the Norton Critical Edition of *Utopia* not least because in doing so she gave me an opportunity to return a favor from a quarter century ago. In 1982, I invited the late Robert M. Adams to collaborate with me in preparing a Latin-English edition of *Utopia*, which would include a revised version of the translation of More's book that Bob had prepared for the first Norton Critical Edition of it (1975), and which was already widely regarded as the best modern translation. W. W. Norton & Company—in the person of the late John Benedict—graciously allowed us to use the translation in this way, and the eventual result was the "Cambridge *Utopia*" (see "Suggestions for Further Reading").

The Norton and Cambridge versions of the translation are significantly different. Bob was a brilliant translator, always passionately engaged with the text and master of a supple and vivid English style. He was also distinctly a translator who was willing to sacrifice the letter of the text to his conception of its spirit. In contrast, I and Clarence H. Miller—who joined me in the preparation of the Cambridge *Utopia* when health problems and the press of other business led Bob to drop out—were, though certainly not unconcerned with the spirit, more concerned with accuracy than Bob had been.

I could not set this latter concern aside when I undertook, for this revision of the Norton Critical Edition, a review of the version of Bob's translation that appeared in the second, 1992 edition. Still, I was determined to leave the Norton *Utopia* as much *Bob's* book as possible and, in particular, not to alter more than necessary a version of his translation that has many admirers (including me): so I have emended it only in those places where the 1992 version either omits something or is not simply *free* but actually misrepresents what More chose to write.

I have also ventured to make minor revisions to Bob's preface, especially to bring what he had said about the "Criticism" section of the volume more closely into alignment with the contents of that section as modified in this new edition. In other parts of the edition, I have felt at liberty to make larger changes. I have pruned Bob's footnotes but have also, where it seemed necessary, added new ones. The "Backgrounds" section has undergone only minor adjustments, but in the selections from modern utopias and dystopias near the end of the book I have omitted the excerpts from *Looking Backward* and *Walden Two* and added excerpts from Ursula K. Le Guin's *The Left Hand of Darkness*. In the "Criticism" section I have restored three excerpts from seminal studies (Seebohm's, Kautsky's, and Ames's) that Bob had included in the first edition but not in the second and have deleted a few items included in the second edition to make room not just for these works but, mainly, for a pair of important studies from the two decades since the second edition was prepared. Fortunately, this exercise of excision and replacement did not need to be a zero-sum game: Norton has permitted me to expand the volume by some 60 pages. Still, I have not been able to find room for a few other items that I would very much like to have included. For an indication of what these are, I refer readers to "Suggestions for Further Reading," which I have entirely recast.

Acknowledgments

Early in the preparation of the edition, my correspondence with Nick Adams, in which he served as an able expositor and advocate for his father's views of translation, greatly helped me in formulating guidelines for my work; I hope Nick will be pleased with the results. Three of my good friends—and favorite scholars—in the More community provided help on particular matters: Dominic Baker-Smith, Elizabeth McCutcheon, and Clarence H. Miller. The prodigious utopian scholar Lyman Tower Sargent gave me advice on the entries for further reading. The fine young classicist Cillian O'Hogan assisted me on a point of Ovidian mythology. Vaughne Hansen of the Virginia Kidd Agency and Susan Allison of Ace Books were of great help to me in a matter relating to the selections from *The Left Hand of Darkness*. At Norton, I want to thank, in addition to Carol Bemis, Rivka Genesen, Candace Levy, and Eric Pier-Hocking. Almost all my work on the edition was done in the utopian setting provided by Massey College.

G.M.L.

Translator's Note[†]

Translations, according to a cynical, sexist wheeze, are like mistresses; the faithful ones are apt to be ugly, and the beautiful ones false. This glib cliché can be supplemented by another one, declaring that the translator's game always involves an effort to have his cake and eat it too. He wants to catch, to savor, to crystallize in his mind the special qualities of his original, and at the same time to transfuse them into an entirely different medium, readable modern English. Thomas More's *Utopia* is not cast in artificial or ornate literary language, as his age understood it. The Latin More uses is simple, conversational, everyday prose such as a lawyer, a diplomat, or a humanist might employ about the normal occasions and business of daily existence. But it is quite unlike modern English in several important respects. The sentences are longer and less tightly knit in patterns of subordination. The main idea of a sentence may be hidden in an ablative absolute, or hung out at a considerable distance in space and syntax. Because it is an inflected language, Latin can scatter the ingredients of a sentence about more loosely than English does, in the assurance that a reader will be able to assemble them within his own mind. An English sentence is expected to do more of the reader's work for him. At the same time, Latin, or at least More's lawyerly Latin, has a whole mass of delicate innuendoes and qualifications at its disposal—double negatives, ironic appositives, pseudo-antitheses, and formal (but only formal) correlatives. To represent the structure of More's Latin syntax in English would create the impression of a whirling chaos; reproducing his stylistic nuances would give rise to a mincing and artificial English, as of a rhetorical sophist. And in either case, the real flavor of More's book, which is casual and colloquial, would be lost completely.

---

† This note originally appeared in the 1975 version of the Norton Critical Edition. It is reproduced here as an illuminating introduction to the nature of More's Latin style, the problems of translation, and the solutions to these problems preferred by Robert M. Adams—who produced translations of unusual grace and verve, not only from Latin but from French and Italian. His characterization of More's Latin can, however, profitably be supplemented by Clarence H. Miller's "Style and Meaning in More's *Utopia*: Hythloday's Sentences and Diction" (see "Suggestions for Further Reading"), which shows that the style of *Utopia* is not as uniform—as consistently simple and straightforward—as Adams suggests [G.M.L.'s note].

A constant temptation of the translator is to go for one quality of his original at the expense of all the others. More's long, loosely articulated sentences can be made swift and clear by rearranging some of their parts and omitting others; his rhetorical structure can be retained, at the cost of sacrificing the colloquial and conversational flavor of his book. In trying to respond to all four demands (for clarity, completeness, colloquial ease, and a sense of contour in the prose), I have consulted from time to time the work of my predecessors. Three in particular proved suggestive and challenging. Ralph Robinson's 1551 rendering is a superb achievement; it still withstands the severest test of any translation, close comparison with the original. To be sure, Robinson is so anxious to squeeze out every drop of More's meaning that he sometimes translates one word by two or four or more; and his language, after more than four hundred years, requires scarcely less glossing and translation than the original text. H. V. S. Ogden (1949) is swift, deft, and modern; but to gain these qualities, he omits not only elements of More's meaning but most of the nuances of More's expression. It is an extraordinarily *flat* translation, as if written for someone in a great hurry; and it occasionally misrepresents to odd effect the actual sense of the Latin. Finally, Father Edward Surtz's recension (1965) of the translation by G. C. Richards (1923) strives as earnestly as Robinson for completeness of expression. But, following a Latinate word order, this version is generally stiff and sometimes wooden; its sentences, with their intricate turnings and grammatical suspensions, often defy articulation by the mouth of anyone who knows and cares for English idiom. Yet all three translations catch intersecting and overlapping sectors of an original that is richer than any of them. In the process of making my own translation, I consulted these various versions freely, and even when dissatisfied with the work of one of my predecessors, drew from it the stimulus of disagreement. A. E. Housman dedicated his great edition of Manilius *in usu editorum*—for the use of those future editors who, he supposed, would *really* study the complexities of a text to which he had merely indicated the first approaches. Less formidably, any "new" translation of a much-translated text can best define itself as a temporary trial balance, for the guidance of future translators in their search for a miracle capable of inverting the action of the old philosopher's stone. For where the alchemist's dream was of turning lead to precious gold, the translator's dream is that he may somehow be kept from reducing gold to common lead.

This translation is dedicated to the memory of Mr. William Nagel of the Horace Mann School for Boys, who more than forty years ago taught me—reluctant and ungrateful infant that I was—the rudiments of the Latin tongue.

R.M.A.

Abbreviations

CW = *The Complete Works of St. Thomas More*, 15 vols. (New Haven and London: Yale University Press, 1963–97)

CWE = *Collected Works of Erasmus*, 86 vols. (Toronto/Buffalo/London: University of Toronto Press, 1974–)

The Text of
UTOPIA

This woodcut image of Utopia first appeared in the March 1518 edition. It was the work of Ambrosius Holbein (brother of the more famous Hans Holbein the Younger). There had been a different and much simpler map of the island in the first (1516) edition (see p. 128 below).

CONCERNING THE BEST
STATE OF A COMMONWEALTH
AND THE NEW ISLAND
OF UTOPIA[1]

A Truly Golden Handbook
No Less Beneficial Than Entertaining
by the Most Distinguished and Eloquent Author
THOMAS MORE
Citizen and Undersheriff[2] of the Famous City
of London

Thomas More to Peter Giles,[3] Greetings

My very dear Peter Giles, I am almost ashamed to be sending you after nearly a year this little book about the Utopian commonwealth, which I'm sure you expected in less than six weeks. For, as you were well aware, I faced no problem in finding my materials, and had no reason to ponder the arrangement of them. All I had to do was repeat what you and I together heard Raphael[4] describe. There was no occasion, either, for labor over the style, since what he said, being extempore and informal, couldn't be couched in fancy terms.[5] And besides, as you know, he's a man not so well versed in Latin as in Greek; so that my language would be nearer the truth, the closer it approached to his casual simplicity. Truth in

1. More coined the word *Utopia* from Greek *ou* ("not") + *topos* ("place"): "Noplace"; perhaps with a pun on *eu* + *topos*, "Happy" or "Fortunate" Place. He wrote the book in Latin, though, and before its publication sometimes called it by a Latin name, *Nusquama* (from *nusquam*, "nowhere"). The whole ornate title here is translated from the title page of the March 1518 edition issued by Johann Froben in Basel. This edition—the third—is usually regarded as the most authoritative of the four published with More's approval, and it forms the basis of the present translation as a whole.
2. As an undersheriff, More's principal duty was to serve as a judge in the Sheriff's Court, a city court that heard a wide variety of cases.
3. Giles—or, in his own language, Pieter Gillis (ca. 1486–1533)—was both a humanistic scholar and a practical man of affairs, city clerk of Antwerp. More's friend the great Dutch humanist Desiderius Erasmus (1466?–1536) had recommended him and More to each other, and they met in Antwerp in the summer of 1515 (see p. 10); *Utopia* seems to have originated in conversations between them, although it was not ready for publication until September 3, 1516, when More sent the manuscript to Erasmus, entrusting him to see it through the press. The first edition—in which this letter is called the Preface—appeared in December, under the imprint of Thierry Martens in Louvain.
4. I.e., the fictitious character Raphael Hythloday. His given name associates him with the archangel Raphael, traditionally a guide and healer.
5. In fact the style of Hythloday's discourse varies, from the informality of most of the account of Utopia to the impassioned eloquence of parts of Book I of the work and the peroration of Book II. Here as elsewhere, the letter is, though a valuable guide to *Utopia*, an oblique and sometimes misleading one, in which very little can be taken simply at face value.

fact is the only quality at which I should have aimed, or did aim, in writing this book.

I confess, friend Peter, that having all these materials ready to hand left hardly anything at all for me to do. Otherwise, thinking through a topic like this from scratch and disposing it in proper order might have demanded no little time and work even if a man were not entirely deficient in talent and learning. And then if the matter had to be set forth with eloquence, not just factually, there's no way I could have done that, however hard I worked, for however long a time. But now when I was relieved of all these problems, over which I could have sweated forever, there was nothing for me to do but simply write down what I had heard. Well, little as it was, that task was rendered almost impossible by my many other obligations. Most of my day is given to the law—pleading some cases, hearing others, compromising others, and deciding still others. I have to visit this man because of his official position and that man because of his business; and so almost the whole day is devoted to other people's business and the rest to my own; and then for myself—that is, my studies—there's nothing left.

For when I get home, I have to talk with my wife, chatter with my children, and consult with the servants. All these matters I consider part of my business, since they have to be done, unless a man wants to be a stranger in his own house. Besides, you are bound to bear yourself as agreeably as you can toward those whom nature or chance or your own choice has made the companions of your life. But of course you mustn't spoil them with your familiarity, or by overindulgence turn the servants into your masters. And so, amid these concerns, the day, the month, and the year slip away.

What time do I find to write, then? especially since I still have taken no account of sleeping or even of eating, to which many people devote as much time as to sleep itself, which consumes almost half of our lives.[6] My own time is only what I steal from sleeping and eating. It isn't very much, but it's something, and so I've finally been able to finish *Utopia,* even though belatedly, and I'm sending it to you now. I hope, my dear Peter, that you'll read it over and let me know if you find anything that I've overlooked. Though I'm not really afraid of having forgotten anything important—I wish my judgment and learning were up to my memory, which isn't half bad—still, I don't feel so sure of it that I would swear I've missed nothing.

For my servant John Clement[7] has raised a great doubt in my mind. As you know, he was there with us, for I always want him to be

---

6. More's 16th-century biographer Thomas Stapleton says he slept four or five hours a night, rising at 2 A.M.

7. Clement (d. 1572) had entered More's household by 1514, as servant and pupil. He later became a respected physician.

present at conversations where there's profit to be gained. (And one of these days I expect we'll get a fine crop of learning from this young sprout, who's already made excellent progress in Greek as well as Latin.) Anyhow, as I recall matters, Hythloday said the bridge over the Anyder at Amaurot[8] was five hundred yards long; but my John says that is two hundred yards too much—that in fact the river is not more than three hundred yards wide there. So I beg you, consult your memory. If your recollection agrees with his, I'll yield to the two of you, and confess myself mistaken. But if you don't recall the point, I'll follow my own memory and keep my present figure. For, as I've taken particular pains to avoid having anything false in the book, so, if anything is in doubt, I'd rather say something untrue than tell a lie. In short, I'd rather be honest than clever.

But the whole matter can easily be cleared up if you'll ask Raphael about it—either face to face or else by letter. And I'm afraid you must do this anyway, because of another problem that has cropped up—whether through my fault, or yours, or Raphael's, I'm not sure. For it didn't occur to us to ask, nor to him to say, in what area of the New World Utopia is to be found. I wouldn't have missed hearing about this for a sizable sum of money, for I'm quite ashamed not to know even the name of the ocean where this island lies about which I've written so much. Besides, there are various people here, and one in particular, a devout man and a professor of theology, who very much wants to go to Utopia. His motive is not by any means idle curiosity, a hankering after new sights, but rather a desire to foster and further the growth of our religion, which has made such a happy start there. To do this properly, he has decided to arrange to be sent there by the pope, and even to be named bishop to the Utopians. He feels no particular scruples about applying for this post, for he considers it a holy ambition, arising not from motives of glory or gain, but simply from religious zeal.[9]

Therefore I beg you, my dear Peter, to get in touch with Hythloday—in person if you can, or by letters if he's gone—and make sure that my work contains nothing false and omits nothing true. It would probably be just as well to show him the book itself. If I've made a mistake, there's nobody better qualified to correct me; but even he cannot do it, unless he reads over my book. Besides, you will be able to discover in this way whether he's pleased or annoyed that I have written the book. If he has decided to write out his own

8. From Greek: "made dark or dim." "Hythloday": its first root is surely Greek *hythlos*, "nonsense"; the second part is probably from *daiein*, "to distribute"—hence, together, "nonsense-peddler." "Anyder": waterless (also from Greek).
9. Tradition has it that this zealous theologian was Rowland Phillips, warden of Merton College, Oxford. But there is no real support for the identification, and the passage may be wholly fabricated.

story himself, he may not want me to do so; and I should be sorry, too, if, in publicizing the Utopian commonwealth, I had robbed him and his story of the flower of novelty.

But to tell the truth, I'm still of two minds as to whether I should publish the book at all.[1] For the tastes of mortals are so various, the tempers of some are so severe, their minds so ungrateful, their judgments so foolish, that there seems no point in publishing something, even if it's intended for their advantage, that they will receive only with contempt and ingratitude. Better simply to follow one's own natural inclinations, lead a merry life, and ignore the vexing problems of publication. Most people know nothing of learning; many despise it. The clod rejects as too difficult whatever isn't cloddish. The pedant dismisses as mere trifling anything that isn't stuffed with obsolete words. Some readers approve only of ancient authors; many men like only their own writing. Here's a man so solemn he won't allow a shadow of levity, and there's one so insipid of taste that he can't endure the salt of a little wit. Some dullards dread satire as a man bitten by a rabid dog dreads water;[2] some are so changeable that they like one thing when they're seated and another when they're standing.

These people lounge around the taverns, and as they swill their ale pass judgment on the intelligence of writers. With complete assurance they condemn every author by his writings, just as they think best, plucking each one, as it were, by the beard. But they themselves remain safe and, as the proverb has it, out of harm's way. No use trying to lay hold of them; they're shaved so close, there's not so much as a hair of their heads to catch them by.[3]

Finally, some people are so ungrateful that even though they're delighted with a work, they don't like the author any better because of it. They are like rude guests who, after they have stuffed themselves with a splendid dinner, go off, carrying their full bellies homeward without a word of thanks to the host who invited them. A fine task, providing at your own expense a banquet for men of such finicky palates and such various tastes, who will remember and reward you with such thanks!

At any rate, my dear Peter, will you take up with Hythloday the points I spoke of? After I've heard from him, I'll take a fresh look at the whole matter. But since I've already taken the pains to write up

---

1. Although More's letters to Erasmus in the fall of 1516 express anxiety about how *Utopia* will be received, there is no indication of ambivalence about publishing it. On the contrary, he told Erasmus "I am most anxious to have it published soon" (ca. September 20) and that "from day to day I look forward to my *Utopia* with the feelings of a mother waiting for her son to return from abroad" (December 15).
2. A late-stage symptom of rabies, which gives the disease its other name, hydrophobia.
3. Evidently wrestling provides the underlying idea.

the subject, it's too late to be wise. In the matter of publication, I hope we can have Hythloday's approval; after that, I'll follow the advice of my friends—and especially yours. Farewell, my dear Peter Giles. My regards to your excellent wife. Love me as you have always done; I am more fond of you than ever.

THE BEST STATE OF A COMMONWEALTH A DISCOURSE BY THE EXTRAORDINARY RAPHAEL HYTHLODAY AS RECORDED BY THE NOTED THOMAS MORE CITIZEN AND UNDERSHERIFF OF LONDON THE FAMOUS CITY OF GREAT BRITAIN

Book I

The most invincible king of England, Henry, the eighth of that name, a prince adorned with the royal virtues beyond any other, had recently some differences of no slight import with Charles, the most serene prince of Castille,[1] and sent me into Flanders as his spokesman to discuss and settle them. I was companion and associate to that incomparable man Cuthbert Tunstall,[2] whom the king has recently created master of the rolls, to everyone's great satisfaction. I will say nothing in praise of this man, not because I fear the judgment of a friend might be questioned, but because his integrity and learning are greater than I can describe and too well known everywhere to need my commendation—unless I would, according to the proverb, "light up the sun with a lantern."

Those appointed by the prince to deal with us, all excellent men, met us at Bruges by prearrangement. Their head and leader was the mayor of Bruges,[3] a most distinguished person. But their main

---

1. Later (1519), as Charles V, he became the Holy Roman Emperor. By 1515 he had already (at age fifteen) inherited the Low Countries, and he was soon to become king of Spain. The matters in dispute between him and Henry VIII were certain Dutch import duties.
   Henry VIII had come to the throne in 1509, at the age of seventeen, and had then seemed to be something close to the humanist ideal of a cultured, just, and peace-loving monarch. By the time *Utopia* appeared, seven years later, this optimistic view had already been somewhat clouded by the king's martial adventurism against France in 1512–14.
2. An admired scholar and influential cleric, Tunstall (1474–1559) was appointed ambassador to Brussels in May 1515 and a year later became master of the rolls (principal clerk of the Chancery Court). Henry made him bishop of London in 1522.
3. J. (for Jean or Jacques) Halewyn, seigneur de Maldeghem, was mayor (margrave) of Bruges. Bruges itself, after a rich commercial flowering in the 14th century (when it was the central distributing point and an important manufacturing center for English wool), was losing some of its commercial clout in the early 16th century, partly because its harbor was silting up.

speaker and guiding spirit was Georgius de Theimseke,[4] the provost
of Cassel, a man eloquent by nature as well as by training, very
learned in the law, and most skillful in diplomatic affairs through
his ability and long practice. After we had met several times, certain points remained on which we could not come to agreement; so
they adjourned the meetings and went to Brussels for some days to
learn their prince's pleasure.

Meanwhile, since my business required it, I went to Antwerp.[5] Of
those who visited me while I was there, no one was more welcome
than Peter Giles. He was a native of Antwerp, a man of high reputation, already appointed to a good position and worthy of the very
best: I hardly know whether the young man is more distinguished in
learning or in character. Apart from being cultured, virtuous, and
courteous to all, with his intimates he is so open-hearted, affectionate, loyal, and sincere that you would be hard-pressed to find anywhere a man comparable to him in all the points of friendship. No
one is more modest or more frank; none better combines simplicity
with wisdom. His conversation is so pleasant, and so witty without
malice, that the ardent desire I felt to see again my native country,
my wife, and my children (from whom I had been separated more
than four months) was much eased by his agreeable company and
delightful talk.

One day after I had heard mass at Nôtre Dame, the most beautiful and most popular church in Antwerp, I was about to return to
my quarters when I happened to see him talking with a stranger, a
man of quite advanced years. The stranger had a sunburned face,
a long beard, and a cloak hanging loosely from his shoulders; from
his appearance and dress, I took him to be a ship's captain. When
Peter saw me, he approached and greeted me. As I was about to
return his greeting, he drew me aside, and, indicating the stranger,
said, "Do you see that fellow? I was just on the point of bringing
him to you."

"He would have been very welcome on your behalf," I answered.

"And on his own too, if you knew him," said Peter, "for there is no
mortal alive today can tell you so much about unknown peoples and
lands; and I know that you're always greedy for such information."

"In that case," said I, "my guess wasn't a bad one, for at first glance
I supposed he was a skipper."

"Then you're far off the mark," he replied, "for his sailing has
not been like that of Palinurus, but more that of Ulysses, or rather

4. Also known as Joris van Themseke. A native of Bruges, he was a distinguished cleric,
diplomat, and royal councilor, whose many offices included the provostship of the
clerical assembly at Cassel.
5. Antwerp and Brussels are about equidistant (sixty miles) from Bruges.

of Plato.[6] This man, who is named Raphael—his family name is Hythloday—knows a good deal of Latin, and is particularly learned in Greek. He studied Greek more than Latin because his main interest is philosophy, and in that field he found that the Romans have left us nothing very valuable except certain works of Seneca and Cicero.[7] Being eager to see the world, he left to his brothers the patrimony to which he was entitled at home (he is a native of Portugal) and took service with Amerigo Vespucci.[8] He was Vespucci's constant companion on the last three of his four voyages, accounts of which are now common reading everywhere; but on the last voyage, he did not return home with the commander. After much persuasion and expostulation he got Amerigo's permission to be one of the twenty-four men who were left in a fort at the farthest point of the last voyage.[9] Being marooned in this way was altogether agreeable to him, as he was more anxious to pursue his travels than afraid of death. He would often say, 'The man who has no grave is covered by the sky,' and 'The road to heaven is the same length from all places.'[1] Yet this frame of mind would have cost him dear, if God had not been gracious to him. After Vespucci's departure, he traveled through many countries with five companions from the garrison. At last, by strange good fortune, he got, via Ceylon, to Calicut, where he opportunely found some Portuguese ships; and so, beyond anyone's expectation, he returned to his own country."[2]

When Peter had told me this, I thanked him for his great kindness in wishing to introduce me to a man whose conversation he hoped I would enjoy, and then I turned to Raphael. After we had greeted each other and exchanged the usual civilities of strangers upon their first meeting, we all went off to my house. There in the garden we sat down on a bench covered with turf, to talk together.

He told us that when Vespucci sailed away, he and his companions who had stayed behind in the fort often met with the people of the countryside, and by ingratiating speeches gradually won their

6. Palinurus was Aeneas's pilot, who dozed over his steering oar and fell overboard (*Aeneid* 5.831ff.) and is an exemplar of the careless traveler; Ulysses, of the person who learns from traveling; and Plato (who made trips to Sicily and Egypt), of the person who travels to learn.
7. The great orator Cicero (106–43 B.C.E.), though not a philosopher, rehearsed at length the views of the various philosophical schools in his writings. Seneca (ca. 4 B.C.E.–65 C.E.) was the foremost Roman Stoic philosopher.
8. The Florentine explorer was sponsored first by the king of Spain and later by the king of Portugal and was reputed to have made four trips to the New World, starting in 1497 (see p. 117 below). Accounts of his voyages published in the opening years of the 16th century were widely circulated and made his exploits more famous than the more substantial explorations of Columbus and Cabot.
9. Reputedly at Cape Frio, east of present-day Rio de Janeiro (see p. 121 below).
1. Both these dicta have classical sources: the first is from the epic poet Lucan (Seneca's nephew), *Pharsalia* 7.819; the second is from Cicero, *Tusculan Disputations* 1.43.104.
2. Thus becoming the first circumnavigator of the globe. (Magellan's men completed the trip in 1522.) Calicut is a seaport on the west coast of India.

The two 1518 editions of *Utopia* included this woodcut by Ambrosius Holbein, showing Hythloday and More seated on the turf-covered bench described in the text. Peter Giles and More's pupil-servant John Clement, who is bringing refreshments, complete the scene.

friendship. Before long they came to dwell with them safely and even affectionately. The prince (I have forgotten his name and that of his country) also gave them his favor, furnishing Raphael and his five companions not only with ample provisions but with means for traveling—rafts when they went by water, wagons when they went by land. In addition, he sent with them a most trusty guide, who was to conduct them to other princes to whom he heartily recommended them. After many days' journey, he said, they came to towns and cities, and to commonwealths that were both very populous and not badly governed.

To be sure, under the equator and as far on both sides of the line as the sun moves, there lie vast empty deserts, scorched with perpetual heat. The whole region is desolate and squalid, grim and uncultivated, inhabited by wild beasts, serpents, and also by men no less wild and dangerous than the beasts themselves. But as you go on, conditions gradually grow milder. The sun is less fierce, the earth greener, the creatures less savage. At last you reach people, cities, and towns which not only trade among themselves and with their neighbors but even carry on commerce by sea and land with remote countries. After that, he said, they were able to visit different lands in every direction, for he and his companions were welcome as passengers aboard any ship about to make a journey.

The first vessels they saw were flat-bottomed, he said, with sails made of stitched papyrus-reeds or wicker, or elsewhere of leather.

Farther on, they found ships with pointed keels and canvas sails, in every respect like our own.[3] The seamen were not unskilled in managing wind and water; but they were most grateful to him, Raphael said, for showing them the use of the compass, of which they had been ignorant. For that reason, they had formerly sailed with great timidity, and only in summer. Now they have such trust in the compass that they no longer fear winter at all, and tend to be overconfident rather than cautious. There is some danger that through their imprudence this device, which they thought would be so advantageous to them, may become the cause of much mischief.

It would take too long to repeat all that Raphael told us he had observed in each place, nor would it make altogether for our present purpose. Perhaps on another occasion we shall tell more about the things that are most profitable, especially the wise and sensible institutions that he observed among the civilized nations. We asked him many eager questions about such things, and he answered us willingly enough. We made no inquiries, however, about monsters, for nothing is less new or strange than they are. Scyllas, ravenous Celaenos, man-eating Lestrygonians,[4] and that sort of monstrosity you can hardly avoid, but well and wisely trained citizens you will hardly find anywhere. While he told us of many ill-considered usages in these new-found nations, he also described quite a few other customs from which our own cities, nations, races, and kingdoms might take example in order to correct their errors. These I shall discuss in another place, as I said. Now I intend to relate only what he told us about the customs and institutions of the Utopians,[5] first recounting the conversation that led him to speak of that commonwealth. Raphael had been talking very sagely about the faulty arrangements and also the wise institutions found in that hemisphere and this (many of both sorts in each), speaking as shrewdly about the manners and governments of each place he had visited as though he had lived there all his life. Peter was amazed.

---

3. As a matter of fact, the Native Americans, when they traveled by water, used canoes made from hollowed logs. In general, More's depiction is fanciful.
4. Scylla and the Lestrygonians were Homeric bogeys: the former, a six-headed sea monster (*Odyssey* 12.73ff.); the latter, giant cannibals (*Odyssey* 10.76ff.). Celaeno, one of the Harpies (birds with women's faces), appears in the *Aeneid* (3.209ff.).
5. According to Erasmus, More wrote Book II of *Utopia* before Book I (see p. 152 below). If so, as J. H. Hexter argues (*More's "Utopia": The Biography of an Idea* [1952; rpt. New York: Harper Torchbooks, 1965], pp. 18–21; *CW* 4:xviii–xx), More presumably first regarded Book II as a complete work, and that work must have had an introduction something like the opening of the present Book I, in which the author later opened a "seam" in order to insert the later-written materials that became the rest of Book I. The present point is almost certainly the seam: the work suddenly goes off on a different tack (the account of Utopia is postponed, and the ensuing conversation includes, among other things, precisely what More has just said he won't relate—Hythloday's accounts of the practices of *other* newfound nations).

"My dear Raphael," he said, "I'm surprised that you don't enter some king's service; for I don't know of a single prince who wouldn't be eager to employ you. Your learning and your knowledge of various countries and peoples would entertain him, while your advice and your supply of examples would be very helpful in the council chamber. Thus you might advance your own interests and be useful at the same time to all your relatives and friends."[6]

"I am not much concerned about my relatives and friends," he replied, "because I consider that I have already done my duty by them. While still young and healthy, I distributed among my relatives and friends the possessions that most men do not part with till they are old and sick (and then only reluctantly, because they can no longer keep them). I think they should be content with this gift of mine, and not expect that for their sake I should enslave myself to any king whatever."

"Well said," Peter replied; "but I do not mean that you should be in servitude to any king, only in his service."

"The difference is only a matter of one syllable," said Raphael.

"All right," said Peter, "but whatever you call it, I do not see any other way in which you can be so useful to your friends or to the general public, in addition to making yourself happier."

"Happier indeed!" exclaimed Raphael. "Would a way of life so absolutely repellent to my spirit make my life happier? As it is now, I live as I please,[7] and I fancy very few courtiers, however splendid, can say that. As a matter of fact, there are so many men soliciting favors from the powerful that it will be no great loss if they have to do without me and a couple of others like me."

Then I said, "It is clear, my dear Raphael, that you seek neither wealth nor power, and indeed I value and revere a man of such a disposition as much as I do the mightiest persons in the world. Yet I think if you would devote your time and energy to public affairs, you would do a thing worthy of a generous and philosophical nature, even if you did not much like it. You could best perform such a ser-

6. The dialogue launched by Giles's suggestion dramatizes a major topic of classical and Renaissance ethical and political thought, the question of whether it behooves an intellectual to enter practical politics (an important case of the general question of the relative merits of the active and contemplative lives). Influential treatments of this issue are found in Plato (*Republic* 6.496C–497B and Epistle 7) and Seneca ("On Leisure" and "On Tranquility of Mind," in *Moral Essays*), who make the case for noninvolvement, and in one of Plutarch's *Moral Essays*, "That a Philosopher Ought to Converse Especially with Men in Power." Cicero sees merit in both courses (*On Moral Obligation* 1.20.69–21.72, 43.153–44.156). For the importance of the topic in Renaissance political thought (including More's) and on its relation to the problem of "counsel" (the problem of ensuring that rulers receive—and follow—good advice), see Hexter's section of the Introduction to *CW* 4, pp. xxii–xl, lxxviii–xcii; Quentin Skinner, *The Foundations of Modern Political Thought*, 2 vols. (Cambridge: Cambridge University Press, 1978), 1:216–20; and, most recently, Eric Nelson (see pp. 274–76 below).

7. Paraphrasing Cicero's definition of philosophic liberty, which occurs in a context similar to this one (*On Moral Obligation* 1.20.69–70).

vice by joining the council of some great prince and inciting him to just and noble actions (as I'm sure you would): for a people's welfare or misery flows in a stream from their prince, as from a never-failing spring. Your learning is so full, even if it weren't combined with experience, and your experience is so great, even apart from your learning, that you would be an extraordinary counselor to any king in the world."

"You are twice mistaken, my dear More," he replied, "first in me and then in the situation itself. I don't have the capacity you ascribe to me, and if I had it in the highest degree, the public would still not be any better off if I exchanged my contemplative leisure for this kind of action. In the first place, most princes apply themselves to the arts of war, in which I have neither ability nor interest, instead of to the good arts of peace. They are generally more set on acquiring new kingdoms by hook or by crook than on governing well those they already have. Moreover, the counselors of kings are all so wise already that they need no advice from anyone else (or at least that's the way they see it). At the same time, they approve and even flatter the most absurd statements of favorites through whose influence they seek to stand well with the prince. It is only natural, of course, that each man should think his own opinions best: the crow loves his fledgling, and the ape his cub.

"Now in a court composed of people who envy everyone else and admire only themselves, if a man should suggest something he had read of in other ages or seen in practice elsewhere, the other counselors would think their reputation for wisdom was endangered and they would look like simpletons, unless they could find fault with his proposal. If all else failed, they would take refuge in some remark like this: 'The way we're doing it was good enough for our ancestors, and I only hope we're as wise as they were.' And with this deep thought they would take their seats, as though they had said the last word on the subject—implying, of course, that it would be a very dangerous matter if anyone were found to be wiser in any point than his ancestors were. As a matter of fact, we have no misgivings about neglecting the best examples they have left us; but if something better is proposed, we eagerly seize upon the excuse of reverence for times past and cling to it desperately. Such proud, obstinate, ridiculous judgments I have encountered many times, and once even in England."

"What!" I said. "Were you ever in my country?"

"Yes," he answered, "I spent several months there. It was not long after the revolt of the Cornishmen against the king had been put down, with the miserable slaughter of the rebels.[8] During my stay I

---

8. Angered by the greedy taxation of Henry VII, an army of Cornishmen marched on London in 1497 but were defeated at the battle of Blackheath.

was deeply beholden to the reverend father John Cardinal Morton,[9] archbishop of Canterbury, and in addition at that time lord chancellor of England. He was a man, my dear Peter (for More knows about him, and can tell what I'm going to say), as much respected for his wisdom and virtue as for his authority. He was of medium height, not bent over despite his years; his looks inspired respect rather than fear. In conversation, he was not forbidding, though serious and grave. When suitors came to him on business, he liked to test their spirit and presence of mind by speaking to them sharply, though not rudely. He liked to uncover these qualities, which were those of his own nature, as long as they were not carried to the point of effrontery; and he thought such men were best qualified to carry on business. His speech was polished and pointed; his knowledge of the law was great; he had an incomparable understanding and a prodigious memory, for he had improved extraordinary natural abilities by study and practice. At the time when I was in England, the king relied heavily on his advice, and he seemed the chief support of the nation as a whole. He had been taken from school to court when scarcely more than a boy, had devoted all his life to important business, and had acquired from weathering violent changes of fortune and many great perils a supply of practical wisdom, which is not soon lost when so purchased.

"One day when I was dining with him, there was present a layman, learned in the laws of your country, who for some reason took occasion to praise the rigid execution of justice then being practiced upon thieves. They were being executed everywhere, he said, with as many as twenty at a time being hanged on a single gallows.[1] And then he declared that he could not understand how so many thieves sprang up everywhere, when so few of them escaped hanging. I ventured to speak freely before the cardinal, and said, 'There is no need to wonder: this way of punishing thieves goes beyond the call of justice, and is not, in any case, for the public good. The penalty is too harsh in itself, yet it isn't an effective deterrent. Simple theft[2] is not so great a crime that it ought to cost a man his life, yet no punishment however severe can withhold those from robbery who have no other way to eat. In this matter not only you in England but a good part of the world seem to imitate bad schoolmasters, who would rather whip their pupils than teach them. Severe and terrible

---

9. Morton (1420–1500) was a distinguished prelate, statesman, and administrator. More's father, following a custom of the age, sent his son to serve as a page for two years (1490–92) in the cardinal's household; the seventy-year-old Morton is said to have been so impressed with the twelve-year-old More that he arranged for his education at Oxford.
1. Later in the 16th century, Holinshed's *Chronicles* recorded that 72,000 thieves and vagabonds were hanged in the reign of Henry VIII alone (*Holinshed's Chronicles [of] England, Scotland, and Ireland*, 6 vols. ([1807; rpt. New York: AMS Press, 1965], 1:314).
2. Theft is "simple" when not accompanied by violence or intimidation.

punishments are enacted against theft, when it would be much better to enable every man to earn his own living, instead of being driven to the awful necessity of stealing and then dying for it.'

"'Oh, we've taken care of that,' said the fellow. 'There are the trades and there is farming, by which men may make a living unless they choose deliberately to be rogues.'

"'Oh no you don't,' I said, 'you won't get out of it that way. We may disregard for the moment the cripples who come home from foreign and civil wars, as lately from the Cornish battle and before that from your wars with France.[3] These men, who have lost limbs in the service of king and country, are too badly crippled to follow their old trades, and too old to learn new ones. But since wars occur only from time to time, let us, I say, disregard these men, and consider what happens every day. There are a great many noblemen who live idly like drones[4] off the labor of others, their tenants whom they bleed white by constantly raising their rents. (This is the only instance of their tightfistedness, because they are prodigal in everything else, ready to spend their way to the poorhouse.) These noblemen drag around with them a great train of idle servants,[5] who have never learned any trade by which they could earn a living. As soon as their master dies, or they themselves fall ill, they are promptly turned out of doors, for lords would rather support idlers than invalids, and the son is often unable to maintain as big a household as his father had, at least at first. Those who are turned off soon set about starving, unless they set about stealing. What else can they do? Then when a wandering life has left their health impaired and their clothes threadbare, when their faces look pinched and their garments tattered, men of rank will not care to engage them. And country people dare not do so, for they don't have to be told that one who has been raised softly to idle pleasures, who has been used to swaggering about with sword and buckler, is likely to look down on the whole neighborhood and despise everybody else as beneath him. Such a man can't be put to work with spade and mattock; he will not serve a poor man faithfully for scant wages and sparse diet.'

"'But we ought to encourage these men in particular,' said the lawyer. 'In case of war the strength and power of our army depend on them, because they have a bolder and nobler spirit than workmen and farmers have.'

---

3. Since the dramatic date of the conversation is 1497 or shortly thereafter, Hythloday may be referring to the English casualties—relatively few—in the sporadic hostilities with France of 1489–92. But the author is probably thinking of the heavier losses of Henry VIII's French excursions of 1512–13.
4. More is thinking of Plato's *Republic* (8.552B–C), where the same metaphor is used to describe monied individuals who contribute nothing to the welfare of society.
5. Some of these were household servants; others were the last vestiges of the private armies by which, under feudalism, every lord was followed.

"'You may as well say that thieves should be encouraged for the
sake of wars,' I answered, 'since you will never lack for thieves as long
as you have men like these. In fact thieves don't make bad soldiers,
and soldiers turn out to be pretty good robbers—so nearly are these
two ways of life related.[6] But the custom of keeping too many retainers is not peculiar to this nation; it is common to almost all of them.
France suffers from an even more grievous plague. Even in peace-
time—if you can call it peace—the whole country is crowded with
foreign mercenaries, imported on the same principle that you've
given for your noblemen keeping idle servants.[7] Wise fools think that
the public safety depends on having ready a strong army, prefera-
bly of veteran soldiers. They think inexperienced men are not reliable, and they sometimes hunt out pretexts for war, just so they may
have trained soldiers and experienced cutthroats—or, as Sallust
neatly puts it, that "hand and spirit may not grow dull through lack
of practice."[8] But France has learned to her cost how pernicious it is
to feed such beasts. The examples of the Romans, the Carthaginians, the Syrians,[9] and many other peoples show the same thing; for
not only their governments but their fields and even their cities were
ruined more than once by their own standing armies. Besides, this
preparedness is unnecessary: not even the French soldiers, practiced
in arms from their cradles, can boast of having often got the best of
your raw recruits.[1] I shall say no more on this point, lest I seem to
flatter present company. At any rate, neither your town workmen nor
your rough farm laborers—except for those whose physiques aren't
suited for strength or boldness, or whose spirits have been cowed by
inability to feed their families—seem to be much afraid of fighting
the idle attendants of noblemen. So you need not fear that retainers,
once strong and vigorous (for that's the only sort noblemen deign to
corrupt), but now soft and flabby because of their idle, effeminate
life, would be weakened if they were taught practical crafts to earn
their living, and trained to manly labor. Anyway, I cannot think it's in
the public interest to maintain for the emergency of war such a vast
multitude of people who trouble and disturb the peace. You never

---

6. A point also made by Erasmus and other humanists (e.g., Erasmus's *Complaint of
   Peace,* CWE 27:316–17).
7. Charles VII of France (reigned 1422–61) had tried to establish a national army, but his
   successors reverted to mercenaries, mostly Swiss infantrymen.
8. Paraphrasing the *Catiline* (16.3) of the Roman historian Sallust (86–35 B.C.E.).
9. The Romans and Carthaginians both had to fight servile wars against gladiators and
   mercenaries. The victimizers of the Syrians that Hythloday has in mind are probably
   the Mamelukes, a military caste of foreign extraction that ruled, from the 13th century
   to the early 16th, a state that included much of the Middle East.
1. Past English victories over the French included Crécy (1346), Poitiers (1356), and
   Henry V's triumph at Agincourt (1415). English chauvinism has always maintained
   that the stout English yeoman, nourished on beef and beer, can overcome ten meager
   Frenchmen, nourished on sour wine and black bread.

have war unless you choose it, and peace is always more to be considered than war. Yet this is not the only circumstance that makes
thieving necessary. There is another one, which, I believe, applies
more especially to you Englishmen.'

"'What is that?' asked the cardinal.

"'Your sheep,' I replied, 'that used to be so meek and eat so little.
Now they have become so greedy and fierce that they devour human
beings themselves, as I hear.[2] They devastate and depopulate fields,
houses, and towns. For in whatever parts of the land the sheep yield
the softest and most expensive wool, there the nobility and gentry,
yes, and even some abbots—holy men—are not content with the old
rents that the land yielded to their predecessors. Living in idleness
and luxury, without doing any good to society, no longer satisfies
them; they have to do positive harm. For they leave no land free for
the plow: they enclose every acre for pasture; they destroy houses
and abolish towns, keeping only the churches, and those for sheep-
barns. And as if enough of your land were not already wasted on
woods and game-preserves, these worthy men turn all human habi-
tations and cultivated fields back to wilderness. Thus one greedy,
insatiable glutton, a frightful plague to his native country, may
enclose many thousand acres of land within a single hedge. The tenants are dismissed; some are stripped of their belongings by trickery
or brute force, or, wearied by constant harassment, are driven to sell
them. By hook or by crook these miserable people—men, women,
husbands, wives, orphans, widows, parents with little children, whole
families (poor but numerous, since farming requires many hands)—
are forced to move out. They leave the only homes familiar to them,
and they can find no place to go. Since they cannot afford to wait for
a buyer, they sell for a pittance all their household goods, which
would not bring much in any case. When that little money is gone
(and it's soon spent in wandering from place to place), what remains
for them but to steal, and so be hanged—justly, you'd say!—or to
wander and beg? And yet if they go tramping, they are jailed as idle
vagrants. They would be glad to work, but they can find no one who
will hire them. There is no need for farm labor, in which they have
been trained, when there is no land left to be planted. One herds-
man or shepherd can look after a flock of beasts large enough to
stock an area that would require many hands if it were plowed and
harvested.

2. This vivid image introduces Hythloday's treatment of the social dislocation brought
about by "enclosure"—the gradual amalgamation and fencing, over a period extending
from the 12th century to the 19th, of the open fields of the feudal system: one incentive
to the practice was the increasing profitability of the wool trade. For a modern historian's view of the pluses and minuses of enclosure, see, pp. 122–23 below.

"'This enclosing has had the effect of raising the price of food in many places. In addition, the price of raw wool has risen so much that poor people who used to make cloth are no longer able to buy it, and so great numbers are forced from work to idleness. One reason is that after the enlarging of the pasture-land, a murrain killed a great number of sheep—as though God were punishing greed by sending a plague upon the animals, which in justice should have fallen on the owners! But even if the number of sheep should increase greatly, their price will not fall a penny. The reason is that the wool trade, though it can't be called a monopoly, because it isn't in the hands of one single person, is concentrated in few hands (an oligopoly, you might say), and these so rich that the owners are never pressed to sell until they have a mind to, and that is only when they can get their price.

"'For the same reason other kinds of livestock also are priced exorbitantly, the more so because with so many farmhouses being pulled down, and farming in a state of decay, there are not enough people to look after the breeding of animals. These rich men will not breed other animals as they do lambs, but buy them lean and cheap, fatten them in their own pastures, and then sell them at a high price. I don't think the full impact of this bad system has yet been felt. We know these dealers raise prices where the fattened animals are sold. But when, over a period of time, they keep buying beasts from other localities faster than they can be bred, then as the supply gradually diminishes where they are purchased, a severe shortage is bound to ensue. So your island, which seemed especially fortunate in this matter, will be ruined by the crass avarice of a few. For the high food prices cause everyone to dismiss as many retainers as he can from his household; and what, I ask, can these men do, but rob or beg? And a man of courage is more likely to steal than to cringe.

"'To make this hideous poverty and scarcity worse, they exist side by side with wanton luxury.[3] Not only the servants of noblemen, but tradespeople, even some farmers, and people of every social rank are given to ostentatious dress and gluttonous greed. Look at the eating houses, the bawdy houses, and those other places just as bad, the wine bars and alehouses. Look at all the crooked games of chance, dice, cards, backgammon, tennis, bowling, and quoits, in which money slips away so fast. Don't all these lead their habitués straight to robbery? Banish these blights, make those who have ruined farmhouses and villages restore them, or hand them over to someone who will rebuild. Restrict the right of the rich to buy up

---

3. Luxurious living was not, in fact, characteristic of the reign of the parsimonious Henry VII (when Hythloday is supposed to be addressing Cardinal Morton). More is projecting onto the earlier period, perhaps unconsciously, a kind of extravagant display that began in 1509 with the accession of Henry VIII.

anything and everything, and then to exercise a kind of monopoly.[4] Let fewer people be brought up in idleness. Let agriculture be restored and the wool manufacture revived as an honest trade, so there will be useful work for the whole crowd of those now idle— whether those whom poverty has already made into thieves, or those whom vagabondage and habits of lazy service are converting, just as surely, into the robbers of the future.

"'If you do not find a cure for these evils, it is futile to boast of your justice in punishing theft. Your policy may look superficially like justice, but in reality it is neither just nor practical. If you allow young folk to be abominably brought up and their characters corrupted, little by little, from childhood; and if then you punish them as grownups for committing crimes to which their early training has inclined them, what else is this, I ask, but first making them thieves and then punishing them for it?'

"As I was speaking thus, the lawyer had made ready his answer, choosing the usual style of disputants who are better at summing up than at replying, and who like to show off their memory. So he said to me, 'You have talked very well for a stranger, but you have heard about more things than you have been able to understand correctly. I will make the matter clear to you in a few words. First, I will summarize what you have said; then I will show how you have been misled by ignorance of our customs; finally, I will demolish all your arguments and reduce them to rubble. And so to begin where I promised, on four points you seemed to me—'

"'Hold your tongue,' said the cardinal, 'for you won't be finished in a few words, if this is the way you start. We will spare you the trouble of answering now, and reserve the pleasure of your reply till our next meeting, which will be tomorrow, if your affairs and Raphael's permit it. Meanwhile, my dear Raphael, I am eager to hear why you think theft should not be punished with death, or what other punishment you think would be more in the public interest. For I'm sure even you don't think it should go unpunished entirely. Even as it is, the fear of death does not restrain evildoers; once they were sure of their lives, as you propose, what force or fear could restrain them? They would look on a lighter penalty as an open invitation to commit more crimes—it would be like offering them a reward.'

"'It seems to me, most kind and reverend father,' I said, 'that it's altogether unjust to take someone's life for taking money. Nothing in the world that fortune can bestow is equal in value to a human life. If they say the thief suffers not for the money, but for violation of justice and transgression of laws, then this extreme justice should

---

4. Laws of these kinds were in fact passed in the reigns of both Henry VII and Henry VIII, but to small effect.

really be called extreme injury.[5] We ought not to approve of these fierce Manlian edicts[6] that invoke the sword for the smallest violations. Neither should we accept the Stoic view that considers all crimes equal,[7] as if there were no difference between killing a man and taking a coin from him. If equity means anything, there is no proportion or relation at all between these two crimes. God has said, "Thou shalt not kill"; shall we kill so readily for the theft of a bit of small change? Perhaps it will be argued that God's commandment against killing does not apply where human law allows it. But then what prevents men from making other laws in the same way— perhaps even laws legalizing rape, adultery, and perjury? God has taken from each person the right not only to kill another, but even to kill himself. If mutual consent to human laws on manslaughter entitles men freely to exempt their agents from divine law and allows them to kill those condemned by human decrees where God has given no precedent, what is this but preferring the law of man to the law of God? The result will be that in every situation men will decide for themselves how far it suits them to observe the laws of God. The law of Moses was harsh and severe, as for an enslaved and stubborn people, but it punished theft with a fine, not death.[8] Let us not think that in his new law of mercy, where he rules us with the tenderness of a father, God has given us greater license to be cruel to one another.

"'These are the reasons why I think it is wrong to put thieves to death. But surely everybody knows how absurd and even harmful to the public welfare it is to punish theft and murder alike. If theft carries the same penalty as murder, the thief will be encouraged to kill the victim whom otherwise he would only have robbed. When the punishment is the same, murder is safer, since one conceals both crimes by killing the witness. Thus while we try to terrify thieves with extreme cruelty, we really invite them to kill the innocent.

"'As for the usual question of what more suitable punishment can be found, in my judgment it would be much easier to find a better one than a worse. Why should we question the value of the punishments long used by the Romans, who were most expert in the arts of government? They condemned those convicted of heinous crimes to work, shackled, for life, in stone quarries and mines. But of all the

---

5. Echoing the classical adage *summum ius, summa iniuria*, long cited in discussions of equity.
6. Manlian edicts (like those imposed by the Roman consul Titus Manlius in the 4th century B.C.E.) are proverbially strict. Manlius executed his own son for disobeying one of them.
7. This view was actually maintained by some of the ancient Stoic philosophers.
8. The Mosaic law is that spelled out in the first verses of Exodus 22. It provides various penalties for theft, but nowhere death. This is contrasted with the "new law" of Christ, under which England is supposed to be operating.

alternatives, I prefer the method which I observed in my Persian travels, among the people commonly called the Polylerites.[9] They are a sizable nation, not badly governed, free and subject only to their own laws, except that they pay annual tribute to the Persian king. Living far from the sea, they are nearly surrounded by mountains. Being contented with the products of their own land, which is by no means unfruitful, they do not visit other nations, nor are they much visited. According to their ancient customs, they do not try to enlarge their boundaries, and easily protect themselves behind their mountains by paying tribute to their overlord. Thus they have no wars and live in a comfortable rather than a showy manner, more contented than renowned or glorious. Indeed, I think they are hardly known by name to anyone but their next-door neighbors.

"'In their land, whoever is found guilty of theft must make restitution to the owner, not (as elsewhere) to the prince;[1] they think the prince has no more right to the stolen goods than the thief. If the stolen property has disappeared, its value is repaid from the thief's possessions. Whatever remains of those is handed over to his wife and children, while the thief himself is sentenced to hard labor.

"'Unless their crimes were compounded with atrocities, thieves are neither imprisoned nor shackled, but go freely and unconstrained about their work on public projects. If they shirk and do their jobs slackly, they are not chained, but they are whipped. If they work hard, they are treated without any indignities, except that at night after roll call they are locked up in their dormitories. Apart from constant work, they undergo no discomfort in living. As they work for the public good, they are decently fed out of the public stores, though arrangements vary from place to place. In some districts they are supported by alms. Unreliable as this support may seem, the Polylerites are so compassionate that no way is found more rewarding. In other places, public revenues are set aside for their support, or a special tax is levied on every individual for their use; and sometimes they do not do public work, but anyone in need of workmen can go to the market and hire some of them by the day at a set rate, a little less than that for free men. If they are lazy, it is lawful to whip them. Thus they never lack for work, and each one of them brings a little profit into the public treasury beyond the cost of his keep.

"'They are all dressed in clothes of the same distinctive color. Their hair is not shaved but trimmed close about the ears,[2] and the

---

9. From Greek: "the People of Much Nonsense."
1. Erasmus condemns this common practice in *The Education of a Christian Prince*, CWE 27:270.
2. At this point in the text, the early editions have a marginal gloss—in translation, "Yet nowadays the servants of noblemen think such a haircut quite handsome." This is one

tip of one ear is cut off. Their friends are allowed to give them food, drink, or clothing, as long as it is of the proper color; but to give them money is death, both to the giver and to the taker. It is just as serious a crime for any free man to take money from them for any reason whatever; and it is also a capital crime for any of these slaves (as the condemned are called) to carry weapons. In each district of the country they are required to wear a special badge. It is a capital crime to throw away the badge, to go beyond one's own district, or to talk with a slave of another district. Plotting escape is no more secure than escape itself: it is death for any other slave to know of a plot to escape, and slavery for a free man. On the other hand, there are rewards for informers—money for a free man, freedom for a slave, and for both of them pardon and amnesty. Thus it can never be safer for them to persist in an illicit scheme than to renounce it.

"'Such are their laws and policies in this matter. It is clear how mild and practical they are, for the aim of the punishment is to destroy vices and save men. The criminals are treated so that they become good of necessity, and for the rest of their lives they atone for the wrong they have done before. There is so little danger of relapse that travelers going from one part of the country to another think slaves the most reliable guides, changing them at the boundary of each district. The slaves have no means of committing robbery, since they are unarmed, and any money in their possession is evidence of a crime. If caught, they would be punished, and there is no hope of escape anywhere. Since every bit of a slave's clothing is unlike the usual clothing of the country, how could a slave escape, unless he fled naked? Even then his cropped ear would give him away. Might not the slaves form a conspiracy against the government? Perhaps. But the slaves of one district could hardly expect to succeed unless they first involved in their plot the slave-gangs of many other districts. And that is impossible, since they are not allowed to meet or talk together or even to greet one another. No one would risk a plot when they all know joining is so dangerous to the participant and betrayal so profitable to the informer. Besides, no one is quite without hope of gaining his freedom eventually if he accepts his punishment in the spirit of obedience and patience, and gives promise of future good conduct. Indeed, every year some are pardoned as a reward for their submissive behavior.'

"When I had finished this account, I added that I saw no reason why this system could not be adopted even in England, and with

---

of a series of some 200 glosses, supplied by Giles (see p. 130 below), which range in length from a single word to a full sentence and provide a valuable record of the response to *Utopia* (especially to Book II, where the glosses are heavily concentrated) by a particularly well-positioned member of the humanist audience for it. The present edition includes a selection of the more pungent glosses, as footnotes.

much greater advantage than the 'justice' which my legal antagonist had praised so highly. But the lawyer replied that such a system could never be established in England without putting the commonwealth in serious peril. And so saying, he shook his head, made a wry face, and fell silent. And all the company sided with him.

"Then the cardinal remarked, 'It is not easy to guess whether this scheme would work well or not, since nobody has yet tried it out. But perhaps when the death sentence has been passed on a thief, the king might reprieve him for a time without right of sanctuary,[3] and thus see how the plan worked. If it turned out well, then he might establish it by law; if not, he could execute immediate punishment on the man formerly condemned. This would be neither less nor more unjust than if the condemned man had been put to death at once, and the experiment would involve no risk. I think vagabonds too might be treated this way, for though we have passed many laws against them, they have had no real effect as yet.'

"When the cardinal had concluded, they all began praising enthusiastically ideas which they had received with contempt when I suggested them; and they particularly liked the idea about vagabonds, because it was the cardinal's addition.

"I don't know whether it is worthwhile telling what followed, because it was silly, but I'll tell it anyhow, for there's no harm in it, and it bears on our subject. There was a hanger-on standing around, who was so good at playing the fool that you could hardly tell him from the real thing. He was constantly making jokes, but so awkwardly that we laughed more at him than at them; yet sometimes a rather clever thing came out, confirming the old proverb that a man who throws the dice often will sooner or later make a lucky cast. One of the company happened to say that in my speech I had taken care of the thieves, and the cardinal had taken care of the vagabonds, so now all that was left to do was to take care of the poor whom sickness or old age had reduced to poverty and kept from earning a living.

"'Leave that to me,' said the fool, 'and I'll set it right at once. These are people I'm eager to get out of my sight, having been so often vexed with them and their woeful complaints. No matter how pitifully they beg for money, they've never whined a single penny out of my pocket. They can't win with me: either I don't want to give them anything, or I haven't anything to give them. Now they're getting wise; they know me so well, they don't waste their breath, but let me pass without a word or a hope—no more, by heaven, than if I

---

3. In earlier days almost any criminal could take sanctuary in any church and be safe from the law. By More's time, the privilege had been abridged considerably, though by no means abolished.

were a priest. But I would make a law sending all these beggars to Benedictine monasteries, where the men could become lay brothers,[4] as they're called, and the women could be nuns.'

"The cardinal smiled and passed it off as a joke; the rest took it seriously. But a certain friar, a theologian, took such pleasure in this jest at the expense of priests and monks that he too began to make merry, though generally he was grave to the point of sourness. 'Even so, you will not get rid of the beggars,' he began, 'unless you take care of us friars[5] too.'

"'You have been taken care of already,' retorted the fool. 'The cardinal provided for you splendidly when he said vagabonds should be arrested and put to work, for you friars are the greatest vagabonds of all.'

"When the company, watching the cardinal closely, saw that he admitted this jest like the other, they all took it up with vigor— except for the friar. He, as you can easily imagine, was stung by the vinegar,[6] and flew into such a rage that he could not keep from abusing the fool. He called him a knave, a slanderer, a sneak, and a 'son of perdition,'[7] quoting the meanwhile terrible denunciations from Holy Scripture. Now the joker began to jest in earnest, for he was clearly on his own ground.

"'Don't get angry, good friar,' he said, 'for it is written, "In your patience possess ye your souls."'[8]

"In reply, the friar said, and I quote his very words, 'I am not angry, you gallows-bird, or at least I do not sin, for the psalmist says, "Be ye angry, and sin not."'[9]

"At this point the cardinal gently cautioned the friar to calm down, but he answered: 'No, my lord, I speak only from righteous zeal, as I ought to. For holy men have had great zeal. That is why Scripture says, "the zeal of thine house hath eaten me up,"[1] and we sing in church, "those who mocked Elisha as he went up to the house of God, felt the zeal of the baldhead,"[2] just as this mocker, this rascal, this guttersnipe may very well feel it.'

---

4. Men who lived and worked in monasteries (mostly performing menial tasks) but who were not admitted to clerical orders.
5. Members of a mendicant (begging) order, as opposed to monks, who live, and labor, in a cloister.
6. Alluding to a phrase in Horace's *Satires* 1.7.32: *italo perfusus aceto*, "soaked in Italian vinegar."
7. John 17.12; 2 Thessalonians 2.3.
8. Luke 21.19.
9. Psalms 4.4. The Vulgate Bible translates as *Irascimini* ("Be angry") the Hebrew word that is rendered as "Stand in awe" in the King James Version.
1. Psalms 69.9.
2. Some children mocked Elisha, son of Elijah the prophet, for his baldness; but he called two bears out of the woods, and they tore the bad children to pieces (2 Kings 23–24). The friar quotes a hymn based on this cautionary tale, by Adam of St. Victor.

" 'Perhaps you mean well,' said the cardinal, 'but you would act in a holier, and certainly in a wiser way, if you didn't set your wit against a fool's wit and try to spar with a buffoon.'

" 'No, my lord,' he replied, 'I would not act more wisely. For Solomon himself, the wisest of men, said, "Answer a fool according to his folly,"[3] and that's what I'm doing now. I am showing him the pit into which he will fall if he does not take care. For if the many mockers of Elisha, who was only one bald man, felt the effects of his zeal, how much more effect shall be felt by a single mocker of many friars, who include a great many baldheads! And besides, we have a papal bull,[4] by which all who mock us are excommunicated.'

"When the cardinal saw there was no end to the matter, he nodded to the fool to leave, and turned the conversation to another subject. Soon after, he rose from table, and, going to hear petitioners, dismissed us.

"Look, my dear More, what a long story I have inflicted on you. I would be quite ashamed, if you had not yourself asked for it, and seemed to listen as if you did not want any part to be left out. Though I ought to have related this conversation more concisely, I did feel bound to recount it, so you might see how those who rejected what I said at first approved of it immediately afterward, when they saw the cardinal did not disapprove. In fact they went so far in their flattery that they indulged and almost took seriously ideas that he tolerated only as the jesting of a fool. From this episode you can see how little courtiers would value me or my advice."

To this I answered, "You have given me great pleasure, my dear Raphael, for everything you've said has been both wise and witty. As you spoke, I seemed to be a child and in my own native land once more, through the pleasant recollection of that cardinal in whose court I was brought up as a lad. Dear as you are to me on other accounts, you cannot imagine how much dearer you are because you honor his memory so highly. Still, my friend Raphael, I don't give up my former opinion: I think if you could overcome your aversion to court life, your advice to a prince would be of the greatest advantage to the public welfare. This, after all, is the chief duty of every good man,[5] including you. Your friend Plato thinks that commonwealths will become happy only when philosophers become kings or kings become philosophers.[6] No wonder we are so far from happiness, when philosophers do not condescend even to assist kings with their counsels."

---

3. Proverbs 26.5. But compare the previous verse: "Answer not a fool according to his folly, lest thou also be like unto him."
4. A formal papal document, named after the seal (Latin *bulla*) that authenticated it.
5. The position, most notably, of Cicero (*On Moral Obligation* 1.43).
6. Plato, *Republic* 5.473; cf. Epistle 7, 326A–B.

"They are not so ungracious," Raphael replied, "but that they would gladly do it; in fact, they have already done it in a great many published books, if the rulers would only read their good advice. But doubtless Plato was right in foreseeing that unless kings became philosophical themselves, they would never take the advice of real philosophers, drenched as they are and infected with false values from boyhood on. Plato certainly had this experience with Dionysius of Syracuse.[7] If I proposed wise laws to some king, and tried to root out of his soul the seeds of evil and corruption, don't you suppose I would be either banished forthwith, or treated with scorn?

"Imagine, if you will, that I am at the court of the king of France.[8] Suppose I were sitting in his royal council, meeting in secret session with the king himself presiding, and all the cleverest councillors were hard at work devising a set of crafty machinations by which the king might keep hold of Milan, recover Naples, which has proved so slippery;[9] then overthrow the Venetians and subdue all Italy; next add Flanders, Brabant, and the whole of Burgundy to his realm, besides some other nations he has in mind to invade. One man urges him to make an alliance with the Venetians for just as long as the king finds it convenient—perhaps to develop a common strategy with them, and even allow them some of the loot, which can be recovered later when things work out according to plan. While one recommends hiring German mercenaries, his neighbor proposes paying the Swiss to stay neutral.[1] A fourth voice suggests soothing the offended divinity of the emperor with an offering of gold.[2] Still another, who is of a different mind, thinks a settlement should be made with the king of Aragon, and that, to cement the peace, he should be allowed to take Navarre from its proper ruler.[3] Meanwhile, someone suggests snaring the prince of Castille into a marriage

---

7. Plato is reported to have made three visits to Syracuse (in Sicily), where his attempts to reform the tyrant Dionysius the Elder, and later his son Dionysius the Younger, were notoriously unsuccessful.
8. At the time of writing, Francis I; at the time of Hythloday's supposed visit to England, either Charles VIII (d. 1498) or Louis XII (d. 1515). All three were would-be imperialists with hereditary claims to Milan and Naples, and all three bogged down in the intricacies of Italian political intrigue.
9. A marginal gloss at this point says, "Indirectly he discourages the French from seizing Italy." France gained Milan in 1499, lost it in 1512, and regained it at the battle of Marignano in September 1515. Naples was won in 1495, lost in 1496, won again in 1501, and lost again in 1504. But, as Hythloday goes on to suggest, French territorial ambitions in the period extended almost limitlessly.
1. Among foot soldiers for hire, the Swiss ranked first, the Germans second.
2. Maximilian of Austria, Holy Roman Emperor, whom Machiavelli sketches sharply in chapter 23 of The Prince, had grandiose schemes (he even dreamed of being pope) but little money. He was always accessible to a bribe.
3. Machiavelli characterizes the tricky Ferdinand of Aragon in chapter 21 of The Prince. Navarre was a small independent enclave astride the Pyrenees, long disputed between Spain and France. In 1512 Ferdinand took most of it from Jean d'Albret.

alliance—a first step would be to buy up some nobles of his court with secret pensions.[4]

"The hardest problem of all is what to do about England. They all agree that peace should be made, and that the alliance, which is weak at best, should be strengthened as much as possible; but while the English are being treated as friends, they should also be suspected as enemies. And so the Scots must be kept in constant readiness, poised to attack the English in case they stir ever so little.[5] Also a banished nobleman with some pretensions to the English throne must be secretly encouraged (there are treaties against doing it openly), and in this way pressure can be brought to bear on the English king, and a ruler kept in check who can't really be trusted.[6]

"Now in a meeting like this one, where so much is at stake, where so many brilliant men are competing to think up intricate strategies of war, what if an insignificant fellow like me were to get up and advise going on another tack entirely? Suppose I said the king should leave Italy alone and stay at home, because the single kingdom of France all by itself is almost too much for one man to govern well, and the king should not dream of adding others to it? Then imagine I told about the decrees of the Achorians,[7] who live off the island of Utopia toward the southeast. Long ago, these people went to war to gain another realm for their king, who had inherited an ancient claim to it through marriage. When they had conquered it, they soon saw that keeping it was going to be as hard as getting it had been. The seeds of war were constantly sprouting, their new subjects were continually rebelling or being attacked by foreign invaders, the Achorians had to be constantly at war for them or against them, and they saw no hope of ever being able to disband their army. In the meantime, they were being heavily taxed, money flowed out of their kingdom, their blood was being shed for the advantage of others, and peace was no closer than it had ever been. The war corrupted their own citizens by encouraging lust for robbery and murder; and the laws fell into contempt because their king, distracted with the cares of two kingdoms, could give neither one his proper attention.

"When they saw that the list of these evils was endless, the Achorians took counsel together and very courteously offered their king his choice of keeping whichever of the two kingdoms he preferred, because he couldn't rule them both. They were too numerous a

---

4. The future emperor Charles V was a great matrimonial and diplomatic catch. (Before he was twenty, he had been engaged ten times.) The question of a French marriage that would unite the two greatest continental and Catholic powers was continually in the air.
5. The Scots, as traditional enemies of England, were traditional allies of France.
6. The French had in fact supported various pretenders to the English throne—most recently, Richard de la Pole, the inheritor of the Yorkist claim.
7. The name arises from Greek *a* ("without") and *chora* ("place"): the People without a Country.

people, they said, to be ruled by half a king; and they added that a man would not even hire a muledriver, if he had to divide his services with somebody else. The worthy king was thus obliged to be content with his own realm and give his new one to a friend, who before long was driven out.

"Finally, suppose I told the French king's council that all this war-mongering, by which so many different nations were kept in turmoil as a result of one man's connivings, would exhaust his treasury and demoralize his people, and yet in the end come to nothing, through some mishap or other.[8] And therefore he should look after his ances-tral kingdom, improve it as much as he could, cultivate it in every conceivable way. He should love his people and be loved by them; he should live among them, govern them kindly, and let other king-doms alone, since his own is big enough, if not too big, for him. How do you think, my dear More, the other councillors would take this speech of mine?"

"Not very well, I'm sure," said I.

"Well, let's go on," he said. "Suppose the councillors of some other king are discussing various schemes for raising money to fill his trea-sury. One man recommends increasing the value of money when the king pays his debts and devaluing it when he collects his revenues.[9] Thus he can discharge a huge debt with a small payment, and collect a large sum when only a small one is due him. Another suggests a make-believe war, so that money can be raised under pretext of carry-ing it on; then, when the money is in, he can conclude a ceremonious peace treaty—which the deluded common people will attribute to the piety of their prince and his careful compassion for the lives of his subjects.[1] Another councillor calls to mind some old motheaten laws, antiquated by long disuse, which no one remembers being made and consequently everyone has transgressed. By imposing fines for break-ing these laws, the king will get great sums of money, as well as credit for upholding law and order, since the whole procedure can be made to look like justice.[2] Another recommendation is that he forbid under

---

8. Francis I lost Milan in 1520 (that is, four years after More wrote this passage) and, in a catastrophic effort to regain it in 1522, was defeated and taken prisoner by Charles V.
9. Both Henry VII and (after Utopia was written) Henry VIII fiddled with the English currency in ways like those suggested here.
1. Something like this happened in 1492, when Henry VII not only pretended war with France on behalf of Brittany and levied taxes for the war (which was hardly fought) but collected a bribe from Charles VIII for not fighting it.
2. This had been common practice under Henry VII, whose ministers Empson and Dudley scratched up many forgotten laws for strictly mercenary purposes. In general, the dis-guised extortion of the policies recommended in this paragraph recalls Aristotle's obser-vation that tyrannies can be preserved in two different ways: by direct oppression or by the tyrant's acting the "role" of a good king. He can, for example, "levy taxes, and require other contributions, in such a way that they can be seen to be intended for the proper management of public services, or to be meant for use . . . on military emergen-cies" (Politics 5.11.21).

particularly heavy fines a lot of practices that are contrary to the public interest; afterward, he can dispense with his own rules for large sums of money. Thus he pleases the people and makes a double profit, one from the heavy fines imposed on lawbreakers, and the other from selling dispensations. Meanwhile he seems careful of his people's welfare, since it is plain he will not allow private citizens to do anything contrary to the public interest, except for a huge price.

"Another councillor proposes that he work on the judges so that they will decide every case in favor of the king. They should be summoned to court often, and invited to debate his affairs in the royal presence. However unjust his claims, one or another of the judges, whether from love of contradiction, or desire to seem original, or simply to serve his own interest, will be bound to find some way of twisting the law in the king's favor. If the judges can be brought to differ, then the clearest matter in the world will be obscured, and the truth itself brought into question. The king is given leverage to interpret the law as he will, and everyone else will acquiesce from shame or fear. The judges will have no hesitation about supporting the royal interest, for there are always plenty of pretexts for giving judgment in favor of the king. Either equity is on his side, or the letter of the law happens to make for him, or the words of the law can be twisted into obscurity—or, if all else fails, he can appeal above the law to the royal prerogative, which is a never-failing argument with judges who know their 'duty.'

"Then all the councillors agree with the famous maxim of Crassus: a king can never have too much gold, because he must maintain an army.[3] Further, that a king, even if he wants to, can do no wrong, for all property belongs to the king, and so do his subjects themselves; a man owns nothing but what the king, in his goodness, sees fit to leave him. The king should in fact leave his subjects as little as possible, because his own safety depends on keeping them from growing insolent with wealth and freedom. For riches and liberty make people less patient to endure harsh and unjust commands, whereas meager poverty blunts their spirits, makes them docile, and grinds out of the oppressed the lofty spirit of rebellion.

"Now at this point, suppose I were to get up again and declare that all these counsels are both dishonorable and ruinous to the king? Suppose I said his honor and his safety alike rest on the people's resources rather than his own? Suppose I said that the people choose a king for their own sake, not for his, so that by his efforts and

---

3. Adapted from Cicero, *On Moral Obligation* 1.8.25. Crassus was a rich Roman who joined with Pompey and Caesar to form the First Triumvirate, which dominated Rome from 60 B.C.E. to Crassus's death seven years later. Legend has it that this came about when a Parthian general, after defeating and capturing Crassus at the battle of Carrhae, disproved his maxim by pouring molten gold down his throat.

troubles they may live in comfort and safety? This is why, I would say, it is the king's duty to take more care of his people's welfare than of his own, just as it is the duty of a shepherd who cares about his job to feed his sheep rather than himself.[4]

"They are absolutely wrong when they say that the people's poverty safeguards public peace—experience shows the contrary. Where will you find more squabbling than among beggars? Who is more eager for revolution than the man who is most discontented with his present position? Who is more reckless about creating disorder than the man who knows he has nothing to lose and thinks he may have something to gain? If a king is so hated or despised by his subjects that he can rule them only by mistreatment, plundering, confiscation, and pauperization of his people, then he'd do much better to abdicate his throne—for under these circumstances, though he keeps the name of authority, he loses all the majesty of a king. A king has no dignity when he exercises authority over beggars, only when he rules over prosperous and happy subjects. This was certainly what that noble and lofty spirit Fabricius meant when he said he would rather be a ruler of rich men than be rich himself.[5]

"A solitary ruler who enjoys a life of pleasure and self-indulgence while all about him are grieving and groaning is acting like a jailer, not a king. Just as an incompetent doctor can cure his patient of one disease only by throwing him into another, so it's an incompetent king who can rule his people only by depriving them of all life's pleasures. Such a king openly confesses that he does not know how to rule free men.

"A king of this stamp should correct his own sloth or arrogance, because these are the vices that cause people to hate or despise him. Let him live on his own income without wronging others, and limit his spending to his income. Let him curb crime, and by wise training of his subjects keep them from misbehavior, instead of letting it breed and then punishing it. Let him not suddenly revive antiquated laws, especially if they have been long forgotten and never missed. And let him never take money as a fine when a judge would regard an ordinary subject as a low fraud for claiming it.

"Suppose I should then describe for them the law of the Macarians,[6] a people who also live not far from Utopia? On the day that their king first assumes office, he must take an oath confirmed by solemn ceremonies that he will never have in his treasury at any one time more than a thousand pounds in gold, or its equivalent in

---

4. This metaphor is one of the great commonplaces. Ezekiel 34.2 reads: "Woe be to the shepherds of Israel that do feed themselves! should not the shepherds feed the flocks?"
5. Gaius Fabricius Luscinus, who took part in the wars against Pyrrhus, king of Epirus (280–275 B.C.E.); the saying attributed to him here was actually coined by his colleague Manius Curius Dentatus, but it is quite in his spirit.
6. From Greek *makarios*, "blessed," "happy."

silver. They say this law was made by an excellent king, who cared more for his country's prosperity than for his own wealth; he established it as a barrier against any king heaping up so much money as to impoverish his people.[7] He thought this sum would enable the king to put down rebellions or repel hostile invasions, but would not tempt him into aggressive adventures. His law was aimed chiefly at keeping the king in check, but he also wanted to ensure an ample supply of money for the daily business transactions of the citizens. Besides, a king who has to distribute all his excess money to the people will not be much disposed to seek out opportunities for extortion. Such a king will be both a terror to evildoers and beloved by the good.—Now, don't you suppose if I set such ideas before men strongly inclined to the contrary, they would turn deaf ears to me?"

"Stone deaf, indeed, there's no doubt about it," I said, "and no wonder! To tell you the truth, I don't think you should offer advice or thrust on people ideas of this sort, that you know will not be listened to. What good can it do? When your listeners are already prepossessed against you and firmly convinced of opposite opinions, how can you win over their minds with such out-of-the-way speeches? This academic philosophy is quite agreeable in the private conversation of close friends, but in the councils of kings, where grave matters are being authoritatively decided, there is no place for it."

"That is just what I was saying," Raphael replied. "There is no place for philosophy in the councils of kings."

"Yes, there is," I said, "but not for this school philosophy which supposes that every topic is suitable for every occasion. There is another philosophy that is better suited for political action, that takes its cue, adapts itself to the drama in hand, and acts its part neatly and appropriately. This is the philosophy for you to use. Otherwise, when a comedy of Plautus is being played, and the household slaves are cracking trivial jokes together, you propose to come on stage in the garb of a philosopher and repeat Seneca's speech to Nero from the *Octavia*.[8] Wouldn't it be better to take a silent role than to say something wholly inappropriate, and thus turn the play into a tragicomedy?

7. Once again More glances at the previous English monarch, Henry VII, who died the richest prince in Christendom and probably the most hated. He combined unscrupulous greed with skinflint stinginess.
8. Most of the plays of the Roman comic dramatist Plautus (ca. 250–184 B.C.E.) involve low intrigue: needy young men, expensive prostitutes, senile moneybags, and clever slaves, in predictable combinations. The tragedy *Octavia*, involving Seneca as a character and long supposed to have been written by him, is full of high seriousness. In the speech More refers to (lines 440–592), Seneca lectures Nero on the abuses of power.

More's position embodies the rhetorical and ethical doctrine of *decorum* (propriety), which, in one of its applications, meant that any utterance should be tailored to take into account the nature of its audience. For rhetoricians, the primary aim of speech or writing is *persuasion*, and the argument between More and Hythloday that here ensues reflects the ancient conflict between rhetoric and philosophy, which centers in the tension between persuasion and *truth*. Renaissance humanism was strongly affiliated with the rhetorical tradition, and humanists often accused scholastic philosophers (as More accuses Hythloday) of naively failing to consider the contexts of utterances.

You pervert and ruin a play when you add irrelevant speeches, even if they are better than the original. So go through with the drama in hand as best you can, and don't spoil it all simply because you happen to think of a play by someone else that would be better.

"That's how things go in the commonwealth, and in the councils of princes. If you cannot pluck up bad ideas by the root, if you cannot cure long-standing evils as completely as you would like, you must not therefore abandon the commonwealth. Don't give up the ship in a storm because you cannot hold back the winds. And don't force strange ideas on people who you know have set their minds on a different course from yours. You must strive to influence policy indirectly, handle the situation tactfully, and thus what you cannot turn to good, you may at least make as little bad as possible. For it is impossible to make everything good unless you make all men good, and that I don't expect to see for a long time to come."

"The only result of this," he answered, "will be that while I try to cure others of madness, I'll be raving along with them myself. If I am to speak the truth, I will simply have to talk in the way I have described. For all I know, it may be the business of a philosopher to tell lies, but it certainly isn't mine. Though my advice may be repugnant and irksome to the king's councillors, I don't see why they should consider it eccentric to the point of folly. What if I told them the kind of thing that Plato advocates in his republic, or that the Utopians actually practice in theirs? However superior those institutions might be (and as a matter of fact they are), yet here they would seem inappropriate, because private property is the rule here, and there all things are held in common.

"People who have made up their minds to rush headlong down the opposite road are never pleased with someone who calls them back and tells them they are on the wrong course. But, apart from that, what did I say that could not and should not be said anywhere and everywhere? If we dismiss as out of the question and absurd everything which the perverse customs of men have made to seem alien to us, we shall have to set aside most of the commandments of Christ, even in a community of Christians. Yet he forbade us to dissemble them, and even ordered that what he had whispered to his disciples should be preached openly from the housetops.[9] Most of his teachings differ more radically from the common customs of mankind than my discourse did. But preachers, like the crafty fellows they are, have found that people would rather not change their lives to conform to Christ's rule, and so, just as you suggest, they have accommodated his teaching to the way people live, as if it were

9. Matthew 10.27; Luke 12.3.

a leaden yardstick.[1] At least in that manner they can get the two things to correspond in some way or other. The only real thing they accomplish that I can see is to make people feel more secure about doing evil.

"And this is all that I could accomplish in the councils of princes. For either I would have different ideas from the others, and that would come to the same thing as having no ideas at all, or else I would agree with them, and that, as Mitio says in Terence, would merely confirm them in their madness.[2] When you say I should 'influence policy indirectly,' I simply don't know what you mean; remember, you said I should try hard to handle the situation tactfully, and what can't be made good I should try to make as little bad as possible. In a council, there is no way to dissemble, no way to shut your eyes to things. You must openly approve the worst proposals, and consent to the most vicious policies. A man who went along only halfheartedly even with the worst decisions would immediately get himself a name as a spy and perhaps a traitor. How can one individual do any good when he is surrounded by colleagues who would more readily corrupt the best of men than do any reforming of themselves? Either they will seduce you by their evil ways or, if you keep yourself honest and innocent, you will be made a screen for the knavery and folly of others. Influencing policy indirectly! You wouldn't have a chance.

"This is why Plato in a very fine comparison declares that wise men are right in keeping clear of public business.[3] They see the people swarming through the streets and getting soaked with rain, and they cannot persuade them to go indoors and get out of the wet. They know if they go out themselves, they can do no good but only get drenched with the rest. So they stay indoors and are content to keep at least themselves dry, since they cannot remedy the folly of others.

"But as a matter of fact, my dear More, to tell you what I really think, as long as you have private property, and as long as money is the measure of all things, it is scarcely ever possible for a commonwealth to be just or happy. For justice cannot exist where all the best things in life are held by the worst people; nor can anyone be happy where property is limited to a few, since even those few are always uneasy, and the many are utterly wretched.

"So I reflect on the wonderfully wise and sacred institutions of the Utopians, who are so well governed with so few laws. Among them virtue has its reward, yet everything is shared equally, and everyone

---

1. A flexible measuring rod of lead was particularly useful in the ancient building style known as the "Lesbian" mode, because of the great number of curved moldings. Aristotle in *Nicomachean Ethics* 5.10.7 uses it as a metaphor for adaptable moral standards.
2. The allusion is to a comedy—*The Brothers*—by the Roman playwright Terence (ca. 190–159 B.C.E.). Speaking of his master, the slave Mitio says, "If I provoke or even listen to his madness, I shall be as crazy as he is" (lines 145–47).
3. *Republic* 6.496.

lives in plenty. I contrast them with the many other nations, which are constantly passing new ordinances and yet can never order their affairs satisfactorily. In these other nations, whatever a man can get he calls his own private property; but all the mass of laws old and new don't enable him to secure his own, or defend it, or even distinguish it from someone else's property—as is shown by innumerable and interminable lawsuits, fresh ones every day. When I consider all these things, I become more sympathetic to Plato and do not wonder that he declined to make laws for any people who refused to share their goods equally.[4] Wisest of men, he saw easily that the one and only road to the welfare of all lies through the absolute equality of goods. I doubt whether such equality can ever be achieved where property belongs to individuals. However abundant goods may be, when everyone tries to get as much as he can for his own exclusive use, a handful of men end up sharing the whole pile, and the rest are left in poverty. The result generally is two sorts of people whose fortunes ought to be interchanged: the rich are rapacious, wicked, and useless, while the poor are unassuming, modest men who work hard, more for the benefit of the public than of themselves.

"Thus I am wholly convinced that unless private property is entirely done away with, there can be no fair or just distribution of goods, nor can the business of mortals be happily conducted. As long as private property remains, by far the largest and the best part of the human race will be oppressed by a heavy and inescapable burden of cares and anxieties. This load, I admit, may be lightened to some extent, but I maintain it cannot be entirely removed. Laws might be made that no one should own more than a certain amount of land or receive more than a certain income. Or laws might be passed to prevent the prince from becoming too powerful and the populace too unruly. It might be made unlawful for public offices to be solicited, or put up for sale, or made burdensome for the officeholder by great expense. Otherwise, officials are tempted to get their money back by fraud or extortion, and only rich men can afford to accept positions which ought to be held by the wise. Laws of this sort, I agree, may have as much effect as poultices continually applied to sick bodies that are past cure. The social evils I mentioned may be alleviated and their effects mitigated for a while, but so long as private property remains, there is no hope at all of effecting a cure and restoring society to good health. While you try to cure one part, you aggravate the

---

4. Diogenes Laertius (3rd century C.E.) reports that the Arcadians and Thebans united to build a great city, and asked Plato to be its legislator. He made communism a condition of his going there, and when the inhabitants would not consent, declined the offer (*Lives of Eminent Philosophers* 3.23). Though in his plan for an ideal commonwealth in the *Republic* Plato espouses communism only for the ruling class (the Guardians: see pp. 101–03 below), in his later political dialogue *The Laws* he argues that the best commonwealth would be entirely communized.

disease in other parts. Suppressing one symptom causes another to break out, since you cannot give something to one person without taking it away from someone else."[5]

"But I don't see it that way," I replied. "It seems to me that people cannot possibly live well where all things are in common. How can there be plenty of commodities where every man stops working? The hope of gain will not spur him on; he will rely on others, and become lazy. If men are driven by need, and yet cannot legally protect what they have gained, what can follow but continual bloodshed and turmoil, especially when respect for magistrates and their authority has been lost? I for one cannot conceive of authority existing among men who are equal to one another in every respect."[6]

"I'm not surprised," said Raphael, "that you think of it this way, since you have no idea, or only a false idea, of such a commonwealth. But you should have been with me in Utopia, and seen with your own eyes their manners and customs as I did—for I lived there more than five years, and would never have left, if it had not been to make that new world known to others. If you had seen them, you would frankly confess that you had never seen a people well governed anywhere but there."

"You will have a hard time persuading me," said Peter Giles, "that people in that new land are better governed than in the world we know. Our minds are not inferior to theirs, and our governments, I believe, are older. Long experience has helped us develop many conveniences of life, and by good luck we have discovered many other things which human ingenuity could never have hit upon."

"As for the relative ages of the governments," Raphael replied, "you might judge more accurately if you had read their histories. If we believe these records, they had cities before there were even people here. What ingenuity has discovered or chance hit upon could have turned up just as well in one place as the other. For the rest, I believe that even if we surpass them in natural intelligence, they leave us far behind in their diligence and zeal to learn.

"According to their chronicles, they had heard nothing of ultra-equatorials (that's their name for us) until we arrived, except that once, some twelve hundred years ago, a ship which a storm had blown toward Utopia was wrecked on their island. Some Romans and Egyptians were cast ashore, and never departed. Now note how the Utopians profited, through their diligence, from this one chance event. They learned every single useful art of the Roman empire either directly from their guests or indirectly from hints and

---

5. Plato similarly employs the metaphor of societal disease, and of the statesman as physician (*Republic* 4.425E–426A; *Statesman* 279E–298E; Epistle 7, 330C–331A).
6. These objections to communism derive from the critique of the *Republic* in Aristotle's *Politics* 2.1–2.

surmises on which they based their own investigations. What benefits from the mere fact that on a single occasion some Europeans landed there![7] If a similar accident has hitherto brought anyone here from their land, the incident has been completely forgotten, as it will perhaps be forgotten in time to come that I was ever in their country. From one such accident they made themselves masters of all our useful inventions, but I suspect it will be a long time before we accept any of their institutions which are better than ours. This willingness to learn is, I think, the really important reason for their being better governed and living more happily than we do, though we are not inferior to them in brains or resources."

"Then let me implore you, my dear Raphael," said I, "to describe that island to us. Do not try to be brief, but explain in order everything relating to their land, their rivers, towns, people, manners, institutions, laws—everything, in short, that you think we would like to know. And you can take it for granted that we want to know everything that we don't know yet."

"There's nothing I'd rather do," he replied, "for these things are fresh in my mind. But it will take quite some time."

"In that case," I said, "let's first go to lunch. Afterward, we shall have all the time we want."

"Agreed," he said. So we went in and had lunch. Then we came back to the same spot, and sat down on the bench. I ordered my servants to take care that no one should interrupt us. Peter Giles and I urged Raphael to keep his promise. When he saw that we were attentive and eager to hear him, he sat silent and thoughtful a moment, and then began as follows.

Book II

[*The Geography of Utopia*][1]

The island of the Utopians is two hundred miles across in the middle part, where it is widest, and is nowhere much narrower than this except toward the two ends, where it gradually tapers. These ends, drawn toward one another as if in a five-hundred-mile circle, make

---

7. In addition to underscoring the benefits of studying the achievements of other societies, the point of this passage seems to be to indicate that Utopia and Christian Europe started about even, on the path of their development, both having the Roman and Egyptian rudiments.

1. The early editions of *Utopia* include, in Book II, eight section headings. These help in locating the treatment of particular topics in Hythloday's rather sprawling discourse, but since in several instances the headings identify only the *initial* topic of a section, they can also be misleading. In the present edition, they are supplemented by additional headings, enclosed in brackets to identify them as editorial insertions. For still further help in locating the treatment of topics in Book II, see the Index, under "Utopia (the country)."

the island crescent-shaped, like a new moon.[2] Between the horns of the crescent, which are about eleven miles apart, the sea enters and spreads into a broad bay. Being sheltered from the wind by the surrounding land, the bay is never rough, but quiet and smooth instead, like a big lake. Thus nearly the whole inner coast is one great harbor, across which ships pass in every direction, to the great advantage of the people. What with shallows on one side and rocks on the other, the entrance into the bay is perilous. Near the middle of the channel, there is one rock that rises above the water, and so presents no danger in itself; on top of it a tower has been built, and there a garrison is kept. Since the other rocks lie underwater, they are very dangerous to navigation. The channels are known only to the Utopians, so hardly any strangers enter the bay without one of their pilots; and even they themselves could not enter safely if they did not direct their course by some landmarks on the coast. If these landmarks were shifted about, the Utopians could easily lure to destruction an enemy fleet coming against them, however big it was.

On the outer side of the island there are likewise occasional harbors; but the coast is rugged by nature, and so well fortified that a few defenders could beat off the attack of a strong force. They say (and the appearance of the place confirms this) that their land was not always an island. But Utopus, who conquered the country and gave it his name (it had previously been called Abraxa),[3] and who brought its rude and uncouth inhabitants to such a high level of culture and humanity that they now excel in that regard almost every other people, also changed its geography. After winning the victory at his first landing, he cut a channel fifteen miles wide where their land joined the continent, and caused the sea to flow around the country. He put not only the natives to work at this task, but all his own soldiers too, so that the vanquished would not think the labor a disgrace.[4] With the work divided among so many hands, the project was finished quickly, and the neighboring peoples, who at first had laughed at his folly, were struck with wonder and terror at his success.

There are fifty-four cities on the island, all spacious and magnificent, identical in language, customs, institutions, and laws. So far

2. The island is similar to England in size, though not at all in shape.
3. The Greek Gnostic Basilides (2nd century C.E.) postulated 365 heavens and called the highest of them Abraxas. The Greek letters that constitute the word have numerical equivalents summing to 365, but what it actually *means* is unknown.
4. This is the first of several passages in the book stressing the dignity of labor. On More's "rehabilitation of the idea of physical labor," which in classical political theory and practice was normally relegated to the lower classes, slaves, and women, see Frank E. and Fritzie P. Manuel, *Utopian Thought in the Western World* (Cambridge, Mass.: Belknap Press of Harvard University Press, 1979), p. 127. Utopus's exploit is probably meant to recall that of the Persian king Xerxes I, who in preparation for his invasion of Greece in 480 B.C.E. had a channel for his warships dug across the isthmus of a peninsula extending from the base of Mount Athos to the Greek mainland. Herodotus recounts this exploit in his *Histories* 7.22–24.

as the location permits, all of them are built on the same plan and
have the same appearance. The nearest are twenty-four miles apart,
and the farthest are not so remote that a person cannot go on foot
from one to the other in a day.

Once a year each city sends three of its old and experienced citizens to Amaurot to consider affairs of common interest to the island.
Amaurot lies at the navel of the land, so to speak, and is convenient
to every other district, so it acts as a capital. Every city has enough
ground assigned to it so that at least twelve miles of farm land
are available in every direction, though where the cities are farther apart, they have much more land.[5] No city wants to enlarge its
boundaries,[6] for the inhabitants consider themselves good tenants
rather than landlords. At proper intervals all over the countryside
they have built houses and furnished them with farm equipment.
These houses are inhabited by citizens who come to the country by
turns. No rural household has fewer than forty men and women
in it, besides two slaves bound to the land. A master and mistress,
serious and mature persons, are in charge of each household. Over
every thirty households is placed a single phylarch.[7] Each year twenty
persons from each household move back to the city, after completing a two-year stint in the country. In their place, twenty others are
sent out from town, to learn farm work from those who have already
been in the country for a year and are therefore better skilled in
farming. They, in turn, will teach those who come the following
year.[8] If all were equally unskilled in farm work, and new to it, they
might harm the crops out of ignorance. This custom of alternating
farm workers is the usual procedure, so that no one will have to do
such hard work unwillingly for more than two years; but many of
them, who take a natural pleasure in farm life, are allowed to stay
longer.

The farm workers till the soil, feed the animals, hew wood, and
take it to the city by land or by water, as is more convenient. They
breed an enormous number of chickens by a marvelous method. The
farmers, not hens, hatch the eggs, by keeping them in a warm place
at an even temperature. As soon as they come out of the shell, the
chicks recognize the humans, follow them around, and are devoted
to them instead of to their mothers.[9]

5. Each consisting of a central metropolis and the surrounding countryside, the Utopian
   cities recall the ancient Greek city-states.
6. The marginal gloss at this point: "But today this is the curse of all countries." Although
   Utopia exists in the present, the glosses repeatedly refer to it as if it belonged to the
   distant past, like classical Greece and Rome.
7. From Greek *phylarchos*, "ruler of a tribe."
8. We learn later (p. 44 below) that everyone studies agriculture in school and gets practical experience of it on field trips.
9. Artificial incubation is mentioned by Pliny the Elder (*Natural History* 10.76.154), but it
   was not practiced in More's time.

They raise very few horses, and those full of mettle, which they keep only to exercise the young people in the art of horsemanship.[1] For all the work of plowing and hauling they use oxen, which they agree are inferior to horses over the short haul, but which can hold out longer under heavy burdens, are less subject to disease (as they suppose), and can be kept with less cost and trouble. Moreover, when oxen are too old for work, they can be used for meat.

Grain they use only to make bread.[2] They drink wine, apple or pear cider, or simple water, which they sometimes boil with honey or licorice, of which they have an abundance. Although they know very well, down to the last detail, how much food each city and its surrounding district will consume, they produce much more grain and cattle than they need for themselves, and share the surplus with their neighbors. Whatever goods the folk in the country need which cannot be produced there, they request of the town magistrates, and since there is nothing to be paid or exchanged, they get what they want without any trouble. They generally go to town once a month in any case, for the feast day. When harvest time approaches, the phylarchs in the country notify the town magistrates how many hands will be needed. Crews of harvesters come just when they're wanted, and in one day of good weather they can usually get in the whole crop.

Their Cities, Especially Amaurot

If you know one of their cities, you know them all, for they're exactly alike, except where geography itself makes a difference. So I'll describe one of them, and no matter which. But what one rather than Amaurot, the most worthy of all?—since its eminence is acknowledged by the other cities, which send representatives to the annual meeting there; besides which, I know it best, because I lived there for five full years.

Well, then, Amaurot lies up against a gently sloping hill; the town is almost square in shape. From a little below the crest of the hill, it runs down about two miles to the river Anyder, and then spreads out along the river bank for a somewhat greater distance. The Anyder rises from a small spring about eighty miles above Amaurot, but other streams flow into it, two of them being pretty big, so that, as it runs past Amaurot, the river has grown to a width of five hundred yards. It continues to grow even larger until at last, sixty miles farther

---

1. In fact, horses were long extinct in the New World before Europeans imported them.
2. I.e., they don't, like the English, use it to make beer and ale, which are strikingly omitted from the following list of utopian drinks. Perhaps More considered them an undue temptation, as being easier to make than wine and more agreeable to the taste of the English workingman. Utopia's drinking habits are more middle class than a plowman accustomed to beer would consider utopian.

along, it is lost in the ocean. In all this stretch between the sea and
the city, and also for some miles above the city, the river is tidal,
ebbing and flowing every six hours with a swift current.[3] When the
tide comes in, it fills the whole Anyder with salt water for about
thirty miles, driving the fresh water back. Even above that, for
several miles farther, the water is brackish; but a little higher up, as
it runs past the city, the water is always fresh, and when the tide
ebbs, the river runs clean and sweet all the way to the sea.

The two banks of the river at Amaurot are linked by a bridge, built
not on wooden piles but on remarkable stone arches. It is placed at
the upper end of the city, farthest removed from the sea, so that ships
can sail along the entire length of the city quays without obstruction.
There is also another stream, not particularly large, but very gentle
and pleasant, which gushes from the hill on which the city is situated,
flows down through the center of town, and into the Anyder. The
inhabitants have walled around the source of this river, which takes
its rise a little outside the town, and joined it to the town proper so
that if they should be attacked, the enemy would not be able to cut
off the stream or divert or poison it. Water from the stream is carried
by tile piping into various sections of the lower town. Where the terrain makes this impractical, they collect rain water in cisterns, which
serve just as well.

The town is surrounded by a thick, high wall, with many towers
and bastions. On three sides it is also surrounded by a dry ditch,
broad and deep and filled with thorn hedges; on its fourth side the
river itself serves as a moat. The streets are conveniently laid out for
use by vehicles and for protection from the wind. Their buildings
are by no means shabby; unbroken rows of houses face each other
across the streets along the whole block. The streets are twenty feet
wide.[4] Behind each row of houses—at the center of every block and
extending the full length of the street—there are large gardens.

Every house has a door to the street and another to the garden.
The doors, which are made with two leaves, open easily and swing
shut automatically, letting anyone enter who wants to—so there is
nothing private anywhere. Every ten years, they change houses by
lot.[5] The Utopians are very fond of these gardens of theirs. They
raise vines, fruits, herbs, and flowers, so well cared for and flourishing that I have never seen any gardens more productive or elegant

3. Many of the details of Amaurot—its situation on a tidal river, its stone bridge (below),
   though not the location of that bridge—are reminiscent of London. Even the little
   second stream (below), which provides Amaurot's water supply, suggests the brook
   known as the Fleet.
4. Lavish, by 16th-century standards.
5. The purpose is, of course, to preclude anything like private property and attachment to
   it. For a striking similarity of custom, founded on a wholly different reason, see Vespucci's account of the American aborigines (pp. 120–21 below).

than theirs. They keep interested in gardening, partly because they delight in it, and also because of the competition between different blocks, which challenge one another to produce the best gardens. Certainly you will not easily find anything else in the whole city more useful or more pleasant to the citizens. And this gives reason to think that the founder of the city paid particular attention to the siting of these gardens.

They say that in the beginning the whole city was planned by Utopus himself, but that he left to posterity matters of adornment and improvement such as could not be perfected in one man's lifetime. Their records began 1,760 years ago with the conquest of the island, have been diligently compiled, and are carefully preserved. From these it appears that the first houses were low, like cabins or peasant huts, built out of any sort of timber, with mud-plastered walls and pointed roofs thatched with straw. But now their houses are all three stories high and handsomely constructed; the fronts are faced with fieldstone, quarried rock, or brick, over rubble construction. The roofs are flat, and are covered with a kind of plaster that is cheap but fireproof, and more weather-resistant even than lead.[6] Glass (which is plentiful there) is used in windows to keep out the weather;[7] and they also use thin linen cloth treated with oil or gum so that it lets in more light and keeps out more wind.

Their Officials

Once a year, every group of thirty households elects an official, formerly called the syphogrant,[8] but now called the phylarch. Over every group of ten syphogrants with their households there is another official, once called the tranibor[9] but now known as the head phylarch. All the syphogrants, two hundred in number, elect the governor. They take an oath to choose the man they think best qualified; and then by secret ballot they elect the governor from among four men nominated by the people of the four sections of the city. The governor holds office for life, unless he is suspected of aiming at

6. Used in More's time to roof important buildings.
7. During More's day in England window glass was not common; oiled cloth and lattices of wicker or wood were more frequent.
8. The word appears to be constructed from Greek *sophos* ("wise")—or perhaps *sypheos* ("of the sty")—plus *gerontes* ("old men"). Each Utopian city is a democratic republic: the syphogrants are elected by the households, and the syphogrants elect the governor (whom they evidently can also remove; see below) as well as the class of scholars, from which all high officials are chosen (see p. 47). Utopia as a whole is a loose federation of these small republics, which, however, seems not to have a central executive. (In a letter to Erasmus of ca. December 4, 1516, though, More reports a daydream of himself as king of Utopia.)
9. The etymology seems to be *traneis* or *tranos* ("clear," "plain," "distinct") plus *boros* ("devouring," "gluttonous"). There is no explanation of why Hythloday consistently uses the "older" form of the titles.

a tyranny. Though the tranibors are elected annually, they are not changed for light or casual reasons. All their other officials hold office for a single year only.

The tranibors meet to consult with the governor every other day, and more often if necessary: they discuss affairs of state, and settle any disputes between private parties (there are very few), acting as quickly as possible.[1] The tranibors always invite two syphogrants to the senate chamber, different ones every day. There is a rule that no decision can be made on a matter of public business unless it has been discussed in the senate on three separate days. It is a capital offense to make plans about public business outside of the senate or the popular assembly. The purpose of these rules, they say, is to prevent the governor and the tranibors from conspiring together to alter the government and enslave the people. Therefore all matters which are considered important are first laid before the assembly of the syphogrants. They talk the matter over with the households they represent, debate it with one another, then report their recommendation to the senate. Sometimes a question is brought before the general council of the whole island.

The senate also has a standing rule never to discuss a matter on the day when it is first introduced; all new business is deferred to the next meeting.[2] They do this so that a man will not blurt out the first thought that occurs to him, and then devote all his energies to defending those foolish impulses, instead of considering impartially the public good. They know that some men would rather jeopardize the general welfare than admit to having been heedless and short-sighted—so perverse and preposterous is their sense of pride. They should have had enough foresight at the beginning to speak with prudence rather than haste.

Their Occupations

Agriculture is the one occupation at which everyone works, men and women alike, with no exceptions. They are trained in it from childhood, partly in the schools, where they learn theory, and partly through field trips to nearby farms, which make something like a game of practical instruction. On these trips they not only watch the work being done, but frequently pitch in and get a workout by doing the jobs themselves.

Besides farm work (which, as I said, everybody performs), each person is taught a particular trade of his own, such as wool-working, linen-making, masonry, metal-work, or carpentry. There is no other

1. Marginal gloss: "A quick ending to disputes, which now are endlessly and deliberately prolonged."
2. Gloss: "Would that the same rule prevailed in our modern councils."

craft that is practiced by any considerable number of them.[3] Through-out the island people wear, and throughout their lives always wear, the same style of clothing, except for the distinction between the sexes, and between married and unmarried persons. Their clothing is attractive, does not hamper bodily movement, and serves for warm as well as cold weather; what is more, each household makes its own.

Every person (and this includes women as well as men) learns a second trade, besides agriculture. As the weaker sex, women prac-tice the lighter crafts, such as working in wool or linen; the heavier jobs are assigned to the men. As a rule, the son is trained to his father's craft, for which most feel a natural inclination. But if any-one is attracted to another occupation, he is transferred by adoption into a family practicing the trade he prefers. Both his father and the authorities make sure that he is assigned to a grave and responsible householder. After someone has learned one trade, if he wants to learn another he gets the same permission. When he has learned both, he pursues whichever he likes better, unless the city needs one more than the other.

The chief and almost the only business of the syphogrants is to manage matters so that no one sits around in idleness, and assure that everyone works hard at his trade. But no one has to exhaust himself with endless toil from early morning to late at night, as if he were a beast of burden. Such wretchedness, really worse than slavery, is the common lot of workmen almost everywhere except Utopia.[4] Of the day's twenty-four hours, the Utopians devote only six to work. They work three hours before noon, when they go to lunch. After lunch they rest for a couple of hours, then go to work for another three hours. Then they have supper, and at eight o'clock (counting the first hour after noon as one) they go to bed, and sleep eight hours.

The other hours of the day, when they are not working, eating, or sleeping, are left to each person's individual discretion, provided that free time is not wasted in roistering or sloth but used properly in some chosen occupation. Generally these periods are devoted to intellectual activity. For they have an established custom of giving daily public lectures before dawn;[5] attendance at these lectures is required only of those who have been specially chosen to devote

3. Would not considerable numbers also be employed making such things as pottery, har-nesses, bread, and books, as well as in mining and the merchant marine? Presumably all the professionals—doctors, for example—are drawn from the class of scholars (see p. 47).
4. In England, for example, a law of 1514–15 required workmen to be present at the work-place from daybreak to nightfall in fall and winter and from 5 A.M. to between 7 and 8 P.M. in spring and summer. (There were breaks for meals and, in summer, for a brief afternoon nap.)
5. Renaissance universities got under way early: first lecture was between 5 and 7 A.M.

themselves to learning, but a great many other people, both men and women, choose voluntarily to attend. Depending on their interests, some go to one lecture, some to another. But if anyone would rather devote his spare time to his trade, as many do who don't care for the intellectual life, this is not discouraged; in fact, such persons are commended as especially useful to the commonwealth.

After supper, they devote an hour to recreation, in their gardens in summer, or during winter in the common halls where they have their meals. There they either play music or amuse themselves with conversation. They know nothing about gambling with dice, or other such foolish and ruinous games.[6] They do play two games not unlike chess. One is a battle of numbers, in which one number captures another. The other is a game in which the vices fight a battle against the virtues. The game is ingeniously set up to show how the vices oppose one another, yet combine against the virtues; then, what vices oppose what virtues, how they try to assault them openly or undermine them insidiously; how the defenses of the virtues can break the strength of the vices or skillfully elude their plots; and finally, by what means one side or the other gains the victory.[7]

But in all this, you may get a wrong impression, if we don't go back and consider one point more carefully. Because they allot only six hours to work, you might think the necessities of life would be in scant supply. This is far from the case. Their working hours are ample to provide not only enough but more than enough of the necessities and even the conveniences of life. You will easily appreciate this if you consider how large a part of the population in other countries exists without doing any work at all. In the first place, hardly any of the women, who are a full half of the population, work;[8] or, if they do, then as a rule their husbands lie snoring in bed. Then there is a great lazy gang of priests and so-called religious.[9] Add to them all the rich, especially the landlords, who are commonly called gentlemen and nobles. Include with them their retainers, that mob of swaggering bullies. Finally, reckon in with these the sturdy and lusty beggars who go about feigning some disease as an excuse for their idleness. You will certainly find that the things which satisfy our needs are produced by far fewer hands than you had supposed.

And now consider how few of those who do work are doing really essential things. For where money is the standard of everything,

---

6. Marginal gloss: "But now dicing is the sport of princes."
7. Moral games of this general character were popular with Renaissance educators.
8. A strange statement, since in More's time most women not only selected, prepared, and cooked the family food; did the family laundry; and performed a thousand other routine tasks of domestic drudgery but also were responsible for taking care of the children. In Utopia, too, they are responsible for at least some of these duties—cooking, child-care—in addition to practicing a craft and taking their turn at farm work.
9. I.e., members of the various religious orders.

many vain, superfluous trades are bound to be carried on simply to satisfy luxury and licentiousness. Suppose the multitude of those who now work were limited to a few trades, and set to producing just those commodities that nature really requires. They would be bound to produce so much that prices would drop and the workmen would be unable to gain a living. But suppose again that all the workers in useless trades were put to useful ones, and that all the idlers (who now guzzle twice as much as the workingmen who make what they consume) were assigned to productive tasks—well, you can easily see how little time would be enough and more than enough to produce all the goods that human needs and conveniences require—yes, and human pleasure too, as long as it's true and natural pleasure.

The experience of Utopia makes this perfectly apparent. In each city and its surrounding countryside barely five hundred of those men and women whose age and strength make them fit for work are exempted from it.[1] Among these are the syphogrants, who by law are free not to work; yet they don't take advantage of the privilege, preferring to set a good example to their fellow citizens. Some others are permanently exempted from work so that they may devote themselves to study, but only on the recommendation of the priests[2] and through a secret vote of the syphogrants. If any of these scholars disappoints their hopes, he becomes a workman again. On the other hand, it happens from time to time that a craftsman devotes his leisure so earnestly to study, and makes such progress as a result, that he is relieved of manual labor and promoted to the class of learned men. From this class of scholars are chosen ambassadors, priests, tranibors, and the governor himself, who used to be called Barzanes, but in their modern tongue is known as Ademus.[3] Since almost all the rest of the population is neither idle nor occupied in useless trades, it is easy to see why they produce so much in so short a working day.

Apart from all this, in several of the necessary crafts their way of life requires less total labor than does that of people elsewhere. In other countries, building and repairing houses requires the constant work of many men, because what a father has built, his thriftless heir lets fall into ruin; and then his successor has to repair, at great expense, what could easily have been maintained at a very small charge. Further, when a man has built a splendid house at

1. I.e., are exempted from manual labor. As Hythloday proceeds to explain, in each city those exempted include the 200 syphogrants and the class of scholars, from which is chosen the other exempted individuals: the twenty tranibors, the governor, ambassadors, and the thirteen (p. 89 below) priests.
2. Who are in charge of the education of children (p. 89).
3. Marginal gloss: "Only the learned hold public office." "Ademus": from Greek for "Without People." "Barzanes": "Son of Zeus" (Hebrew—*bar*—plus Greek). A powerful Chaldean magician named "Mithrobarzanes" figures in the dialogue "Menippus" by the Greek satirist Lucian (2nd century C.E.). More had published Latin translations of this and other brief works by him (see p. 107 below).

vast cost, someone else may think he has finer taste, let the first house fall to ruin, and then build another one somewhere else for just as much money. But among the Utopians, where everything has been well ordered and the commonwealth properly established, building a brand-new home on a new site is a rare event. They are not only quick to repair damage, but foresighted in preventing it. The result is that their buildings last for a very long time with minimal repairs; and the carpenters and masons sometimes have so little to do that they are set to hewing timber and cutting stone in case some future need for it should arise.

Consider, too, how little labor their clothing requires. Their work clothes are unpretentious garments made of leather, which last seven years. When they go out in public, they cover these rough working-clothes with a cloak. Throughout the entire island, these cloaks are of the same color, which is that of natural wool.[4] As a result, they not only need less wool than people in other countries, but what they do need is less expensive. Even so, they use linen cloth most, because it requires least labor. They like linen cloth to be white and wool cloth to be clean; but they put no price on fineness of texture. Elsewhere a man may not be satisfied with four or five woolen cloaks of different colors and as many silk shirts; or if he's a clothes-horse, even ten are not enough. But there everyone is content with a single cloak, and generally wears it for two years. There is no reason at all why he should want any others, for if he had them, he would not be better protected against the cold, nor would he appear in any way better dressed.

Since there is an abundance of everything, as a result of everyone working at useful trades and the trades requiring less work, they sometimes assemble great numbers of people to work on the roads, if any of them need repairing. And when there is no need even for this sort of work, then the officials very often proclaim a shorter workday, since they never force their citizens to perform useless labor. The chief aim of their constitution is that, whenever public needs permit, all citizens should be free to withdraw as much time as possible from the service of the body and devote themselves to the freedom and culture of the mind. For in that, they think, is the real happiness of life.

Social Relations

Now I must explain how the citizens behave toward one another, the nature of their social relations, and how they distribute their goods within the society.

4. In a passage of his letter to Erasmus of ca. December 4, 1516, More identifies this garment as the habit of a Franciscan friar.

Each city, then, consists of households, the households consisting generally of blood-relations. When the women grow up and are married, they move into their husbands' households. On the other hand, male children and after them grandchildren remain in the family, and are subject to the oldest member, unless his mind has started to fail, in which case the next oldest takes his place. To keep the cities from becoming too large or too small, they take care that there should be no more than six thousand households in each (exclusive of the surrounding countryside), each family containing between ten and sixteen adults.[5] They do not, of course, try to regulate the number of minor children in a family. The limit on adults is easily observed by transferring individuals from a household with too many into a household with not enough. Likewise if a city has too many people, the extra persons serve to make up a shortage of population in other cities. And if the population throughout the entire island exceeds the quota, they enroll citizens out of every city and plant a colony under their own laws on the mainland near them, wherever the natives have plenty of unoccupied and uncultivated land.[6] Those natives who want to live with the Utopian settlers are taken in. When such a merger occurs, the two peoples gradually and easily blend together, sharing the same way of life and customs, much to the advantage of both. For by their policies the Utopians make the land yield an abundance for all, though previously it had seemed too poor and barren even to support the natives. But if the natives will not join in living under their laws, the Utopians drive them out of the land they claim for themselves, and if they resist make war on them. They think it is perfectly justifiable to make war on people who leave their land idle and waste, yet forbid the use of it to others who, by the law of nature, ought to be supported from it.[7]

If for any reason one of their cities shrinks so sharply in population that it cannot be made up from other cities without bringing

5. If an average household includes thirteen adults, and there are 6,000 households per city (not counting those on the surrounding farms), then there are about 78,000 adults per city; allowing for children and slaves, the total population must be well in excess of 100,000, making every Utopian city larger than all but the greatest European cities of the time. Whether More actually made these calculations (or whether there is really much point in making them) is another matter.
6. Among previous works of political theory, the closest parallel to the Utopian arrangements for population control is found in Plato's Laws (5.740A–741A), where the set figure of 5,040 households for the city-state is maintained by redistributing children, manipulating the birthrate (using such techniques as enforced abstinence for the overly fertile and rewards or censure to stimulate underbreeders), and establishing colonies.
7. Such rationalizations have long been the stock in trade of imperialism. For centuries, they found their most respectable underpinnings (as here) in the classical concept of the law of nature, an unchanging, universally valid body of law that human beings were thought to apprehend through reason and instinct. A fundamental principle of natural law is that all things are common property; from this it follows that a nation may appropriate "wasteland" necessary to its survival. Such arguments were applied, for example, to European colonization of the New World.

them too under proper strength, the numbers are restored by bringing people back from the colonies. This has happened only twice,
they say, in their whole history, both times as a result of a frightful
plague. They would rather that their colonies disappeared than that
any of the cities on their island should get too small.

But to return to their manner of living. The oldest of every
household, as I said, is the ruler. Wives are subject to their husbands,
children to their parents, and generally the younger to their elders.[8]
Every city is divided into four equal districts, and in the middle of
each district is a market for all kinds of commodities. Whatever each
household produces is brought here and stored in warehouses, each
kind of goods in its own place. Here the head of each household
looks for what he or his family needs, and carries off what he wants
without any sort of payment or compensation. Why should anything
be refused him? There is plenty of everything, and no reason to fear
that anyone will claim more than he needs. Why would anyone be
suspected of asking for more than is needed, when everyone knows
there will never be any shortage? Fear of want, no doubt, makes
every living creature greedy and rapacious—and, in addition, man
develops these qualities out of sheer pride, pride which glories in getting ahead of others by a superfluous display of possessions. But this
kind of vice has no place whatever in the Utopian way of life.

Next to the marketplace of which I just spoke are the food markets, where people bring all sorts of vegetables, fruit, and bread.
Fish, meat, and poultry are also brought there from designated places
outside the city, where running water can carry away all the blood
and refuse. Bondsmen do the slaughtering and cleaning in these
places: citizens are not allowed to do such work. The Utopians feel
that slaughtering our fellow creatures gradually destroys the sense
of compassion, which is the finest sentiment of which our human
nature is capable. Besides, they don't allow anything dirty or filthy to
be brought into the city, lest the air become tainted by putrefaction
and thus infectious.

Each block has its own spacious halls, equally distant from one
another, and each known by a special name. In these halls live the
syphogrants. Thirty families are assigned to each hall, to take their
meals in common[9]—fifteen live on one side of the hall, fifteen on

8. Utopian women enjoy considerably more equality with men than did their 16th-century
   European counterparts, but Utopian social relations as a whole exhibit the same patri-
   archal structure that had always been prevalent in Europe and was sanctioned in classical and biblical texts (e.g., Aristotle, *Politics* 1.5.1–2; Ephesians 5.22–6.4) as well as
   in many later ones.
9. The institution of the common messes has precedents in ancient Sparta and in the
   designs for an ideal commonwealth by Plato (*Republic* 3.416E) and Aristotle (*Politics*
   7.10.10). It has also been a feature of other communities with a utopian bent—for
   example, the Israeli kibbutzim.

the other. The stewards of all the halls meet at a fixed time in the market and get food according to the number of persons for whom each is responsible.

But first consideration goes to the sick, who are cared for in public hospitals. Every city has four of these, built at the city limits, slightly outside the walls, and spacious enough to appear like little towns. The hospitals are large for two reasons: so that the sick, however numerous they may be, will not be packed closely and uncomfortably together, and also so that those who have a contagious disease, such as might pass from one to the other, may be isolated. The hospitals are well ordered and supplied with everything needed to cure the patients, who are nursed with tender and watchful care. Highly skilled physicians are in constant attendance. Consequently, though nobody is sent there against his will, there is hardly anyone in the city who would not rather be treated for an illness at the hospital than at home.

When the hospital steward has received the food prescribed for the sick by their doctors, the best of the remainder is fairly divided among the halls according to the number in each, except that special regard is paid to the governor, the high priest, and the tranibors, as well as to ambassadors and foreigners, if there are any. In fact, foreigners are very few; but when they do come, they have certain furnished houses assigned to them.

At the hours of lunch and supper, a brazen trumpet summons the entire syphogranty to assemble in their hall, except for those who are bedridden in the hospitals or at home. After the halls have been served with their quotas of food, nothing prevents an individual from taking food home from the marketplace. They realize that no one would do this without good reason. For while it is not forbidden to eat at home, no one does it willingly, because it is not thought proper; and besides, it would be stupid to take the trouble of preparing a worse meal at home when there is an elegant and sumptuous one near at hand in the hall.

In this hall, slaves do all the particularly dirty and heavy work. But planning the meal, as well as preparing and cooking the food, is carried out by the women alone, with each family taking its turn. Depending on their number, they sit down at three or more tables. The men sit with their backs to the wall, the women on the outside, so that if a woman has a sudden qualm or pain, such as occasionally happens during pregnancy, she may get up without disturbing the others and go off to the nurses.

A separate dining room is assigned to the nurses and infants, with a plentiful supply of cradles, clean water, and a warm fire. Thus the nurses may lay the infants down, or remove their swaddling clothes and let them refresh themselves by playing freely before the fire.

Each child is nursed by its own mother, unless death or illness prevents. When that happens, the wives of the syphogrants quickly find a nurse. The problem is not difficult. Any woman who can, gladly volunteers for the job, since everyone applauds her kindness and the child itself regards its nurse as its natural mother.

Children under the age of five sit together in the nursery. All other minors, both boys and girls up to the age of marriage, either wait on table or, if not old and strong enough for that, stand by in absolute silence. Both groups eat whatever is handed to them by those sitting at the table, and have no other set time for their meals.

The syphogrant with his wife sits at the middle of the first table, in the highest part of the dining hall. This is the place of greatest honor, and from this table, which is placed crosswise to the others, the whole gathering can be seen. Two of the eldest sit with them, for they always sit in groups of four; if there is a church in the district, the priest and his wife sit with the syphogrant, so as to preside.[1] On both sides of them sit younger people, next to them older people again, and so through the hall: those of about the same age sit together, yet are mingled with others of a different age. The reason for this, as they explain it, is that the dignity of the aged, and the respect due them, may restrain the younger people from improper freedom of words and gestures, since nothing said or done at table can pass unnoticed by the old, who are present on every side.

Dishes of food are not served down the tables in order from top to bottom, but all the old persons, who are seated in conspicuous places, are served with the best food; and then equal shares are given to the rest. The old people, as they feel inclined, give their neighbors a share of those delicacies which are not plentiful enough to be served to everyone. Thus due respect is paid to seniority, yet everyone enjoys some of the benefits.

They begin every lunch and supper with some reading on a moral topic,[2] but keep it brief lest it become a bore. Taking that as an occasion, the elders introduce proper topics of conversation, which they try not to make gloomy or dull. They never monopolize the conversation with long monologues, but are eager to hear what the young people say. In fact, they deliberately draw them out, in order to discover the natural temper and quality of each one's mind, as revealed in the freedom of mealtime talk.

Their lunches are light, their suppers rather more elaborate, because lunch is followed by work, supper by rest and a night's sleep, which they think particularly helpful to good digestion. No evening

1. Marginal gloss: "Priest before prince. But now even bishops act as servants to royalty."
2. Humanists were fond of this social custom, the origins of which were part monastic, part classical.

meal passes without music, and the dessert course is never scanted; during the meal, they burn incense and scatter perfume, omitting nothing which will make the occasion festive. For they are somewhat inclined to think that no kind of pleasure is forbidden, provided harm does not come of it.

This is the pattern of life in the city; but in the country, where they are farther removed from neighbors, they all eat in their own homes. No family lacks for food, since, after all, whatever the city-dwellers eat comes originally from those in the country.

The Travels [and Trade] of the Utopians

Anyone who wants to visit friends in another city, or simply to see the place itself, can easily obtain permission from his syphogrant and tranibor, unless for some special reason he is needed at home. They travel together in groups, taking a letter from the governor granting leave to travel and fixing a day of return. They are given a wagon and a public slave to drive the oxen and look after them, but unless women are in the company they dispense with the wagon as an unnecessary bother. Wherever they go, though they take nothing with them, they never lack for anything, because they are at home everywhere. If they stay more than a day in one place, each one practices his trade there, and is kindly received by his fellow artisans.

Anyone who takes upon himself to leave his district without permission, and is caught without the governor's letter, is treated with contempt, brought back as a runaway, and severely punished. If he is bold enough to try it a second time, he is made a slave. Anyone who wants to stroll about and explore the extent of his own district is not prevented, provided he first obtains his father's permission and his wife's consent. But wherever he goes in the countryside, he gets no food until he has completed either a morning's or an afternoon's stint of work. On these terms, he may go where he pleases within his own district, yet be just as useful to the city as if he were at home.

So you see there is no chance to loaf or any pretext for evading work; there are no wine bars or alehouses or brothels, no chances for corruption, no hiding places, no spots for secret meetings. Because they live in the full view of all, they are bound to be either working at their usual trades or enjoying their leisure in a respectable way. Such customs must necessarily result in plenty of life's good things, and since they share everything equally, it follows that no one can ever be reduced to poverty or forced to beg.

In the senate at Amaurot (to which, as I said before, three representatives come every year from each city), they survey the island to find out where there are shortages and surpluses, and promptly satisfy one district's shortage with another's surplus. These are outright gifts; those who give receive nothing in return from those to whom they give. Though they give freely to one city, asking nothing in return, they get freely from another to which they gave nothing; and thus the whole island is like a single family.

After they have accumulated enough for themselves—and this they consider to be a full two-years' store, because next year's crop is always uncertain—then they export their surpluses to other countries: great quantities of grain, honey, wool, flax, timber, scarlet and purple dyestuffs, hides, wax, tallow, and leather, as well as livestock. One-seventh of their cargo they give freely to the poor of the importing country, and the rest they sell at moderate prices. In exchange they receive not only such goods as they lack at home (in fact, about the only important thing they lack is iron) but immense quantities of silver and gold. They have been carrying on trade for a long time now, and have accumulated a greater supply of the precious metals than you would believe possible. As a result, they now care very little whether they sell for cash or on credit, and most payments to them actually take the form of promissory notes. However, in all such transactions, they never trust individuals but insist that the foreign city become officially responsible. When the day of payment comes, the city collects the money due from private debtors, puts it into the treasury, and enjoys the use of it till the Utopians claim payment. Most of it, in fact, is never claimed. The Utopians think it hardly right to take what they don't need away from people who do need it. But if they need to lend some part of the money to another nation, then they call it in—as they do also when they must wage war. This is the only reason that they keep such an immense treasure at home, as a protection against extreme peril or sudden emergency. They use it above all to hire, at extravagant rates of pay, foreign mercenaries, whom they would much rather risk in battle than their own citizens. They know very well that for large enough sums of money many of the enemy's soldiers can themselves be bought off or set at odds with one another, either secretly or openly.[3]

[Their Attitude to Gold and Silver]

For this reason, therefore, they have accumulated a vast treasure; but they do not keep it like a treasure. I'm really quite ashamed to tell you how they do keep it, because you probably won't believe me. I would not have believed it myself if someone had just told me about it; but I was there, and saw it with my own eyes. It is a general rule that the more different anything is from what people are used

3. Marginal gloss: "Better to avoid war by bribery or guile than to wage it with great loss of human blood."

to, the harder it is to accept. But, considering that all their other customs are so unlike ours, a sensible judge will perhaps not be surprised that they treat gold and silver quite differently from the way we do. After all, they never do use money among themselves, but keep it only for a contingency which may or may not actually arise. So in the meanwhile they take care that no one shall overvalue gold and silver, of which money is made, beyond what the metals themselves deserve. Anyone can see, for example, that iron is far superior to either; men could not live without iron, by heaven, any more than without fire or water. But Nature granted to gold and silver no function with which we cannot easily dispense. Human folly has made them precious because they are rare. In contrast, Nature, like a most indulgent mother, has placed the best things out in the open, like air, water, and the earth itself; but vain and unprofitable things she has hidden away in remote places.

If in Utopia gold and silver were kept locked up in some tower, foolish heads among the common people might concoct a story that the governor and senate were out to cheat ordinary folk and get some advantage for themselves. They might indeed put the gold and silver into plate-ware and such handiwork, but then in case of necessity the people would not want to give up such articles, on which they had begun to fix their hearts, only to melt them down for soldiers' pay. To avoid all these inconveniences, they thought of a plan which conforms with their institutions as clearly as it contrasts with our own. Unless one has actually seen it working, their plan may seem incredible, because we prize gold so highly and are so careful about protecting it. While they eat from pottery dishes and drink from glass cups, well made but inexpensive, their chamber pots and all their humblest vessels, for use in the common halls and even in private homes, are made of gold and silver.[4] The chains and heavy fetters of slaves are also made of these metals. Finally, criminals who are to bear the mark of some disgraceful act are forced to wear golden rings in their ears and on their fingers, golden chains around their necks, and even golden headbands. Thus they hold gold and silver up to scorn in every conceivable way. As a result, if they had to part with their entire supply of these metals, which other nations give up with as much agony as if they were being disemboweled, the Utopians would feel it no more than the loss of a penny.

4. Marginal gloss: "O magnificent scorn for gold!" Vespucci had reported Native Americans' indifference to gold and gems (p. 121 below), as had the historian Pietro Martire d'Anghiera (1457–1526), who wrote of a tribe that "used kitchen and other common utensils made of gold" (De Orbe Novo [On the New World], trans. Francis A. MacNutt, 2 vols. [New York and London: G. P. Putnam's Sons, 1912; rpt. New York: B. Franklin, 1970], 1:221).

They pick up pearls by the seashore, and diamonds and garnets from certain cliffs, but never go out of set purpose to look for them. If they happen to find some, they polish them and give them to the children, who, when they are small, feel proud and pleased with such gaudy decorations. But after, when they grow a bit older, and notice that only babies like such toys, they lay them aside. Their parents don't have to say anything; the children simply put these trifles away out of shame, just as our children when they grow up put away their marbles, baubles, and dolls.

These customs so different from those of other people produce quite different attitudes: this never became clearer to me than it did in the case of the Anemolian[5] ambassadors, who came to Amaurot while I was there. Because they came to discuss important business, the national council had assembled ahead of time, three citizens from each city. The ambassadors from nearby nations, who had visited Utopia before and knew something of their customs, understood that fine clothing was not respected in that land, silk was despised, and gold a badge of contempt; therefore they always came in the very plainest of their clothes. But the Anemolians, who lived farther off and had had fewer dealings with the Utopians, had heard only that they all dressed alike and very simply; so they took for granted that their hosts had nothing to wear that they didn't put on. Being themselves rather more proud than wise, they decided to dress as resplendently as the very gods, and dazzle the eyes of the poor Utopians by the glitter of their garb.

Consequently the three ambassadors made a grand entry with a suite of a hundred attendants, all in clothing of many colors, and most in silk. Being noblemen at home, the ambassadors were arrayed in cloth of gold, with heavy gold chains on their necks, gold earrings, gold rings on their fingers, and sparkling strings of pearls and gems on their caps. In fact, they were decked out in all the articles which in Utopia are used to punish slaves, shame wrongdoers, or entertain infants. It was a sight to see how they strutted when they compared their finery with the dress of the Utopians, who had poured out into the streets to see them pass. But it was just as funny

---

5. From Greek *anemolios,* "windy." The story of the Anemolian ambassadors owes much to "Nigrinus," a dialogue by Lucian in which a rich Roman makes a fool of himself by stalking around Athens, where people are "brought up . . . to poverty and to philosophy[,] . . . in all the vulgar pomp of retinue and gold and gorgeous raiment, expecting that every eye would be turned upon him in envy of his lot; instead of which, they heartily pitied the poor worm. . . . They soon eased him of his embroidery and purple, by playful allusions to flower and colour. 'Spring is early.'—'How did that peacock get here?'—'His mother must have lent him that shawl,'—and so on. The same with the rest, his rings, his elaborate coiffure. . . . Little by little he came to his senses, and left Athens very much the better for the public education he had received." Quoted from *The Works of Lucian of Samosata,* ed. H. W. Fowler and F. G. Fowler, 4 vols. (Oxford: Clarendon Press, 1905), 1:16 (sect. 12–13).

to see how wide they fell of the mark, and how far they were from
getting the consideration they wanted and expected. Except for a
very few Utopians who for some special reason had visited foreign
countries, all the onlookers considered this pomp and splendor a
mark of disgrace. They therefore bowed to the humblest of the party
as lords, and took the ambassadors, because of their golden chains,
to be slaves, passing them by without any reverence at all. You might
have seen children, who had themselves thrown away their pearls
and gems, nudge their mothers when they saw the ambassadors' jew-
eled caps, and say:

"Look at that big lummox, mother, who's still wearing pearls and
jewels as if he were a little boy!"

But the mother, in all seriousness, would answer:

"Hush, son, I think he is one of the ambassadors' fools."

Others found fault with the golden chains as useless, because
they were so flimsy any slave could break them, and so loose that he
could easily shake them off and run away whenever he wanted, foot-
loose and fancy-free. But after the ambassadors had spent a couple
of days among the Utopians, they saw the immense amounts of gold
which were as thoroughly despised there as they were prized at home.
They saw too that more gold and silver went into making the chains
and fetters of a single runaway slave than into costuming all three of
them. Somewhat ashamed and crestfallen, they put away all the
finery in which they had strutted so arrogantly, especially after they
had talked with the Utopians enough to learn their customs and
opinions.

[Their Philosophy]

The Utopians marvel that any mortal can take pleasure in the
dubious sparkle of a little jewel or bright gemstone, when he has a
star, or the sun itself, to look at. They are amazed at the foolishness
of any man who considers himself a nobler fellow because he wears
clothing of specially fine wool. No matter how delicate the thread,
they say, a sheep wore it once, and still was nothing but a sheep.[6]
They are surprised that gold, a useless commodity in itself, is everywhere valued so highly that man himself, who for his own purposes
conferred this value on it, is considered far less valuable than the
gold. They do not understand why a dunderhead with no more brains
than a post, and who is as depraved as he is foolish, should command
a great many wise and good men simply because he happens to have
a great pile of gold. Yet if this master should lose his money to the
lowest rascal in his household (as can happen by chance, or through

6. Echoing Lucian's "Demonax" (sect. 41).

some legal trick—for the law can produce reversals as violent as Fortune herself), he would promptly become the servant of his servant, as if he were personally attached to the coins, and a mere appendage to them.[7] Even more than this, the Utopians are appalled at those people who practically worship a rich man, though they neither owe him anything nor are obligated to him in any way. What impresses them is simply that the man is rich. Yet all the while they know he is so mean and grasping that as long as he lives not a single penny out of that great mound of money will ever come their way.

These and the like attitudes the Utopians have picked up partly from their upbringing, since the institutions of their commonwealth are completely opposed to such folly, and partly from instruction and their reading of good books. For though not many people in each city are excused from labor and assigned to scholarship full-time (these are persons who from childhood have given evidence of excellent character, unusual intelligence, and devotion to learning), every child gets an introduction to good literature, and throughout their lives a large part of the people, men and women alike, spend their leisure time in reading.

They study all the branches of learning in their native tongue, which is not deficient in terminology or unpleasant in sound, and adapts itself as well as any to the expression of thought. Just about the same language is spoken throughout that entire area of the world, though elsewhere it is corrupted to various degrees.

Before we came there, the Utopians had never so much as heard about a single one of those philosophers[8] whose names are so celebrated in our part of the world. Yet in music, dialectic, arithmetic, and geometry they have found out just about the same things as our great men of the past. But while they equal the ancients in almost all subjects, they are far from matching the inventions of our modern logicians.[9] In fact they have not discovered even one of those elaborate rules about restrictions, amplifications, and suppositions which our own young men study in the *Litle Logicbook*.[1] They are so far from being able to speculate on "second intentions" that not one of them was able to see "man-in-general,"[2] though I pointed straight

7. Alongside this passage and obviously applying to several sentences in it, a marginal gloss proclaims, "How much wiser are the Utopians than the ruck of Christians!"
8. As the next sentence indicates, the idea of "philosophy" here is the old, broad one that encompasses learning in general (the sense that survives in the title Doctor of Philosophy).
9. The scholastic philosophers, constantly deprecated by humanists.
1. Probably the *Parva logicalia*, a textbook of logic by Peter of Spain, later Pope John XXI (d. 1277).
2. Man conceived of as a "universal." "Second intentions": in scholastic discourse, purely abstract conceptions, derived from "first intentions" (the direct apprehensions of things). The sentence is typical of the way humanists liked to ridicule, in the name of common sense, the scholastics' abstractions.

at him with my finger, and he is, as you well know, bigger than any giant, maybe even a colossus. On the other hand, they have learned to plot expertly the courses of the stars and the movements of the heavenly bodies. They have devised a number of different instruments by which they compute with the greatest exactness the course and position of the sun, the moon, and the other stars that are visible in their area of the sky. As for the conjunctions and oppositions of the planets, and that whole deceitful business of divination by the stars, they have never so much as dreamed of it.[3] From long experience in observation, they are able to forecast rains, winds, and other changes in the weather. But as to the causes of the weather, of the tides in the sea and its saltiness, and the origins and nature of the heavens and the earth, they have various opinions. They agree with our ancient philosophers on some matters, but on others, just as the ancients disagreed with one another, so the Utopians differ from all the ancients and yet reach no consensus among themselves.

In matters of moral philosophy, they carry on the same arguments as we do. They inquire into the nature of the good, distinguishing goods of the body from goods of the mind and external goods.[4] They ask whether the name of "good" may be applied to all three, or applies only to goods of the mind. They discuss virtue and pleasure, but their chief concern is what to think of human happiness, and whether it consists of one thing or of more. On this point, they seem overly inclined to the view of those who think that all or most human happiness consists of pleasure.[5] And what is more surprising, they seek support for this comfortable opinion from their religion, which is serious and strict, indeed almost stern and forbidding. For they

3. Marginal gloss: "Yet these astrologers are revered by Christians to this day."
4. This threefold classification of goods appears in Plato (*Laws* 3.697B, 5.743E), but it is associated especially with Aristotle (*Nicomachean Ethics* 1.8.2, *Politics* 7.1.3–4) and Aristotelian tradition. Recall that, despite their long-ago visit by a shipwrecked boatload of Romans and Egyptians (p. 37 above), the Utopians had never, before Hythloday's arrival, heard of any European philosophers. Thus one point of the account of Utopian philosophy is evidently to show that reason will at any time or place lead thoughtful people to the same set of philosophical problems and positions. The other, main point is surely to suggest that the moral norms derivable from reason are consistent with those divinely revealed to Christians.
5. I.e., the Utopians' primary affinity in moral philosophy is with the hedonistic school founded by Epicurus (341–271 B.C.E.). Cf. Vespucci on the Native Americans: "I deem their manner of life to be Epicurean" (see p. 120 below). Contrary to popular opinion, however, Epicurus himself did not mean, by the pursuit of pleasure, mere undiscriminating sensual indulgence: like the Utopians, he placed primary emphasis on the pleasures of a virtuous, rational life. The long passage on Utopian hedonism that begins here is in fact a contribution to the gradual, qualified rehabilitation of Epicurus that began with Petrarch and Boccaccio and was continued by a series of Renaissance humanists and philosophers. See *The Cambridge History of Renaissance Philosophy*, ed. Charles B. Schmitt et al. (Cambridge: Cambridge University Press, 1988), pp. 374–86. Note, though, that the Utopians do not share the Epicureans' denial of human immortality or their conviction that the gods are unconcerned with humankind. The Utopians' belief in the soul's immortality is crucial to their development of an ethical position similar to the Christian one.

never discuss happiness without joining to their philosophic ratio-
nalism certain principles drawn from religion. Without these religious principles, they think that reason by itself is weak and defective
in its efforts to investigate true happiness.

Their religious principles are of this nature: that the soul of man is
immortal, and by God's goodness born for happiness; that after this
life, rewards are appointed for our virtues and good deeds, punishments for our sins. Though these are indeed religious beliefs, they
think that reason leads us to believe and accept them. And they add
unhesitatingly that if these beliefs were rejected, no one would be so
stupid as not to feel that he should seek pleasure, regardless of right
and wrong. His only care would be to keep a lesser pleasure from
standing in the way of a greater one, and to avoid pleasures that are
inevitably followed by pain.[6] They think you would have to be actually crazy to pursue harsh and painful virtue, give up the pleasures of
life, and suffer pain from which you can expect no advantage. For if
there is no reward after death, you have no compensation for having
passed your entire existence without pleasure, that is, miserably.

To be sure, they believe happiness is found, not in every kind of
pleasure, but only in good and honest pleasure. Virtue itself, they
say, draws our nature to this kind of pleasure, as to the supreme
good. There is an opposed school which declares that virtue is itself
happiness.[7]

They define virtue as living according to nature; and God, they
say, created us to that end. When an individual obeys the dictates
of reason in choosing one thing and avoiding another, he is following nature. Now the first rule of reason is to love and venerate the
Divine Majesty to whom we owe our existence and our capacity for
happiness. The second rule of nature is to lead a life as free of anxiety and as full of joy as possible, and to help all one's fellow men
toward that end. The most hard-faced eulogist of virtue and the
grimmest enemy of pleasure, while they invite us to toil and sleepless nights and self-laceration, still admonish us to relieve the
poverty and misfortune of others as best we can. It is especially
praiseworthy, they tell us, when we provide for our fellow creatures'
comfort and welfare. Nothing is more humane (and humanity is the
virtue most proper to human beings) than to relieve the misery of
others and, by removing all sadness from their lives, restore them to
enjoyment, that is, pleasure. Well, if this is the case, why doesn't
nature equally invite us to do the same thing for ourselves? Either a

---

6. These rules for choosing among pleasures are attributed to Epicurus (Diogenes Laertius, *Lives of Eminent Philosophers* 10.129).
7. This is the position of the Stoics, who asserted that virtue constitutes happiness
whether or not it leads to pleasure. The definition of *virtue* as "living according to
nature" (below) is also Stoic.

joyful life (that is, one of pleasure) is a good thing, or it isn't. If it isn't, then you should not help anyone to it—indeed, you ought to take it away from everyone you can, as being harmful and deadly to them. But if such a life is good, and if we are supposed, indeed obliged, to help others to it, why shouldn't we first of all seek it for ourselves, to whom we owe no less charity than to anyone else? When nature prompts you to be kind to your neighbors, she does not mean that you should be cruel and merciless to yourself.[8] Thus they say that nature herself prescribes for us a joyous life, in other words, pleasure, as the goal of our actions; and living according to her prescriptions is to be defined as virtue. But as nature bids mortals to make one another's lives merrier, to the extent that they can, so she warns us constantly not to seek our own advantage in ways that cause misfortune to our fellows. And the reason for this is an excellent one; for no one is placed so far above the rest that he is nature's sole concern: she cherishes alike all those living beings to whom she has granted the same form.

Consequently, the Utopians maintain that one should not only abide by private agreements but also obey all those public laws which control the distribution of vital goods, such as are the very substance of pleasure. Any such laws, provided they have been properly promulgated by a good king, or ratified by a people free of force and fraud, should be observed; and as long as they are observed, to pursue your own interests is prudent; to pursue the public interest as well is pious; but to pursue your own pleasure by depriving others of theirs is unjust. On the other hand, deliberately to decrease one's own pleasure in order to augment that of others is a work of humanity and benevolence which never fails to reward the doer over and above his sacrifice. You may be repaid for your kindness; and in any case you are conscious of having done a good deed. Your mind draws more joy from recalling the affection and good will of those whom you have benefited than your body would have drawn pleasure from the things you gave up. Finally, they believe (as religion easily persuades a well-disposed mind to believe) that God will recompense us, for surrendering a brief and transitory pleasure here, with immense and neverending joy in heaven. And so they conclude, after carefully considering and weighing the matter, that all our actions and the virtues exercised within them look toward pleasure and happiness as their ultimate end.

By pleasure they understand every state or movement of body or mind in which we find delight in accordance with the behests of

_____

8. Marginal gloss: "But now some people cultivate pain as if it were the essence of religion, rather than incidental to performance of a pious duty or the result of natural necessity—and thus to be borne, not pursued."

nature. They are right in adding that the desire must accord with
nature. By simply following our senses and right reason[9] we may discover what is pleasant by nature: it is a delight that does not injure
others, that does not preclude a greater pleasure, and that is not followed by pain. But a pleasure which is against nature, and which
men call "delightful" only by the emptiest of fictions (as if one could
change the real nature of things just by changing their names), does
not, they hold, really make for happiness; in fact, they say it often
precludes happiness. And the reason is that men whose minds are
filled with false ideas of pleasure have no room left for true and
genuine delight. As a matter of fact, there are a great many things
which have no genuine sweetness in them but are for the most part
actually bitter, yet which, through the perverse enticements of evil
desires, are considered very great pleasures, and even included
among the supreme goals of life.

Among the devotees of this false pleasure, they include those
whom I mentioned before, the people who think themselves finer
fellows because they wear finer clothes. These people are twice mistaken: first in thinking their clothes better than anyone else's, and
then in thinking themselves better because of their clothes. As far
as a garment's usefulness goes, what does it matter if it was woven of
fine thread or coarse? Yet they act as if they were set apart by nature
herself, rather than their own fantasies; they strut about, and put on
airs. Because they have a fancy suit, they think themselves entitled
to honors they would never have expected if they were dressed in
homespun, and they grow indignant if someone passes them by
without showing special respect.

It is the same kind of absurdity to be pleased by empty, ceremonial
honors. What true and natural pleasure can you get from someone's bent knee or bared head? Will the creaks in your own knees
be eased thereby, or the madness in your head? The phantom of
false pleasure is illustrated by others who run mad with delight over
their own blue blood, plume themselves on their nobility, and applaud
themselves for all their rich ancestors (the only ancestors that count
nowadays), and especially for all their ancient family estates. Even
if they don't have the shred of an estate themselves, or if they've
squandered every penny of their inheritance, they don't consider
themselves a bit less noble.

In the same class the Utopians put those people I described before
who are mad for jewelry and gems, and think themselves divinely
happy if they find a good specimen, especially of the sort that happens to be fashionable in their country at the time—for stones vary

9. The power, thought to have been implanted by God in all humankind, to apprehend
truth and moral law; conscience.

in value from one market to another. The collector will not make an offer for a stone till it's taken out of its gold setting, and even then he will not buy unless the dealer guarantees and gives security that it is a true and genuine stone. What he fears is that his eyes will be deceived by a counterfeit. But if you consider the matter, why should a counterfeit give any less pleasure, when your eyes cannot distinguish it from a real gem? Both should be of equal value to you—as they would be, in fact, to a blind man.[1]

What about those who pile up money not because they want to do anything with the heap, but so they can sit and look at it? Is that true pleasure they experience, or aren't they simply cheated by a show of pleasure? Or what of those with the opposite vice, who hide away gold they will never use and perhaps never even see again? In their anxiety to hold onto it, they actually lose it. For what else happens when you deprive yourself, and perhaps other people too, of a chance to use your gold, by burying it in the ground? And yet when you've hidden your treasure away, you exult over it as if your mind were now free to rejoice. Suppose someone stole it, and you died ten years later, knowing nothing of the theft. During all those ten years, what did it matter whether the money was stolen or not? In either case, it was equally useless to you.

To these false and foolish pleasures they add gambling, which they have heard about, though they've never tried it, as well as hunting and hawking. What pleasure can there be, they wonder, in throwing dice on a table? If there were any pleasure in the action, wouldn't doing it over and over again quickly make one tired of it? What pleasure can there be in listening to the barking and yelping of dogs— isn't that rather a disgusting noise? Is there any more pleasure felt when a dog chases a hare than when a dog chases a dog? If what you like is fast running, there's plenty of that in both cases; they're just about the same. But if what you really want is slaughter, if you want to see a living creature torn apart under your eyes—you ought to feel nothing but pity when you see the little hare fleeing from the hound, the weak creature tormented by the stronger, the fearful and timid beast brutalized by the savage one, the harmless hare killed by the cruel dog. The Utopians, who regard this whole activity of hunting as unworthy of free men, have assigned it, accordingly, to their butchers, who, as I said before, are all slaves.[2] In their eyes, hunting is the

---

1. In *The Praise of Folly*, Erasmus tells a story about More giving his wife some false gems, which he passed off as being real and highly valuable: "Now, if the young woman was just as happy feasting her eyes and thoughts on coloured glass, what did it matter to her if she was keeping such trinkets hidden carefully away in her room as if they were some rare treasure? Meanwhile her husband saved expense, enjoyed his wife's illusion, and kept her as closely bound in gratitude to him as if he'd given her something which had cost him a fortune" (*CWE* 27:118–19)
2. Marginal gloss: "Yet today this is the chosen art of our court-divinities."

lowest thing even butchers can do. In the slaughterhouse, their work is more useful and honest, since there they kill animals only from necessity; but the hunter seeks merely his own pleasure from the killing and mutilating of some poor little creature. Even in beasts, taking such relish in the sight of death reveals, in the Utopians' opinion, a cruel disposition, or else one that has become so through the constant practice of such brutal pleasures.

Common opinion considers these activities, and countless others like them, to be pleasures; but the Utopians say flatly they have nothing at all to do with real pleasure, since there's nothing naturally pleasant about them. They often please the senses, and in this they are like pleasure, but that does not alter their basic nature. The enjoyment doesn't arise from the experience itself, but only from the perverse habits of the mob, as a result of which they mistake the bitter for the sweet, just as pregnant women, whose taste has been turned awry, sometimes think pitch and tallow taste sweeter than honey. A person's taste may be similarly depraved by disease or by custom, but that does not change the nature of pleasure, or of anything else.

They distinguish several different classes of true pleasure, some being pleasures of the mind and others pleasures of the body. Those of the mind are knowledge and the delight which rises from contemplating the truth, also the gratification of looking back on a well-spent life and the unquestioning hope of happiness to come.

Pleasures of the body they also divide into two classes. The first is that which fills the senses with immediate delight. Sometimes this happens when bodily organs that have been weakened by natural heat are restored with food and drink; sometimes it happens when we eliminate some excess in the body, as when we move our bowels, generate children, or relieve an itch somewhere by rubbing or scratching it. Now and then pleasure arises, not from restoring a deficiency or discharging an excess, but from something that excites our senses with a hidden but unmistakable force, and attracts them to itself. Such is the power of music.

The second kind of bodily pleasure they describe as nothing but the calm and harmonious state of the body, its state of health when undisturbed by any disorder. Health itself, when not oppressed by pain, gives pleasure, without any external excitement at all. Even though it appeals less directly to the senses than the gross gratifications of eating and drinking, many consider this to be the greatest pleasure of all. Most of the Utopians regard it as the foundation and basis of all the pleasures, since by itself alone it can make life peaceful and desirable, whereas without it there is no possibility of any other pleasure. Mere absence of pain, without positive health, they regard as insensibility, not pleasure.

Some have maintained that a stable and tranquil state of health is not really a pleasure, on the grounds that the presence of health cannot be felt except through some external stimulus.[3] The Utopians (who have considered the matter thoroughly) long ago rejected this opinion. On the contrary, they nearly all agree that health is crucial to pleasure. Since pain is inherent in disease, they argue, and pain is the bitter enemy of pleasure, just as disease is the enemy of health, then pleasure must be inherent in quiet good health. You may say pain is not the disease itself, simply an accompanying effect; but they argue that that makes no difference, since the effect is the same either way. For whether health is itself a pleasure or is merely the cause of pleasure (as fire is the cause of heat), the fact remains that those who have stable health must also have pleasure.

When we eat, they say, what happens is that health, which was starting to fade, takes food as its ally in the fight against hunger. While our health gains strength, the simple process of returning vigor gives us pleasure and refreshment. If our health feels delight in the struggle, will it not rejoice when the victory has been won? When at last it is restored to its original strength, which was its aim all through the conflict, will it at once become insensible, and fail to recognize and embrace its own good? The idea that health cannot be felt they consider completely wrong. Every man who's awake, they say, feels that he's in good health—unless he isn't. Is anyone so torpid and dull that he won't admit health is delightfully agreeable to him? And what is delight except pleasure under another name?

Of all the different pleasures, they seek primarily those of the mind, and prize them most highly. The foremost mental pleasure, they believe, arises from the practice of the virtues and the consciousness of a good life. Among the pleasures of the body, they give the first place to health. As for eating and drinking and other delights of that sort, they consider them desirable, but only for the sake of health. They are not pleasant in themselves, but only as ways to withstand the insidious attacks of sickness. A wise man would rather escape sickness altogether than have a good cure for it; he would rather prevent pain than find a palliative for it. And so it would be better not to need this kind of pleasure at all than to be assuaged by it.

Anyone who thinks happiness consists of this sort of pleasure must confess that his ideal life would be one spent in an endless round of hunger, thirst, and itching, followed by eating, drinking, scratching, and rubbing. Who can fail to see that such an existence is not only disgusting but miserable? These pleasures are certainly the lowest of all, as they are the most adulterate—for they never

3. This is, especially, the position of Plato, e.g., *Republic* 9.583C–585A.

occur except in connection with the pains that are their contraries. Hunger, for example, is linked to the pleasure of eating, and far from equally, since the pain is sharper and lasts longer; it precedes the pleasure, and ends only when the pleasure ends with it. So the Utopians think pleasures of this sort should not be much valued, except insofar as they are necessary to life. Yet they enjoy these pleasures too, and acknowledge gratefully the kindness of Mother Nature, who coaxes her children with allurements and cajolery to do what in any case they must do from necessity. How wretched life would be if the daily diseases of hunger and thirst had to be overcome by bitter potions and drugs, like some other diseases that afflict us less often!

Beauty, strength, and agility, as special and pleasant gifts of nature, they joyfully accept. The pleasures of sound, sight, and smell they also pursue as the special seasonings of life, recognizing that nature intended these delights to be the particular province of man. No other kind of animal admires the shape and loveliness of the universe, or enjoys odors, except in the way of searching for food, or distinguishes harmonious from dissonant sounds. But in all their pleasures, the Utopians observe this rule, that the lesser pleasure must not interfere with the greater, and that no pleasure shall carry pain with it as a consequence. If a pleasure is dishonorable, they think it will inevitably lead to pain.

Moreover, they think it is crazy for a man to despise beauty of form, to impair his own strength, to grind his energy down to lethargy, to exhaust his body with fasts, to ruin his health, and to scorn all other natural delights, unless by so doing he can better serve the welfare of others or the public good. Then indeed he may expect a greater reward from God. But otherwise for a man to inflict pain on himself does no one any good. He gains, perhaps, the empty and shadowy reputation of virtue; and no doubt he hardens himself against fantastic adversities which may never occur. But such a person the Utopians consider absolutely crazy—cruel to himself, as well as most ungrateful to nature—as if, to avoid being in her debt, he rejects all her gifts.

This is the way they think about virtue and pleasure. Human reason, they believe, can attain to no surer conclusions than these, unless a revelation from heaven should inspire men with holier notions. In all this, I have no time now to consider whether they are right or wrong, and don't feel obliged to do so. I have undertaken only to describe their principles, not to defend them. But of this I am sure, that whatever you think of their ideas, there is not a more excellent people or a happier commonwealth anywhere in the whole world.

In body they are nimble and lively, and stronger than you would expect from their stature, though they're by no means tiny. Their soil is not very fertile, nor their climate of the best, but they protect themselves against the weather by temperate living, and improve their soil by industry, so that nowhere do grain and cattle flourish more plentifully, nowhere are people more vigorous, and liable to fewer diseases. There you can see not only that they do all the things farmers usually do to improve poor soil by hard work and technical knowledge, but you can see a forest which they uprooted with their own hands and moved to another site. They did this not so much for the sake of better growth but to make transport easier, by having wood closer to the sea, the rivers, or the cities themselves. For grain is easier than wood to carry by land over a long distance.

[Their Delight in Learning]

The people in general are easygoing, cheerful, clever, and like their leisure. When they must, they can stand heavy labor, but otherwise they are not very fond of it. In intellectual pursuits, they are tireless. When they heard from us about the literature and learning of the Greeks (for we thought there was nothing in Latin, except the historians and poets, that they would value), it was wonderful to behold how eagerly they sought to be instructed in Greek. We therefore began to study a little of it with them, at first more to avoid seeming lazy than out of any expectation that they would profit by it. But after a short trial, their diligence convinced us that our efforts would not be wasted. They picked up the forms of the letters so easily, pronounced the language so aptly, memorized it so quickly, and began to recite so accurately that it seemed like a miracle. Most of our pupils were established scholars, of course, picked for their unusual ability and mature minds; and they studied with us, not just of their own free will, but at the command of the senate.[4] Thus in less than three years they had perfect control of the language and could read the best authors fluently, unless the text was corrupt. I have a feeling they picked up Greek more easily because it was somewhat related to their own tongue. Though their language resembles Persian in most respects, I suspect their race descends from the Greeks, because their language retains some vestiges of Greek in the names of cities and in official titles.

Before leaving on the fourth voyage, I placed on board, instead of merchandise, a good-sized packet of books; for I had resolved not to return at all rather than come home soon. Thus they received from me most of Plato's works and more of Aristotle's, as well as Theophrastus's book *On Plants*, though the latter, I'm sorry to say, was somewhat mutilated.[5] During the voyage I carelessly left it lying around, a monkey got hold of it, and from sheer mischief ripped out

4. Marginal gloss: "But now clods and blockheads are assigned to learning, while the best minds are corrupted by pleasures."
5. Theophrastus, Aristotle's pupil, was studied in the Renaissance not as a quaint curiosity but because his views were still current in botany.

a b c d e f g h i k l m n o p q r s t u x y

⊖⊕⊕⊙⊖⊖⊙⊃⊖⊙⊗⊗⊿⅃⌐⌐⊓⊡⊟⊞⊟⊟

TETRASTICHON VERNACVLA VTO-
PIENSIVM LINGVA.

Vtopos   ha   Boccas   peula   chama.

polta   chamaan

Bargol   he   maglomi   baccan

foma   gymnofophaon

Agrama   gymnofophon   labarem

bacha   bodamilomin

Voluala   barchin   heman   la

lauoluola   dramme   pagloni.

HORVM VERSVVM AD VERBVM HAEC
EST SENTENTIA.

Vtopus me dux ex non infula fecit infulam.
Vna ego terrarum omnium abfq; philofophia.
Ciuitatem philofophicam expreffi mortalibus.
Libenter impartio mea, non grauatim accipio meliora.

b ﾞ

This sample of the Utopian language, which first appeared in the earliest edition of More's book (1516), reveals affinities with Greek and Latin and has enough internal consistency to suggest that it was worked out with care (evidently by Peter Giles; see p. 130 below). The stilted Latin quatrain at the end, which purports to be a literal translation, can itself be translated as follows: "Me, once a peninsula, Utopus the king made an island. / Alone among all nations, and without complex abstractions, / I set before men's eyes the philosophical city. / What I give is free; what is better I am not slow to take from others."

a few pages here and there and tore them up. Of the grammarians they have only Lascaris, for I did not take Theodorus with me, nor any dictionary except that of Hesychius; and they have Dioscorides.[6] They are very fond of Plutarch's writings, and delighted with the witty persiflage of Lucian.[7] Among the poets they have Aristophanes, Homer, and Euripides, together with Sophocles in the small typeface of the Aldine edition.[8] Of the historians they possess Thucydides and Herodotus, as well as Herodian.[9]

As for medical books, a comrade of mine named Tricius Apinatus brought with him some small treatises by Hippocrates, and the *Microtechne* of Galen.[1] They were delighted to have these books. Even though there's hardly a country in the world that needs doctors less, medicine is nowhere held in greater honor: they consider it one of the finest and most useful parts of philosophy. They think that when, with the help of philosophy, they explore the secrets of nature they are gratifying not only themselves but the author and maker of nature. They suppose that, like other artists, he created this beautiful mechanism of the world to be admired—and by whom, if not by man, who is alone in being able to appreciate so great a thing? Therefore he is bound to prefer a careful observer and sensitive admirer of his work before one who, like a brute beast, looks on the grand spectacle with a stupid and blockish mind.

Once stimulated by learning, the minds of the Utopians are wonderfully quick to seek out those various arts which make life more agreeable. Two inventions, to be sure, they owe to us: the art of printing and the manufacture of paper. At least they owe these arts partly to us, though partly to their own ingenuity. While we were showing them the Aldine editions of various works, we talked about papermaking and how letters are printed, though without going into detail, for none of us had had any practical experience of either skill. But

6. Dioscorides (1st century C.E.) wrote a treatise on drugs and herbs that was printed in 1499. The Renaissance scholars Constantine Lascaris and Theodore of Gaza wrote grammars of Greek. The Greek dictionary of Hesychius of Alexandria (5th century C.E.?) was published in 1514.

7. The Syrian-born ironist who was admired, translated, and imitated by both More and Erasmus (see p. 107 below). The writings of Plutarch (ca. 46–ca. 120 C.E.) referred to presumably include his *Moral Essays* as well as his *Parallel Lives* of eminent Greeks and Romans.

8. The first printed edition of Sophocles was that of Aldus Manutius in 1502. The house of Aldus, established in Venice toward the end of the 15th century, was not only the first establishment to print Greek texts in Greek type but was responsible for some of the best-designed books in the history of the art.

9. Thucydides and Herodotus (both 5th century B.C.E.) are the preeminent Greek historians. Herodian (ca. 175–250 C.E.) wrote a history of the Roman emperors of the 2nd and 3rd centuries.

1. Hippocrates (5th century B.C.E.) and Galen (2nd century C.E.) were the most influential Greek medical writers. The *Microtechne* is a medieval summary of Galen's ideas. The name Tricius Apinatus (like Hythloday) is a learned joke: in classical Italy, Trica and Apina were extinct towns whose names, taken together, were proverbial for trifling, worthless things.

with great sharpness of mind they immediately grasped the basic principles. While previously they had written only on vellum, bark, and papyrus, they now undertook to make paper and to print with type. Their first attempts were not altogether successful, but with practice they soon mastered both arts. They became so proficient that, if they had texts of the Greek authors, they would soon have no lack of volumes; but as they have no more than those I mentioned, they have contented themselves with reprinting each in thousands of copies.

Any sightseer coming to their land who has some special intellectual gift, or who has traveled widely and seen many countries, is sure of a warm welcome, for they love to hear what is happening throughout the world. This is why we were received so kindly. Few merchants, however, go there to trade. What could they import except iron—or else gold and silver, which everyone would rather bring home than send abroad? As for the export trade, the Utopians prefer to do their own transportation, rather than invite strangers to do it. By carrying their own cargos they are able to learn more about foreign countries on all sides, and keep up their skill in navigation.

Slaves[2]

The only prisoners of war the Utopians enslave are those captured in wars they fight themselves. The children of slaves are not automatically enslaved,[3] nor are slaves obtained from foreign countries. Their slaves are either their own citizens, enslaved for some heinous offense, or else foreigners who were condemned to death in their own land. Most are of the latter sort. Sometimes the Utopians buy them at a very modest rate, more often they ask for them, get them for nothing, and bring them home in considerable numbers. Both kinds of slaves are kept constantly at work, and are always fettered. But the Utopians deal with their own people more harshly than with the others, feeling that their crimes are worse and deserve stricter punishment because they had an excellent education and the best of moral training, yet still couldn't be restrained from wrongdoing. A third class of slaves consists of hardworking penniless drudges from other nations who voluntarily choose to become slaves in Utopia.

2. The institution of slavery—with prisoners of war (civilians as well as combatants) as a major source of the slaves—was ubiquitous in the ancient world, including the Greek and Roman civilizations that Utopia resembles in various ways. In Europe, slavery declined in the Middle Ages, being replaced as a source of labor by feudal serfdom, in which individuals were bound to the land rather than to a particular owner. Chattel slavery, however, revived strongly in the European colonies in the New World: the enslavement of Native Americans began with the earliest settlements, in the 1490s, and the first African slaves were imported in 1502.
3. This fact sharply distinguishes Utopian slavery from both classical slavery and medieval serfdom.

Such people are treated well, almost as well as citizens, except that they are given a little extra work, on the score that they're used to it. If one of them wants to leave, which seldom happens, no obstacles are put in his way, nor is he sent off emptyhanded.

[Suicide and Euthanasia]

As I said before, the sick are carefully tended, and nothing is neglected in the way of medicine or diet which might cure them. Everything possible is done to mitigate the pain of those who are suffering from incurable diseases; and visitors do their best to console them by sitting and talking with them. But if the disease is not only incurable but excruciatingly and constantly painful, then the priests and public officials come and urge the invalid not to endure such agony any longer. They remind him that he is now unfit for any of life's duties, a burden to himself and to others; he has really outlived his own death. They tell him he should not let the disease prey on him any longer, but now that life is simply torture, he should not hesitate to die but should rely on hope for something better. Since life has become a mere prison cell, where he is bitterly tormented, he should free himself, or let others free him, from the rack of living. This would be a wise act, they say, since for him death would put an end not to pleasure but to agony. In addition, he would be obeying the advice of the priests, who are the interpreters of God's will; which ensures that it would be a holy and pious act.[4]

Those who have been persuaded by these arguments either starve themselves to death or, having been put to sleep, are freed from life without any sensation of dying. But they never force this step on a man against his will; nor, if he decides against it, do they lessen their care of him. Under these circumstances, when death is advised by the authorities, they consider self-destruction honorable. But the suicide, who takes his own life without the approval of priests and senate, they consider unworthy either of earth or fire, and throw his body, unburied and disgraced, into a bog.

[Marriage and Divorce]

Women do not marry till they are eighteen, nor men till they are twenty-two. Premarital intercourse, if discovered and proved, brings severe punishment on both man and woman, and the guilty parties are forbidden to marry during their whole lives, unless the governor by his pardon remits the sentence. In addition both the father and

---

4. In ancient Rome, suicide was regarded as an honorable way out of deep personal or political difficulties, but neither suicide nor euthanasia has ever been acceptable in Catholic Christianity. Cf. Hythloday's earlier reference to God's prohibition of suicide (p. 22).

mother of the household where the offense occurred suffer public disgrace for having been remiss in their duty. The reason they punish this offense so severely is that they suppose few people would join in married love—with confinement to a single partner, and all the petty annoyances that married life involves—unless they were strictly restrained from a life of promiscuity.

In choosing marriage partners, they solemnly and seriously follow a custom which seemed to us foolish and absurd in the extreme. Whether she is a widow or a virgin, the woman is shown naked to the suitor by a responsible and respectable matron; and similarly, some respectable man presents the suitor naked to the woman.[5] We laughed at this custom and called it absurd; but they were just as amazed at the folly of all other peoples. When men go to buy a colt, where they are risking only a little money, they are so suspicious that, though the beast is almost bare, they won't close the deal until the saddle and blanket have been taken off, lest there be a hidden sore underneath. Yet in the choice of a mate, which may cause either delight or disgust for the rest of their lives, people are completely careless. They leave all the rest of her body covered up with clothes and estimate the attractiveness of a woman from a mere handsbreadth of her person, the face, which is all they can see. And so they marry, running great risk of bitter discord, if something in either's person should offend the other. Not all people are so wise as to concern themselves solely with character; and even the wise appreciate physical beauty, as a supplement to the virtues of the mind.[6] There's no question but that deformity may lurk under clothing, serious enough to make a man hate his wife when it's too late to be separated from her. If some disfiguring accident occurs after marriage, each person must bear his own fate; but beforehand everyone should be legally protected from deception.

There is extra reason for them to be careful, because in that part of the world they are the only people who practice monogamy. Their marriages are seldom terminated except by death, though they do

5. Marginal gloss: "Not very modest, but not so imprudent, either."
6. More wrote several Latin epigrams (i.e., short poems) on the topic of choosing a wife. His own performance in the matter—according to the biography by his son-in-law William Roper, he chose a less-favored eldest daughter to avoid hurting her feelings, though the middle one attracted him more—was decorous to the point of seeming a little chilly. When he compared taking a wife to buying a colt, he can hardly have failed to recall that the maiden name of that first wife was Joanna Colt. (After she died in childbirth, More—left with four children from six years of marriage—remarried within a month, to a widow, Alice Middleton.)

Plato's *Laws* commends a practice of premarital inspection similar to the Utopians': since it is vital that people who are potential marital partners have "the fullest possible information" about each other, "boys and girls must dance together at an age when plausible occasions can be found for their doing so, in order that they may have a reasonable look at each other; and they should dance naked, provided sufficient modesty and restraint are displayed by all concerned" (6.771E–772A). Quoted from *The Laws*, trans. Trevor J. Saunders (Harmondsworth, Middlesex: Penguin Books, 1970), p. 250.

allow divorce for adultery or for intolerably offensive behavior. A husband or wife who is the aggrieved party in such a divorce is granted permission by the senate to remarry, but the guilty party is considered disreputable and is permanently forbidden to take another mate.[7] They absolutely forbid a husband to put away his wife against her will and without any fault on her part, just because of some bodily misfortune; they think it cruel that a person should be abandoned when most in need of comfort; and they add that old age, since it not only entails disease but is actually a disease itself,[8] needs more than a precarious fidelity.

It happens occasionally that a married couple cannot get along, and have both found other persons with whom they hope to live more harmoniously. After getting the approval of the senate, they may then separate by mutual consent and contract new marriages. But such divorces are allowed only after the senators and their wives have carefully investigated the case. They allow divorce only very reluctantly, because they know that husbands and wives will find it hard to settle down together if each has in mind that a new marriage is easily available.

They punish adulterers with the strictest form of slavery. If both parties were married, they are both divorced, and the injured parties may marry one another, if they want, or someone else. But if one of the injured parties continues to love such an undeserving spouse, the marriage may go on, providing the innocent person chooses to share in the labor to which the slave is condemned. And sometimes it happens that the repentance of the guilty and the devotion of the innocent party move the governor to pity, so that he restores both to freedom. But a second conviction of adultery is punished by death.

[Punishments and Rewards; Customs and Laws]

No other crimes carry fixed penalties; the senate sets specific penalties for each particular misdeed, as it is considered atrocious or venial. Husbands chastise their wives, and parents their children, unless the offense is so serious that public punishment is called for. Generally, the gravest crimes are punished by slavery, for they think this deters offenders just as much as getting rid of them by immediate capital punishment, and is more beneficial to the commonwealth. In addition, slaves contribute more by their labor than by their death, and they are permanent and visible reminders that crime does not pay. If the slaves rebel against their condition, then, like savage beasts which neither bars nor chains can tame, they are finally put

---

7. In Europe, the Catholic Church allowed separation in cases of adultery but did not allow even the aggrieved party to remarry.
8. Echoing Terence's *Phormio* 4.1; line 575.

to death. But if they are patient, they are not left altogether without hope. When subdued by long hardships, if they show by their behavior that they regret the crime more than the punishment, their slavery is lightened or remitted altogether, sometimes by the governor's pardon, sometimes by popular vote.

Attempted seduction is subject to the same penalty as seduction itself. They think that a crime clearly and deliberately attempted is as bad as one committed, and that failure should not confer advantages on a criminal who did all he could to succeed.

They are very fond of fools, and think it contemptible to insult them.[9] There is no prohibition against enjoying their foolishness, and they even regard this as beneficial to the fools. If anyone is so serious and solemn that the foolish behavior and comic patter of a clown do not amuse him, they don't entrust him with the care of such a person, for fear that a man who gets not only no use from a fool but not even any amusement—a fool's only gift—will not treat him kindly.

To mock a person for being deformed or crippled is considered ugly and disfiguring, not to the victim but to the mocker, who stupidly reproaches the cripple for something he cannot help.

They think it a sign of a weak and sluggish character to neglect one's natural beauty, but they consider cosmetics a detestable affectation. From experience they have learned that no physical beauty recommends a wife to her husband so effectually as goodness and respect. Though some men are captured by beauty alone, none are held except by virtue and compliance.

As they deter people from crime by penalties, so they incite them to virtue by public honors. They set up in the marketplace statues of distinguished men who have served their country well, thinking thereby to preserve the memory of their good deeds and to spur on the citizens to emulate the glory of their ancestors.

Any man who campaigns for a public office is disqualified for all of them. They live together harmoniously, and the public officials are never arrogant or unapproachable. Instead, they are called "fathers," and that is the way they behave. Because the officials never extort respect from the people against their will, the people respect them spontaneously, as they should. Not even the governor is distinguished from his fellow citizens by a robe or crown; he is known only by a sheaf of grain he carries, just as the high priest is distinguished by a wax candle borne before him.[1]

They have very few laws, and their training is such that they need no more. The chief fault they find with other nations is that, even with infinite volumes of laws and interpretations, they cannot man-

9. More's household included a fool, Henry Patenson.
1. Grain and candle evidently symbolize the special function of each ruler: to ensure prosperity and to provide spiritual vision.

age their affairs properly. They think it completely unjust to bind people by a set of laws that are too many to be read and too obscure for anyone to understand. As for lawyers, a class of men whose trade it is to manipulate cases and multiply quibbles, they exclude them entirely.[2] They think it is better for each man to plead his own case, and say the same thing to the judge that he would tell his lawyer. This makes for less ambiguity, and readier access to the truth. A man speaks his mind without tricky instructions from a lawyer, and the judge examines each point carefully, taking pains to protect simple folk against the false accusations of the crafty. It is hard to find this kind of plain dealing in other countries, where they have such a multitude of incomprehensibly intricate laws. But in Utopia everyone is a legal expert. For the laws are very few, as I said, and they consider the most obvious interpretation of any law to be the fairest. As they see things, all laws are promulgated for the single purpose of teaching every man his duty. Subtle interpretations teach very few, since hardly anybody is able to understand them, whereas the more simple and apparent sense of the law is open to everyone. If laws are not clear, they are useless; for simpleminded men (and most men are of this sort, and need to be told where their duty lies), there might as well be no laws at all as laws which can be interpreted only by devious minds after endless disputes. The dull common man cannot understand this legal chicanery, and couldn't even if he studied it his whole life, since he has to earn a living in the meantime.

[Foreign Relations]

Some of the Utopians' free and independent neighbors (many of whom were previously liberated by them from tyranny), having learned to admire Utopian virtues, have made a practice of asking the Utopians to supply magistrates for them. Some of these magistrates serve one year, others five. When their service is over, they bring them home with honor and praise, and take back new ones to their country. These peoples seem to have settled on an excellent scheme to safeguard the commonwealth. Since the welfare or ruin of a commonwealth depends on the character of its officials, where could they make a more prudent choice than among Utopians, who cannot be tempted by money? For money is useless to them when they go home, as they soon must, and they can have no partisan or factional feelings, since they are strangers in the city over which they rule. Wherever they take root in men's minds, these two evils, greed and faction, are the destruction of all justice—and justice is the strongest bond of any society. The Utopians call these people

---

2. Marginal gloss: "The useless crowd of lawyers." More was, of course, one himself.

who have borrowed magistrates from them their *allies*; others whom they have benefited they call simply *friends*.

While other nations are constantly making treaties, breaking them, and renewing them, the Utopians never make any treaties at all. If nature, they say, doesn't bind man adequately to his fellow man, will an alliance do so? If a man scorns nature herself, is there any reason to think he will care about mere words? They are confirmed in this view by the fact that in that part of the world, treaties and alliances between kings are not generally observed with much good faith.

In Europe, of course, the dignity of treaties is everywhere kept sacred and inviolable, especially in those regions where the Christian religion prevails. This is partly because the kings are all so just and virtuous, partly also because of the reverence and fear that everyone feels toward the popes.[3] Just as the popes themselves never promise anything which they do not most conscientiously perform, so they command all other princes to abide by their promises in every way. If someone declines to do so, they compel him to obey by means of pastoral censure and sharp reproof. The popes rightly declare that it would be particularly disgraceful if people who are specifically called "the faithful" acted in bad faith.

But in that new world, which is as distant from ours in customs and way of life as in the distance the equator puts between us, nobody trusts treaties. The greater the formalities, the more numerous and solemn the oaths, the sooner the treaty will be broken. The rulers will easily find some defect in the wording of it, which often enough they deliberately inserted themselves. No treaty can be made so strong and explicit that a government will not be able to worm out of it, breaking in the process both the treaty and its own word. If such craft, deceit, and fraud were practiced in private contracts, the politicians would raise a great outcry against both parties, calling them sacrilegious and worthy of the gallows. Yet the very same politicians think themselves clever fellows when they give this sort of advice to kings. As a consequence, people are apt to think that justice is a humble, plebeian virtue, far beneath the majesty of kings. Or else they conclude that there are two kinds of justice, one which is only for the common herd, a lowly justice that creeps along the ground, hedged in everywhere and encumbered with chains; and the other, which is the justice of princes, much more free and majestic, so that it can do anything it wants and nothing it doesn't want.

This royal practice of keeping treaties badly there is, I suppose, the reason the Utopians don't make any; doubtless if they lived here in Europe they would change their minds. However, they think it a

---

3. In fact the crowned heads of Europe and the popes alike were ruthless and casual violators of treaties.

bad idea to make treaties at all, even if they are faithfully observed. A treaty implies that people who are separated by some natural obstacle as slight as a hill or a brook are joined by no bond of nature; it assumes that they are born rivals and enemies, and are right in aiming to destroy one another except insofar as a treaty restrains them. Moreover, they see that treaties do not really promote friendship; for both parties still retain the right to prey upon one another to whatever extent incautious drafting has left the treaty without sufficient provisions against it. The Utopians think, on the other hand, that no one should be considered an enemy who has done you no harm, that the fellowship of nature is as good as a treaty, and that men are united more firmly by good will than by pacts, by their hearts than by their words.

Military Practices

They despise war as an activity fit only for beasts,[4] yet practiced more by man than by any other creature. Unlike almost every other people in the world, they think nothing so inglorious as the glory won in battle. Yet on certain fixed days, men and women alike carry on vigorous military training, so they will be fit to fight should the need arise.[5] But they go to war only for good reasons: to protect their own land, to protect their friends from an invading army, or to liberate an oppressed people from tyranny and servitude. Out of human sympathy, they not only protect their friends from present danger but sometimes avenge previous injuries; they do this, however, only if they themselves have previously been consulted, have approved the cause, and have demanded restitution in vain. Then and only then they think themselves free to declare war. They take this final step not only when their friends have been plundered but also, and even more fiercely, when their friends' merchants have been subjected to extortion in another country, either on the pretext of laws unjust in themselves or through the perversion of good laws.

This and no other was the cause of the war which the Utopians waged a little before our time on behalf of the Nephelogetes against

---

4. A common false etymology derived *bellum* ("war") from *belua* ("beast"). Erasmus refers to it in one of the most famous essays in his ever-expanding dictionary of proverbs (each with an accompanying commentary): "Dulce bellum inexpertis" ("War is sweet, to those who have not tried it"), *Adages* IV.i.1 (*CWE* 35:405). In general, the Utopians' attitude toward war and their distinctly anti-chivalric military practices harmonize with the views of More's Erasmian humanist circle. See Robert P. Adams, *The Better Part of Valor: More, Erasmus, Colet, and Vives, on Humanism, War, and Peace, 1496–1535* (Seattle: University of Washington Press, 1962).
5. The citizen soldier has been idealized since classical times, and in More's time was, for example, the object of the fondest hopes of Machiavelli (e.g., *The Prince*, chap. 13). Cf. Hythloday's earlier comments (p. 18) on the superiority of English "raw recruits" to the professional soldiers of France.

the Alaopolitans.[6] Under pretext of right, a wrong (as they saw it) had been inflicted on some Nephelogete traders residing among the Alaopolitans. Whatever the rights and wrongs of the quarrel, it developed into a fierce war, into which, apart from the hostile forces of the two parties themselves, the neighboring nations poured their efforts and resources. Some prosperous nations were ruined completely, others badly shaken. One trouble led to another, and in the end the Alaopolitans were crushed and reduced to slavery (since the Utopians weren't involved on their own account) by the Nephelogetes—a people who, before the war, had not been remotely comparable in power to their rivals.

So severely do the Utopians punish wrong done to their friends, even in matters of mere money; but they are not so strict in enforcing their own rights. When they are cheated out of their goods, so long as no bodily harm is done, their anger goes no further than cutting off trade relations with that nation till restitution is made. The reason is not that they care more for their allies' citizens than for their own, but simply this: when the merchants of their friends are cheated, it is their own property that is lost, but when the Utopians lose something, it comes from the common stock, and is bound to be in plentiful supply at home; otherwise they wouldn't have been exporting it. Hence no one individual even notices the loss. So small an injury, which affects neither the life nor the livelihood of any of their own people, they consider it cruel to avenge by the deaths of many soldiers. On the other hand, if one of their own is maimed or killed anywhere, whether by a government or by a private citizen, they first send envoys to look into the circumstances; then they demand that the guilty persons be surrendered; and if that demand is refused, they are not to be put off, but at once declare war. If the guilty persons are surrendered, their punishment is death or slavery.

The Utopians are not only troubled but ashamed when their forces gain a bloody victory, thinking it folly to pay too high a price even for the best goods. But if they overcome the enemy by skill and cunning, they exult mightily, celebrate a public triumph, and raise a monument as for a hard-won victory. They think they have really acted with manly virtue when they have won a victory such as no animal except man could have won—a victory achieved by strength of understanding. Bears, lions, boars, wolves, dogs, and other wild beasts fight with their bodies, they say; and most of them are superior to us in strength and ferocity; but we outdo them all in shrewdness and rationality.

The only thing they aim at, in going to war, is to secure what would have prevented the declaration of war, if the enemy had conceded it beforehand. Or if they cannot get that, they try to take

6. "People Born from the Clouds" versus "Citizens of a Country without People."

such bitter revenge on those who have provoked them that they will be afraid ever to do it again. These are their chief aims, which they try to achieve quickly, yet in such a way as to avoid danger rather than to win fame and glory.

As soon as war is declared, therefore, they have their secret agents simultaneously post many placards, each marked with their official seal, in the most conspicuous places throughout the enemy territory. In these proclamations they promise immense rewards to anyone who will kill the enemy's king. They offer smaller but still very substantial sums for killing any of a list of other individuals whom they name. These are the persons whom they regard as most responsible, after the king, for plotting aggression against them. The reward for an assassin is doubled for anyone who succeeds in bringing in one of the proscribed men alive. The same reward, plus a guarantee of personal safety, is offered to any one of the proscribed men who turns against his comrades. As a result, the enemies of the Utopians quickly come to suspect everyone, particularly one another; and the many perils of their situation lead to panic. They know perfectly well that many of them, including their princes, have been betrayed by those in whom they placed complete trust—so effective are bribes as an incitement to crime. Knowing this, the Utopians are lavish in their promises of bounty. Being well aware of the risks their agents must run, they make sure that the payments are in proportion to the peril; thus they not only offer, but actually deliver, enormous sums of gold, as well as large landed estates in very secure locations on the territory of their friends.

Everywhere else in the world, this process of bidding for and buying the life of an enemy is condemned as the cruel villainy of a degenerate mind; but the Utopians consider it good policy, both wise and merciful. In the first place, it enables them to win tremendous wars without fighting any actual battles; and in the second place it enables them, by the sacrifice of a few guilty men, to spare the lives of many innocent persons who would have died in battle, some on their side, some on the enemy's. They pity the mass of the enemy's soldiers almost as much as their own citizens, for they know common people do not go to war of their own accord, but are driven to it by the madness of princes.

If assassination does not work, they sow the seeds of dissension in enemy ranks by inciting the prince's brother or some other member of the nobility to scheme for the crown.[7] If internal discord dies down, they try to rouse up neighboring peoples against the enemy by reviving forgotten claims to dominion, of which kings always have an ample supply.

---

7. Cf. Hythloday's condemnation of this device in his satiric account of an imagined meeting of the French privy council (p. 29 above).

When they promise their resources to help in a war, they send money very freely, but commit their own citizens only sparingly. They hold their own people dear, and value them so highly that they would not willingly exchange one of their citizens for an enemy's prince. Since they keep their gold and silver for the purpose of war alone, they spend it without hesitation; after all, they will continue to live just as well even if they expend the whole sum. Besides the wealth they have at home, they have a vast treasure abroad, since, as I said before, many nations owe them money. So they hire mercenary soldiers from all sides, especially the Zapoletes.[8]

These people live five hundred miles to the east of Utopia, and are rude, rough, and fierce. The forests and mountains where they are bred are the kind of country they like: tough and rugged. They are a hard race, capable of standing heat, cold, and drudgery, unacquainted with any luxuries, careless of what houses they live in or what they wear; they don't till the fields but raise cattle instead. Most of them survive by hunting and stealing. These people are born for battle and are always eager for a fight; they seek one out at every opportunity. Leaving their own country in great numbers, they offer themselves for cheap hire to anyone in need of warriors. The only art they know for earning a living is the art of taking life.

They fight with great courage and incorruptible loyalty for the people who pay them, but they will not bind themselves to serve for any fixed period of time. If someone, even the enemy, offers them more money tomorrow, they will take his side; and day after tomorrow, if a trifle more is offered to bring them back, they'll return to their first employers. Hardly a war is fought in which a good number of them are not engaged on both sides. It happens every day that men who are united by ties of blood and have served together in friendship, but who are now separated into opposing armies, meet in battle. Forgetful of kinship and comradeship alike, they furiously run one another through, driven to mutual destruction for no other reason than that they were hired for paltry pay by opposing princes. They care so much about money that they can easily be induced to change sides for an increase of only a penny a day. They have picked up the habit of avarice, but none of the profit; for what they earn by shedding blood, they quickly squander on debauchery of the most squalid sort.

Because the Utopians give higher pay than anyone else, these people are ready to serve them against any enemy whatever. And the Utopians, who seek out the best possible men for proper uses, hire these, the worst possible men, for improper uses. When the

---

8. "Busy sellers." The Zapoletes resemble the Swiss, who produced the best and most feared mercenaries of Europe (a remnant still survives as the Swiss Guard in the Vatican).

situation requires, they thrust the Zapoletes into the positions of greatest danger by offering them immense rewards. Most of them never come back to collect their pay, but the Utopians faithfully pay off those who do survive, to encourage them to try it again. As for how many Zapoletes get killed, the Utopians never worry about that, for they think they would deserve very well of all mankind if they could exterminate from the face of the earth that entire disgusting and vicious race.

Besides the Zapoletes, they employ as auxiliaries the soldiers of the people for whom they have taken up arms, and then squadrons of their other friends. Last, they add their own citizens, including some man of known bravery to command the entire army. In addition, they appoint two substitutes for him, who hold no rank as long as he is safe. But if the commander is captured or killed, the first of these two substitutes becomes his successor, and in case of a mishap to him, the other. Thus, though the accidents of war cannot be foreseen, they make sure that the whole army will not be disorganized through the loss of their leader.

In each city, soldiers are chosen from those who have volunteered. No one is forced to fight abroad against his will, because they think a man who is naturally fearful will act weakly at best, and may even spread panic among his comrades. But if their own country is invaded, they call everyone to arms, posting the fearful (as long as they are physically fit) on shipboard among braver men, or here and there along fortifications, where there is no place to run away. Thus shame at failing their countrymen, desperation at the immediate presence of the enemy, and the impossibility of flight often combine to overcome their fear, and they make a virtue out of sheer necessity.

Just as no man is forced into a foreign war against his will, so women are allowed to accompany their men on military service if they want to—not only not forbidden, but encouraged and praised for doing so. Each goes with her husband to the front, and stands shoulder to shoulder with him in the line of battle; in addition, they place around a man his children and blood- or marriage-relations, so that those who by nature have most reason to help one another may be closest at hand for mutual aid. It is a matter of great reproach for either partner to come home without the other, or for a son to return after losing a parent. The result is that if the enemy stands his ground, the hand-to-hand fighting is apt to be long and bitter, ending only when everyone is dead.

As I observed, they take every precaution to avoid having to fight in person, so long as they can bring the war to an end with mercenaries. But when they are forced to take part in battle, they are as bold in the struggle as they were prudent in avoiding it while they could. In the first charge they are not fierce, but gradually as the fighting goes on they grow more determined, putting up a steady, stubborn resistance. Their spirit is so strong that they will die rather than yield ground. They are certain that everyone at home will be provided for, and they have no worries about the future of their families (and that sort of worry often daunts the boldest courage); so their spirit is exalted and unconquerable. Their skill in the arts of war gives them extra confidence; also from childhood they have been trained in sound principles of conduct (which their education and the good institutions of their commonwealth reinforce); and that too adds to their courage. They don't hold life so cheap that they throw it away recklessly, nor so dear as to grasp it avidly at the price of shame, when duty bids them give it up.

At the height of the battle, a band of the bravest young men, who have taken a special oath, devote themselves to seeking out the opposing general. They attack him directly, they lay secret traps for him, they hit at him from near and far. A long and continuous supply of fresh men keep up the assault as the exhausted drop out. In the end, they rarely fail to kill or capture him, unless he takes to flight.

When they win a battle, it never ends in a massacre, for they would much rather take prisoners than cut throats. They never pursue fugitives without keeping one line of their army drawn up under the colors. They are so careful of this that if they win the victory with this last reserve force (supposing the rest of their army has been beaten), they would rather let the enemy army escape than pursue fugitives with their own ranks in disorder. They remember what has happened more than once to themselves: that when the enemy seemed to have the best of the day, had routed the main Utopian force and, exulting in their victory, had scattered to pursue the fugitives, a few Utopians held in reserve and watching their opportunity have suddenly attacked the dispersed and scattered enemy at the very moment when he felt safe and had lowered his guard. Thereby they changed the fortune of the day, snatched certain victory out of the enemy's hands, and, though conquered themselves, conquered their conquerors.

It is not easy to say whether they are more crafty in laying ambushes or more cautious in avoiding those laid for them. Sometimes they seem to be on the point of breaking and running when that is the last thing they have in mind; but when they really are ready to retreat, you would never guess it. If they are outnumbered, or if the terrain is unsuitable, they shift their ground silently by night or slip away from the enemy by some stratagem. Or if they have to withdraw by day, they do so gradually, and in such good order that they are as dangerous to attack then as if they were advancing. They fortify their camps very carefully with a deep, broad ditch all around them, the earth being thrown inward to make a wall; the work is done not by workmen but by the soldiers themselves with their own hands. The whole army pitches in, except for an armed guard posted around the rampart to prevent a surprise attack. With so many hands at work, they complete great fortifications, enclosing wide areas with unbelievable speed.

The armor they wear is strong enough to protect them from blows, but does not prevent easy movement of the body; in fact, it doesn't interfere even with their swimming, and part of their military training consists of swimming in armor. For long-range fighting they use arrows, which they fire with great force and accuracy, and from horseback as well as on foot. At close quarters they use not swords but battle-axes, which because of their sharp edge and great weight are lethal weapons, whether used in slashing or thrusting. They are very skillful in inventing machines of war, but conceal them with the greatest care, since if they were made known before they were needed, they might be more ridiculous than useful. Their first consideration in designing them is to make them easy to move and aim.[9]

When the Utopians make a truce with the enemy, they observe it religiously, and will not break it even if provoked. They do not ravage the enemy's territory or burn his crops; indeed, so far as possible, they avoid any trampling of the fields by men or horses, thinking they may need the grain themselves later on. Unless he is a spy, they injure no unarmed man. When cities are surrendered to them, they keep them intact; even when they have stormed a place, they do not plunder it, but put to death the men who prevented surrender, enslave the other defenders, and do no harm to the civilians. If they find any inhabitants who recommended surrender, they give them a share in the property of the condemned, and present their auxiliaries with the rest; for the Utopians themselves never take any booty.

After a war is ended, they collect the cost of it, not from the allies for whose sake they undertook it, but from the conquered. They take as indemnity not only money, which they set aside to finance future wars, but also landed estates, from which they may enjoy forever a substantial annual income. They now have revenues of this sort in many different countries, acquired little by little in various ways, till it now amounts to over seven hundred thousand ducats a year.[1] As managers of these estates, they send abroad some of their own citizens to

9. The military devices of the Utopians are a patchwork of different notions from the common knowledge of the day. Their camps are fortified like Roman ones. Their reliance on archery links them with the English, whose archers had played key roles in the famous victories over the French at Crécy (1346) and Agincourt (1415)—though the Utopians' skill in shooting arrows from horseback recalls the ancient Parthians and Scythians. Their "machines" are presumably like Roman dart hurlers, battering rams, and stone throwers, but the emphasis on their portability probably reflects contemporary experience with cannon, which were terribly hard to drag over the muddy roads of the time.
1. Gold coins of this name were minted by the governments of Venice and several other European states. Four ducats of Venice, Burgundy, or Hungary were roughly equivalent to an English pound, and the pound itself was worth several hundred times its value today. The point is that the Utopians' annual income from the estates is huge.

serve as collectors of revenue. Though they live on the properties in grand style and conduct themselves like great lords, plenty of income is still left over to be put in the public treasury, unless they choose to give the conquered nation credit. They often do the latter, until they happen to need the money, and even then it's rare for them to call in the entire debt. Some of the estates are given, as I've already described, to those who have risked great dangers on their behalf.

If any prince takes up arms and prepares to invade their land, they immediately attack him in full force outside their own borders. They are most reluctant to wage war on their own soil, and no necessity could ever compel them to admit foreign auxiliaries onto their island.

The Religions of the Utopians

There are different forms of religion throughout the island, and even in individual cities. Some worship as a god the sun, others the moon, and still others one of the planets. There are some who worship a man of past ages who was conspicuous either for virtue or glory; they consider him not only a god but the supreme god. The vast majority, however, and these by far the wisest, believe nothing of the sort: they believe in a single power, unknown, eternal, infinite, inexplicable, beyond the grasp of the human mind, and diffused throughout the universe, not physically, but in influence. Him they call their parent, and to him alone they attribute the origin, increase, progress, changes, and ends of all things; they do not offer divine honors to any other.

Though the other sects of the Utopians differ from this main group in various particular doctrines, they agree with them in this single head, that there is one supreme power, the maker and ruler of the universe, whom they all call in their native language Mithra.[2] Different people define him differently, and each supposes the object of his worship is that one and only nature to whose divine majesty, by the consensus of all nations, the creation of all things is attributed. But gradually they are coming to forsake this mixture of superstitions, and to unite in that one religion which seems more reasonable than any of the others. And there is no doubt that the other religions would have disappeared long ago, had not various unlucky accidents that befell certain Utopians who were thinking about changing their religion been interpreted, out of fear, as signs of divine anger, not chance, as if the deity who was being abandoned were avenging an insult against himself.

---

2. In ancient Persian religion, Mithra (or Mithras) was the spirit of light. Recall that the Utopian language is said to resemble Persian (p. 67 above).

But after they had heard from us the name of Christ, and learned of his teachings, his life, his miracles, and the no less marvelous constancy of the many martyrs whose blood, freely shed, has drawn many nations far and near into the Christian fellowship, you would not believe how eagerly they assented to it, either through the mysterious inspiration of God, or because Christianity seemed very like the religion already prevailing among them. But I think they were also much influenced by the fact that Christ approved a communal way of life for his disciples, and that among the truest communities of Christians the practice still prevails.[3] Whatever the reason, no small number of them chose to join our communion, and received the holy water of baptism. By that time, two of our group had died, and among us four survivors there was, I am sorry to say, no priest; so, though they received the other sacraments, they still lack those which in our religion can be administered only by priests.[4] They do, however, understand what these are, and earnestly desire them. In fact, they dispute vigorously whether a man chosen from among themselves could legitimately assume the functions of a priest without the dispatch of a Christian bishop. Though they seemed on the point of selecting such a person, they had not yet done so when I left.

Those who have not accepted Christianity make no effort to restrain others from it, nor do they criticize new converts to it. While I was there, only one of the Christians was interfered with. As soon as he was baptized, he took upon himself to preach the Christian religion publicly, with more zeal than discretion. We warned him not to do so, but he soon worked himself up to a pitch where he not only set our religion above the rest but condemned all others as profane in themselves, leading their impious and sacrilegious followers to the hell-flames they richly deserved. After he had been going on in this style for a long time, they arrested him. He was tried on a charge, not of despising their religion, but of creating a public disorder, convicted, and sentenced to exile. For it is one of their oldest rules that no man's religion, as such, shall be held against him.

Utopus had heard that before his arrival the inhabitants were continually quarreling over religious matters. In fact, he found it was easy to conquer the country because the different sects were too busy fighting one another to oppose him. As soon as he had gained the victory, therefore, he decreed that everyone could cultivate the religion of his choice, and strenuously proselytize for it too, provided he did so quietly, modestly, rationally, and without bitterness toward

---

3. The communist practice of the early Christians is described in Acts 2.44–45 and 4.32–35 (see pp. 105–06 below). Many monastic and ascetic orders still made a practice of abolishing private property for their members.
4. Of the seven Catholic sacraments, only baptism and matrimony can be conferred by laymen. Priests are created by ordination by a bishop (cf. below).

others. If persuasion failed, no one was allowed to resort to abuse or violence. Anyone who fights wantonly about religion is punished by exile or enslavement.

Utopus laid down these rules not simply for the sake of peace, which he saw was in danger of being destroyed by constant quarrels and implacable hatreds, but also for the sake of religion itself. In matters of religion, he was not at all quick to dogmatize, because he suspected that God perhaps likes diverse and manifold forms of worship and has therefore deliberately inspired different people with different views. On the other hand, he was quite sure that it was arrogant folly for anyone to enforce conformity with his own beliefs on everyone else by means of threats or violence.[5] He supposed that if one religion is really true and the rest false, the true one will sooner or later emerge and prevail by its own natural strength, provided only that men consider the matter reasonably and moderately. But if they try to decide these matters by fighting and rioting, since the worst men are always the most headstrong, the best and holiest religion in the world will be crowded out by blind superstitions, like grain choked out of a field by thorns and briars. So he left the whole matter open, allowing each individual to choose what he would believe. The only exception he made was a solemn and strict law against any person who should sink so far below the dignity of human nature as to think that the soul perishes with the body, or that the universe is ruled by mere chance rather than divine providence.

Thus the Utopians all believe that after this life vices are to be punished and virtue rewarded; and they consider that anyone who denies this proposition is not even one of the human race, since he has degraded the sublimity of his own soul to the base level of a beast's wretched body. Still less will they count him as one of their citizens, since he would openly despise all the laws and customs of society, if not prevented by fear. Who can doubt that a man who has nothing to fear but the law, and no hope of life beyond the grave, will do anything he can to evade his country's laws by craft or break them by violence, in order to gratify his own private greed? Therefore a person who holds such views is offered no honors, entrusted with no offices, and given no public responsibility; he is universally regarded as low and torpid. Yet they do not afflict him

---

5. This was not the attitude More took a decade after *Utopia*, when, the Reformation schism having begun, he was involved in the prosecution of Protestant heretics, sometimes to the death. In the *Dialogue Concerning Heresies*, he wrote that "if it were now doubtful and ambiguous whether the church of Christ were in the right rule of doctrine or not, then were it very necessary to give them all good audience that could and would anything dispute on either party for it or against it, to the end that if we were now in a wrong way, we might leave it and walk in some better" (CW 6:345–46; spelling modernized). *Utopia* was in this hypothetical situation; England, in More's view, was not.

with punishments, because they are persuaded that no one can choose to believe by a mere act of the will. They do not compel him by threats to dissemble his views, nor do they tolerate in the matter any deceit or lying, which they detest as next door to deliberate malice. The man may not argue with the common people in behalf of his opinion; but in the presence of the priests and other important persons, in private, they not only permit but encourage it. For they are confident that in the end his madness will yield to reason.

There are some others, in fact no small number of them, who err in the opposite direction, in supposing that animals too have immortal souls,[6] though not comparable to ours in excellence, nor destined to equal felicity. These people are not thought to be evil, their opinion is not thought to be wholly unreasonable, and so they are not interfered with.

Almost all the Utopians are absolutely convinced that human bliss after death will be enormous; thus they lament every individual's sickness, but mourn over a death only if the person was torn from life anxiously and unwillingly. Such behavior they take to be a very bad sign, as if the soul, despairing and conscious of guilt, dreaded death through a secret premonition of punishments to come. Besides, they suppose God can hardly be well pleased with the coming of one who, when he is summoned, does not come gladly but is dragged off reluctantly and against his will. Such a death fills the onlookers with horror, and they carry the corpse out to burial in melancholy silence. There, after begging God to have mercy on his spirit and to pardon his infirmities, they commit his body to the earth. But when someone dies blithely and full of good hope, they do not mourn for him but carry the body cheerfully away, singing and commending the dead man's soul to God. They cremate him in a spirit more of reverence than of grief, and erect a column on which the dead man's honors are inscribed. After they have returned home, they talk of his character and deeds, and no part of his life is mentioned more frequently or more gladly than his joyful death.

They think that recollecting the dead person's goodness helps the living to behave virtuously and is also the most acceptable form of honor to the dead. For they think that dead people are actually present among us, and hear what we say about them, though through the dullness of human sight they are invisible to our eyes. Given their state of bliss, the dead must be able to travel freely where they please, and it would be unkind of them to cast off every desire of revisiting their friends, to whom they had been bound by mutual affection and charity during their lives. Like all other good things,

---

6. These Utopians resemble the ancient Pythagoreans, who, as a facet of their doctrine of the transmigration of souls, conceded them to animals.

they think that after death charity is increased rather than decreased in good men; and thus they believe the dead come frequently among the living, to observe their words and actions. Hence they go about their business the more confidently because of their trust in such protectors; and the belief that their forefathers are physically present keeps them from any secret dishonorable deed.

Fortune-telling and other vain forms of superstitious divination, such as other peoples take very seriously, they have no part of and consider ridiculous. But they venerate miracles which occur without the help of nature, considering them direct and visible manifestations of the divine power. Indeed, they report that miracles have frequently occurred in their country. Sometimes in great and dangerous crises they pray publicly for a miracle, which they then anticipate with great confidence, and obtain.

They think that the contemplation of nature, and the sense of reverence arising from it, are acts of worship to God. There are some people, however, and not just a few of them, who from religious motives reject learning and pursue no studies; but none of them is the least bit idle. Constant dedication to the offices of charity, these people think, will increase their chances of happiness after death; and so they are always busy in the service of others. Some tend the sick; others repair roads, clean ditches, rebuild bridges, dig turf, sand, or stones; still others fell trees and cut them up, and transport wood, grain, or other commodities into the cities by wagon. They work for private citizens as well as for the public, and work even harder than slaves. They undertake with cheery good will any task that is so rough, hard, and dirty that most people refuse to tackle it because of the toil, boredom, and frustration involved. While constantly engaged in heavy labor themselves, they secure leisure for others, and yet they claim no credit for it.[7] They do not criticize the way other people live, nor do they boast of their own doings. The more they put themselves in the position of slaves, the more highly they are honored by everyone.

These people are of two sects. The first are celibates who abstain not only from sex but also from eating meat, and some of them from any sort of animal food whatever. They reject all the pleasures of this life as harmful, and look forward only to the joys of the life to come, which they hope to deserve by hard labor and all-night vigils. As they hope to attain it soon, they are cheerful and active in the here and now. The other kind are just as fond of hard work, but prefer to marry. They don't despise the comforts of marriage, but think

---

7. The constant labor of these ascetics, often on disagreeable and painful tasks, contrasts with the sloth Hythloday had previously attributed to the "great lazy gang of priests and so-called religious [i.e., members of the various religious orders]" in Europe (p. 46). A strain of penitential, self-mortifying feeling ran deep in More himself.

that, as their duty to nature requires work, so their duty to their country requires them to beget children. They avoid no pleasure unless it interferes with their labor, and gladly eat meat, precisely because they think it makes them stronger for any sort of heavy work. The Utopians regard the second sort as more sensible, but the first sort as holier. If they claimed to prefer celibacy to marriage, and a hard life to a comfortable one, on grounds of reason alone, the Utopians would think them absurd. But since these men claim to be motivated by religion, the Utopians respect and revere them. There is no subject on which they are warier of jumping to conclusions than in this matter of religion. These then are the men whom in their own language they call Buthrescas, a term which may be translated as "the especially religious."

Their priests are of great holiness, and therefore very few. In each city, there are no more than thirteen, one for each church.[8] In case of war, seven of them go out with the army, and seven substitutes are appointed to fill their places for the time being. When the regular priests come back, the substitutes return to their former posts— that is, they serve as assistants to the high priest, until one of the regular thirteen dies, and then one of them succeeds to his position. The high priest is, of course, in authority over all the others. Priests are elected, just like all other officials, by secret popular vote, in order to avoid partisan feeling. After election they are ordained by the college of priests.

They preside over divine worship, attend to religious matters, and act as censors of public morality.[9] For a man to be summoned before them and scolded for not living an honorable life is considered a great disgrace. As the duty of the priests is simply to counsel and advise, so correcting and punishing offenders is the duty of the governor and the other officials, though the priests do exclude from divine service persons whom they find to be extraordinarily wicked. Hardly any punishment is more dreaded than this; the excommunicate incurs great disgrace, and is tortured by the fear of damnation. Not even his body is safe for long, for unless he quickly convinces the priests of his repentance he will be seized and punished by the senate for impiety.

The priests are entrusted with teaching the children and young people.[1] Instruction in morality and virtue is considered just as important as the accumulation of learning. From the very first they

8. Since there are well over 100,000 inhabitants in each city (see p. 49, n. 5), the thirteen churches of each must be able to accommodate, no doubt in several shifts, some 10,000 worshipers apiece.
9. Priests do not seem to hold secular office in Utopia, as, for example, the lord chancellors Cardinal Morton and Cardinal Wolsey did in More's England.
1. Presumably the priests only *supervise* the teaching: there are only thirteen of them per city, whereas each city is home to thousands of children.

try to instill in the pupils' minds, while they are still young and tender, principles which will be useful to preserve the commonwealth.
What is planted in the minds of children lives on in the minds of
adults, and is of great value in strengthening the commonwealth:
the decline of society can always be traced to vices which arise from
wrong attitudes.

Women are not debarred from the priesthood, but only a widow
of advanced years is ever chosen, and it doesn't happen often.[2] The
wives of the male priests are the very finest women in the whole
country.

No official in Utopia is more honored than the priest. Even if one
of them commits a crime, he is not brought into a court of law, but
left to God and his own conscience. They think it is wrong to lay
human hands on a man, however guilty, who has been specially
consecrated to God as a holy offering, so to speak. This custom is
the easier for them to observe because their priests are very few and
very carefully chosen. Besides, it rarely happens that a man selected
for his goodness and raised to high dignities wholly because of his
moral character will fall into corruption and vice. And even if such
a thing should happen, human nature being as changeable as it is, no
great harm is to be feared, because the priests are so few and have no
power beyond that which derives from their good reputation. In fact,
the reason for having so few priests is to prevent the order, which the
Utopians now esteem so highly, from being cheapened by numbers.[3]
Besides, they think it would be hard to find many men qualified for
a dignity for which merely ordinary virtues are not sufficient.

Their priests are esteemed no less highly abroad than at home,
which can be seen from the following fact: Whenever their armies
join in battle, the Utopian priests are to be found, a little removed
from the fray but not far, wearing their sacred vestments and down
on their knees. With hands raised to heaven, they pray first of all for
peace, and then for victory to their own side, but without much
bloodshed on either hand.[4] Should their side be victorious, they rush
among the combatants and restrain the rage of their own men against
the enemy. If any of the enemy see these priests and call to them, it is
enough to save their lives; to touch the flowing robes of a priest will
save all their property from confiscation. This custom has brought
them such veneration among all peoples, and given them such genu-

2. There were female priests in classical Greek and Roman religions, and women had
   performed some priest-like functions in various early Christian groups. In England, a
   few communities among the Wycliffite dissenters ("Lollards") who arose in the late
   14th century allowed female preachers. But there were not (and are not) female priests
   in the Roman Catholic Church. And of course Catholic priests, vowed to celibacy, cannot marry.
3. Marginal gloss: "But what a crowd of them we have!"
4. Gloss: "O priests far holier than our own!"

ine authority, that they have saved the Utopians from the rage of the enemy as often as they have protected the enemy from Utopians. Instances of this are well known. Sometimes when the Utopian line has buckled, when the field was lost, and the enemy was rushing in to kill and plunder, the priests have intervened to stop the carnage and separate the armies, and an equitable peace has been concluded. There was never anywhere a tribe so fierce, cruel, and barbarous as not to hold their persons sacrosanct and inviolable.

The Utopians celebrate the first and last days of every month, and likewise of each year, as feast days. They divide the year into months which they measure by the orbit of the moon, just as they measure the year itself by the course of the sun. In their language, the first days are known as the Cynemerns and the last days as the Trapemerns, which is to say "First-feasts" and "Last-feasts."[5] Their churches are beautifully constructed, finely adorned, and large enough to hold a great many people. This is a necessity, since churches are so few. Their interiors are all rather dark, not from architectural ignorance but from deliberate policy; for the priests think that in bright light the congregation's thoughts will go wandering, whereas a dim light tends to concentrate the mind and encourage devotion.

Though there are various religions in Utopia, all of them, even the most diverse, agree in the main point, which is worship of the divine nature; they are like travelers going to one destination by different roads. So nothing is seen or heard in the churches that does not square with all the creeds. If any sect has a special rite of its own, that is celebrated in a private house; the public service is ordered by a ritual which in no way derogates from any of the private services. Therefore in the churches no image of the gods is to be seen, so that each person may be free to form his own image of God according to his own religion, in any shape he pleases. They do not invoke God by any name except Mithra. Whatever the nature of the divine majesty may be, they all agree to refer to it by that single word, and their prayers are so phrased as to accommodate the beliefs of all the different sects.

On the evening of the "Last-feast" they meet in their churches, and while still fasting they thank God for their prosperity during that month or year which is just ending. Next day, which is "First-feast," they all flock to the churches in the morning, to pray for prosperity and happiness in the month or year which is just beginning. On the day of "Last-feast," in the home before they go to church, wives kneel before their husbands and children before their parents, to confess their various sins of commission or of negligence and beg

---

5. Cynemerns really means, in Greek, "dog-days" (or perhaps "starting-days"); Trapemerns, "turning-days."

forgiveness for their offenses. Thus if any cloud of anger or resentment has arisen in the family, it is dispersed, and they can attend divine services with clear and untroubled minds—for they consider it sacrilege to worship with a rankling conscience. If they are conscious of hatred or anger toward anyone, they do not take part in divine services till they have been reconciled and have cleansed their hearts, for fear of some swift and terrible punishment.

As they enter the church, they separate, men going to the right side and women to the left.[6] Then they take their seats so that the males of each household are placed in front of the head of that household, while the womenfolk are directly in front of the mother of the family. In this way they ensure that everyone's behavior in public is supervised by the same person whose authority and discipline direct him at home. They take great care that the young are everywhere placed in the company of their elders. For if children were trusted to the care of other children, they might spend in childish foolery the time they should devote to developing a religious fear of the gods, which is the greatest and almost the only incitement to virtue.

They do not slaughter animals in their sacrifices, and do not think that a merciful God, who gave life to all creatures precisely so that they might live, will be gratified with the shedding of blood. They burn incense, scatter perfumes, and display a great number of candles—not that they think these practices profit the divine nature in any way, any more than human prayers do; but they like this harmless kind of worship. They feel that sweet smells, lights, and other such rituals elevate the mind and lift it with a livelier devotion toward the adoration of God.

When they go to church, the people all wear white. The priest wears robes of various colors, wonderful for their workmanship and decoration, though not of materials as costly as one would suppose. The robes have no gold embroidery nor any precious stones, but are decorated with the feathers of different birds so skillfully woven together that the value of the handiwork far exceeds the cost of the most precious materials.[7] Also, certain symbolic mysteries are hidden in the patterning of the feathers on the robes, the meaning of which is carefully handed down among the priests. These messages serve to remind them of God's benefits toward them, and consequently of the devotion they owe to God, as well as of their duty to one another.

6. Separation of the sexes in church had been customary since the early Christian centuries.
7. Perhaps related to Vespucci's observation that the Native Americans' wealth "consists of feathers of many-hued birds . . . and of many other things to which we attach no value" (p. 121 below).

As the priest in his robes appears from the vestibule, the people all fall to the ground in reverence. The stillness is so complete that the scene strikes one with awe, as if a divinity were actually present. After remaining in this posture for some time, they rise at a signal from the priest. Then they sing hymns to the accompaniment of musical instruments, most of them quite different in shape from those in our part of the world. Many of them produce sweeter tones than ours, but others are not even comparable. In one respect, however, they are beyond doubt far ahead of us, because all their music, both vocal and instrumental, renders and expresses natural feelings and perfectly matches the sound to the subject. Whether the words of the hymn are supplicatory, cheerful, troubled, mournful, or angry, the music represents the meaning through the contour of the melody so admirably that it penetrates and inspires the minds of the ardent hearers. Finally, the priest and the people together recite certain fixed forms of prayer, so composed that what they all repeat in unison each individual can apply to himself.

In these prayers, the worshipers acknowledge God to be the creator and ruler of the universe and the author of all good things. They thank God for benefits received, and particularly for the divine favor which placed them in the happiest of commonwealths and inspired them with religious ideas which they hope are the truest. If they are wrong in this, and if there is some sort of society or religion more acceptable to God, they pray that he will, in his goodness, reveal it to them, for they are ready to follow wherever he leads. But if their form of society is the best and their religion the truest, then they pray that God will keep them steadfast, and bring other mortals to the same way of life and the same religious faith—unless, indeed, there is something in this variety of religions which delights his inscrutable will.

Then they pray that after an easy death God will receive each of them to himself, how soon or how late it is not for them to say. But if God's divine majesty so please, they ask to be brought to him soon, even by the hardest possible death, rather than be kept away from him longer, even by the most fortunate of earthly lives. When this prayer has been said, they prostrate themselves on the ground again; then after a little while they rise and go to lunch. The rest of the day they pass in games and military training.

Now I have described to you as accurately as I could the structure of that commonwealth which I consider not only the best but indeed the only one that can rightfully claim that name. In other places men talk very liberally of the commonwealth, but what they mean is simply their own wealth; in Utopia, where there is no private business, everyone zealously pursues the public business. And in both places people are right to act as they do. For among us, even though the commonwealth may flourish, there are very few who do not know that unless they make separate provision for themselves, they may perfectly well die of hunger. Bitter necessity, then, forces them to think that they must look out for themselves rather than for others, that is, for the people. But in Utopia, where everything belongs to everybody, no one need fear that, so long as the public warehouses are filled, anyone will ever lack for anything he needs. For the distribution of goods is not niggardly; in Utopia no one is poor, there are no beggars, and though no one owns anything, everyone is rich.

For what can be greater riches than to live joyfully and peacefully, free from all anxieties, and without worries about making a living? No man is bothered by his wife's querulous entreaties about money, no man fears poverty for his son, or struggles to scrape up a dowry for his daughter. Everyone can feel secure of his own livelihood and happiness, and of his whole family's as well: wife, sons, grandsons, great-grandsons, great-great-grandsons, and that whole long line of descendants that gentlefolk are so fond of contemplating. Indeed, even those who once worked but can no longer do so are cared for just as well as those who are still working.

Now here I'd like to see anyone try to compare this equity of the Utopians with the so-called justice that prevails among other peoples—among whom let me perish if I can discover the slightest scrap of justice or fairness. What kind of justice is it when a nobleman or a goldsmith[8] or a moneylender, or someone else who makes his living by doing either nothing at all or something completely useless to the commonwealth, gets to live a life of luxury and grandeur, while in the meantime a laborer, a carter, a carpenter, or a farmer works so hard and so constantly that even a beast of burden could scarcely endure it? Although this work of theirs is so necessary that no commonwealth could survive a year without it, they earn so meager a living and lead such miserable lives that beasts of burden would really seem to be better off. Beasts do not have to work every minute, and their food is not much worse; in fact they like it better. And besides, they do not have to worry about their future. But workingmen not only have to sweat and suffer without present reward, but agonize over the prospect of a penniless old age. Their daily wage is inadequate even for their present needs, so there is no possible chance of their saving toward the future.

Now isn't this an unjust and ungrateful commonwealth? It lavishes rich rewards on so-called gentry, goldsmiths, and the rest of that crew, who don't work at all or are mere parasites, purveyors of empty

---

8. Besides making what the Utopians would regard as worthless objects, goldsmiths in More's time often functioned as bankers.

pleasures. And yet it makes no provision whatever for the welfare of farmers and colliers, laborers, carters, and carpenters, without whom the commonwealth would simply cease to exist. After society has taken the labor of their best years, when they are worn out by age and sickness and utter destitution, then the thankless commonwealth, forgetting all their sleepless nights and great services, throws them out to die a miserable death. What is worse, the rich constantly try to grind out of the poor part of their meager wages, not only by private swindling but by public laws. Before, it appeared to be unjust that people who deserve most from the commonwealth should receive least; but now, by promulgating law, they have palmed injustice off as "legal." When I run over in my mind the various commonwealths flourishing today, so help me God, I can see in them nothing but a conspiracy of the rich, who are fattening up their own interests under the name and title of the commonwealth.[9] They invent ways and means to hang onto whatever they have acquired by sharp practice, and then they scheme to oppress the poor by buying up their toil and labor as cheaply as possible. These devices become law as soon as the rich, speaking for the commonwealth—which, of course, includes the poor as well—say they must be observed.

And yet, when these insatiably greedy and evil men have divided among themselves all the goods which would have sufficed for the entire people, how far they remain from the happiness of the Utopian republic, which has abolished not only money but with it greed! What a mass of trouble was cut away by that one step! What a multitude of crimes was pulled up by the roots! Everyone knows that if money were abolished, fraud, theft, robbery, quarrels, brawls, altercations, seditions, murders, treasons, poisonings, and a whole set of crimes which are avenged but not prevented by the hangman would at once die out. If money disappeared, so would fear, anxiety, worry, toil, and sleepless nights. Even poverty, the one condition which seems more than anything else to need money for its relief, would die away if money were entirely abolished.

Consider, if you will, this example. Take a barren year of failed harvests, when many thousands of people have been carried off by famine. If at the end of the scarcity the barns of the rich were searched, I dare say positively that enough grain would be found in them to have kept all those who died of starvation and disease from even realizing that a shortage ever existed—if only it had been divided among them. So easily might people get the necessities of

9. Marginal gloss: "Reader, note well!" In the text at this point, More may be alluding to the judgment of St. Augustine in *The City of God* 4.4: "*Remota itaque iustitia quid sunt regna nisi magna latrocinia?*" ("Take away justice, and what are kingdoms except great robber-bands?") As a young man, More had given a series of public lectures on Augustine's book.

life if that cursed money, that marvelous invention which is supposed to provide access to them, were not in fact the only barrier to
our getting what we need to live. Even the rich, I'm sure, understand
this. They must know that it's better to have enough of what we really
need than an abundance of superfluities, much better to escape from
our many present troubles than to be burdened with great masses
of wealth. And in fact I have no doubt that every man's perception
of where his true interest lies, along with the authority of Christ
our Savior (whose wisdom could not fail to recognize the best, and
whose goodness would not fail to counsel it), would long ago have
brought the whole world to adopt Utopian laws, if it were not for
one single monster, the prime plague and begetter of all others—I
mean Pride.

Pride measures her advantages not by what she has but by what
others lack. Pride would not condescend even to be made a goddess,
if there were no wretches for her to sneer at and domineer over. Her
good fortune is dazzling only by contrast with the miseries of others,
her riches are valuable only as they torment and tantalize the poverty
of others. Pride is a serpent from hell that twines itself around the
hearts of men; and it acts like a suckfish[1] in holding them back from
choosing a better way of life.

Pride is too deeply fixed in human nature to be easily plucked
out. So I am glad that the Utopians at least have been lucky enough
to achieve this commonwealth, which I wish all mankind would
imitate. The institutions they have adopted have made their community most happy, and, as far as anyone can tell, capable of lasting
forever. Now that they have rooted up the seeds of ambition and
faction at home, along with most other vices, they are in no danger
from internal strife, which alone has been the ruin of many cities
that seemed secure. As long as they preserve harmony at home, and
keep their institutions healthy, the Utopians can never be overcome
or even shaken by all the envious princes of neighboring countries,
who have often attempted their ruin, but always in vain.

When Raphael had finished his story, I was left thinking that not
a few of the customs and laws he had described as existing among
the Utopians were quite absurd. These included their methods of
waging war, their religious practices, as well as other customs of
theirs, but my chief objection was to the basis of their whole system, that is, their communal living and their moneyless economy.
This one thing alone takes away all the nobility, magnificence,

---

1. Or remora. It has a suction plate atop its head, by which it attaches itself to the under-
belly of larger fishes or the hulls of ships. Impressed by the tenacity of its grip, the
ancients fabled that it could stop ships in their courses.

splendor, and majesty which (in the popular view) are the true ornaments and glory of any commonwealth. But I saw Raphael was tired with talking, and I was not sure he could take contradiction in these matters, particularly when I remembered what he had said about certain people who were afraid they might not appear wise unless they found out something to criticize in the ideas of others. So with praise for the Utopian way of life and his account of it, I took him by the hand and led him in to supper. But first I said that we would find some other time for thinking of these matters more deeply, and for talking them over in more detail. And I still hope such an opportunity will present itself someday.

Meanwhile, though he is a man of unquestionable learning, and highly experienced in the ways of the world, I cannot agree with everything he said. Yet I freely confess there are very many things in the Utopian commonwealth that in our own societies I would wish rather than expect to see.

BACKGROUNDS

PLATO

(*Fourth Century B.C.E.*)

In the background of *Utopia*, no other book is as important as Plato's *Republic*, the perennially stimulating and controversial work that inaugurated the tradition of writing to which *Utopia* belongs: the discussion of the best possible organization of a polity. (This is not necessarily to say that the commonwealth of Utopia *is* More's ideal state.) More's book resonates with Plato's in a number of ways, but the most striking feature that the Utopian republic shares with Plato's pattern for an ideal state is communism. In Plato's envisioned state, however, the prohibition of private property is restricted to the ruling caste, the Guardians (though in his last political work, *The Laws*, Plato declares that the best commonwealth would be communistic across the board). The Guardians are the philosopher-warrior-kings of the ideal state, whose training is the subject of the third of the *Republic*'s ten books.

Guardians are to be trained from youth on a deliberate lie or myth, the first element of which informs them that they are not children of particular fathers or mothers, but rather children of the land herself, to whom they owe absolute loyalty. They will also be told, by a peculiar socializing of the myth of the Four Ages of Man (for which, see Ovid, pp. 103–05 below), that they are the golden or at least the silver people—the lower castes over whom they rule are mere creatures of brass or iron. Partly as a way of fostering this myth, the Guardians and their chosen women will consort strenuously and promiscuously together, and their children will be removed to nurseries as soon as they are born. Thus no child will ever know its own mother or father, and no dynasty founded on wealth or kinship will ever be in danger of springing up. Far removed from these common temptations of ordinary humanity, the Guardians—athletes of the ideal, shock troops of the mind—will be able to bring perfect disinterested justice to the state over which they rule.

As usual in Plato's dialogues, Socrates is the main speaker. In the excerpts here, his interlocutor is Glaucon, who, like his younger brother Plato, was in real life one of Socrates's pupils. In the first passage, Socrates is expounding the myth on which he would have the Guardians raised; the second passage comes about a page later and constitutes the ending of Book 3.

[The Guardians]†

Citizens, we shall say to them in our tale, you are brothers, yet God has framed you differently. Some of you have the power of command,

---

† From *The Republic of Plato*, translated by Benjamin Jowett, 3rd ed. (Oxford: Clarendon Press, 1888), pp. 104–06 (3.415A–D, 416D–417B), with minor modifications of spelling and capitalization.

and in the composition of these he has mingled gold, wherefore also they have the greatest honor; others he has made of silver, to be auxiliaries; others again who are to be husbandmen and craftsmen he has composed of brass and iron; and the species will generally be preserved in the children. But as all are of the same original stock, a golden parent will sometimes have a silver son, or a silver parent a golden son. And God proclaims as a first principle to the rulers, and above all else, that there is nothing which they should so anxiously guard, or of which they are to be such good guardians, as of the purity of the race. They should observe what elements mingle in their offspring; for if the son of a golden or silver parent has an admixture of brass and iron, then nature orders a transposition of ranks, and the eye of the ruler must not be pitiful toward the child because he has to descend in the scale and become a husbandman or artisan, just as there may be sons of artisans who having an admixture of gold or silver in them are raised to honor, and become guardians or auxiliaries. For an oracle says that when a man of brass or iron guards the state, it will be destroyed. Such is the tale; is there any possibility of making our citizens believe in it?

Not in the present generation, he replied; there is no way of accomplishing this; but their sons may be made to believe in the tale, and their sons' sons, and posterity after them.

* * *

Then now let us consider what will be their way of life, if they are to realize our idea of them. In the first place, none of them should have any property of his own beyond what is absolutely necessary; neither should they have a private house or store closed against anyone who has a mind to enter; their provisions should be only such as are required by trained warriors, who are men of temperance and courage; they should agree to receive from the citizens a fixed rate of pay, enough to meet the expenses of the year and no more; and they will go to mess and live together like soldiers in a camp. Gold and silver we will tell them that they have from God; the diviner metal is within them, and they have therefore no need of the dross which is current among men, and ought not to pollute the divine by any such earthly admixture; for that commoner metal has been the source of many unholy deeds, but their own is undefiled. And they alone of all the citizens may not touch or handle silver or gold, or be under the same roof with them, or wear them, or drink from them. And this will be their salvation, and they will be the saviours of the state. But should they ever acquire homes or lands or moneys of their own, they will become good housekeepers and husbandmen instead of guardians, enemies and tyrants instead of allies of the other citizens; hating and being hated, plotting and being plotted against, they will pass their whole life in much greater terror of internal than of external enemies, and the hour of ruin, both to themselves and to the rest of the state, will be at hand. For all which reasons may we not say that thus shall our state be ordered, and that these shall be the regulations appointed by us for our Guardians concerning their houses and all other matters?

Yes, said Glaucon.

OVID

(*First Century C.E.*)

The myth of a Golden Age, from which humankind sprang and to which we may someday hope to return, is immemorial and universal: as it has no one point of origin, so also it has no fixed limits, precise definition, or single significance. Viewed from a Judeo-Christian perspective, for example, the Age of Gold was easily conflated with the Garden of Eden; whereas psychological interpreters have had no difficulty reading it as nostalgia for the womb; and messianic revolutionaries, by simply transferring it to the other end of the historical time scale, have converted it to the classless society or the New Jerusalem. For Western literary culture, the Roman poet Ovid (47 B.C.E.–17 C.E.), who under his urbane, up-to-date Augustan surface had a deep feeling for the remote past, gave the most memorable expression to the myth, in the first book of his *Metamorphoses* (a huge collection of brilliant retellings of myths and legends of transformation). Ovid's poem had enormous impact on Renaissance literature, but for More's *Utopia* its influence was not so much direct and specific as through a diffused and pervasive atmosphere of thought that identified a life of innocence, equality, peace, and closeness to nature as the first and last state of humankind.

[The Golden Age and After]†

The age was formed of gold; in those first days
No law or force was needed; men did right
Freely; without duress they kept their word.
No punishment or fear of it; no threats
Inscribed on brazen tablets; no jostling crowds
Beseeching mercy from a lofty judge;
For without law or judge all men were safe.
High on its native hills the pine tree stood,
Unlopped as yet, nor yet compelled to cross

† *Metamorphoses* 1.89–136; translation by R. M. Adams.

Ocean's wide waves, and help men leave their homes.
Towns had no moats; no horns of winding brass
Nor trumpets straight, nor swords nor shields existed.
The nations dozed through ages of soft time,
Safe without armies; while the earth herself,
Untouched by spade or plowshare, freely gave,
As of her own volition, all men needed:
And men were well content with what she gave
Unforced and uncompelled; they found the fruit
Of the arbutus bush, and cornel-cherries,
Gathered wild berries from the mountain-sides,
Eating ripe fruit plucked from the thorny canes,
And acorns as they fell from Jove's wide oak.[1]
Spring lasted all year long; the warm west wind
Played gently over flowers sprung from no seed:
Soon too the untilled earth brought forth profuse
Her crops of grain; and fields, uncultivated,
Whitened beneath their stalks of bearded wheat.
Streams flowed profuse, now milk, now nectar, and
The living oak poured streams of golden honey.

    Later, with Saturn sent to gloomy Hell,
Jove ruled the world;[2] the Age of Silver came,
Worse than the Age of Gold, though not so bad
As was to be the Age of tawny Bronze.
Jove cut the old spring short and turned the year
To the four changing seasons, winter, spring
(Brief now), hot summer, and contrarious fall.
Then first the air burnt white with summer heat,
And icicles hung down, gripped by the winds:
Then men first sought out homes; they used to live
In caves, or else in thickets, where they wove
Together twigs and withes with strips of bark.
Then first the seeds of grain were set in rows,
And bullocks groaned, under the heavy yoke.

    Third of the ages came the Age of Bronze,
Harder of mind, quicker to savage arms,
But not yet brutal. Last was the Age of Iron.
Evil at once broke forth; from such coarse stuff
Modesty, truth, and faith withdrew; their place
Was filled by tricks, deceitful plots, brute force,
Treachery, and the shameful lust for gain.

---

1. In Latin, the oak is sometimes called (as by Ovid here) *Iovis arbor*, "Jove's tree."
2. With the help of his brothers and sisters, Jove, Saturn's youngest child, deposed him as king of heaven and earth.

Sails now spread to the winds—at first, the sailors
Knew little of their use—while keels of wood
That long had stood on lofty mountaintops
Now leaped exultantly over strange waves.
And now the ground itself, which once had been
Common to all, like sunlight and the air,
Fell under the surveyor's drawn-out lines.

* * *

THE ACTS OF THE APOSTLES

(*First Century c.e.*)

The last verses of Chapter 4 in the Acts of the Apostles describe the life
of the primitive—that is, the very early—Christians. The spirit of God
was strongly on the little group—half a community, half a church—
from which the entire body of Christian believers was to derive. In
many matters for which Jesus left no explicit commandments, later
ages assumed he meant the example set by these earliest Christians to
prevail. Among their distinctive practices was community of material
goods; none of them claimed anything as his own, but all things were
held in common. Sometimes, however, this practice evidently needed
the reinforcement (opening of Chapter 5) of a cautionary tale.

[The Community]†

From *Chapter 4*

* * *

31. And when they had prayed, the place was shaken where they
were assembled together; and they were all filled with the Holy
Ghost, and they spake the word of God with boldness.

32. And the multitude of them that believed were of one heart
and of one soul: neither said any of them that ought of the things
which he possessed was his own; but they had all things common.

33. And with great power gave the apostles witness of the resur-
rection of the Lord Jesus: and great grace was upon them all.

34. Neither was there any among them that lacked: for as many
as were possessors of lands or houses sold them, and brought the
prices of the things that were sold,

---

† In the King James Version (1611). More, of course, read the Bible in the Latin Vulgate.

35. And laid them down at the apostles' feet: and distribution was made unto every man according as he had need.

* * *

From *Chapter 5*

1. But a certain man named Ananias, with Sapphira his wife, sold a possession,

2. And kept back part of the price, his wife also being privy to it, and brought a certain part, and laid it at the apostles' feet.

3. But Peter said, Ananias, why hath Satan filled thine heart to lie to the Holy Ghost, and to keep back part of the price of the land?

4. Whiles it remained, was it not thine own? and after it was sold, was it not in thine own power? why hast thou conceived this thing in thine heart? thou has not lied unto men, but unto God.

5. And Ananias hearing these words fell down, and gave up the ghost: and great fear came on all of them that heard these things.

6. And the young men arose, wound him up, and carried him out, and buried him.

7. And it was about the space of three hours after, when his wife, not knowing what was done, came in.

8. And Peter answered unto her, Tell me whether ye sold the land for so much? And she said, Yea, for so much.

9. Then Peter said unto her, How is it that ye have agreed together to tempt the Spirit of the Lord? behold, the feet of them which have buried thy husband are at the door, and shall carry thee out.

10. Then fell she down straightway at his feet, and yielded up the ghost: and the young men came in, and found her dead, and, carrying her forth, buried her by her husband.

11. And great fear came upon all the church, and upon as many as heard these things.

* * *

LUCIAN OF SAMOSATA

(*Second Century C.E.*)

Lucian's "Saturnalian Letters" are addressed to the Greek god Cronus (who was identified with the Roman Saturn), the father and predecessor of Zeus, on the occasion of his particular festival, the Saturnalia. This festival (eventually a full week long) fell just about the same time as Christmas, in the latter half of December. During the festival all schools were closed, no battles were fought, and no punishments were inflicted; distinctions of rank were (at least ostensibly) abolished, slaves and servants sat at tables alongside their masters and were even waited on by them, and gifts were exchanged, particularly wax tapers and clay dolls. Behind all these observances lay the myth that Saturn's age was an Age of Gold, when life was simpler, people were better, and nature, as the common heritage of the human race, shared out its blessings equally to all.

Lucian, who was a cynical Syrian rhetorician who wrote in Greek, doesn't take any of this mythology very seriously. He writes to the god, asking that the simulated, temporary equality of his festival be made real and permanent. His letter suffers the usual fate of such communications in the modern world: Cronus says it doesn't come within the mandate of his department and shuffles it off to Zeus, who will no doubt conveniently mislay it. Still, it provides Lucian with a chance to revive that dream of the Golden Age in which nobody had too much but everybody had what he needed, and to contrast it with his own society, whose gross disparities between rich and poor are very like those in More's society (as described in Book I of *Utopia*) and in ours.

Lucian was a special favorite of both More and Erasmus, each of whom translated several of his short works from Greek into Latin for a volume they published together in 1506. For both men, Lucian was the most congenial and instructive model for how wit and irony could be the vehicle of a pungent social criticism. Erasmus's *Praise of Folly* (written in More's house in 1509 and published in 1511) is the best large-scale example of the kind of writing that resulted, but in *Utopia*, the account of the discomfiture of the Anemolian ambassadors (pp. 56–57) relies directly on Lucian, and there is some degree—how much is a disputed matter—of kinship between the book as a whole and Lucian's parody of lying travelers' tales, *A True History*. It is not surprising that works of Lucian were among the books Hythloday took with him to South America and then Utopia, or that when he shared his books with the Utopians they were "delighted with the witty persiflage of Lucian" (p. 69).

[Saturn's Age][†]

I to Cronus, Greeting.

I have written to you before telling you of my condition, how poverty was likely to exclude me from the festival you have proclaimed. I remember observing how unreasonable it was that some of us should be in the lap of wealth and luxury, and never give a share of their good things to the poor, while others are dying of hunger with

† From "Saturnalian Letters" 1 and 2, in *The Works of Lucian of Samosata*, translated by H. W. Fowler and F. G. Fowler, 4 vols. (Oxford: Clarendon Press, 1905), 4:117–21.

your holy season just upon them. But as you did not answer, I thought I might as well refresh your memory. Dear good Cronus, you ought really to remove this inequality and pool all the good things before telling us to make merry. The world is peopled with camels and ants now, nothing between the two. Or, to put it another way, kindly imagine an actor, with one foot mounted on the tragic stilt[1] and the other bare; if he walks like that, he must be a giant or a dwarf according to the leg he stands on; our lives are about as equal as his heights. Those who are taken on by manager Fortune and supplied with stilts come the hero over us, while the rest pad it on the ground, though you may take my word for it we could rant and stalk with the best of them if we were given the same chance.

Now the poets inform me that in the old days when you were king it was otherwise with men; earth bestowed her gifts upon them unsown and unploughed, every man's table was spread automatically, rivers ran wine and milk and honey. Most wonderful of all, the men themselves were gold, and poverty never came near them. As for us, we can hardly pass for lead; some yet meaner material must be found. In the sweat of our face the most of us eat bread. Poverty, distress, and helplessness, sighs and lamentations and pinings for what is not, such is the staple of man's life, the poor man's at least. All which, believe me, would be much less painful to us, if there were not the felicity of the rich to emphasize it. They have their chests of gold and silver, their stored wardrobes, their slaves and carriages and house property and farms, and, not content with keeping to themselves their superfluity in all these, they will scarce fling a glance to the generality of us.

Ah, Cronus, there is the sting that rankles beyond endurance—that one should loll on cloth of finest purple, overload his stomach with all delicacies, and keep perpetual feast with guests to wish him joy, while I and my like dream over the problematic acquisition of a sixpence to provide us a loaf white or brown, and send us to bed with a smack of cress or thyme or onion in our mouths. Now, good Cronus, either reform this altogether and feed us alike, or at the least induce the rich not to enjoy their good things alone; from their bushels of gold let them scatter a poor pint among us; the raiment that they would never feel the loss of though the moth were to consume it utterly, seeing that in any case it must perish by mere lapse of time, let them devote to covering our nakedness rather than to propagating mildew in their chests and drawers.

*   *   *

---

1. I.e., the buskin, the thick-soled boot worn by actors in classical tragedies.

These things if you correct and reform, you will have made life life, and your feast a feast. If not, we will leave the feasting to them, and just kneel down and pray that as they come from the bath the slave may knock down and spill their wine, the cook smoke their sauce and absentmindedly pour the pea-soup over the caviare, the dog steal in while the scullions are busy and make away with the whole of the sausage and most of the pastry.

* * *

* * * These are specimens of the petitions we will send up, if they will not moderate their selfishness, acknowledge themselves trustees for the public, and let us have our fair share.

Cronus to his well-beloved me, Greeting.

My good man, why this absurdity of writing to me about the state of the world, and advising redistribution of property? It is none of my business; the present ruler must see to that. It is an odd thing you should be the only person unaware that I have long abdicated;[2] my sons now administer various departments, of which the one that concerns you is mainly in the hands of Zeus; my own charge is confined to draughts[3] and merry-making, song and good cheer, and that for one week only. As for the weightier matters you speak of, removal of inequalities and reducing of all men to one level of poverty or riches, Zeus must do your business for you.

* * *

ST. AMBROSE

(*Fourth Century*)

The most forceful exponent of the tradition of Christian communism that informs *Utopia* was St. Ambrose (ca. 340–397 c.e.), bishop of Milan and one of the greatest and most influential of Christian theologians. Interpreting the Genesis story in the light of the myth of the Golden Age, Ambrose concluded that the institution of private property was a direct and deeply regrettable consequence of the Fall of Adam and Eve; and no preacher has ever railed more furiously against the evildoing of the rich. One of Ambrose's treatments of this theme,

---

2. Cronus did not abdicate but was deposed by his children: his sons, Zeus, Hades, and Poseidon, and his daughters, Hera, Demeter, and Hestia.
3. The British name for checkers—which is in fact an ancient game, though Lucian in the Greek actually refers to dicing.

a treatise perhaps originating in a series of sermons, takes its starting
point from the biblical story of Naboth, in 1 Kings 21: when Naboth
declined to sell his vineyard to the wicked King Ahab, Queen Jezebel
arranged to have him killed, so that the vineyard could be appropri-
ated. From Ambrose's treatise, the eminent historian of ideas Arthur
O. Lovejoy pieced together the following translated excerpts. The original source is the massive—221-volume—collection of writings of the
Latin "Church Fathers" edited by J. P. Migne and known to scholars as
"*MPL*" (Migne, *Patrologia Latina*), 14:767–72, 784. (Migne also edited
the Greek Fathers, in 165 volumes.)

[Naboth's Vineyard]†

How far, ye rich, will you carry your insane cupidity? . . . Why do
you reject nature's partnership of goods, and claim possession of
nature for yourselves? The earth was established to be in common
for all, rich and poor; why do ye rich alone arrogate it to yourselves
as your rightful property? Nature knows no rich, since she brings
forth all men poor. For we are born without clothes and are brought
forth without silver or gold. Naked she brings us to the light of day,
and in want of food and covering and drink; and naked the earth
receives back what she has brought forth, nor can she stretch men's
tombs to cover their possessions. A narrow mound of turf is enough
for rich and poor alike; and a bit of land of which the rich man when
alive took no heed now takes in the whole of him. Nature makes no
distinctions among us at our birth, and none at our death. All alike
she creates us, all alike she seals us in the tomb. Who can tell the
dead apart? Open up the graves, and, if you can, tell which was a
rich man. . . .

But why do you think that, even while you live, you have abundance of all things? Rich man, you know not how poor you are, how
destitute you would seem even to yourself, who call yourself
wealthy. The more you have, the more you want; and whatever you
may acquire, you nevertheless remain as needy as before. Avarice is
inflamed by gain, not diminished by it. . . .

You crave possessions not so much for their utility to yourself, as
because you want to exclude others from them. You are more concerned with despoiling the poor than with your own advantage. You
think yourself injured if a poor man possesses anything which you
consider a suitable belonging for a rich man; whatever belongs to

† From Arthur O. Lovejoy, "The Communism of St. Ambrose," *Essays in the History of Ideas*
(Baltimore: Johns Hopkins University Press, 1948), pp. 299–300. Reprinted by permission of Professor Gerald Monsman, University of Arizona.

others you look upon as something of which you are deprived. Why do you delight in what to nature are losses? The world, which you few rich men try to keep for yourselves, was created for all men. For not alone the soil, but the very heaven, the air, the sea, are claimed for the use of the few rich. . . . Do the angels in heaven, think you, have their separate regions of space, as you divide up the earth by fixed boundaries? . . .

How many men are killed to procure the means of your enjoyment! A deadly thing is your greed, and deadly your luxury. One man falls to death from a roof, in order that you may have your big granaries. Another tumbles from the top of a high tree while seeking for certain kinds of grapes, so that you may have the right sort of wine for your banquet. Another is drowned in the sea while making sure that fish or oysters shall not be lacking on your table. Another is frozen to death while tracking hares or trying to catch birds with traps. Another is beaten to death before your eyes, if he chances to have displeased you, and your very viands are bespattered with his blood. . . .

Do you think your great halls (*atria*) exalt you—when they ought rather to cause you remorse because, though they are big enough to take in multitudes, they shut out the voice of the poor? Though, indeed, nothing is gained by your hearing their voice if, when you hear it, you do nothing about it. In fine, does not your very dwelling-place admonish you of your shame, in that in building it you wished to show that your riches surpass [those of others]—and yet you do not succeed? You cover walls, but you leave men bare. Naked they cry out before your house, and you heed them not: a naked man cries out, but you are busy considering what sort of marbles you will have to cover your floors. A poor man asks for money, and does not get it; a human being begs for bread, and your horse champs a golden bit. You gratify yourself with costly ornaments, while other men go without food. How great a judgment, O rich man, do you draw down upon yourself! The people go hungry, and you close your granaries; the people weep, and you turn your finger-ring about. Unhappy man, who have the power but not the will to save so many souls from death: the cost of the jewel in your ring would have sufficed to save the lives of a whole people.

*   *   *

ST. BENEDICT

(Sixth Century)

The Utopians turned readily to Christianity in part because the early disciples set an example of communal living and because certain Christian communities continued to practice it. These were the monastic orders, of which the best known and most widespread was that founded by St. Benedict (ca. 480–543) His famous Rule—the foundational document of Western monasticism—was developed for use by monks of the newly established house of Monte Cassino, southeast of Rome. Though it has a reputation for strictness and austerity, the Rule was not in fact very severe; various suborders of Benedictines (for example, the Cistercians) split off from the main order in search of greater purity and stricter discipline. But on the question of personal property within the monastery, the Rule of Saint Benedict was, and remained, crisp and uncompromising. Chapters 33 and 34 present the core of the Rule's teaching on this point.

[Monastic Rules]†

Chapter 33

Whether Monks Should Have Anything of Their Own

This vice especially ought to be utterly rooted out of the monastery. Let no one presume to give or receive anything without the abbot's leave, or to have anything as his own, anything whatever, whether book or tablets or pen or whatever it may be; for monks should not have even their bodies and wills at their own disposal. But let them look to the father of the monastery for all that they require, and let it be unlawful to have anything which the abbot has not given or allowed. And, as the Scripture saith, *let all things be common to all, nor let anyone say that anything is his own*[1] or claim it for himself. But if anyone shall be found to indulge in this most wicked vice, let him be admonished once and a second time; if he do not amend, let him undergo punishment.

---

† From *The Rule of Saint Benedict in Latin and English*, edited and translated by Abbot Justin McCann (London: Burns Oates, 1952), pp. 85–87.
1. Cf. Acts 4.32 (p. 105 above).

Chapter 34

Whether All Should Receive Necessaries in Like Measure

Let us follow the Scripture: *Distribution was made to every man according as he had need.*[2] By this we do not mean that there should be respect of persons (God forbid), but consideration for infirmities. He that needeth less, let him thank God and not be discontented; he that needeth more, let him be humbled for his infirmity and not made proud by the mercy shown to him: so will all the members be at peace. Above all, let not the vice of murmuring[3] show itself in any word or sign, for any reason whatever. But if a brother be found guilty of it, let him undergo strict punishment.

ANONYMOUS

(Thirteenth Century)

The mythical land of Cockayne—the subject of many literary treatments in later medieval Europe (and, in the sixteenth century, of the famous painting reproduced on p. 115)—was a sort of peasant's version of the Golden Age and Saturnalia rolled into one. In Cockayne, all rules are abrogated or reversed and life is an endless round of gluttony, sloth, and carefree lechery. Roasted pigs amble by, eager to be eaten, on streets of pastry strewn with edible buildings and bordered by rivers of wine; the weather is always good; and youth is eternal. (Such fantasies are, of course, perennial. A familiar American example, from the turn of the twentieth century, is the hobo song "Big Rock Candy Mountain.")

In the famous English treatment of the myth—a 190-line poem from the thirteenth century known as "The Land of Cockayne"—the idlers' utopia is used as a vehicle for anti-clerical satire: the poem purports to find Cockayne behind a monastery's walls. More, like Erasmus, was a frequent, and often satiric, critic of corrupt clergy: recall Hythloday's inclusion, in his list of idlers who are a drag on Old World economies, of "a great lazy gang of priests and so-called religious" (p. 46 above). But More must also have been anxious to have readers distinguish sharply between Cockayne and *his* island "Far out to sea and west of Spain," and perhaps the desire to avoid any possible confusion encouraged him to stress so strongly the rigid discipline of life in Utopia and to make its monks—the "Buthrescas" (pp. 88–89)—the hardest-working and most abstemious Utopians of all.

---

2. Acts 4.35.
3. I.e., grumbling.

From The Land of Cockayne[†]

Far out to sea and west of Spain
Lies a land known as Cockayne;
There is no place beneath the sky
Where men live more deliciously.
5   Though Paradise is brisk and bright,[1]
Cockayne is a more glorious sight;
For what has Paradise to show
But plants and more plants row on row?
Flowers are red there, grasses green,
10 The moral atmosphere's serene,
But though the bliss is absolute,
The only thing to eat is fruit,
And water's all you get to drink—
Not much excitement there, I think.
15 Society is pretty meager, too;
After Elias and Enoch, I wonder who
There is to talk to?[2] Fine men, no doubt,
But everyone else you do without.
     Cockayne o'erflows with meat and drink,
20 No need to sweat or strain or swink,[3]
The meat is free, the drink flows clear,
Nothing to pay, nothing to fear,
Yours for the asking noon and night,
Everything for your delight.

                    *   *   *

     A noble abbey, proud in its array,
Crowded with monks both white and gray,[4]
Raises its banners through the air;
Many bowers and halls are there;
55 The walls are made of pasty-pies,
Rising in turrets to the skies,
Stuffed all with fish and good red meat
The finest any man could eat;
The roofs of gingerbread, each and all,
60 Whether of church or cloister, tower or hall;

---

† The Middle English of the original has been freely modernized.
1. Legends of the survival, somewhere in the East, of the Edenic paradise were common in the later Middle Ages.
2. The Old Testament figures Elias (Elijah) and Enoch, spared death, were thought to be awaiting the end of the world as the sole inhabitants of the earthly paradise.
3. Work.
4. I.e., both white-frocked Carmelites and gray-frocked Franciscans.

Some typical gustatory delights of Cockayne, with their stupefying consequences for the human inhabitants (one of them a scholar who has forgotten about his book), are vividly represented in Pieter Brueghel the Elder's celebrated painting *The Land of Cockayne* (1567). Courtesy of The Bridgeman Art Library.

The postern gates[5] are fat pudding,
Fit for the feast of prince or king.
People may eat their fill, and stuff
Themselves enough and more than enough;
65 For all is common to young and old,
To stout and stern, to meek and bold.

* * *

There the young monks every day
After dinner go out to play;
There is no hawk or quail so swift,
Half as nimble or as deft,
125 As these monks in joyous mood,
Their long sleeves flying and their hood
Floating on the evening air
As they dance across the lawn.
When the abbot sees them flee,
130 Who more joyous is than he?
Till he summons them along,
Crying, "Time for even-song!"

5. Back or side gates.

But feisty monks absorbed in play
Romp over the hills and far away.
135 When the abbot sees his crew
Frolic off, far from his view,
He picks a maiden from the flock
And gathers up her pretty smock,
And loudly sounds the recall drum
140 Upon the tabor of her bum.

* * *

Another abbey is thereby,
Forsooth a great fine nunnery,
On a river of sweet milk
150 The countryside as soft as silk.
When a summer's day is hot,
The younger nuns take out a boat
And in the stream with active oar
Set boldly onward from the shore,
155 And having left their home behind
Strip to enjoy both wave and wind,
Then leaping boldly in the brim,
Dispose themselves to splash and swim.
The young monks, having them in sight,
160 Approach in haste, with great delight,
And coming to the nuns anon,
Each makes selection of his own,
And quickly leadeth back his prize
Out of the range of curious eyes,
165 Back to the abbey's private cot,
Where they may tie the true love's knot.
Each girl performs her act of true devotion
Contributing her own peculiar motion.
The monk who is reputed good,
170 And carries high aloft his hood,
He shall enjoy for his good cheer
At least a dozen wives a year,
By his own right and not through grace,
For his own pleasure and solace;
175 And for the monk whose eager zest
Keeps his lady all night from rest,
There is good grounds to hope he may
Himself be named abbot some day.

* * *

AMERIGO VESPUCCI

(Early Sixteenth Century)

The Florentine explorer Amerigo Vespucci (1454–1512), sailing first for
the king of Spain and then for the king of Portugal, made at least two
voyages to the New World, in the period 1497–1502. The opening five
years of the sixteenth century saw the publication of two accounts of his
travels, purportedly by Amerigo himself: *New World* (in Latin) and *The
Four Voyages of Amerigo Vespucci* (in Italian). The latter was republished
in a Latin translation in 1507 as an appendix to Martin Waldseemüller's
Introduction to Cosmography—the book that bestowed on the newly discovered lands a Latinized version of the explorer's name: America.

The authorship of both early accounts of Vespucci's voyages is now
disputed, but in the sixteenth century their authenticity does not seem
to have been questioned, and they were, as More says in *Utopia*, "common reading everywhere." *Utopia* exhibits parallels with both, and its
fiction is grafted directly onto *Four Voyages* in the claim that Hythloday
accompanied Vespucci on the last three of his four supposed voyages
and went on to discover Utopia after becoming one of the twenty-four
men whom Vespucci is said to have left behind at the farthest point of
his last voyage (see "The Fourth Voyage"). Moreover, the account of
New World natives in *Four Voyages*—especially the characterization
of them as Epicureans and the assertion that they were indifferent to
gold and jewels—clearly helped set More's imagination working on the
contours of his alternative society. The account in *Four Voyages* itself
is far from soberly factual, though, and readers should bear in mind
that it is excerpted here not as reliable history or ethnography but as a
typically sensationalized traveler's tale, which happened to play a part
in the genesis of *Utopia*.

From The Four Voyages[†]

The First Voyage

* * * [We] sailed north-west, for thus the coast trended,[1] ever in
sight of land, continually seeing people along the beach, until, after
having voyaged two days, we found a tolerably safe place for the
ships. And we anchored a half league[2] from shore, where we saw an

---

[†] Reprinted from Amerigo Vespucci, *Letter to Piero Soderini*, Vespucci Reprints, Texts
and Studies IV, translated by George Tyler Northup (Princeton, N.J.: Princeton University Press, 1916), pp. 4–9, 44.
1. *Four Voyages* recounts that Vespucci's first expedition set out from Cadiz in May 1497.
Sailing first to the Canary Islands (off the northwest coast of Africa) and from there
across the main body of the Atlantic, the four ships made landfall at Honduras, and
then made their way along the coast seeking safe harbor.
2. One league is roughly three miles.

immense number of people. And this same day we went ashore with
the boats. And we leaped ashore, full 40 well equipped men, and
the people ashore still showed themselves shy of associating with
us. And we could not so reassure them that they would come to talk
with us. And this day we so persistently endeavored in giving them
of our wares, such as bells, mirrors, glass beads and other trash
that some of them were rendered confident, and came to converse
with us. And when we had established kindly relations with them,
inasmuch as night was falling, we took leave of them and returned
to the ships. And the next day, when dawn broke, we saw that infinite hordes were on the beach; and they had with them their wives
and children. We put ashore and found that all came laden with
their possessions, which are such as will be told in its place. And
before we reached land, many of them dove and came to meet us a
cross-bow shot out to sea, for they are very great swimmers, with
just as much confidence as if they had associated with us for a long
time. And we were pleased at this confidence of theirs.

What we ascertained concerning their manner of life and customs was that they go about wholly naked, men and women alike,
without covering any shameful part, not otherwise than they issued
from their mothers' wombs. They are of medium stature, very well
proportioned. Their skin is of a color which inclines to red, like a
lion's mane; and I believe that if they went clothed, they would be
white like ourselves. They have no hair at all on the body, except
long and black hair on the head, especially the women, which renders them beautiful. They are not very fair of countenance, because
they have broad faces, so that their appearance may be that of the
Tartar. They do not let any hair grow in the eyebrows nor in the eye-
lashes, nor in any other place whatsoever, exception made of the
hair of the head; for they hold hair to be something ugly. They are
very swift of their bodies, in walking and in running, both men and
women; for a woman recks nothing of running a league or two, as
we frequently saw; and in this they have a very great advantage over
us Christians. They swim past all belief, and the women better than
the men; because many times we have found and seen them swimming along two leagues out at sea without any support. Their weapons are bows and arrows, very well wrought, except that they have
no iron or other sort of hard metal; and in place of iron they put
animals' or fishes' teeth or a splinter of stout wood burnt at the tip.
They are sure shots, for they hit wherever they please; and in some
places the women use these bows. And they have other weapons,
such as fire-hardened spears and other clubs with knobs of most
excellent workmanship. They practise war among themselves with
peoples who are not of their own speech, very cruelly, without spar-
ing anybody's life except for a greater punishment. When they go to

war, they take with them their wives; not that these may wage war, but because they carry their supplies after them. For one woman bears on her back a burden such as no man will carry, thirty or forty leagues; for we often saw it. It is not their custom to have any captain, nor do they walk in orderly array; for each is master of himself. And the occasion of their wars is not desire of rule, nor to widen their boundaries, nor any inordinate covetousness; it is due merely to some old hostility which in the past has sprung up among them. And, when asked why they waged war, they could give us no other reason than that they did so to avenge the death of their ancestors or of their parents. These have neither king nor master, nor do they obey anybody; for they live in their individual liberty. And the way in which they are incited to go to war is that when the enemy has killed or captured some of them, his eldest relative rises and goes through the streets, exhorting them to go with him to avenge the death of such and such a relative of his; and thus they are stirred by pity. They do not practise justice, nor punish the criminal, nor do father and mother punish their children; and whether or not it was something unusual, we never saw disputing amongst them. They show themselves simple in their speech, yet they are very crafty and sharp in that which comes within their province. They speak little and with subdued voice. They use the same accents as ourselves, because they form the words either on the palate, or the teeth, or the lips, except that they use other names for things. Great are the varieties of dialects, for at every hundred leagues we found a change of tongues such that these were mutually unintelligible. The manner of their living is very barbarous, because they do not eat at fixed times, but as often as they please. And it matters little to them that they should be seized with a desire to eat at midnight rather than by day, for at all times they eat. And their eating is done upon the ground, without tablecloth or any other cloth, because they hold their food either in earthen basins which they make or in half gourds. They sleep in certain nets made of cotton, very big, and hung in the air. And although this their way of sleeping may appear uncomfortable, I say that it is a soft way to sleep; because it was very frequently our lot to sleep in them, and we slept better in them than in quilts. They are people neat and clean of person, owing to the constant washing they practise. When, begging your pardon, they evacuate the bowels, they do everything to avoid being seen; and just as in this they are clean and modest, the more dirty and shameless are they in making water, both men and women. Because, even while talking to us, they let fly such filth, without turning around or showing shame, that in this they have no modesty. They do not practise marriage amongst themselves. Each one takes all the wives he pleases; and when he desires to repudiate them, he does repudiate them without it being considered a wrong on his part or a disgrace to the woman; for in this the woman has as much liberty as the man. They are not very jealous, and are libidinous beyond measure, and the women far more than the men; for I refrain out of decency from telling you the trick which they play to satisfy their immoderate lust. They are very fertile women, and in their pregnancies avoid no toil. Their parturitions are so easy that one day after giving birth they go out everywhere, and especially to bathe in the rivers; and they are sound as fish. They are so heartless and cruel that, if they become angry with their husbands, they immediately resort to a trick whereby they kill the child within the womb, and a miscarriage is brought about, and for this reason they kill a great many babies. They are women of pleasing person, very well proportioned, so that one does not see on their bodies any ill-formed feature or limb. And although they go about utterly naked, they are fleshy women, and that part of their privies which he who has not seen them would think to see is invisible; for they cover all with their thighs, save that part for which nature made no provision, and which is modestly speaking, the *mons veneris*. In short they are no more ashamed of their shameful parts than we are in displaying the nose and mouth. Only exceptionally will you see a woman with drooping breasts, or with belly shrunken through frequent parturition, or with other wrinkles; for all look as though they had never given birth. They showed themselves very desirous of copulating with us Christians. While among these people we did not learn that they had any religion. They can be termed neither Moors nor Jews; and they are worse than heathen; because we did not see that they offered any sacrifice, nor yet did they have any house of prayer. I deem their manner of life to be Epicurean. Their dwellings are in common,[3] and their houses built after the fashion of huts, but stoutly wrought and constructed out of very large trees and thatched with palm leaves, safe against tempests and winds, and in some places of such breadth and length that in a single house we found there were 600 souls; and we saw towns of only thirteen houses where there were 4,000 souls. Every eight to ten years they shift their towns. And when asked why they

---

3. In *New World*, Vespucci depicts the indigenous Americans as communitarian in all respects: "neither do they have goods of their own, but all things are held in common" (*Mundus novus: Letter to Lorenzo Pietro di Medici*, translated by G. T. Northup [Princeton: Princeton University Press, 1916], p. 6). So too the historian Pietro Martire d'Anghiera, expatiating in the first part of his *De Orbe Novo* [*On the New World*] (1511) on what he had learned about Columbus's encounters with the natives of Cuba, writes that "with them the earth, like the sun and water, is common, nor do 'mine and yours,' the seeds of all evils, fall among them. * * * Theirs is a golden age: they do not hedge their estates with ditches, walls or hedges; they live with open gardens; without laws, without books, without judges, of their own nature, they cultivate what is right" (*Selections from Peter Martyr*, edited and translated by Geoffrey Eatough, *Repertorium Columbianum*, Vol. 5 [Turnhout, Belgium: Brepols, 1998], p. 69).

put themselves to so much trouble, they made us a very plausible answer. They said that they did so on account of the soil, which, when once rendered infectious and unhealthful by filth, occasioned disease in their bodies, which seemed to us a good reason. Their wealth consists of feathers of many-hued birds, or of little rosaries which they make out of fish bones, or of white or green stones which they stick through cheeks, lips, and ears, and of many other things to which we attach no value. They engage in no barter whatsoever; they neither buy nor sell. In short, they live and are contented with what nature gives them. The wealth which we affect in this our Europe and elsewhere, such as gold, jewels, pearls, and other riches, they hold of no value at all; and although they have them in their lands they do not work to get them, nor do they care for them.

* * *

The Fourth Voyage

* * * We sailed 260 leagues farther until we reached a harbor where we decided to build a fort.[4] We did so, and left in it 24 Christian men who were aboard my consort, and whom she had received from the wrecked flag-ship.[5] In that harbor we stayed full five months, building the fort and loading our ships with brazil wood; for we could not go farther, because we had no crews and I lacked much gear. When this was accomplished, we decided to return to Portugal, which was on our course between north and north-east. We left the 24 men who remained in the fort with supplies for six months, 12 mortars, and many other weapons. We pacified all the natives, of whom I have made no mention in this voyage, not because we did not see and associate with countless natives; because full 30 of us men went inland 40 leagues, where I saw so many things that I refrain from telling them, reserving them for my *Four Journeys.*[6]

* * *

4. Reputedly at Cape Frio, seventy miles east of the site of Rio de Janeiro. They had sailed from the Bahia de Todos os Santos (All Saints' Bay), now the site of the Brazilian city Salvador.
5. Wrecked and sunk as a consequence, the narrator has previously claimed, of the folly of the unnamed admiral of the expedition. "Consort": in the sense of a ship that accompanies another.
6. A supposed book based on diaries written during the voyages. It never appeared.

G. R. ELTON

Born in Germany, Sir Geoffrey Rudolf Elton (1921–1994) became a highly distinguished British historian of Tudor England. The opening chapter of his *Reform and Reformation: England 1509–1558* includes a brief, balanced overview—with all the advantages of hindsight—of the set of social and economic problems that Hythloday discusses in Book I of *Utopia*.

[The Problems of the Realm]†

* * * The fundamental problems of the realm were of long standing and had received attention before, but it is apparent that as Henry VIII ascended the throne¹ a good many people expected to see real changes. The country was passing through a period of economic upheaval, drastic enough for an agrarian society in which change is always bound to be slow, and rendered more drastic still by the inability of contemporaries to understand what was happening. For some two generations the population had been rising. We have no reliable figures, but since the disputed calculations range around a mean of about two and a half millions it will be clear that even ten thousand more mouths to feed, twenty thousand more hands to employ, would cause some real convulsions in that economy. The pressure was heaviest on the peasantry, the men who had benefited from the shortage of labour created in the demographic disasters of the fourteenth century² and who now found the terms of life turn against them. Prices were also rising, not yet dramatically but with a certain ominousness, and it increasingly became inadvisable to live on fixed incomes. All men with assets to develop saw reason why they should do so. In particular this meant pressure on rents and efforts to increase the premiums charged to incoming tenants (entry fines). It is often alleged that the early sixteenth century was an exceptionally materialist and unspiritual age, but this is to take contemporary laments at face value and to forget that business letters have a better chance of surviving than less 'materialist' effusions. Agrarian troubles and unrest did not spring from the greed of landlords and the

---

† From G. R. Elton, *Reform and Reformation: England 1509–1558* (London: Edward Arnold, 1977), pp. 2–5. Reprinted by permission. All footnotes are by the editor.
1. In 1509.
2. These included not only famines and frequent periods of warfare—with Scotland in the earlier part of the century and with France in the Hundred Years' War that began in 1337—but, far more devastating, the ravages of plague. The most horrific epidemic was the Black Death of 1348 (perhaps a combination of bubonic and pneumonic plague), which killed from a third to a half of the population.

harshness of bailiffs whose activities represented an often necessary and usually understandable reaction to the impact of change.

The most obvious manifestation of that change was enclosure against which a comprehensive but unenforceable act had been passed in 1489. It was widely believed that for the sake of profit from wool production landlords were converting arable to pasture, destroying units of agriculture, and ejecting tenants. The true situation was much too complex to be subsumed under so ready a generalization. Quite apart from the often effective limitations that the peasant's legal and customary rights placed upon the landlord's freedom of action (as a result of which agrarian changes differed greatly from region to region, even when economic circumstances were very similar), enclosure meant several practices, some laudable, some disastrous. It could signify the amalgamation of dispersed strips in the open field into efficient arable farms, as well as the enclosing of wastes and commons for the grazing of an entrepreneur's sheep or cattle; and the first was as advantageous to the commonweal as the second was likely to lead to depopulation and the disappearance of villages which could not survive without their commons. Most of this enclosure, good or bad, had taken place before 1489, so that the act caught relatively few enclosers. The most insidious rural problem of Henry VIII's reign, which the age had not yet diagnosed, was not touched on in the statute—the practice of buying up leaseholds and taking them out of husbandry. In this game the entrepreneurs were as often graziers (cattlemen) as sheepfarmers, and clergy as well as laity; by allowing a derelict building to survive on the converted property, they could evade the legislation directed at the 'decay of houses'.

Unquestionably all this drove some men off the land, though no one could then, or can now, tell the numbers affected. Some of these products of rural unemployment joined bands of vagrants, mostly young people seeking work, though contemporaries were far from wrong in supposing that the freedom of the roads and the attractions of crime helped to create those bands of wandering beggars which by giving means of physical violence to people disconnected from the normal forms of social control soon threatened the peace of mind and even the stability of this society. Population growth played its part; even without the agrarian changes many men would have found difficulties in getting work. This unsettled state was aggravated by changes in industry, too, especially in England's premier manufacture, that of woollen cloth. In the course of the fifteenth century, the clothing industry had shifted location, so that old centres of manufacture like Bristol and Gloucester declined while new areas of prosperity opened up in the Yorkshire dales and the villages of Suffolk. The measures taken by Henry VII to encourage the trade in cloth assisted a major shift both in manufacturing regions and the types of cloth produced. His commercial treaties with the Netherlands promoted the specialist trade between London and Antwerp monopolized by the unchartered association of the London Merchant Adventurers who rose to wealth and eminence by supplying the Antwerp market with what it wanted—white (unfinished) cloth for the finishing trades that flourished in that great entrepôt[3] of the first half of the sixteenth century. In consequence the English finishing trades declined, unable to compete in quality and in the cost of materials; in London, for instance, the Mercers' Company, engaged in selling white cloth, took over the primacy hitherto occupied by the drapers who coordinated the production of finished cloth. Another consequence was seen in the gradual decline of the so-called outports—Hull, Bristol, Southampton—as more and more of England's export trade flowed through London, with its easy access to the main continental inlet.

Thanks above all to its export of woollen products, but also because it supplied such other materials as grain, leather and tin to foreign countries, the English economy was very definitely tied to a European complex which itself was being affected by changes in population and wealth, and by an inflation of prices. Englishmen, however, for the most part did not look beyond the boundaries of the realm, shire or even village; and they naturally sought the causes of distress close to home. The agitation against enclosers and engrossers always revived in times of corn shortage and harvest failure, as did (more rationally) the attempts to prevent unlicensed exports of grain. As it happened, the beginning of the reign was blessed with good weather, and it was only in 1515[4] that the argument rose high again. Exports of cloth, too, remained buoyant from early in Henry VIII's reign until the end of the second decade of the sixteenth century. Thus few outward signs of the underlying causes of unrest made themselves felt in about 1510: while people could not but sense that uncomfortable changes were coming over the commonwealth, relative prosperity cushioned shocks and confined really ill effects for the moment to the truly powerless and necessarily silent. However, though the reign opened in an atmosphere of economic euphoria, it must be remembered that changes in population, shifts of wealth, transformations of manufacture and trade, and the insidious beginnings of price inflation were all present. At the foundations of society, stability was under attack, not necessarily to the disadvantage of society as a whole (for profit and prosperity lurked in the cracks opening in the traditional structure) but certainly to the detriment of a social phi-

3. Commercial center; hub of distribution of goods.
4. A famine year.

losophy which saw security and hope solely in maintaining what had always been. Men's daily lives passed against a background of increasingly rapid change, but apart from at intervals lamenting the fact they had no thought to offer.

Above all, nothing so far suggested that anybody was really attempting to analyse the inwardness of the changes or thought of prescribing remedies designed to control them constructively, beyond forbidding whatever seemed contrary to past practice—a practice identified with the natural order of the universe. Even the complaints testify to a striking absence of radical thinking, being marked by an undeviating belief in a past good order that these recent and degenerate days had managed to lose. * * * Men, it was held, could not so much alter the terms of their lives as manage themselves within them by obeying God's injunctions against envy, covetousness and anger. Certainly it was thought possible to apply positive controls to such anarchic and selfish instincts when self-control failed to suffice, and society had a duty to take the necessary action. That was what the Church preached, diligently though ineffectually, in sermons that made no impact even on ecclesiastical possessors, as pressed in their growingly insufficient income as their lay brethren and on the whole more competent at taking the allegedly antisocial steps required to meet the crisis. And that, too, was what the law supposedly stood for—the maintenance of an existing order, not the creation of a new one. Society existed in and by a known system of law which supposedly regulated each man's rights and duties and which provided remedies and punishments when men ruptured concord by innovatory abuses. The prevalent attitude treated law as the guarantee of continuity and not as a fruitful instrument of change.

* * *

The Humanist Circle: Letters

Shortly after entrusting the manuscript of *Utopia* to Erasmus, More wrote to his friend again (ca. September 20, 1516), to say that he hoped the published book would "be handsomely set off with the highest of recommendations, if possible, from several people, both intellectuals and distinguished statesmen." He was surely gratified with the results of this request. When the first edition appeared, at the end of 1516, More's prefatory letter to Peter Giles was preceded in it by a number of letters, poems, and other items by various hands. The buttressing of published books with commendations was a common practice then as now, but the number and range of ancillary materials in More's little book was unusually large. There was, first, a map of Utopia (cruder than the one by Ambrosius Holbein that appeared in the 1518 editions and that is reproduced early in this one), which was followed by a page, supplied by Giles, giving the Utopian alphabet and a poem in Utopian (see p. 68 above). Next came a six-line poem, of unknown authorship but purporting to be by the Utopian poet laureate. These items were in turn succeeded by a letter from Giles (written at the instigation of Erasmus) to Jérôme de Busleyden, a Burgundian statesman and patron of learning. Jean Desmarez, public orator and professor at the University of Louvain, contributed a letter and a poem, and there were also two other short poems, by two Dutch humanists, Gerard Geldenhouwer and Cornelis de Schrijver. Best of all, Busleyden, prompted (like Giles) by Erasmus, contributed a letter of his own, addressed to More—so that there was one commendation, at least, from the ranks of the "distinguished statesmen" whom More had hoped would join his fellow humanists in praising his book.

In subsequent editions, these items appeared in different configurations (some were placed at the back of the book; for the 1518 editions, Desmarez's contributions were ignominiously omitted), and a few new ones were added. In the second edition (published in Paris in 1517), the longest of the letters debuted: a ponderous effusion by the preeminent French humanist of the time, Guillaume Budé. For the same edition, More wrote a second letter to Giles, which was printed just after the text of Book II. Erasmus's own commendatory letter, however, did not (for whatever reason) appear until the third and fourth editions, published in Basel in March and November 1518.

The main purpose of the commendatory letters and poems—like that of the signed blurbs that frequently adorn the covers or jackets of our modern books—was to entice prospective readers of More's little work to take the plunge. All of them praise the book; some of them also

This woodcut map of Utopia, by an unknown artist, appears on the reverse of the title page of the first edition (Louvain, 1516). Compare the much more elaborate map found in the two Basel editions of 1518 (see p. 3 above). The difference in fanciness is indicative of that between the Louvain and Basel editions in general.

offer useful insights or analysis. Collectively they indicate how *Utopia*
struck the kind of readers for whom More primarily intended it. At the
same time, though, the letters and poems (like the map and the page on
the Utopian language) continue the Lucianic (or, to post-Renaissance
readers, Swiftian) game of the book: they all maintain, and in some
cases venture to extend, the pretence that Utopia is a real place and
Raphael Hythloday a real visitor to it. For sophisticated readers, this
pretence was transparent and comic. How many less cunning readers
were actually taken in by it, we do not know. More alludes to two such
readers (one is mentioned in each of the letters to Giles—though the
second is said to be uncertain whether the book is truth or fiction), but
there is no telling whether he simply invented them.

Reprinted here is a selection of the most interesting of the letters,
together with the 1516 map and, finally, a biographical account of More
by Erasmus, which—far longer, warmer, more personal, and more interesting than the letter Erasmus contributed to the 1518 editions—
appeared not in *Utopia* but in a passage of a letter to the German humanist and religious reformer Ulrich von Hutten.

Peter Giles to Jérôme de Busleyden

[On October 17, 1516, Erasmus, who had received the manuscript of
Utopia from More shortly before, wrote to Giles asking him to prepare
a prefatory letter for the book, addressed to Busleyden: Giles's letter—
which was printed first among the commendatory letters in the 1516
edition—constitutes the dedication of *Utopia*. Busleyden, whom More
had met the previous year, was a prominent Burgundian statesman, a
wealthy man, and a patron of the arts, most notably in his endowment
of the Trilingual College of Louvain, a humanist institution dedicated
to the teaching of Greek, Latin, and Hebrew. Giles, taking his cue from
More's prefatory letter to *him*, used his own letter in part to elaborate
on the Utopian fiction, and in doing so he also slyly alludes to the fact
that the book had originated in conversations (in the summer of 1515)
between himself and More.]

Most distinguished Busleyden, the other day Thomas More (who,
as you very well know from your intimate acquaintance with him, is
one of the great ornaments of our age) sent me his *Island of Utopia*.
It is a place known so far to only a few men, but which should be
known by everyone, as going far beyond Plato's Republic. It is particularly interesting because it has been so vividly described, so carefully depicted and brought before our very eyes, by a man of such
great eloquence. As often as I read it, I seem to see even more than I
heard from the actual mouth of Raphael Hythloday—for I was present at his discourse as much as More himself. As a matter of fact,
Hythloday himself showed no mean rhetorical gifts in setting forth

his topic; it was perfectly plain that he wasn't just repeating what he had heard from other people but was describing exactly what he had seen close at hand with his own eyes and experienced in his own person, over a long period of time. I consider him a man with more knowledge of nations, peoples, and business than even the famous Ulysses. Such a man as this has not, I think, been born in the last eight hundred years; by comparison with him, Vespucci[1] seems to have seen nothing at all. Apart from the fact that we naturally describe what we have seen better than what we have only heard about, the man had a particular skill in explaining things. And yet when I contemplate the same matters as sketched by More's pen, I am so affected by them that I sometimes seem to be living in Utopia itself. I can scarcely believe, by heaven, that Raphael saw as much in the five years he lived on the island as can be seen in More's description. That description contains, in every part of it, so many wonders that I don't know what to marvel at first or most. Perhaps it should be the accuracy of his splendid memory, which could recite almost word for word so many different things that he had heard only once; or else his good judgment, which traced back to sources of which the common man is completely ignorant the evils that arise in commonwealths and the blessings that could arise in them. Or finally I might marvel at the strength and amplitude of his language, in which, while preserving a pure and vigorous Latin style, he has gathered together so much matter. This is all the more remarkable in a man distracted, as he is, by a mass of public business and private concerns. But of course none of these remarks will surprise you, most erudite Busleyden, since you have already learned from your intimate acquaintance with him to appreciate the more-than-human, the almost-divine genius of the man.

For the rest, I can add nothing to what he has written. There is, indeed, a quatrain written in the Utopian tongue, which Hythloday showed to me after More had gone away. I've prefixed to it the alphabet of the Utopians, and added to the volume some marginal notes.[2]

As for More's difficulties about locating the island, Raphael did not try in any way to suppress that information, but he mentioned it only briefly and in passing, as if saving it for another occasion. And then an unlucky accident caused both of us to miss what he said. For while Raphael was speaking of it, one of More's servants came in to whisper something in his ear; and though I was listening, for that very reason, more intently than ever, one of the company, who I suppose had caught cold on shipboard, coughed so loudly that some of Raphael's

---

1. Amerigo Vespucci, Florentine explorer of America, with whom Hythloday sailed (see pp. 11 and 117 above).
2. See pp. 23–24, n. 2 above, and, for the alphabet and quatrain, p. 68.

words escaped me. But I will never rest till I have full information on this point, not just the general position of the island but its exact latitude—provided only that our friend Hythloday is safe and alive.

For we hear various stories about him, some people asserting that he died on the way home, others that he got home but could not bear the ways of his countrymen,[3] retained his old hankering for Utopia, and so made his way back.

It's true, of course, that the name of this island is not to be found among the cosmographers, but Hythloday himself had an elegant answer for that. For, he said, either the name that the ancients gave it has changed over the ages, or else they never discovered the island at all. Nowadays we find all sorts of lands turning up which the old geographers never mentioned. But what's the point of piling up these arguments authenticating the story, when we already have it on the word of More himself?

His uncertainty about having the book published I attribute to his modesty, and very creditable it is. But on many scores, it seems to me a work that should not be suppressed any longer; on the contrary, it eminently deserves to be sent forth into the hands of men, especially under the powerful protection of your name. Nobody knows More's good qualities better than you do, and no one is better suited than you to serve the commonwealth with good counsels. At this work you have labored for many years, earning the highest praise for wisdom as well as integrity. Farewell, then, you Maecenas[4] of learning, and ornament of our era.

Antwerp, November 1, 1516

Jérôme de Busleyden to Thomas More

[More visited Busleyden during his embassy to Flanders in 1515 and later wrote two Latin poems in praise of his host's magnificent house and its artistic and archaeological treasures. Writing to Erasmus in October 1516, he singled out Busleyden as one of the "distinguished statesmen" who he hoped would endorse *Utopia*. Erasmus, a good friend of Busleyden, asked him to do so, and the resulting letter was printed among the commendations of *Utopia*, in all four early editions. The feature of the Utopian republic that Busleyden chose to endorse with special fervor was its communism, which he praises as a pattern for all the nations of the world—a judgment that may strike us as odd, given his own lordly way of life.]

3. Cf. More's second letter to Giles (printed in the 1517 edition of *Utopia*), which says that Hythloday has returned to his native Portugal (see p. 143 below).
4. Maecenas was the patron of Virgil, Horace, and other Roman writers. To call someone a "Maecenas" was to accord him the highest possible praise for generosity and discriminating taste.

For you, my most distinguished friend More, it was not enough to have devoted all your care, labor, and energy to the interest and advantage of individuals: such is your goodness and liberality that you must bestow them on the public at large. You saw that this goodness of yours, however great it might be, would deserve more favor, gain more gratitude, and aim at greater glory, the more widely it was diffused, the more people shared in it and were benefited by it. This is what you've always tried to do on other occasions, and now by a singular stroke of luck you've attained it again—I mean by that afternoon's discussion which you've recorded and now published, about the right and proper constitution (which everyone must long for) of the Utopian republic.

It is a delightful description of a wonderful system, an account replete with profound erudition and a consummate knowledge of human affairs. Both qualities meet in this work so equally and so congenially that neither yields to the other, but both contend on an even footing. You enjoy such a wide range of learning and such profound experience that whatever you write comes from full experience, and whatever you decide to say carries a full weight of learning. A rare and wonderful happiness! and all the more remarkable in that it withdraws itself from the multitude and imparts itself only to the few—to such, above all, as have the candor to wish, the erudition to understand, the trustworthiness to put into practice, and the authority to judge in the common interest as honorably, accurately, and practically as you do now. For you don't consider yourself born for yourself alone, but for the whole world; and so by this splendid work you have thought it worth your while to place the whole world in your debt.

You could hardly have accomplished this end more effectually and correctly than by setting before rational men this pattern of a commonwealth, this model and perfect image of proper conduct. And the world has never seen a model more perfect than yours, more solidly established or fully executed or more desirable. It far surpasses the many celebrated commonwealths of which so much has been said, those of Sparta, Athens, and Rome. Had they been founded under the same auspices as your commonwealth, and governed by the same institutions, laws, regulations, and customs, certainly they would not now be fallen, leveled to the ground, and extinguished—alas!—beyond all hope of rebirth. On the contrary, they would now be intact, fortunate and prosperous, leading a happy existence—mistresses of the world besides, and dividing a far-flung empire by land and by sea.

Feeling pity for the pitiable fate of these commonwealths, you feared lest others, which now hold supreme power, should undergo the same fate; so you drew the portrait of a perfect commonwealth, one which devoted its energies less to setting up laws than to form-

ing the very best men to administer them. And in this they were absolutely right; for without good rulers, even the best laws (if we take
Plato's word for it)[1] would be nothing but dead letters. It is according to the pattern of such rulers as these—models of probity, specimens of good conduct, images of justice—that the whole existence
and proper character of any commonwealth should be imagined.
What is needed is prudence in the rulers, courage in the military,
temperance in the private citizenry, and justice in all.[2]

Since the commonwealth you praise so lavishly is clearly formed
on these principles, no wonder if it seems not only a challenge to
many nations but an object of reverence to all peoples and an achievement to be celebrated among future generations. Its great strength
lies in the fact that all squabbles over private property are removed,
and no one has anything of his own. Instead, everyone has everything in common for the sake of the common good, and thus every
action and each decision, whether public or private, trifling or important, is not directed by the greed of the many or the lusts of the
few, but aims solely at upholding one uniform rule of justice, equality, and community solidarity. Where the common good is fully
respected, there is bound to be a clean sweep of everything that
might serve as torch, kindling, or fuel for the fires of ambition, luxury, injury, and injustice. These are vices into which men are sometimes pushed against their will, and to their own immense and
incomparable loss, by private property or lust for gain or that most
miserable of passions, ambition. From these sources rise mental
quarrels, martial clashes, and wars worse than civil,[3] which not
only overthrow the flourishing state of supremely happy republics
but cause their previous glories, their past triumphs, rich prizes,
and proud spoils to be utterly obliterated.

If my thoughts on this point should be less than absolutely convincing, only consider the swarm of perfectly reliable witnesses I can
call to my support—I mean the many great cities destroyed in times
past, the states crushed, the republics beaten down, the towns burnt
up. Today not only are there scarcely any remains or vestiges of those
great calamities—not even the names of the places are reliably preserved by any history, however far back it reaches.

Such terrible downfalls, devastations, disasters, and other calamities of war our commonwealths (if we have any) could easily escape,

---

1. E.g., *Laws* 6.751B–C.
2. Prudence (or wisdom), courage, temperance, and justice are the four Cardinal Virtues
   of Greek and Roman ethics. Busleyden's remark summarizes the main argument of
   Book 4 of the *Republic* (especially 427D–434C).
3. "*Bella plus quam civilia,*" as in Busleyden's Latin, is the famous opening phrase of the
   Pharsalia (more properly, *De bello civili*), the unfinished epic by the Roman poet Lucan
   (39–65 C.E.) on the civil war between Caesar and Pompey (which culminated in Caesar's victory at the battle of Pharsalia, in 48 B.C.E.).

if they would only adapt themselves exactly to the Utopian pattern and not swerve from it, as people say, by a hair's breadth. If they act so, the result will fully convince them how much they have profited by the service you have done them; especially since in this way they will have learned to keep their republic healthy, unharmed, and victorious. Their debt to you, their most ready and willing savior, will be no less than that owed to a man who has saved not just one citizen of a country, but the entire country itself.

Farewell for now. May you continue to prosper, ever contriving, carrying out, and completing new plans which will bring long life to the commonwealth, and to yourself immortality. Farewell, most learned and humane More, supreme ornament of your Britain and of this world of ours.

From my house at Mechlin, 1516.

Guillaume Budé to Thomas Lupset[†]

[In 1517, Thomas Lupset, a precocious young humanistic scholar born in London about 1498, went to Paris to continue his studies. While there, he also oversaw the printing of several humanist works, including two of Thomas Linacre's translations of Galen from Greek into Latin, and the second edition of *Utopia*. Lupset had met Guillaume Budé, the preeminent French humanist of the time, and gave him a copy of More's book (in February, Erasmus had urged him to buy one), evidently hoping that he would write a commendatory letter for the new edition. Budé complied with manifest enthusiasm, writing what was by far the longest letter among the commendations in the early editions. Like Busleyden, Budé was a man of considerable personal property who was especially enthusiastic about Utopian communism: with the eminently respectable precedents of Plato and the communist practice of the early Christians (see pp. 101, 105), and with no actual communist states in existence or at all likely to exist in the foreseeable future, it was easy to be enthusiastic about communism in theory. Erasmus's *Adages*, for example, opens with an essay ardently endorsing the classical maxim "*Amicorum communia omnia*" ("Among friends all things are in common"): "it is extraordinary how Christians dislike this common ownership of Plato's, how in fact they cast stones at it, although nothing was ever said by a pagan philosopher which comes closer to the mind of Christ" (*CWE* 31:30). Budé's letter is a valuable document for understanding *Utopia* and its early reception; for an appreciation, see Dominic Baker-Smith, *More's "Utopia"* (Toronto: University of Toronto Press, 2000; orig. publ. 1991), pp. 229–30. (For Edward Surtz on the letter, see pp.

[†] The translation is that of J. H. Lupton in his edition of *Utopia* (Oxford: Clarendon Press, 1895), pp. lxxx–xcii, but with minor modifications of spelling and punctuation. All footnotes are by the editors.

208–09 below.) But even admirers of Budé's scholarship, such as Erasmus, have found his writing sometimes obscure, overweighed with erudition, and florid in its rhetoric.]

I owe you many thanks, my learned young friend Lupset, for having sent me Thomas More's *Utopia*, and so drawn my attention to what is very pleasant, and likely to be very profitable, reading.

It is not long ago since you prevailed upon me (your entreaties seconding my own strong inclination) to read the six books of Galen *On the Preservation of the Health*, to which that master of the Greek and Latin tongues Dr. Thomas Linacre has lately rendered the service—or rather, paid the compliment—of translating them from the extant originals into Latin.[1] So well has the task been performed, that if all that author's works (which I consider worth all other medical lore put together) be in time translated, the want of a knowledge of Greek is not likely to be seriously felt by our schools of medicine.

I have hastily skimmed over that work, as it stands in Linacre's papers (for the courteous loan of which, for so long a time, I am very greatly indebted to you), with the result that I deem myself much benefited by the perusal. But I promise myself still greater profit when the book itself, on the publication of which at the presses of this city you are now busily engaged, shall have appeared in print.

While I thought myself already under a sufficient obligation to you on this account, here you have presented to me More's *Utopia*, as an appendix or supplement to your former kindness. He is a man of the keenest discernment, of a pleasant disposition, well versed in knowledge of the world. I have had the book by me in the country, where my time was taken up with running about and giving directions to workpeople (for you know something, and have heard more, of my having been occupied for more than a twelvemonth on business connected with my country house); and was so impressed by reading it, as I learnt and studied the manners and customs of the Utopians, that I well-nigh forgot, nay, even abandoned, the management of my family affairs. For I perceived that all the theory and practice of domestic economy, all care whatever for increasing one's income, was mere waste of time.

And yet, as all see and are aware, the whole race of mankind is goaded on by this very thing, as if some gadfly were bred within them

---

1. Galen (129–199 C.E.) was the foremost medical authority of ancient Greece, and his unparalleled influence on medicine continued into the Renaissance and beyond. His translator Linacre (ca. 1460–1524) was educated at Oxford and subsequently in Italy, where he perfected his knowledge of Latin and Greek and earned his medical degree. A friend of Erasmus's, and one of More's instructors in Greek, Linacre was appointed physician to Henry VIII in 1509, and in 1518 he became the founder and first president of the Royal College of Physicians.

to sting them. The result is that we must needs confess the object of nearly all legal and civil qualification and training to be this: that with jealous and watchful cunning, as each one has a neighbor with whom he is connected by ties of citizenship, or even, at times, of relationship, he should be ever conveying or abstracting something from him; should pare away, repudiate, squeeze, chouse,[2] chisel, cozen, extort, pillage, purloin, thieve, filch, rob, and—partly with the connivance, partly with the sanction of, the laws—be ever plundering and appropriating.

This goes on all the more in countries where the civil and canon law, as they are called, have greater authority in the two courts.[3] For it is evident that their customs and institutions are pervaded by the principle that those are to be deemed the high priests of law and equity who are skilled in *caveats*—or *capiats*,[4] rather; men who hawk at their unwary fellow citizens; artists in formulas, that is, in gudgeon traps; adepts in concocted law; getters-up of cases; jurisconsults of a controverted, perverted, inverted *ius*.[5] These are the only fit persons to give opinions as to what is fair and good; nay, what is far more, to settle with plenary power what each one is to be allowed to have, and what not to have, and the extent and limit of his tenure. How deluded must public opinion be to have determined matters thus!

The truth is that most of us, blind with the thick rheum of ignorance in our eyes, suppose that each one's cause, as a rule, is *just*, in proportion to its accordance with the requirements of the *law*, or to the way in which he has based his claim on the law. Whereas, were we agreed to demand our rights in accordance with the rule of *truth*, and what the simple Gospel prescribes, the dullest would understand, and the most senseless admit, if we put it to them, that, in the decrees of the canonists, the divine law differs as much from the human, and, in our civil laws and royal enactments, true equity differs as much from law, as the principles laid down by Christ, the founder of human society, and the usages of his disciples, differ from the decrees and enactments of those who think the *summum bonum* and perfection of happiness to lie in the moneybags of a Croesus or a Midas.[6] So that, if you chose to define Justice nowadays in the way that early writers[7] liked to do, as the power who assigns to each his due, you would either find her non-existent in public, or, if I may

2. Swindle.
3. I.e., countries where the strict letter of the law, rather than natural equity or evangelical principle, is the most important factor in decisions of both the secular (civil-law) and ecclesiastical (canon-law) courts.
4. Approximating the legal wordplay of Budé's Latin: "caveats" are warnings (of a person's interest in a title or litigation), "capiats" are *takings* (a "writ of capias" commands the arrest of a person).
5. Law, justice (Latin).
6. Proverbially rich men of antiquity. "*Summum bonum*": supreme good.
7. E.g., Cicero, *On the Supreme Good and Evil* 5.23.65; Justinian, *Digests* 1.1.10.

use such a comparison, you would have to admit that she was a kind of kitchen stewardess: and this, alike whether you regard the character of our present rulers, or the disposition of fellow citizens and fellow countrymen one towards another.

Perhaps indeed it may be argued that the law I speak of has been derived from that inherent, world-old justice called natural law; which teaches that the stronger a man is, the more he should possess;[8] and the more he possesses, the more eminent among his countrymen he ought to be: with the result that now we see it an accepted principle in the law of nations that persons who are unable to help their fellows by any art or practice worth mentioning, if only they are adepts in those complicated knots and stringent bonds by which men's properties are tied up (things accounted a mixture of Gordian knots and charlatanry, with nothing very wonderful about them, by the ignorant multitude and by scholars living, for the sake of recreation or of investigating the truth, at a distance from the courts)—that these persons, I say, should have an income equal to that of a thousand of their countrymen, nay, even of a whole state, and sometimes more than that; and that they should then be greeted with the honorable titles of wealthy men, thrifty men, makers of splendid fortunes. Such in truth is the age in which we live, such our manners and customs, such our national character. These have pronounced it lawful for a man's credit and influence to be high in proportion to the way in which he has been the architect of his own fortunes and of those of his heirs: an influence, in fact, which goes on increasing according as their descendants, in turn, to the remotest generation, vie in heaping up with fine additions the property gained by their ancestors— which amounts to saying, according as they have ousted more and more extensively their connections, kindred, and even their blood relations.

But the founder and regulator of all property, Jesus Christ, left among his followers a Pythagorean communion and love, and ratified it by a plain example, when Ananias was condemned to death for breaking this law of communion.[9] By laying down this

---

8. The concept of an unchanging, universally valid body of natural law, which human beings apprehend by reason and instinct, was a foundation of legal and political theory from classical antiquity until the 19th century. Since human equality was a fundamental precept of natural law, the doctrine that might makes right could be derived from it only by a thoroughly perverse interpretation. The "law of nations" (below) denotes a body of legal principles common to the different peoples—universally accepted, but not necessarily consistent with natural law. For an exposition of the development and relations of these concepts, see R. W. Carlyle and A. J. Carlyle, *A History of Mediaeval Political Theory in the West*, 6 vols., 3rd ed. (London: Blackwood, 1930), esp. 1:33–44; see also p. 204 below.

9. Ananias sold a property and gave the Apostles only part of the price, instead of the whole gain, as he should have done. See Acts 5.1–11, on p. 106 above. "Pythagorean communion": The Greek philosopher and mathematician Pythagoras (6th century B.C.E.) was believed to have instituted a communal life among his followers.

principle, Christ seems to me to have abolished, at any rate among his followers, all the voluminous quibbles of the civil law, and still more of the later canon law; which latter[1] we see at the present day holding the highest position in jurisprudence, and controlling our destiny.

As for the island of Utopia, which I hear is also called Udepotia,[2] it is said (if we are to believe the story), by what must be owned a singular good fortune, to have adopted Christian usages both in public and in private, to have imbibed the wisdom thereto belonging, and to have kept it undefiled to this very day. The reason is, that it holds with firm grip to three divine institutions: namely, the absolute equality, or, if you prefer to call it so, the civil communication,[3] of all things good and bad among fellow citizens; a settled and unwavering love of peace and quietness; and a contempt for gold and silver. Three things these, which overturn, one may say, all fraud, all imposture, cheating, roguery, and unprincipled deception. Would that the gods, by their own power,[4] would cause these three principles of Utopian law to be fixed in the minds of all men by the rivets of a strong and settled conviction. We should soon see pride, covetousness, insane competition, and almost all other deadly weapons of our adversary the Devil fall powerless; we should see the interminable array of law books, the work of so many excellent and solid understandings, that occupy men till the very day of their death, consigned to bookworms, as mere hollow and empty things, or else given up to make wrapping paper for shops.

Good heavens! What holiness of the Utopians has had the power of earning such a blessing from above that greed and covetousness have for so many ages failed to enter, either by force or stealth, into that island alone? that they have failed to drive out from it, by wanton effrontery, justice and honor?

Would that great Heaven in its goodness had dealt so kindly with the countries which keep, and would not part with, the appellation they bear, derived from His most holy name![5] Of a truth, greed, which perverts and sinks down so many minds, otherwise noble and elevated, would be gone from hence once for all, and the Golden Age of Saturn[6] would return. In Utopia, one might verily suppose that

---

1. I.e., the law of "voluminous quibbles" rather than that of simple natural or Christian justice. (Canon law is "later" than civil law because the latter is based on Roman law that preceded the Christian era.)
2. *Utopia* = "Noplace"; *Udepotia* = "Never place."
3. "Civic sharing" might be a better translation.
4. Emending Lupton's "Providence, on its own behalf," which is based on a reading (*nomine* instead of *numine*) found only in the last of the four early editions.
5. I.e., the appellation "Christian."
6. The Roman god (equated with the Greek Cronus) who ruled in the first and best of the mythological Four Ages of Man (see pp. 103–05 above), which ended when he was replaced by his son Jupiter (Zeus).

there is a risk of Aratus and the early poets having been mistaken in their opinion, when they made Justice depart from earth, and placed her in the Zodiac.[7] For, if we are to believe Hythloday, she must needs have stayed behind in that island and not yet made her way to heaven.

But in truth I have ascertained by full inquiry that Utopia lies outside the bounds of the known world. It is in fact one of the Fortunate Isles, perhaps very close to the Elysian Fields;[8] for More himself testifies that Hythloday has not yet stated its position definitely. It is itself divided into a number of cities, but all uniting or confederating into one state, named Hagnopolis[9]—a state contented with its own customs, its own goods, blest with innocence, leading a kind of heavenly life, on a lower level indeed than heaven, but above the defilements of this world we know, which amid the endless pursuits of mankind, as empty and vain as they are keen and eager, is being hurried in a swollen and eddying tide to the cataract.

It is to Thomas More, then, that we owe our knowledge of this island. It is he who, in our generation, has made public this model of a happy life and rule for leading it; the discovery, as he tells us, of Hythloday: for he ascribes all to him. For while Hythloday has built the Utopians their state and established for them their rites and customs; while, in so doing, he has borrowed from them and brought home for us the representation of a happy life; it is beyond question More who has set off by his literary style the subject of that island and its customs. He it is who has perfected, as by rule and square, the City of the Hagnopolitans itself, adding all those touches by which grace and beauty and weight accrue to the noble work; even though in executing that work he has claimed for himself only a common mason's share. We see that it has been a matter of conscientious scruple with him not to assume too important a part in the work, lest Hythloday should have just cause for complaint on the ground of More having plucked the first flowers of that fame which would have been left for him, if he had himself ever decided to give an account of his adventures to the world. *He was afraid, of course, that Hythloday, who was residing of his own choice in the island of Udepotia, might someday come in person upon the scene and be vexed and aggrieved at this unkindness on his part, in leaving him the glory of this discovery*

---

7. The Greek poet Aratus (fl. 3rd century C.E.) recounts that the goddess of justice, Astraea (identified with the constellation Virgo), departed earth in the face of mounting human wickedness.
8. In classical culture, the Fortunate Isles or Islands of the Blest—situated, like Utopia, in the remotest west—were the eternal paradise of heroes. They were sometimes loosely identified with the Elysian Fields, that part of Hades where the virtuous pass eternity in the favorite pursuits of their mortal lives.
9. From Greek for "Holy City" or "City of the Saints."

with the best flowers plucked off. To be of this persuasion is the part of good men and wise.[1]

Now while More is one who of himself carries weight, and has great authority to rest upon, I am led to place unreserved confidence in him by the testimony of Peter Giles of Antwerp. Though I have never made his acquaintance in person—apart from recommendations of his learning and character that have reached me—I love him on account of his being the intimate friend of the illustrious Erasmus, who has deserved so well of letters of every kind, whether sacred or profane; with whom personally I have long corresponded and formed ties of friendship.

Farewell, my dear Lupset. Greet for me, at the first opportunity, either by word of mouth or by letter, Linacre, that pillar of the British name in all that concerns good learning; one who is now, as I hope, not more yours than ours. He is one of the few whose good opinion I should be very glad, if possible, to gain. When he was himself known to be staying here, he gained in the highest degree the good opinion of me and of Jean Du Ruel, my friend and the sharer in my studies.[2] And his singular learning and careful industry I should be the first to look up to and strive to copy.

Greet More also once and again for me, either by message, as I said before, or by word of mouth. As I think and often repeat, Minerva[3] has long entered his name on her selectest album; and I love and revere him in the highest degree for what he has written about this isle of the New World, Utopia.

In his history, our age and those which succeed it will have a nursery, so to speak, of polite and useful institutions, from which men may borrow customs, and introduce and adapt them each to his own state. Farewell.

Paris, July 31 [1517]

Erasmus of Rotterdam to Johann Froben

[Johann Froben (ca. 1460–1527) was among the most celebrated printers of his time, known especially for the series of distinguished editions of works of humanistic scholarship that issued from his shop, in Basel. In 1517, his good friend Erasmus—godfather to one of his sons—persuaded Froben to produce a new edition of *Utopia*, for which More evidently supplied a corrected copy of the 1516 edition. The Froben edition—the last one in which the author could have had a hand—appeared in March 1518 and was reprinted with small changes in No-

---

1. The italicized passage is in Greek.
2. Du Ruel, like Linacre, was a distinguished physician and translator.
3. The Roman goddess of wisdom and the arts, identified with the Greek Athena.

vember. It is the most authoritative of the early editions and by far the handsomest. Erasmus provided this commendatory letter for it.]

While heretofore I have always thought extremely well of all of my friend More's writings, yet I rather mistrusted my own judgment because of the very close friendship between us. But when I see all the learned unanimously subscribe to my opinion, and esteem even more highly than I the divine genius of this man, not because they love him better but because they see more deeply into his merits, I am wholly confirmed in my opinion and no longer shrink from saying openly what I feel. How admirably would his fortunate disposition have stood forth if his genius had been nurtured in Italy![1] if he had devoted his whole energy to the service of the Muses, maturing gradually, as it were, toward his own proper harvest! As a youth, he toyed with epigrams,[2] many written when he was only a boy. He has never left Britain except a couple of times to serve his prince as an ambassador to Flanders.[3] Apart from the cares of a married man and the responsibilities of his household, apart from his official post and floods of legal cases, he is distracted by so many and such important matters of state business that you would marvel he finds any free time at all for books.

For this reason I am sending you his *Exercises*[4] and his *Utopia*, so that, if you think proper, their appearance under your imprint may commend them to the world and to posterity. For the authority of your firm is such that a book is sure of pleasing the learned as soon as it is known to issue from the house of Froben. Farewell to you, to your excellent father-in-law, your dear wife, and your delightful children. Make sure that Erasmus, the little son we share in common, and who was born among books, is educated in the best of them.

Louvain, August 25, 1517

1. I.e., in the homeland of humanist learning.
2. I.e., short Latin poems.
3. Erasmus exaggerates: in 1508, More had visited the universities of Louvain and Paris. (Since Erasmus sometimes wrote as many as forty letters in a day, it's no wonder he occasionally misspoke.) The embassies to Flanders are the one during which More began *Utopia* (1515) and another one two years later.
4. The *Exercises* (*Progymnasmata*) is a series of rival translations by More and the grammarian William Lyly, who both made Latin translations of the same Greek epigrams. These are bound with *Utopia* in the Froben edition, along with additional Latin epigrams by More and a collection of poems by Erasmus.

Thomas More to Peter Giles

[This second letter of More to Giles appeared only in the second edition of *Utopia* (Paris, 1517), where it immediately follows Book II. The
letter praises, with characteristic Morean irony, the supposedly per-
spicacious critique of *Utopia* by a "very sharp fellow," whose identity is
unknown—if indeed More didn't simply invent him.]

Thomas More to His Friend Peter Giles, Warmest Greetings

My dear Peter, I was absolutely delighted with the judgment of
that very sharp fellow you recall, who posed this dilemma about
my *Utopia*: if the story is put forward as fact, he said, then I see a
number of absurdities in it; but if it's fiction, then it seems to me
that in various respects More's usual good judgment is at fault. I
suspect this fellow of being learned, and I see that he's a friend;
but whoever he is, I'm much obliged to him. By this frank opinion
of his, he has pleased me more than anyone else since the book was
published.

For in the first place, either out of fondness for me or for the
work itself, he seems to have borne up under the burden of reading
the book all the way through—and that not perfunctorily or hastily,
the way priests read the divine office—those, at least, who read it at
all.[1] No, he read slowly and attentively, noting all the particular
points. Then, having singled out certain matters for criticism, and
not very many, as a matter of fact, he gives careful and considered
approval to the rest. And finally, in the very expressions he uses to
criticize me, he implies higher praises than some of those who have
put all their energies into compliment. It's easy to see what a high
opinion he has of me, when he expresses disappointment over reading something imperfect or inexact—whereas I don't expect, in
treating so many different matters, to be able to say more than a
few things which aren't totally ridiculous.

Still, I'd like to be just as frank with him as he was with me; and,
in fact, I don't see why he should think himself so acute (so "sharp-
sighted," as the Greeks would say) just because he's discovered some
absurdities in the institutions of Utopia, or caught me putting forth
some half-baked ideas about the constitution of a republic. Aren't
there any absurdities elsewhere in the world? And did any one of
the philosophers who've offered a pattern of a society, a ruler, or even
a private household set down everything so well that nothing ought
to be changed? Actually, if it weren't for the great respect I retain

---

1. Priests read the "divine office"—the daily round of prescribed prayers to be recited at
   set hours—with varying degrees of enthusiasm, according to More.

for certain highly distinguished names, I could easily produce from each of them a number of notions which I can hardly doubt would be universally condemned as absurd.

But when he wonders whether *Utopia* is fact or fiction, then I find *his* judgment, in turn, sorely at fault. I do not deny that if I'd decided to write about a commonwealth, and a tale of this sort had occurred to me, I might have spread a little fiction, like so much honey, over the truth, to make it more acceptable. But I would certainly have tempered the fiction a little, so that, while it deceived the common folk, I gave hints to the more learned which would enable them to see what I was about. So, if I'd done nothing but give special names to the governor, the river, the city, and the island, which hinted to the learned that the island was nowhere, the city a phantom, the river waterless, and that the governor had no people,[2] that would not have been hard to do, and would have been far more clever than what I actually did. Unless I had a historian's devotion to fact, I am not so stupid as to have used those barbarous and senseless names of Utopia, Anyder, Amaurot, and Ademus.

Still, my dear Giles, I see some people are so suspicious that what we simple-minded and credulous fellows have written down of Hythloday's account can hardly find any credence at all with these circumspect and sagacious persons. I'm afraid my personal reputation, as well as my authority as a historian, may be threatened by their skepticism; so it's a good thing that I can defend myself by saying, as Terence's Mysis says about Glycerium's boy, to confirm his legitimacy, "Praise be to God there were some free women present at his birth."[3] And so it was a good thing for me that Raphael told his story not just to you and me, but to a great many perfectly respectable and serious-minded men. Whether he told them more things, and more important things, I don't know; but I'm sure he told them no fewer and no less important things than he told us.

Well, if these doubters won't believe such witnesses, let them consult Hythloday himself, for he is still alive. I heard only recently from some travelers coming out of Portugal that on the first of last March he was as healthy and vigorous a man as he ever was. Let them get the truth from him—dig it out of him with questions, if they want. I only want them to understand that I'm responsible for my own work, and my own work alone, not for anyone else's credibility.

Farewell, my dearest Peter, to you, your charming wife, and your clever little girl—to all, my wife sends her very best wishes.

2. This is of course precisely what the names do mean.
3. *The Lady of Andros*, lines 770–71.

From Erasmus to Ulrich von Hutten[†]

[Three years after the first publication of *Utopia*, the German human-ist Ulrich von Hutten, author, most famously, of some of the *Letters of Obscure Men* (which satirized degenerate scholasticism and clerical cor-ruption), asked Erasmus about Thomas More, whom he admired but had never met. The pen portrait that Erasmus wrote in response to this query is remarkably detailed, precise, and candid about a number of matters, including More's appearance and personal habits; and it is striking in how many respects More as described by Erasmus resem-bles the Utopians as described by More.]

Erasmus of Rotterdam to the Honourable Ulrich von Hutten, Knight, Greeting

The affection—one might almost say, the passion—that you feel for that gifted man Thomas More, fired as of course you are by reading his books, which you rightly call as brilliant as they are scholarly—all this, believe me my dear Hutten, you share with many of us, and between you and More it works both ways: he in his turn is so delighted with the originality of your own work that I am almost jealous of you.[1] Surely this is an example of that wisdom which Plato calls the most desirable of all things, which rouses far more passion-ate desire in mortal hearts than the most splendid physical beauty. The eyes of the body cannot perceive it, but the mind has its own eyes, so that here too we find the truth of the old Greek saying that the eye is the gateway to the heart. They are the means through which the most cordial affection sometimes unites men who have never exchanged a word or set bodily eyes on one another. It is a com-mon experience that for some obscure reason one man is captivated by this form of beauty and another by something different; and in the same way between one man's spirit and another's there seems to be a kind of unspoken kinship, which makes us take great delight in cer-tain special people, and less in others.

Be that as it may, you ask me to draw a picture of More for you at full length, and I wish I were as skilful as you are eager. For me too it would be nothing but a pleasure to spend a little time thinking about the friend I love best. But there are difficulties: it is not every-one can appreciate all More's gifts, and I doubt if he would endure to be depicted by any and every artist. It is, I suspect, no easier to

---

[†] Reprinted with permission, from *The Correspondence of Erasmus*, Vol. 7, translated by R. A. B. Mynors, annotated by Peter G. Bietenholz, in the *Collected Works of Erasmus* (Toronto/Buffalo/London: University of Toronto Press, 1987), pp. 16–24. All footnotes are by the editor of the present volume, often drawing on notes in the Toronto edition.

1. After Hutten became, in the early 1520s, a vigorous—even violent—supporter of the Reformation, Erasmus retracted the claim of Hutten's compatibility with More.

produce a portrait of More than one of Alexander the Great or Achilles, nor did they deserve their immortality any more than he does. Such a sitter demands the skill of an Apelles, and I fear there is less of Apelles in me than of Fulvius or Rutuba.[2] I will try, however, to do you not so much a picture as an outline sketch of the whole man, based on long-standing and intimate acquaintance, as far as my observation or memory will serve. Should any mission overseas eventually bring you together, you will realize what an incompetent artist you have selected for this task, and I am afraid that you will think me either envious or purblind—too blind to detect, or too envious to be willing to record more than a few of all his good qualities.

To begin with one aspect of More which is quite unknown to you, in stature and habit of body he is not tall, without being noticeably short, but the general harmony of his proportions is such that nothing seems amiss. He has a fair skin; his complexion tends to be warm rather than pale, though with no tendency to a high colour, except for a very delicate flush which suffuses it all. His hair blackish-brown, or brownish-black if you prefer; beard[3] somewhat thin; eyes rather greyish-blue, with a kind of fleck in them, the sort that usually indicates a gifted intelligence, and among the English is thought attractive, while our own people prefer dark eyes. No kind of eye, they say, is so immune from defects. His expression shows the sort of man he is, always friendly and cheerful, with something of the air of one who smiles easily, and (to speak frankly) disposed to be merry rather than serious or solemn, but without a hint of the fool or the buffoon. His right shoulder looks a little higher than his left, especially when walking, not by nature but from force of habit, like so many human tricks. Otherwise there is nothing to criticize in his physique. Only his hands are a trifle coarse, at least if one compares them with his other bodily features. As for the care of his personal appearance, he has taken absolutely no heed of it ever since boyhood, to the extent of devoting very little care even to those niceties allotted to the gentlemen by Ovid.[4] How good-looking he was as a young man, one can guess even now by what remains—though I knew him myself when he was not more than three-and-twenty, for even now he is scarcely past his fortieth year.

He enjoys good, but not rude, health, adequate at any rate to support all the duties of a good citizen, and is subject to no complaints

2. Roman gladiators mentioned in Horace's *Satires* 2.7.97. By saying that he is more like Fulvius and Rutuba than like Apelles—the most celebrated painter of classical antiquity—Erasmus reinforces his protest of inadequacy for the job of creating a pen portrait of More.
3. More did not have a beard, but Hans Holbein the Younger's famous portrait of him (in the Frick Collection, New York) indicates that he did not shave every day, either.
4. In *The Art of Love* (1.505–24), Ovid cautions would-be seducers not to be dandies but does advise them to keep clean and neat.

or very few; there is every hope that he will enjoy long life, for his father is still alive at a great age,[5] but wonderfully active and vigorous for his years. I have never seen a man less particular about his food. Until he reached manhood he was content to drink nothing but water, a habit inherited from his father. Only, for fear of causing any embarrassment in this regard, he used to drink his beer out of a pewter tankard, so that the guests did not know—small beer next door to water, and often just water. As for wine, the habit in those parts being to invite your neighbour to drink in his turn from the same cup, he sometimes barely sipped it, so as not to seem entirely to dislike it, and at the same time to learn to follow common usage. Beef, salt fish, and coarse bread with much yeast in it he preferred to the dishes of which most people are fond, though in other ways he was by no means averse from all the things that bring harmless pleasure, be it only to the body. Dairy produce and all the fruit which grows on trees have always had a great attraction for him, and he is particularly devoted to eggs. His voice is not loud, yet not particularly soft, but of a sort to strike clearly on the ear; no music in it, no subtlety, a straightforward speaking voice, for he does not seem framed by nature to be a singer, though he is fond of music of all kinds. His language is remarkably clear and precise, without a trace of hurry or hesitation.

Simple clothes please him best, and he never wears silk or scarlet or a gold chain, except when it is not open to him to lay it aside. He sets surprisingly little store by the ceremonies which ordinary men regard as a touchstone of good breeding; these he neither demands from other people nor tenders meticulously himself either in public assemblies or in private parties, although he is familiar with them should he wish to use them. But he thinks it effeminate and unworthy of a man to waste a good part of his time in such frivolities.

Court life and the friendship of princes were formerly not to his taste, for he has always had a special hatred of absolute rule[6] and a corresponding love for equality. You will hardly find any court, however modest, that is not full of turmoil and self-seeking, of pretence and luxury, and is really free from any taint of despotic power. Even the court of Henry VIII he could not be induced to enter except by great efforts,[7] although it would be difficult to wish for anything more

5. John More was about sixty-eight when Erasmus wrote. A successful lawyer, he had recently been made a judge. "Rude": robust, vigorous.
6. The Latin word that Erasmus uses here—*tyrannis*—is usually translated "tyranny," though "absolute rule" (i.e., without a necessarily pejorative connotation) is also an acceptable rendering. More's writings, especially his Latin epigrams and his *History of King Richard the Third*, abundantly confirm his hostility to *tyrannis* in both senses.
7. In fact, appointment to the king's service was a natural culmination of More's legal career, and, though *Utopia* shows that he understood quite clearly the negatives of such service, it does not seem that it was nearly as difficult to induce him to join Henry's court as Erasmus thought. Erasmus himself (like Hythloday) spurned all such offers.

cultured and more unassuming than the present king.[8] By nature he has a great love of liberty and leisure; but dearly as he loves to enjoy leisure when he can, no one displays more energy or more endurance at the call of duty.

Friendship he seems born and designed for; no one is more open-hearted in making friends or more tenacious in keeping them, nor has he any fear of that plethora of friendships against which Hesiod warns us.[9] The road to a secure place in his affections is open to anyone. In the choice of friends he is never difficult to please, in keeping up with them the most compliant of men, and in retaining them the most unfailing. If by any chance he has picked on someone whose faults he cannot mend, he waits for an opportunity to be quit of him, loosening the knot of friendship and not breaking it off. When he finds open-hearted people naturally suited to him, he enjoys their company and conversation so much that one would think he reckoned such things the chief pleasure in life. For ball games, games of chance, and cards he hates, and all the other pastimes with which the common run of grandees normally beguile their tedious hours. Besides which, though somewhat negligent in his own affairs, no one could take more trouble in furthering the business of his friends. In a word, whoever desires a perfect example of true friendship, will seek it nowhere to better purpose than in More.

In society he shows such rare courtesy and sweetness of disposition that there is no man so melancholy by nature that More does not enliven him, no disaster so great that he does not dissipate its unpleasantness. From boyhood he has taken such pleasure in jesting that he might seem born for it, but in this he never goes as far as buffoonery, and he has never liked bitterness. In his youth he both wrote brief comedies and acted in them.[1] Any remark with more wit in it than ordinary always gave him pleasure, even if directed against himself; such is his delight in witty sayings that betray a lively mind. Hence his trying his hand as a young man at epigrams, and his special devotion to Lucian; in fact it was he

---

8. This view of Henry—the standard one among humanists for the first several years after he came to the throne (1509)—had in fact already begun to be undermined by the time of this 1519 letter (see p. 9, n. 1 above).
9. The great early Greek poet Hesiod (fl. 700 B.C.E.) issues this warning in his *Works and Days*, line 715.
1. While there are no other contemporary references to More as a playwright, his earliest surviving letter (ca. November 1501) refers to his additions to a comedy about Solomon, and the *Life* by his son-in-law William Roper says that while More was a page at Cardinal Morton's, where plays were presented on festive occasions, he would "suddenly sometimes step in among the players, and never studying for the matter, make a part of his own there presently among them, which made the lookers-on more sport than all the players beside." See Richard S. Sylvester and Davis P. Harding, eds., *Two Early Tudor Lives* (New Haven and London: Yale University Press, 1962), p. 198.

(yes, he can make the camel dance) who persuaded me to write my *Moriae encomium*.[2]

In fact there is nothing in human life to which he cannot look for entertainment, even in most serious moments. If he has to do with educated and intelligent people, he enjoys their gifts; if they are ignorant and stupid, he is amused by their absurdity. He has no objection to professional buffoons, such is the skill with which he adapts himself to the mood of anyone. With women as a rule, and even with his wife, he confines himself to humour and pleasantry. You would think him Democritus[3] reborn, or rather that Pythagorean philosopher who strolled unthinking through the market-place watching the crowds of people buying and selling. Nobody is less swayed by public opinion, and yet nobody is closer to the feelings of ordinary men.

He takes a particular pleasure in contemplating the shapes, character, and behaviour of different living creatures. Thus there is hardly any kind of bird of which he does not keep one in his household, and the same with any animal that as a rule is rarely seen, such as monkey, fox, ferret, weasel, and the like. Besides these, if he sees anything outlandish or otherwise remarkable, he buys it greedily, and has his house stocked with such things from all sources, so that everywhere you may see something to attract the eyes of the visitor; and when he sees other people pleased, his own pleasure begins anew. In his younger days he was not averse from affairs[4] with young women, but always without dishonour, enjoying such things when they came his way without going out to seek them, and attracted by the mingling of minds rather than bodies.

A liberal education he had imbibed from his very earliest years. As a young man he devoted himself to the study of Greek literature and philosophy, with so little support from his father, a man in other respects of good sense and high character, that his efforts were deprived of all outside help and he was treated almost as if disinherited because he was thought to be deserting his father's profession; for his father is a specialist in English law. The law as a profession has little in common with literature truly so called; but in England those who have made themselves authorities in that subject are in the first rank for eminence and distinction. Nor is it easy in that country to find any other career more likely to lead to wealth and reputation;

---

2. *The Praise of Folly*, which Erasmus wrote in More's house in 1509 (though there seems to be an exaggeration in the claim that More prompted him to write it). A camel dancing is a proverbial expression for something done against one's natural bent. (Thus in *Folly*, Erasmus says that if you take a sage to a ball, you'll see how a camel dances.) On Lucian, see, pp. 106–07 above.
3. The pre-Socratic Greek thinker Democritus was sometimes called "the laughing philosopher" because of the mirth aroused in him by the human spectacle.
4. Given Erasmus's insistence on the honorable nature of More's youthful romances, "affairs" is probably a misleading translation of Latin *amores* ("loves").

and in fact most of the nobility of the island owes its rank to studies of this kind. In the law, they say, no one can perfect himself without many years of hard work. So it was not surprising that, when he was a young man, More's nature should swerve away from the law, being made for better things; but after a taste of the subjects studied at the university, he betook himself to it with such good effect that there was no one whose advice was more freely sought by litigants, nor was a larger income made by any of those who gave their whole time to the law. Such was the force and quickness of his intelligence.

Besides this he devoted himself actively to reading the works of the orthodox Fathers. On St Augustine's *De civitate Dei* he gave public lectures before large audiences while still quite a young man;[5] priests and old men were not ashamed to seek instruction in holy things from a young man and a layman, or sorry they had done so. And all the time he applied his whole mind to the pursuit of piety, with vigils and fasts and prayer and similar exercises preparing himself for the priesthood. In this indeed he showed not a little more sense than those who plunge headlong into so exacting a vocation without first making trial of themselves. Nor did anything stand in the way of his devoting himself to this kind of life, except that he could not shake off the desire to get married. And so he chose to be a god-fearing husband rather than an immoral priest.

However, he chose for his wife an unmarried girl[6] who was still very young, of good family, and quite inexperienced as yet, having always lived in the country with her parents and her sisters, which gave him the more opportunity to mould her character to match his own. He arranged for her education and made her skilled in music of every kind, and had (it is clear) almost succeeded in making her a person with whom he would gladly have shared his whole life, had not an early death removed her from the scene, after she had borne him several children. Of these there survive three daughters, Margaret, Alice,[7] and Cecily, and one son, John. Nor did he endure to remain a widower for very long, though the advice of his friends urged a different course. A few months after his wife's death, he married a widow,[8] more to have someone to look after his household than for his own pleasure, for she was neither beautiful nor in her first youth, as he used to remark in jest, but a capable and watchful housewife, though they lived on as close and affectionate terms as if she had been a girl of the most winning appearance. Few husbands

---

5. More lectured on Augustine's *City of God* about 1501, in the London church of St. Lawrence Jewry.
6. Joanna (or Joan) Colt, who died in 1511, at age twenty-three, after bearing More's four children.
7. Actually Elizabeth. (Alice was the daughter of More's second wife.)
8. Dame Alice Middleton (1475–1551), whose first husband had died in 1509. More, with four small children, married her within *one* month of Joanna's death.

secure as much obedience from their wives by severity and giving them orders as he did by his kindness and his merry humour. He could make her do anything: did he not cause a woman already past the prime of life, of a far from elastic disposition, and devoted to her household affairs, to learn to play the zither, the lute, the monochord,[9] and the recorder, and in this department to produce a set piece of work every day to please her exacting husband?

He shows the same geniality in the management of his household, in which there are no troubles and no disputes. If anything should go wrong, he puts it right promptly or makes them agree; nor has he ever dismissed anyone as a result of ill feeling on either side. In fact his household seems to enjoy a kind of natural felicity, for no one has ever been a member of it without bettering his fortune later, and no one has ever earned the least shadow on his reputation. Indeed you would hardly find such close relations anywhere between a man and his mother as exists between him and his stepmother;[1] for his father had now remarried for the second time, and he loved them both as if they had been his own mother. The father has lately remarried a third time; and More solemnly swears that he has never seen a better person. Such moreover is his affection for his kinsmen, his children, and his sisters[2] that his relations with them are never oppressive, nor yet does he ever fall short in his family duties.

From any love of filthy lucre he is absolutely free. To provide for his children he has earmarked as much of his resources as he considers sufficient for them; and the rest he spends liberally. In the days when he was still dependent on the income from his clients, he gave everyone helpful and reliable advice, thinking much more of their advantage than of his own; the majority he used to persuade to settle their actions, on the ground that this would save them expense. If that was not successful, he then tried to show them how to carry on their litigation at the least cost to themselves; for some men are so made that they actually enjoy going to law. In the city of London, in which he was born, he has for some years acted as judge[3] in civil cases. This office is by no means onerous, for the court sits only on Thursdays until dinner-time, but it carries much prestige. No one ever determined more cases, and no one showed more absolute integrity. Many people have had the money returned to them which according to precedent must be paid by litigants; for before the action comes into court, the plaintiff must deposit three

9. An ancient single-stringed instrument, with pitch varied by a movable bridge.
1. After the death of his first wife, who bore all his children, Sir John More married three more times; his last wife survived him.
2. More had three sisters and two brothers. Only two sisters and one brother lived to adulthood.
3. In his capacity as an undersheriff of London (see p. 5, n. 2 above). More had resigned this position in 1518 after becoming a royal councillor.

drachmas,[4] and the defendant the same, nor is it permissible to demand any more. The result of this behaviour was that his native city held him in deep affection.

He had made up his mind to be content with this station in life, which gave him quite sufficient standing and at the same time was not exposed to serious risks. More than once he was forced to go on a diplomatic mission; and as he conducted these with great intelligence, his serene Majesty King Henry VIII would not rest until he had dragged the man to his court. I use the word 'dragged' advisedly, for no man was ever more consumed with ambition to enter a court than he was to avoid it.[5] But since that excellent king had it in mind to fill his household with learned, wise, intelligent, and upright men, he summoned a great many others, and especially More; whom he keeps so close to him that he never allows him leave to go. If serious business is afoot, no better counsellor than he; if the king wishes to relax his mind with more cheerful topics, no man's company more gay. Often difficult issues demand an authoritative and able judge; and More can settle these in such a way that both parties are grateful. Yet no one has succeeded in persuading him to take a present from anybody. Happy indeed a commonwealth would be, if the prince would appoint to each post a magistrate like More. And all the time no pride has touched him.

Amidst such masses of business he does not forget his old and ordinary friends, and returns to his beloved literature from time to time. Whatever power his station gives him, whatever his influence can do with so powerful a king, is all devoted to the good of the commonwealth and of his friends. His disposition was always most ready to do good unto all men, and wonderfully prone to show mercy; and he now gives it more play, because he has more power to do good. Some men he helps with money, to some he gives the protection of his authority, others he advances in life by his recommendation. Those whom he cannot help in any other way he aids with good advice. He has never sent anyone away with a long face. You might call More the general resource of everyone who needs help. He thinks some great stroke of luck has come his way if he has been able to relieve the oppressed, to help the perplexed and entangled out of their troubles, or to reconcile the parties to a quarrel. No one more enjoys doing a kindness or less demands gratitude for doing one. And yet, though he is very fortunate on so many counts, and though good fortune is often accompanied by self-conceit, it has never yet been my fortune to see a man more free from that fault than he.

---

4. Writing humanist Latin, Erasmus uses the name of an ancient silver coin. The money in question formed part of judges' remuneration.
5. But see p. 146, n. 7 above.

But to return to tell of his literary pursuits, which have been the chief bond between More and myself in both directions. His earlier years were exercised principally in poetry; after that came a long struggle to acquire a more supple style in prose by practising his pen in every sort of writing. What his style is like now, I need not set down, especially for your benefit, for you have his books always in your hands. He has taken delight especially in declamations,[6] and, in that department, in paradoxical themes, as offering more lively practice to one's ingenuity. As a youth he even worked on a dialogue in which he supported Plato's doctrine of communalism, extending it even to wives.[7] He wrote an answer to Lucian's *Tyrannicida*, on which topic it was his wish to have me as an opponent, to test more accurately what progress he had made in this sort of composition.[8] *Utopia* he published with the purpose of showing the reasons for the shortcomings of a commonwealth; but he represented the English commonwealth in particular, because he had studied it and knew it best. The second book he had written earlier, when at leisure; at a later opportunity he added the first in the heat of the moment.[9] Hence there is a certain unevenness in the style.

It would be difficult to find a more felicitous extempore speaker, so fertile are both his mind and the tongue that does its bidding. His mind is always ready, ever passing nimbly to the next point; his memory always at his elbow, and as everything in it is held, so to say, in ready cash, it puts forward promptly and without hesitation whatever time or place demand. In disputations nothing more acute can be imagined, so that he has often taken on even the most eminent theologians in their own field and been almost too much for them. John Colet,[1] a sensitive and experienced critic, used to say sometimes in conversation that there was only one able man in the whole of England, though the island is blessed with so many men of outstanding ability.

True piety finds in him a practising follower, though far removed from all superstition. He has his fixed hours at which he says his prayers, and they are not conventional but come from the heart. When he talks with friends about the life after death, you recognize that he is speaking from conviction, and not without good hope.

---

6. The declamation, a standard rhetorical exercise, was a speech on a paradoxical or otherwise ingenious topic, often involving the impersonation of some historical or mythological figure.
7. As it had been among the Guardian class in the *Republic* (5.457B–466D); see p. 101 above.
8. Erasmus and More included their rival answers to Lucian's declamation on a fictitious and farfetched tyrannicide in the volume they published (1506) of translations—some by Erasmus, others by More—of selected brief works of Lucian.
9. See p. 13, n. 5 above.
1. More's mentor and friend John Colet (1467–1519) was dean of St. Paul's Cathedral, where he established a great humanist grammar school.

And More is like this even at court. What becomes then of those people who think that Christians are not to be found except in monasteries?

Such are the men whom that most intelligent king admits to his household and his privy chamber;[2] admits, yes, and invites, and even forces them to come. These are the continual spectators and witnesses of the way he lives; these form his council; these are the companions of his journeys. He rejoices to have them round him rather than young men or women dissolute and vicious, or even rich men in their splendid collars, or all the blandishments of insincerity, where one man would divert him to aimless pleasures, another would heat his blood with thoughts of tyranny, another put forward fresh tricks with which to fleece his people. Had you lived in this court, my dear Hutten, I have no doubt you would quite rewrite your *Aula*,[3] and cease to be a professed enemy of court life, though you too live with as honourable a prince as you could wish, nor do you lack men who look for a better state of things, such as Stromer and Kopp.[4]

*   *   *

Antwerp, July 23, 1519

---

2. Private quarters.
3. "*Aula*": a dialogue (*aula*: "court").
4. Humanist physicians at the court of Albert of Brandenburg, archbishop of Mainz, to which Hutten was also attached.

CRITICISM

OVERVIEW: THE CRITICAL TRADITIONS

Although the earliest commentators on *Utopia*—the humanists who contributed letters and poems to buttress the first four editions—sometimes evince an awareness of the ironies of More's book, those of them who express a view on the Utopian republic (a group that notably does not include the author's closest friend among the commentators, Erasmus) uniformly seem to take the account of it seriously as More's blueprint for an ideal commonwealth (which is not to say that they indicate a confidence that it could—at least in its entirety—be realized in practice). In the succeeding decades and centuries, this was a widespread, perhaps ubiquitous, understanding of Book II of the work: whether or not readers *approved* of Utopia, they took it as the author's ideal. The meanings that More's Greek-based coinage—*Utopia* ("Noplace")—acquired as a common noun—*utopia*—both reflected and supported this interpretation of the book. The great *Oxford English Dictionary* documents the fact that by the early seventeenth century *utopia* was used to mean "a place, state, or condition ideally perfect in respect of politics, laws, customs, and conditions"—though by the early eighteenth century the word was also used to mean "an impossibly ideal scheme, especially for social improvement."

The central feature of the Utopian commonwealth is of course its communism; and when, with Karl Marx and Friedrich Engels (who published their *Communist Manifesto* in 1848), communism emerged as a fully developed economic and political theory and a platform for social revolution, it is not surprising that the movement seized on More's book as a precursor and More himself as a visionary. Marx quotes *Utopia* in *Das Kapital*; and Engels's close associate Karl Kautsky wrote a book—the *first* book—about *Utopia*: *Thomas More and His Utopia* appeared (in German) in 1888.

Kautsky's book had been preceded, in 1867, by another important work dealing (in this case only partly) with *Utopia*, Frederic Seebohm's *The Oxford Reformers of 1498*, and these two very different books are the best markers of the beginning of the modern era of scholarship and criticism on *Utopia*. Seebohm interprets *Utopia* by putting it into the context of More's affiliation with the Erasmiam humanists of England in the early sixteenth century. (Erasmus himself, who in a series of visits spent a total of about six years in England in the period 1499–1516, was the central member of the group.) After Seebohm, explaining *Utopia* in terms of More's links with humanism, and with the classical Greek and Roman works on which the humanists focused much of their attention, became (as it has remained) the dominant critical approach to the book; while Kautsky's appropriation of More for the communist pantheon—an appropriation that proved highly controversial—determined the main battleground for interpreters. Among the exponents of the humanistic interpretation, some—with More's early-twentieth-century biographer R. W. Chambers and, later in the century, the Jesuit scholar Edward Surtz foremost among them—argued that More was not seriously espousing communism as a social program;

others—and here the leading figures include Russell Ames, J. H. Hexter, Quentin Skinner, and, most recently, Eric Nelson—argued that More meant exactly what he had made Hythloday say: that communist Utopia is not only the best commonwealth but the only one that can rightfully claim the *name* of commonwealth (see p. 93).

Though exponents of the humanistic interpretation of *Utopia* vary greatly on the extent to which they take the book as a blueprint for reform, they all take it as serious social commentary and political theory—as a book that belongs on the same shelf as Plato's *Republic*. A very different note was sounded by C. S. Lewis, in his volume in the Oxford History of English Literature, *English Literature in the Sixteenth Century Excluding Drama* (1954). Lewis argued that the book's "real place is not in the history of political thought so much as in that of fiction and satire"; it is "a revel of debate, paradox, comedy, and (above all) of invention, which starts many hares and kills none" (see pp. 198–99, 200–201 below). His views prefigured the emergence, in the following decades, of a new strand of criticism of *Utopia*, dominated by literary critics (as the humanistic interpretation has been dominated by historians) and employing the increasingly diverse and sophisticated critical methodologies that emerged in the latter half of the twentieth century. In some cases (such as Elizabeth McCutcheon's subtle article on More's use of the rhetorical figure litotes—ironic understatement—and Northrop Frye's deep taxonomy of utopian and anti-utopian fiction) these studies illuminate *Utopia* in ways that can be regarded as extending the humanistic interpretation or at least as compatible with it. In other cases, especially those in which the focus is on the implications of the book's complex narrative technique (as in studies by Harry Berger Jr., Richard S. Sylvester, and Alistair Fox), these works constitute in effect a *counter*-tradition: criticism of this kind often focuses on contradictions in Hythloday's arguments and on unattractive aspects of his personality, and this focus is often linked with a stress on unattractive aspects of Utopia itself, which is sometimes viewed as less utopian than dystopian. Arguably, though, the most important effect of this strand of criticism has been to bring a new sophistication to the humanistic interpretation, whose recent exponents, such as Dominic Baker-Smith, have understood that it is not enough simply to *assert* that Hythloday speaks for his creator and who have in fact often argued that the key to the book's meaning is found in the interplay *between* Hythloday and the character "More."

What follows is a selection of the most influential Utopian criticism of the past century and a half. None of these studies is included, however, simply because it has *been* influential. Literary criticism usually builds on previous criticism, but this does not mean that the latest work necessarily replaces or invalidates all earlier work. Everything collected here has something to say to current-day students of *Utopia* that can help them not just to understand the history of Utopian criticism but to respond to and understand *Utopia* itself. Regrettably, limitations of space have made it necessary to reprint extracts rather than entire studies. Readers are encouraged to seek out the complete works, as well as other major studies that could not be included even in abbreviated form. For the latter, see "Suggestions for Further Reading."

FREDERIC SEEBOHM
[A Satire on Crying Abuses]†

The point of the *Utopia* consisted in the contrast presented by its ideal commonwealth to the condition and habits of the European commonwealths of the period. This contrast is most often left to be drawn by the reader from his own knowledge of contemporary politics, and hence the peculiar advantage of the choice by More of such a vehicle for the bold satire it contained. Upon any other hypothesis than that the evils against which its satire was directed were admitted to be *real*, the romance of *Utopia* must also be admitted to be harmless. To pronounce it to be dangerous was to admit its truth.

Take, *e.g.*, the following passage relating to the international policy of the Utopians:

'While other nations are always entering into leagues,[1] and breaking and renewing them, the Utopians never enter into a league with any nation. For what is the use of a league? they say. As though there were no natural tie between man and man! and as though anyone who despised this natural tie would, forsooth, regard mere words! They hold this opinion all the more strongly, because in that quarter of the world the leagues and treaties of princes are not observed as faithfully as they should be. For in Europe, and especially in those parts of it where the Christian faith and religion are professed, the sanctity of leagues is held sacred and inviolate. * * *'[2]

Read without reference to the international history of the period, these passages appear perfectly harmless. But read in the light of that political history which, during the past few years, had become so mixed up with the personal history of the Oxford Reformers, recollecting '*how* religiously' treaties had been made and broken by almost every sovereign in Europe—Henry VIII and the Pope included—the words in which the justice and goodness of European

---

† Reprinted, with small changes of punctuation, from Frederic Seebohm, *The Oxford Reformers: John Colet, Erasmus, and Thomas More*, 3rd ed. (London: Longman, Green, and Co., 1887; 1st ed. 1867), pp. 348–54. All footnotes are by the editors. Seebohm's book launched the modern "humanistic interpretation" of *Utopia* (see p. 157 above).
1. Treaties.
2. Seebohm continues with Hythloday's heavily ironic remarks, through his surmise that if the Utopians lived in Europe they would doubtless change their minds about treaties (see p. 76 above).

princes is so mildly and modestly extolled become almost as bitter in their tone as the cutting censure of Erasmus in the *Praise of Folly*, or his more recent and open satire upon kings.[3]

Again, bearing in mind the wars of Henry VIII,[4] and how evidently the love of military glory was the motive which induced him to engage in them, the following passage contains almost as direct and pointed a censure of the King's passion for war as the sermon preached by Colet[5] in his presence:

'The Utopians hate war as plainly brutal, although practised more eagerly by man than by any other animal. And contrary to the sentiment of nearly every other nation, they regard nothing more inglorious than glory derived from war.'[6]

Turning from international politics to questions of internal policy, and bearing in mind the hint of Erasmus that More had in view chiefly the politics of his own country,[7] it is impossible not to recognise in the *Utopia* the expression, again and again, of the *sense of wrong* stirred up in More's heart, as he had witnessed how every interest of the commonwealth had been sacrificed to Henry VIII's passion for war; and how, in sharing the burdens it entailed, and dealing with the social evils it brought to the surface, the interests of the poor had been sacrificed to spare the pockets of the rich; how, whilst the very wages of the labourer had been taxed to support the long-continued war expenditure, a selfish Parliament, under colour of the old 'statutes of labourers,' had attempted to cut down the amount of his wages, and to rob him of that fair rise in the price of his labour which the drain upon the labour market had produced.[8]

It is impossible not to recognise that the recent statutes of labourers was the target against which More's satire was specially directed in the following paragraph:

'Let any one dare to compare with the even justice which rules in Utopia, the justice of other nations; amongst whom, let me die, if I find any trace at all of equity and justice. For where is the jus-

---

3. The 1515 edition of Erasmus's *Adages* included several harsh denunciations of kings, and especially of their wars. Among these are the essays on the proverbs "*Sileni Alcibiadis*" ("The Sileni of Alcibiades"), "*Scarabaeus aquilam quaerit*" ("A dung-beetle hunting an eagle"), and, above all, "*Dulce bellum inexpertis*" ("War is sweet, to those who have not tried it"). For translations of these essays, see *CWE* 34:262–82, 35:178–214, 399–440.

4. Against France, 1512–14.

5. On John Colet, see p. 152, n. 1 above. Erasmus reported that Colet had argued in a sermon that "an unjust peace was preferable to the most just of wars," and that he had later told Henry VIII that "for Christians there can never be a just war" (*CWE* 8:242, 243).

6. See p. 77 above.

7. See p. 152 above.

8. Responding to a scarcity of labor, which would naturally tend to drive up wages, a parliamentary act of 1514–15 imposed rigid maxima on pay.

tice, that noblemen, goldsmiths, and usurers, and those classes who either do nothing at all or, in what they do, are of no great service to the commonwealth, should live a genteel and splendid life in idleness or unproductive labour; whilst in the meantime the servant, the waggoner, the mechanic, and the peasant, toiling almost longer and harder than the horse, in labour so necessary that no commonwealth could endure a year without it, lead a life so wretched that the condition of the horse seems more to be envied. * * *'9

* * *

The whole framework of the Utopian commonwealth bears witness to More's conviction that what should be aimed at in his own country and elsewhere was a true *community*—not a rich and educated aristocracy on the one hand, existing side by side with a poor and ignorant peasantry on the other—but one people, well-to-do and educated throughout.

Thus More's opinion was that in England in his time, 'far more than four parts of all the whole [people], divided into ten, could never read English';[1] and probably the education of the other six-tenths was anything but satisfactory. He shared Colet's faith in education, and represented that in Utopia every child was properly educated.[2]

Again, the great object of the social economy of Utopia was not to increase the abundance of luxuries, or to amass a vast accumulation in few hands, or even in national or royal hands, but to lessen the hours of labour to the working man. By spreading the burden of labour more evenly over the whole community—by taking care that there shall be no idle classes, be they beggars or begging friars—More expressed the opinion that hours of labour to the working man might probably be reduced to six.[3]

Again: living himself in Bucklersbury,[4] in the midst of all the dirt and filth of London's narrow streets; surrounded by the unclean, ill-ventilated houses of the poor, whose floors of clay and rushes, never cleansed, were pointed out by Erasmus as breeding pestilence and inviting the ravages of the sweating sickness; himself a commissioner of sewers, and having thus some practical knowledge of London's sanitary arrangements;[5] More described the towns of Utopia as well and regularly built, with wide streets, waterworks, hospitals, and

9. Seebohm's quotation from Hythloday's peroration concludes with the bitter observation that the schemes of the rich to oppress the poor—which include devices to "grind out of . . . [them] part of their meager wages"—are enacted into law in the name of the commonwealth (see pp. 94–95 above).
1. *Apology*, CW 9:13.
2. See p. 58 above.
3. Cf. p. 45 above.
4. Bucklersbury Street, London, where More had lived for more than a decade when he wrote *Utopia*.
5. In 1514, More was appointed one of the commissioners of sewers for the Thames bank.

numerous common halls; all the houses well protected from the
weather, as nearly as might be fireproof, three stories high, with
plenty of windows, and doors both back and front, the back door
always opening into a well-kept garden.[6] All this was utopian, doubtless, and the result in Utopia of the still more utopian abolition of
private property; but the gist and point of it consisted in the contrast it presented with what he saw around him in Europe, and
especially in England, and men could hardly fail to draw the lesson
he intended to teach.

KARL KAUTSKY

From The Roots of More's Socialism[†]

As a Humanist and a politician, More was in the front rank of his
contemporaries, as a Socialist he was far ahead of them all. His
political, religious, and Humanist writings are to-day only read by a
small number of historians. Had he not written *Utopia* his name
would scarcely be better known to-day than that of the friend who
shared his fate, Bishop Fisher of Rochester.[1] His socialism made
him immortal.

Whence originated this socialism?

Unlike the historians of the idealistic school, we do not believe
in a Holy Spirit which illumines minds and fills them with ideas, to
which the political and economic development adapts itself. We
rather start from the assumption that the contradictions and antagonisms which the economic development creates in society stimulate thought and provoke investigations by men who are favourably
situated to prosecute such researches, so that they may understand
what is going on before their eyes and remove the suffering which
contemporary conditions entail. In this way arise political and social
ideas which influence contemporary thought, or at least, particular
classes, in the degree that they respond to the actual conditions,
and which are correct so far as they coincide with the interests of
the aspiring classes.

---

6. See pp. 42–43 above.
† From Karl Kautsky, *Thomas More and His Utopia*, translated by H. J. Stenning (London: A. & C. Black, Ltd., 1927), pp. 159–63, 168–71 (Part III, chap. 1, sect. 1). First
   German edition 1888. Copyright 1927 by International Publishers Co., Inc. Reprinted
   by permission of the publisher. Footnotes are by the editors. On Kautsky, and the
   importance of his book in the history of *Utopia* criticism, see p. 157 above and the critique by Russell Ames on pp. 184–87 below.
1. Exemplary bishop, chancellor of the University of Cambridge, and distinguished theologian, John Fisher preceded his friend Thomas More by two weeks as a martyr to their
   Catholic faith and was canonized with him on May 19, 1935. He is hardly the obscure
   figure that he evidently was to Kautsky (nor, of course, does More's celebrity depend
   exclusively on *Utopia*).

* * *

It is clear that ideas must be fermenting for some time before they can exercise any influence on the masses. There is a tendency to reproach the masses with running after novelties, whereas the truth is that they cling most obstinately to the old. The antagonism of the new economic conditions to the transmitted conditions and the ideas which accord therewith must be fairly pronounced before it penetrates to the mind of the masses. Where the acumen of the investigator perceives unbridgeable antagonisms of classes, the average man sees only accidental personal disputes; where the investigator sees social evils which could only be removed by social transformations, the average man consoles himself with the hope that times are only temporarily bad and will soon improve. We are not speaking of the members of classes on the decline, most of whom will not face facts, but have in mind the nascent classes, whose interests it is to see, but who cannot see until they bump right up against the new conditions. Their ideas also were conditioned by the newly developing material conditions, but these conditions were not yet sharply defined enough to render the aspiring classes accessible to these ideas.

But a thinker who takes his stand on the material conditions may be a whole epoch in advance of his time, if he perceives a newly evolving mode of production and its social consequences not only sooner than most of his contemporaries, but straining far into the future, also glimpses the more rational mode of production into which it will develop.

Thomas More is one of the few who have been capable of this bold intellectual leap; at a time when the capitalist mode of production was in its infancy, he mastered its essential features so thoroughly that the alternative mode of production which he elaborated and contrasted with it as a remedy for its evils contained several of the most important ingredients of Modern Socialism. The drift of his speculations, of course, escaped his contemporaries, and can only be properly appreciated by us to-day. Despite the immense economic and technical transformations of the last three hundred years, we find in *Utopia* a number of tendencies which are still operative in the Socialist Movement of our time.

* * *

More's personal character may * * * be regarded as one of the causes of his Socialism. Erasmus tells us how amiable, helpful, and full of sympathy with the poor and oppressed More was: he called him the protector of all the poor.[2]

2. Cf. p. 151 above.

Only in the northern countries of Western Europe were the material conditions in the sixteenth century favourable to the formation of such a disinterested character. In the mercantile republics of Italy, as in the Courts of the Romance monarchies,[3] egotism, the grand feature of the new mode of production, reigned absolutely; it reigned openly, boldly, full of revolutionary defiance. It was a vast egotism, quite different from the cowardly, mendacious, despicable egotism of to-day, which hides itself behind conventional hypocrisy.

*   *   *

At the commencement of the sixteenth century the primitive agrarian communism still existed in England.[4] It had survived under cover of feudalism, and only then began to yield place to another system of agriculture. The features which corresponded to primitive communism still existed, especially among the lower population, and we meet them in More only slightly glossed over with the Humanistic and courtier traits and the self-censure which the conditions imposed upon him. In his serenity, tenacity, unyieldingness, selflessness, and helpfulness we see the impress of all the characteristics of communistic "Merry England."

But sympathy with the poor does not make one a socialist, although without that sympathy no one is likely to become a socialist. In order that socialist sentiments and ideas should grow out of this interest, it must be conjoined with a special economic situation, the existence of a working proletariat as a permanent mass phenomenon, and on the other hand profound economic insight.

*   *   *

When capitalism first invades industry and then turns to agriculture, it seems at the onset to wear a benevolent aspect. It must aim at a constant extending of the market, of production, while the importation of labour-power proceeds but slowly. In its early stages, such an industry is always complaining of the lack of labour-power. Capitalists must outbid handicraftsmen and peasants in order to entice away from them their journeymen and bondsmen: wages rise.

In this way capitalism began in many countries; it was hailed as a blessing. Not so in England, where it first invaded and revolutionised agriculture. Improvements in methods of cultivation made many

3. The monarchies—especially those of France and Spain—that developed in former Roman colonies.
4. Though Kautsky probably overstates the prevalence in medieval England of "primitive communism"—the sharing of goods among agricultural peasants, more or less on the basis of need—this "primitive" (i.e., pre-Marxist) communism was a monastic practice (see p. 112 above), and the rightness of communal sharing was a frequent theme of religious reformers.

workers superfluous.[5] Capitalism in agriculture meant the direct setting-free of workers. In England this process of setting-free proceeded in its severest forms, at a time when industry was developing but slowly and required only small supplies of labour-power; least of all, the ignorant country labourer.

And hand in hand with the separation of the workers from the land, from their means of production, a rapid concentration of landed property into a few hands was going on.

Nowhere else in Europe, therefore, were the unfavourable reactions of the capitalist mode of production upon the working classes so immediately obvious as in England; nowhere did the unhappy workers clamour so urgently for assistance.

That such an economic situation should cause a man of More's character to reflect and to cast about for means of alleviating the intolerable conditions is what we should expect.

More was not the only person who sought for and propounded such expedients. From numerous writings of that time, from numerous Acts of Parliament we may perceive how deep was the impression made by the economic revolution then proceeding, and how generally the shabby practices of the landlords and their tenants were condemned.

But none of those who put forward remedies had a wider outlook, to none of them came the conviction that the sufferings incident to the new mode of production could only be ended by a transition to another and higher mode of production; none of them, save More, was a Socialist.

A theory of Socialism could only arise within the realm of Humanism. As a Humanist, More learned to think methodically and to generalise. As a Humanist he was enabled to look beyond the horizon of his time and his country: in the writings of classical antiquity he became acquainted with social conditions different from those of his own time. Plato's ideal of an aristocratic-communist community[6] must have prompted him to imagine social conditions which, being the opposite of those existing, were free from their concomitant poverty. Plato's authority must have encouraged him to regard such a community as more than a mere figment of the imagination, and to set it up as a goal which humanity should strive to attain.

In so far was Humanism favourable to More's development. But the situation in England was, in a scientific respect,[7] similar to that in Germany: English Humanism remained an imported, exotic growth, without roots in the national life, a mere academic affair.

5. Cf. Hythloday's analysis on p. 19 above.
6. I.e., in the *Republic*; see p. 101 above.
7. I.e., as understood through Marxist "scientific" analysis.

Had More been a mere Humanist, he would hardly have attained to Socialism. We know, however, that More's father, much to the regret of Erasmus and his other Humanist friends, soon tore him away from his studies, in order to put him to the study of law and then to launch him on a practical career. We know in what close relationship More stood to the London merchants, how he was entrusted with the care of their interests on every important occasion.[8] The majority of the positions which More filled impelled him to deal with economic questions; the fact that he was appointed to these posts also proves that he was regarded as an expert in economic matters.

We know that he was a popular advocate, that in 1509 he was appointed Under-Sheriff, in which position he had sufficient opportunity to gain an insight into the economic life of the people.[9] We have also mentioned several missions of which he was a member, for the conduct of commercial negotiations. The first was to Bruges in 1515. In the same year Parliament appointed him a Commissioner of Sewers.[1] His second mission was to Calais in 1517, in order to compose disputes between English and French merchants. In 1520 we find him on a mission to Bruges, to settle disputes between English merchants and the Hansa.[2] Then he became Treasurer,[3] and, in 1523, Speaker in the Commons, both positions presupposing experience in financial matters, and shortly afterwards Chancellor of the Duchy of Lancaster: truly, if anybody had an opportunity to become acquainted with the economic life of his time, it was More. And he became acquainted with it from the most modern standpoint that was then possible, from that of the English merchant, for whom world trade was then opening up. In our view, this close connection of More with mercantile capital cannot be too strongly emphasised. To this we attribute the fact that More thought on modern lines, that his Socialism was of a modern kind.

We believe that we have disclosed the most essential roots of More's Socialism: his amiable character in harmony with primitive communism; the economic situation of England, which brought into sharp relief the disadvantageous consequences of capitalism for the working class; the fortunate union of classical philosophy with activity in practical affairs—all these circumstances combined must have induced in a mind so acute, so fearless, so truth-loving as More's an ideal which may be regarded as a foregleam of Modern Socialism.

8. More belonged to the Mercers' Company of London and did in fact represent its interests on several occasions.
9. As an undersheriff of London (1510–18), More sat as judge in the Sheriff's Court, hearing cases involving debt, assault, and many other matters.
1. See p. 161, n. 5 above.
2. The Hanseatic League was a powerful alliance of northern European mercantile associations in the 13th to 17th centuries.
3. In 1521 More was appointed under-treasurer of the exchequer, and knighted.

R. W. CHAMBERS

The Meaning of *Utopia*[†]

An ex-Cabinet minister is still alive who dates his political career from the accidental purchase of a copy of *Utopia* at a second-hand bookstall. One of his colleagues in the Cabinet has written of *Utopia*, that no treatise is better calculated to nourish the heart of a Radical. *Utopia* has become a text-book of Socialist propaganda. It did more to make William Morris a Socialist than ever Karl Marx did.[1] All this testifies to its abiding power; yet we must never think of More as writing it for Nineteenth-Century Radicals or Twentieth-Century Socialists. Even he could not do that.

The first step to an appreciation of *Utopia* is to understand how it must have struck a scholar in the early Sixteenth Century. That is a difficult task, yet not an impossible one; and if we would understand More himself, it is a task which we must undertake.

We shall then find, I think, that few books have been more misunderstood than *Utopia*. It has given the English language a word 'Utopian' to signify something visionary and unpractical. Yet the remarkable thing about *Utopia* is the extent to which it adumbrates social and political reforms which have either been actually carried into practice, or which have come to be regarded as very practical politics. Utopia is depicted as a sternly righteous and puritanical State, where few of us would feel quite happy; yet we go on using the word 'Utopia' to signify an easy-going paradise, whose only fault is that it is too happy and ideal to be realized. *Utopia* is the first of a series which we have christened 'Ideal Commonwealths'. Some of these, for example William Morris' *News from Nowhere*, really *are* ideal. They are 'Utopian' in the current sense, that is to say, they are quite unpractical fancies of what this world might be like if the dreamer could shatter it to bits, and then remould it nearer to the heart's desire. For instance, in *News from Nowhere* we might be sure

---

† This and the following excerpt are from *Thomas More* (London: Jonathan Cape, 1938; orig. publ. 1935), pp. 125–33, 134–38, 143–44. Reprinted by permission of Jonathan Cape Ltd. on behalf of the estate of R. W. Chambers. Footnotes are by the editors, unless otherwise indicated.

    Raymond Wilson Chambers (1874–1942) spent his entire academic career at University College London (a constituent college of the University of London), writing on a broad range of topics in English literature and history, especially of the medieval and early-modern eras. His *Thomas More*—published in 1935, to coincide with More's canonization—has been the most widely read and influential biography, and its treatment of *Utopia* the single most influential account of that work. The impact of Chambers's work is attributable in no small part to the lightness with which he wore his great learning and the grace of his prose. For Russell Ames's critique of Chambers's account of *Utopia*, see pp. 179–80, 187–90 below.

1. The multitalented William Morris (1834–1896)—writer, painter, designer of household furnishings, weaver, printer—was also a socialist agitator. *News from Nowhere*, his utopian romance, is Marxism with a thick overlay of nostalgia for the medieval.

that the Divine Worship of the citizens would be Morris' ideal. If
he gives them no Divine Worship, that also tells its tale. Now, More
does not make his Utopians Christian. So modern scholars have
argued: 'Utopia is an ideal commonwealth; *argal*[2] More thought
the vague deism of his Utopians more ideal than the popular religious beliefs of his time.'

Such argument might be reasonable if *Utopia* were a modern
'Ideal Commonwealth'. But we must never forget that More's education fell not in the Nineteenth but in the Fifteenth Century. To a
man educated in that century, the distinction was obvious between
the virtues which might be taught by human reason alone, and the
further virtues taught by Catholic orthodoxy. It was part of the medieval system to divide the virtues into the Four Cardinal Virtues (to
which the heathen might attain) and the Three Christian Virtues.
The Four Cardinal Virtues—Wisdom, Fortitude, Temperance, and
Justice—are the foundation of Plato's commonwealths, as outlined
in the *Republic* and the *Laws*.[3] These virtues were taken into the
medieval system—part of the immense debt it owes to Greek philosophy. The Three Christian Virtues—Faith, Hope, and Charity—
come of course from St. Paul's *First Epistle to the Corinthians*. Four
and Three make Seven—the Perfect Number, which was extremely
comforting. The perfect Christian character must comprise all seven.
But the four heathen virtues were sufficient to ensure that a man or
a State might be a model of conduct in secular matters. In Dante's
Divine Comedy Virgil represents Philosophy, Reason, Human Wisdom. He is able to rescue Dante from the dark wood (although he
was one of those who had not the three sacred virtues) because he
knew and followed the four other virtues without fault. So Virgil can
guide Dante till he meets Beatrice, but can go no further.

For a pattern of a State, Dante turns to Heathen Rome or to Heathen Greece. And it is not because of his deep learning that Dante
does this. Our great English medieval poet, William Langland, the
author of *Piers Plowman*, had but a commonplace education, but
his system is similar. *Do Well* is the virtue of secular life, and the
examples of it are the great non-Christian philosophers and rulers:
Aristotle, Solomon, Socrates, Trajan. *Do Better* and *Do Best* represent forms of Christian virtues. And so More's friend, Busleiden, in
his introductory letter to *Utopia*, tells us that the perfect commonwealth must unite 'Wisdom in the ruler, Fortitude in the soldiers,
Temperance in private individuals, and Justice in all.'[4]

---

2. Corruption of Latin *ergo* ("therefore"): used facetiously, to suggest that the reasoning
that precedes it is absurd.
3. *Republic*, Book IV; *Laws*, Book XII [Chambers's note].
4. See p. 133 above.

In basing his *Utopia* upon these four heathen virtues, More is following medieval tradition; further, he is following his great examples, Plato's *Republic* and *Laws*; but, above all, he makes his satire
upon contemporary European abuses more pointed. The virtues of
Heathen Utopia show up by contrast the vices of Christian Europe.
But the Four Cardinal Virtues are subsidiary to, not a substitute for,
the Christian virtues. More has done his best to make this clear. It
is not his fault if he has been misunderstood, as the following example will show.

Most of us would agree with Dame Alice in deploring More's
extreme austerities. We have seen that, years before *Utopia* was written, she had complained to More's confessor about that shirt of hair.[5]
It was no good. It may have been some ten years after *Utopia* was
written that, as Roper tells us, More's daughter-in-law, young Anne
Cresacre, noticed it:

> My sister More, in the summer as he sat at supper, singly[6] in his
> doublet and hose, wearing thereupon a plain shirt, without ruff
> or collar, chancing to spy, began to laugh at it. My wife [Marga-
> ret Roper] not ignorant of his manner, perceiving the same,
> privily told him of it; and he, being sorry that she saw it, pres-
> ently amended it. He used also sometimes to punish his body
> with whips, the cords knotted, which was known only to my
> wife, whom for her secrecy above all other he specially trusted,
> causing her, as need required, to wash the same shirt of hair.[7]

Now, despite all this, we are told that the Utopians condemn bodily
austerities as 'a point of extreme madness, and a token of a man cruelly minded toward himself'.[8]

More's biographers and commentators have been puzzled. Yet the
very next sentence of *Utopia* explains the puzzle. The Utopians have
only reason to guide them, and they believe that *by man's reason* nothing can be found truer than their view, *'unless any godlier be inspired
into man from Heaven'*. The same point is made by More later. There
are orders of ascetics in *Utopia*: if the ascetics grounded their action
on reason the Utopians would mock them; but as they base it on
religion, the Utopians honour them and regard them as holy.[9]

---

5. Alice Middleton, More's second wife, had no sympathy for his strict ascetic practices
   and, as Chambers had recorded (p. 109), had at one point asked her husband's priest to
   advise him to give up the hair shirt that he wore to mortify his flesh.
6. Simply.
7. The passage comes from the highly engaging biography of More by his son-in-law William Roper (the husband of his favorite child, Margaret). See Richard S. Sylvester and
   Davis P. Harding, eds., *Two Early Tudor Lives* (New Haven and London: Yale University
   Press, 1962), p. 224.
8. Cf. p. 66 above. Chambers quotes *Utopia* from the first English translation, that of
   Ralph Robinson (1551), modernizing the spelling.
9. See p. 89 above.

We find More, a dozen years later, urging against the Reformers this same doctrine which lies at the root of *Utopia*: 'That Reason is servant to Faith, not enemy.' More argues that Reason, Philosophy, and even Poetry have their part to play: zealots who, neglecting 'a good mother wit' would cast away all learning except the Bible are, says More, 'in a mad mind',[1] and he quotes St. Jerome to prove that pagan Philosophy and Poetry have their use for Christians. By 'Poetry' More of course means any work of the imagination: his Protestant critics deride *Utopia* as 'poetry', and More himself as a 'poet'. When a Sixteenth-Century Catholic depicts a pagan state founded on Reason and Philosophy, he is not depicting his ultimate ideal. Erasmus tells us that More's object was 'to show whence spring the evils of States, with special reference to the English State, with which he was most familiar'.[2] The underlying thought of *Utopia* always is, *With nothing save Reason to guide them, the Utopians do this; and yet we Christian Englishmen, we Christian Europeans . . . !*

Just as More scored a point against the wickedness of Christian Europe, by making his philosophers heathen, so Jonathan Swift scored a point against the wickedness of mankind by representing *his* philosophers, the Houyhnhnms, as having the bodies of horses. Yet we do not call Swift inconsistent, because he did not live on a diet of oats, or, like poor Gulliver, fall into the voice and manner of horses in speaking. Swift did not mean that all horses are better than all men. He meant that some men are worse than horses. More did not mean that Heathendom is better than Christianity. He meant that some Christians are worse than heathen.

Dante and Langland and innumerable medieval writers had said the same before him. The conviction that life might be nobly lived on the basis of the four heathen cardinal virtues was one which the Catholic Middle Ages had inherited from Greek philosophy.

So, naturally, More is interested in the problem which for half a lifetime tormented Dante and Langland; what will be the fate, in the next world, of the just heathen, who are an example to us in the affairs of this world? More's answer is tentative, but he quotes with approval the 'comfortable saying' of Master Nicholas de Lyra,[3] the Franciscan, Dante's younger contemporary. Nicholas de Lyra argued that, though a much fuller faith is demanded from Christians, it suffices for the heathen to have believed 'that God is, and that He is the rewarder of them that seek Him'; these are, says de Lyra, 'two points such as every man may attain by natural reason, holpen forth with such grace as God keepeth from no man'.

---

1. See More's *Dialogue Concerning Heresies*, CW 6:132.
2. See p. 152 above.
3. One of the most influential of scriptural exegetes (1270–1349).

And More quoted this, not in his alleged 'emancipated' youth, but in his last book, the *Treatise upon the Passion*,[4] written in the Tower, when he had dismissed all worldly affairs, and was awaiting martyrdom 'for the faith of the Catholic Church'.

What, then, is the attitude of *Utopia* as to these two articles, which represent, in More's view, the orthodoxy to which a heathen may attain? King Utopus tolerated all varieties of belief and disbelief, save on these two points; he forbade, 'ernestly and straitly' that any man should disbelieve in either (1) Divine Providence, or (2) a future life in which, as the Utopians believed, the just would be rewarded by God's presence.[5]

So far was this simple creed from appearing lax to More's friends, that the marginal note (written either by Erasmus or by Peter Giles)[6] contrasts the Utopian faith in immortality with the laxity and doubts of many Christians: '*The immortality of the soul, concerning which not a few, though Christians, to-day doubt or dispute.*' But in Utopia, the man who disbelieves either of these articles is not counted as a citizen, or even as a man; he is excluded from all office, and despised, as being necessarily of a base and vile nature. To suffer lifelong public contumely, in a land where all life is lived in public, and where, save as a citizen, a man has and is nothing, is a punishment which many would feel to be worse than death. Yet the sceptic may not, publicly, argue in his own defence. Then comes the sentence which has been so often quoted, out of its context. In the old translation it runs, 'Howbeit they put him to no punishment'. Of course, More did not write such nonsense. What he really says is, 'They do not put him to any bodily punishment'[7]—so long, that is, as he humbly submits to the disgrace and to the silence which his heresies involve. The charge against More of inconsistency rests upon refusing to notice his distinction between liberty to hold an opinion, and liberty to preach that opinion; between a man being in More's phrase 'a heretic alone by himself', and being 'a seditious heretic'.

Bishop Creighton, to prove that More in later life 'put his principles aside,' quotes the passage which tells how King Utopus, when settling the Utopian constitution, found many religions prevalent in the land, and ordained that they should all be tolerated.[8] Creighton

---

4. See CW 13:42–43. (Though late, the *Treatise* is no longer thought to be More's last book.)
5. See p. 86 above.
6. For Giles's claim to have authored the marginal glosses that appear in the early editions of *Utopia*, see p. 130 above. But the title page of the second, 1517, edition attributes them to Erasmus.
7. The Latin is *nullo adficiunt supplicio*: "they do not punish [him]." But Chambers is surely right that the *meaning* is "no corporal punishment."
8. See Mandell Creighton, *Persecution and Tolerance* (London: Longman, Green, and Co., 1895), pp. 104–05, 108. The Anglican bishop Creighton (1843–1901) was an influential historian.

then omits the passage about Utopus disgracing and muzzling those who held the opinions he thought pernicious. But this passage is vital; for, in the light of it, we find that Utopus did *not* tolerate the preaching of all views, but only of those which he, in his wisdom, thought tolerable. Then Creighton begins to quote again. Even those who held most noxious opinions 'were put to no punishment'. They are put to no bodily punishment, so long as they will submit to being disfranchised, despised, and silenced.

But, as the watchman says to Dogberry, 'How if they will not?'[9]

We can tell what would happen *then*, when we remember that, even in the discussion of such opinions as the State allows, any violent or seditious speech is punished in Utopia by banishment or bondage. And, in Utopia, if a man condemned to bondage jibs at his punishment, he is slain out of hand like a wild beast. Suppose that two sceptics, who did not believe the soul of man to be immortal, had discussed, in private, in Utopia, how they could get the law repealed which silenced and disenfranchised them. They would have incurred the penalty imposed on those who plot against the fundamental laws of Utopia. And, even for the highest magistrats, that penalty is death.[1]

Still, within these narrow limits, the Utopian has liberty of conscience. He may not spread among the common people a belief which the State thinks harmful, nor may he discuss the most innocent opinions in a way likely to cause sedition and dissension. He may not, in private, discuss any affair of State.[2] But, if he submits to these restrictions, he is left alone; he is not to be terrorized into saying that he believes what he does not believe.

It may be a low ideal of liberty which allows, to a man who holds views disapproved by the authorities, freedom of thought only on condition that he does not claim freedom of speech. But that *is* the liberty Utopia allows. I shall try, later,[3] to show how far More stuck to that ideal.

From *Utopia* and the Problems of 1516

But we merely confuse the issues if we use our modern question-begging terminology, and contrast More's alleged 'emancipated youth'

---

9. Cf. *Much Ado About Nothing* 3.3.24.
1. For the passages of *Utopia* referred to in this paragraph, see pp. 85–86, 73–74, 44 above.
2. Though More's Latin in the passage Chambers refers to here is often construed in this way, it actually means something less spine-chilling: that it is a capital offense "to make plans for public business outside of the senate or the popular assembly" (p. 44). This is a law against political conspiracy, not innocent private discussion.
3. See *Thomas More*, pp. 264–67, 366–68.

with his orthodox old age. If we try to judge it in relation to the early Sixteenth Century, we shall find that *Utopia* is by no means 'emancipated'; it is rather a protest against undue 'emancipation'.

Utopia is, in part, a protest against the New Statesmanship: against the new idea of the autocratic prince to whom everything is allowed. I do not say that it is an impartial protest. The evil counsellors, who are represented in the First Book of *Utopia* egging the prince to despotism, might have replied that their ideal was not necessarily base or sycophantic. Patriots have sometimes seen in tyranny the only force strong enough to make their country great; reformers have sometimes seen in it the only force strong enough to carry through the reformation they desire. But *Utopia* is hostile to it.

Again, *Utopia* is, in part, a protest against the New Economics: the enclosures of the great landowners, breaking down old law and custom, destroying the old common-field agriculture. Here again, we must not suppose that *Utopia* gives us the full story. There was much more in the problem of enclosures than the greed of the great landlord, 'the very plague of his native country'.[1] The up-to-date farmer was also in favour of sweeping away all traces of the older communal husbandry. Thomas Tusser, a humble but practical agriculturist, says:

> Where all things in common do rest,
> Yet what doth it stand ye in stead?[2]

Now, in contrast to this changing world, More depicts a state where 'all things in common do rest', and where there is no place for the grabbing superman. More's theoretical *Utopia*, looking back to Plato's *Republic* and to corporate life in the Middle Ages, probably seemed to some contemporaries the reverse of 'progressive'. Cardinal Pole has told of a conversation he had in his youth with Thomas Cromwell. Cromwell ridiculed the *Republic* of Plato, which, after so many centuries, has led to nothing. *He* had a book on statesmanship in manuscript, by a practical modern writer, based on experience. The book, which Cromwell offered to lend to Pole, was *The Prince* of Nicholas Machiavelli.[3]

It is noteworthy that the two most potent books on the State written in the Sixteenth Century were written within so few years

---

1. See p. 19 above.
2. I.e., "where all things are held in common, what good does it do you?" The lines come from a poem in praise of enclosure found in Tusser's collection of rough-and-ready poems on agriculture, *Five Hundred Sundry Points of Good Husbandry* (1573).
3. Reginald Pole (1500–1558) broke with Henry VIII over the king's desire to divorce Catherine of Aragon. He went into self-imposed exile in 1532 and was made a cardinal in 1536. Thomas Cromwell (1485?–1540) was Henry's chief adviser during the period of the separation of the English church from Rome.

of each other. Parts of *Utopia* read like a commentary on parts of *The Prince*, as Johnson's *Rasselas* reads like a commentary on Voltaire's *Candide*, though we know that in neither case can the English writer have read his continental predecessor.[4] There is a reason for the coincidence; before *The Prince* was written, ideas used in *The Prince* had been gaining ground. They were the 'progressive' ideas, and we may regard *Utopia* as a 'reaction' against them. Over and over again, in Book I of *Utopia*, Raphael Hythlodaye imagines himself as counselling a prince, telling him what he ought to do, against those who are telling him what he *can* do; and always Raphael admits that these ideas of justice which he has brought from Utopia are opposed to all that the most-up-to-date statesmen of Europe are thinking and doing.

And so, from the point of view of the new age of Machiavellian statesmanship and commercial exploitation, *Utopia* is old-fashioned. The King is to 'live of his own', in medieval wise, and to turn a deaf ear to the counsellors who would make him all-powerful. The big landlords are to have mercy on their tenants, and not to allow them to be sacrificed to economic progress, and the law of supply and demand in the wool market.[5]

* * *

Another leading problem of controversy was the immortality of the soul. Did philosophy and human reason, apart from revelation, teach such immortality? There were philosophers who said 'No'; and, three years before *Utopia* was published, this matter also had come before the Lateran Council.[6] Teachers of philosophy were enjoined to point out how Christian philosophy corrected the views of the heathen on immortality; they were to refute these heathen errors, and steps were taken to ensure that the student *in sacris ordinibus constitutus*[7] should not spend more than five years upon philosophy and poetry, before diluting them with the safer studies of theology and pontifical law.

Now, let us try and look at *Utopia* from the point of view of 1516. Here is a heathen community, whose religion is founded on philosophy and natural reason. Yet, so far from doubting the immortality of the soul, they base their whole polity upon it. No disbeliever in

4. Dr. Johnson published *Rasselas* and Voltaire *Candide* within a few weeks of each other in 1759. Machiavelli's *Prince* was written in 1513, two years before More began *Utopia*, but it was not published until 1532.
5. Chambers next turns to argue that "the outlook of *Utopia*" on three great ecclesiastical problems of 1516 is also "conservative and orthodox." The first of the problems is clerical immunity (the exemption of clerics from prosecution by the civil courts); the following excerpt constitutes Chambers's treatment of the other two.
6. Held in the Roman church of St. John Lateran, the council was the last of five going under that name. It was in session from 1512 to 1517.
7. Students studying for holy orders, theology students.

immortality may be a citizen of Utopia. In life, and in death, every true Utopian has a firm trust in the communion of saints.

So that, in the eyes of More's friends, Erasmus or Peter Giles, *Utopia* is a striking defence of a vital tenet of the Christian faith. More will not tolerate the ambiguous formula: 'As an orthodox Catholic I believe in immortality; as a philosopher I doubt.' Reason and philosophy teach the Utopian to affirm that he is somehow in touch with the souls of the noble dead, mighty overseers whose presence encourages him to do his duty the more courageously.

Thus here we find More in *Utopia* opposing the scepticism of his age, precisely as we have seen him opposing its Machiavellian statecraft. And so thoroughly is *Utopia* a book of the hour, that here again More seems to be making a comment on a book which he had never seen. For it was in the very same November of 1516, in which Peter Giles was writing the dedicatory epistle of *Utopia*, that the professor of Philosophy at Bologna, Pomponazzi, published his famous treatise on the Immortality of the Soul. Pomponazzi submitted to the Church in all matters of faith, but, as a philosopher, he stubbornly upheld his doubt as to the doctrine of immortality.[8]

Therefore More's *Utopia*, among other things, is a contribution to this current controversy. More attacks the enemy in their philosophical camp, and makes his heathen Utopians into unexpected allies of the Catholic faith with regard to this great dogma—and, as we shall see later, with regard to other things as well.

But the imminent problem was monasticism. There was an incompatibility between the declining spirit of the monastic common life, and the rising commercialism of the grasping 'new rich'. Within a quarter of a century commercialism was to destroy monasticism in England. More stands, as it were, at the crossways, and asks, 'Why not destroy commercialism? Is not the spirit of the common life really better worth preserving?' It is significant that *the religious houses are the one European institution which the Utopians are said to approve.*[9] And with reason, for in Utopia, though the rule of celibacy is necessarily absent, the monastic idea is at work. The Utopian State is as sumptuous as many a religious house was. But the Utopian, like the monk or friar, may possess nothing. Everyone in Utopia must wear the common habit (in a letter to Erasmus we shall find More calling it Franciscan).[1] There are four varieties,

---

8. Pietro Pomponazzi's treatise *On the Immortality of the Soul* is handily available in *The Renaissance Philosophy of Man*, edited by Ernst Cassirer, Paul Oskar Kristeller, and John Herman Randall Jr. (Chicago and London: The University of Chicago Press, 1948). For Giles's dedicatory letter to Busleyden, see p. 129 above.

9. Cf. p. 85.

1. St. Thomas More, *Selected Letters*, edited by Elizabeth Frances Rogers (New Haven and London: Yale University Press, 1961), p. 85.

for men and women, married and unmarried. 'The cloaks of the
Utopians are all of one colour, and that is the natural colour of the
wool.'[2] Their hours of work, of recreation, the very games they may
play, are all regulated. There are no foolish and pernicious games
like dice. Instead, the Utopians have two games, one of which is
intended to teach mathematics, and the other to teach morals. The
Utopians eat in refectories, beginning every dinner and supper by
reading something pertaining to good manners and virtue. Talk at
table is initiated and directed by the elders, who graciously encourage the younger married people to join in the discussion, by turning
it into a kind of oral examination. As for the men below twenty-two
and the girls below eighteen: they serve, or else stand by, in marvel-
lous silence, watching their elders eat and talk.[3]

In much of this, More is perhaps joking; it was his way to utter his
jests with such a solemn face as to puzzle his own household.[4] But,
underneath More's fun, was a creed as stern as that of Dante, just as,
underneath his gold chain, was the shirt of hair. And, quite certainly,
the ideal of *Utopia* is discipline, not liberty. It is influenced by some
of the most severe disciplines the world has ever known. Through
Plato's *Republic* it goes back to the barrack life of a Spartan warrior;
through More's own experience to the life of a Charterhouse monk.[5]
And the discipline of Utopia is enforced rigidly, even ferociously. If
the Utopian attempts to break the laws of his native land, there is the
penalty of bondage, and, if that fails, of death. We have seen that
even to speak of State affairs, except at the licensed place and hour,
is punishable in Utopia with death,[6] lest permission to discuss politics might lead to revolution. Has any State, at any time, carried terrorism quite so far?

Many framers of ideal commonwealths have shirked the question
of compulsion, by imagining their citizens to have all become moral
overnight. More does not choose this easy way. He recognizes that
there will be a minority, to whom higher motives do not appeal. For
them, there is penal servitude; if that fails, death.

But no great State can be founded on terrorism. For the mass of
its citizens, Utopia is founded on religious enthusiasm. Faith in God,
and in the immortal destiny of the human soul, supplies the driving

---

2. On Utopian clothes, see pp. 45, 48 above.
3. Utopian men and women marry at the ages of twenty-two and eighteen, respectively
   (see p. 71 above); up to that age, boys and girls wait on tables in the communal dining
   halls or, if not old or strong enough for that, stand by silently (p. 52 above).
4. According to the biography by his great-grandson Cresacre More.
5. Roper reports that as a young man More tried out the life of the strictest monastic
   order, the Carthusians: "he gave himself to devotion and prayer in the Charterhouse of
   London, religiously living there without vow about four years" (*Two Early Tudor Lives*,
   p. 198).
6. On Chambers's error here, see p. 172, n. 2 above.

power which is to quench human passion and human greed.[7] Based on religion, Utopia is supported by a belief in the dignity of manual labour. Even rulers and magistrates, although legally exempt, share in this work as an example to others.[8] So a six-hours' day suffices, and the rest of the time is free for those intellectual and artistic pursuits in which, to the Utopians, pleasure consists.[9] But religion is the basis of all.

Now a monk of to-day, Dom Ursmer Berlière, of the Abbey of Maredsous, has pointed out how at the beginning of the Middle Ages, monasticism, as St. Benedict shaped it, gave a pattern to the State. St. Benedict's monastery 'was a little State, which could serve as a model for the new Christian society which was arising from the fusion of the conquered and conquering races—a little State which had for its basis, religion; for its support, the honour given to work; for its crown a new intellectual and artistic culture.'[1] The writer was not thinking of *Utopia*. I do not know if he had ever read it. But, at the end of the Middle Ages, we find More depicting a State founded on just these things: the common life, based on religion; honour given to manual labour; intellectual and artistic culture. However far these things might sometimes be from monastic practice, the writer of *Utopia* could never have approved of the destruction of monasticism; he looked for its reform.

✻ ✻ ✻

We can only understand *Utopia* if we remember the Europe for which it was written; at home John Rastell preaching exploration to the More household; abroad the travels of Vespucci in every man's hands; Vespucci, who had found folk holding property in common, and not esteeming gold, pearls, or jewels.[2] (It is important to remember that the Inca empire of Peru, which in more than one detail had a likeness to Utopia, was not known till some fourteen years later; Cortes had not yet conquered Mexico.)

The problem of poverty and unemployment (destined in England to be aggravated by the dissolution of the Monasteries) was already a European one. Ten years after *Utopia*, More's friend Vives[3] wrote a tract on it. At the root of More's interest in colonization lies his pity for the unemployed labourers:

---

7. Cf. pp. 86–88 above.
8. See p. 47 above.
9. See pp. 45, 48 above.
1. *L'ordre monastique des origines au XIIᵉ siècle*, 2nd ed. (Paris, 1921), p. 45 [Chambers's note]. For St. Benedict's rule, see p. 112 above.
2. See pp. 120–21 above. The extraordinary John Rastell—historian, dramatist, printer, lawyer, would-be North American colonizer—was More's brother-in-law.
3. Juan Luis Vives (1492–1540), Spanish humanist, wrote prodigiously on a vast range of subjects.

'Poor silly[4] wretched souls; away they trudge out of their known
and accustomed houses; all their household stuff, being suddenly thrust out, they be constrained to sell it for a thing of
naught. And when they have, wandering about, soon spent
that, what can they do but steal, and then be hanged, or else go
about abegging. Whom no man will set awork, though they
never so willingly offer themselves thereto.'[5]

But the fact that *Utopia* belongs to its age does not mean that it is the
less epoch-making. Some things which may now seem commonplaces to us were less so then. It may seem quite natural to us that in
Utopia there should be no class distinctions. It was less obvious to a
scholar of the Renaissance. Plato's Commonwealths had been based
on class distinction. In the *Laws* the citizens fall into four classes.
In the *Republic*, also, there are classes, although so much attention
is given to the warrior class, and their common life, that we almost
forget the others. Plato is emphatic that every man should have one
job only, and he does not waste words on his artisans, except to urge
that they must be experts in their own business, and must stick to
it. The Middle Ages inherited the same idea of the State: ploughmen
and artisans to labour, clerks to pray and study, knights to fight. But
the Utopian citizen does all three things; he labours with his hands,
studies in his spare hours, and, though he hates warfare, is, at need,
a soldier.

It is noteworthy that, despite his admiration for Greek life and
thought, More did not build Utopia after the Hellenic pattern. His
free citizens are not a privileged class dependent on slave labour, nor
are his bondmen a distinct class. Bondage in Utopia is penal servitude—a humane substitute for the death penalty. The repentant
bondman is restored to freedom, the incorrigible bondman is slain.[6]
But the citizens themselves are all workers.

Finally the outstanding feature of *Utopia* is implied in the great
sentence with which Raphael ends his story:

> When I consider all these commonwealths which nowadays any-
> where do flourish, so God help me, I can perceive nothing but
> a conspiracy of rich men, procuring their own commodities
> under the name and title of the commonwealth.[7]

The Middle Ages had often been charitable to the poor, and More's
age had inherited vast charitable endowments. More altogether
approved of these endowments, and, later, we shall find him defend-

---

4. Pitiable; helpless.
5. Cf. p. 19 above. Here and elsewhere, Chambers silently omits phrases of Robinson's
   translation (though not so as to change the meaning of the passages).
6. See pp. 73–74 above.
7. Cf. p. 95 above. This is not in fact Hythloday's final sentence. "Commodities": advantages.

ing them against the fanaticism of reformers who wished to hand them over to a conspiracy of rich men procuring their own commodities under the title of the commonwealth.[8] But More's claim for *justice* goes far beyond medieval admonitions to charity. Its publication throughout Europe by the printing press marks an epoch.

RUSSELL AMES

[More the Social Critic][†]

More's *Utopia* expresses the various reforming purposes of the statesman, the lawyer, the merchant, the humanist, and the man of religion. These purposes were, of course, intertwined and overlapping as well as distinguishable. The middle class, in its inconsistent and only partly conscious campaign against feudalism, had the merchants as its chief economic power and the humanists as its ideological shock troops—with More active in both groups. The *Utopia*, incorporating many views acceptable to the London merchants, presented a program of social reform, and was, first of all, a humanist tract. Its form and spirit owed much to classical literature and to religious tradition, but its substance was contemporary and secular.

The hypothesis may be very seriously projected that the *Utopia* in every detail had a practical meaning in More's day. This is not to say that More was urging his contemporaries immediately to institute in their societies every practice of the Utopians. The hypothesis implies, rather, that those Utopian practices which were fantastic consistently indicated a practical line of conduct which would be understood by sympathetic readers.

R. W. Chambers, in the most notable of recent books on More, shows that many Utopian customs and ordinances directly reflect More's opinions of current problems, particularly religious problems. Chambers believes, however, that More often makes his Utopians do things which are not approved because the Utopians follow reason rather than the imperatives of the Christian religion. It is

---

8. Chambers refers to his later discussion (*Thomas More*, pp. 257–62) of More's opposition to proposals for the dissolution of monasteries and other religious institutions, including hospitals.

† From Russell Ames, "Introduction," *Citizen Thomas More and His Utopia* (Princeton, N.J.: Princeton University Press, 1949), pp. 8–21. Except where otherwise indicated, footnotes are by the editors.

   Around 1950, not one but two important books on *Utopia* emerged from Queens College in New York City. Ames, an English professor, produced the first; the second, by the historian J. H. Hexter, appeared three years later (see p. 190 below). During the gestation of the books, there was some polemic between their authors, but it is greatly softened in the final version of both works, and each man thanks the other in his preface for critiquing his book in manuscript. For Ames's major thesis, see p. 187 below.

more accurate to say that even when the Utopians depart from practices acceptable to Christianity, they do so in such a way as to indicate how a sixteenth century European should behave. Chambers feels that "The underlying thought of *Utopia* always is, *With nothing save Reason to guide them, the Utopians do this; and yet we Christian Englishmen, we Christian Europeans . . . !*"[1] This is certainly part of the meaning of Utopia; but it may be better phrased thus: *The Utopians, guided by Reason and also by their basically sound religion, have almost achieved a truly Christian ideal which they live by while we Christians do not.* In short, though More was limited by the necessities of keeping his fiction logical, consistent, and an adequate disguise for his attacks and proposals, he makes every effort within this framework to teach social and religious truth. The Utopians "joine unto the reasons of Philosophye certeyne principles taken oute of religion: wythoute the whyche . . . they thynke reason of it selfe weake and unperfecte."[2] The Utopians have more than reason to guide them, and are quite conscious of the fact; their only real difference from Europeans is that they actually follow reason, which leads them closer and closer to Christian religion and to ideal Christian behavior.[3]

The hypothesis outlined above suggests the following type of analysis. Utopian children confess their misdeeds to their parents.[4] This does not mean that More advises English children to stop confessing to priests. It means two quite different things: first, the Utopians, though not in contact with Christianity, by reason and natural religion found their way to confession, and this proves that the confessional as ordained by the church is both a godly and a rational institution; secondly, the Utopian practice suggests that a virtuous Utopian parent is a better confessor than a corrupt European priest, and that the latter had better reform himself. Thus, the institution of confession is upheld, and at the same time reform is advocated. Similarly, when we see that in *Utopia* many religions are permitted, we should not assume that More advocates the dismemberment of European Christianity and the institution of many new religions. More does mean, however, in these years before Luther appeared on his horizon, that true faith will peacefully conquer false ideas, that bigoted repressions may halt that revival of true religion which Colet[5] and Erasmus were attempting, and that it is unchristian for Portuguese gold-hunters to drive Indians into church with the sword.

1. *Thomas More*, p. 128 (p. 170 above).
2. Ames quotes *Utopia* from Robinson's translation (see p. 169, n. 8 above). In the present edition, the passage appears on pp. 59–60.
3. Budé wrote that the Utopians "have adopted Christian usages both in public and in private" [Ames's note]. See p. 138 above.
4. See p. 91 above.
5. On Colet, see p. 152, n. 1 above.

More's general discussion of religion in Utopia is meant to prove, not the superiority of agnosticism to Christianity, but that Christianity has nothing to fear from peace, freedom, and rational criticism.

The meaning of More's apparent advocacy of communism—a question more closely related to the main interest of this study—can be understood through a similar type of analysis. It is improbable, though possible, that More was a practical advocate of communism in England, however much he *may* have been drawn to the theory of it. The lesson of Utopian communism is, however, that economic conditions are the cause of social evils and that the English ruling classes will not make themselves happier and wealthier by overworking, dispossessing, hanging, or failing to employ the poor, or even by exhorting the poor with pious phrases to a better life. In such futile ways they will only impoverish their country. Instead, they must revive husbandry and cloth-working, improve law and government, and extend trade. Most critics of *Utopia* have spent so much time trying to prove either that communism won't work, or that More was not a communist, that they have ignored the immediate and practical significance of his economic criticism.

Many other aspects of the *Utopia* need detailed rather than abstract attention. More the lawyer, as well as More the saint, the humanist, and the statesman, wrote the book. His actual practice as a lawyer clearly led him to the severest criticism of legal trickery and injustice. His legal studies, however, probably gave him part of his social ideals. The Roman law, to which he had some attachment as a member of a society of Roman lawyers, did support the claims of absolute monarchy, but it also, in the Justinian code, proposed a harmonious commonwealth of nations[6] which was an ideal of More's both in Utopia and in England. John Rastell, More's brother-in-law, in his preface to a *Book of Assizes* which he printed in 1513, praises the function of good laws as a curb upon greed: "Wealth, power and glory are . . . in themselves evil things, since they cannot be achieved except at the cost of impoverishment, subjection and humiliation. They cannot, for that reason, constitute the commonweal."[7]

Similarly, the influence of primitive Christian communism on *Utopia* has not been emphasized, though *Utopia* itself emphasizes it.[8] The direct effect of the Gospels must have been strong. Even more

6. Ames cites J. N. Figgis, *Studies of Political Thought from Gerson to Grotius, 1414–1625*, 2nd ed. (Cambridge: Cambridge University Press, 1931), p. 9. "A society of Roman lawyers": i.e., Doctors' Commons, a London association of practitioners and aficionados of canon law and civil law. The latter, in contrast to the English common law, was based on Roman law. "Justinian code": the codification of laws under the emperor Justinian (482–565 C.E.) was one of the great and enduring achievements of the late Roman Empire.
7. Ames quotes the abbreviated paraphrase in A. W. Reed, *Early Tudor Drama* (London: Methuen & Co. Ltd., 1926), p. 207.
8. See p. 85 above.

important was the republican, and more or less radical economic
character of northern humanism. From this, which is not the main
subject of the present study, probably flows the major influence on
Utopia.

That the first book refers in a general way to contemporary social
evils is, of course, obvious to all readers. That the whole work refers
frequently to specific events with which More was often personally
acquainted, is not so well known.

Some of the more obvious examples can show how specific these
references were. Hythlodaye, telling why he will not take service as
an adviser to princes, asked More how the king of France would
respond if advised to govern his own land well and give up foreign
invasion, and More admitted that the king would not be pleased
with the advice.[9] This is no general, classical attack on war but a
definite reference to the invasion of Italy by Francis I in the preceding year (1515) which culminated in the victory of Marignano in
September. Clearly the advice against invasion applied equally
well to Henry VIII's invasions of France (1512–1514). Hythlodaye's
description of the way kings are advised to get money[1] perfectly
describes the recent practices of Henry VII: juggling the value of
currency, feigning war and taxing for it, reviving old laws to collect
new fines, establishing new regulations to sell exemption from
them. Particularly, the attack on the revival of old Crown privileges
points to Henry VII's collection of dues for the knighting of his
dead son Arthur, which More resisted in the parliament of 1504.[2] It
was noted above that shafts directed against Francis I also struck
Henry VIII: similarly criticism of Henry VII applied in part to
Henry VIII. Both the French and the Utopian practice of bribing
and corrupting enemy populations suggested the intrigues of Henry
VIII and his minister Dacre, who sowed treason among the Scotch
lords. It is reasonable to assume that every item of criticism in *Utopia*
recalled to well-informed readers precise events in current history,
many of which may not be easy to identify today.

More's connections with the merchants of London, with the Court,
and with humanists, kept him familiar also with more remote continental affairs and even with some African, Asian, and American
conditions. Reports at this time from Sir Robert Wingfield, English
ambassador to the Emperor Maximilian, are rich in references to
the politics of eastern Europe, the Turkish threat, and Italian conditions. The direct attack on international intrigues in the first

---

9. See p. 30 above.
1. See pp. 30–31 above.
2. Whether More was a member of the parliament of 1504 is not certain: the sole authority for the claim is the biography by his son-in-law William Roper, written a half-
century later.

book of *Utopia*, as well as the ironic attack in the second book,[3] were unusually apropos in these two years (1515–1516) when the book was being written. International relations were peculiarly unstable. Peace had just come in 1514 after England's successful wars against France. In 1515 France invaded Italy and won an unexpected victory which sharply changed the balance of forces. The new peace following was of the most fluid character, and the diplomatic correspondence of the time shows that all cats were ready to jump in any direction at any moment.

The influence of foreign events and conditions on Utopia has hardly been mentioned by its students, though Chambers discusses the problem of the unity of Christendom against the Turk, and points out, concerning More's embassy of 1515, that "Everywhere in *Utopia* we can trace the influence of these [Flemish] foreign scholars and foreign men of affairs, as well as of the civilization of the noble Flemish cities."[4] This was probably the most important continental influence, for More did not travel much elsewhere. It is noted by J. H. Lupton, who contrasts London with the towns of Flanders.[5]

Also important among the influences on *Utopia* were ideals of city and gild[6] life, and a popular English devotion to the common weal. It is surprising that Kautsky, a socialist, neglects these, though he pays general tribute to the liberty-loving sentiments of the English and emphasizes his belief that More, in peculiar English conditions, differed from other humanists in his concern for the people. The youthful radicalism of John Rastell, More's brother-in-law, and his ideal of the commonwealth expressed in legal theory,[7] the common weal advocated by economists like Clement Armstrong[8]—all these, mentioned below, are native parallels to *Utopia*, and express its practical content, rather than its literary form as Plato's *Republic* does.

To summarize the problem of the general character of *Utopia*: rather abstract polemics over religion and communism, divorced from the detailed events of More's experience, have obscured *Utopia's* nature as an effort at practical social reform. The obscurity has been lighted up by Chambers, Seebohm, and Kautsky more than by other writers.

3. See pp. 28–29 and 76–77 above.
4. *Thomas More*, p. 120.
5. *Utopia*, edited by J. H. Lupton (Oxford: Clarendon Press, 1895), pp. xxix–xxx.
6. I.e., guild. Guilds were associations of merchants or craftsmen, formed to protect and promote their common interests.
7. Preface to the *Book of Assizes* (1513) [Ames's note].
8. "A treatise concerninge the Staple and the commodities of the realme" (ca. 1519–35), in R. H. Tawney and Eileen Power, eds., *Tudor Economic Documents*, 3 vols. (London: Longmans, Green and Co., 1924), 3:90–114. A staple was, by royal appointment, a port town containing a body of merchants granted exclusive right to purchase certain classes of goods for export. The term was also sometimes applied to the merchant body itself.

The two best books on More, those by Kautsky and Chambers, may now be given a general criticism. This is none too grateful a task, for the critic's sword is very likely to develop a reverse edge when he also attempts an interpretation of More and his *Utopia*. More's experience was so rich and varied, the society in which he lived so fast changing and contradictory in nature, his book so disguised in meaning, so many-sided, constructed on so many levels of reference, that almost any foolish speculation concerning *Utopia* is likely to have a little truth in it, and almost any well-founded hypothesis is bound to be incomplete and somewhat one-sided. A few claims and excuses can be made for the present study. It does not pretend to exhaust the subject: it does not concentrate on that aspect of *Utopia* which the present writer considers central—its nature as a pamphlet written to promote humanistic, Erasmian social reform. Secondly, this writer is quite certain that he has felt little or no compulsion to dress More in his own political and religious clothing. Lastly, this study consciously employs throughout the weakest of all forms of argument—analogy. The *Utopia* being itself the best evidence of what More was thinking when he wrote it, at the same time hiding much of his thought within many levels of meaning, interpretation must proceed by probability, by hopeful comparisons.

Kautsky's study, *Thomas More and His Utopia*, is the only one which gives full attention to the book as an expression of the views of the English middle class, particularly of the London merchants. It is a brilliant work but, unfortunately, little read. Kautsky, in much of his general historical view and in his detailed analysis of *Utopia*, is sound and flexible. Occasionally, however, his generalizations are loose and his applications of them mechanical. On a number of important points new materials and more concrete analysis suggest changes of emphasis, and even reversal of his interpretation.

Most of the faulty generalizations in Kautsky's work are rooted in what this study holds to be a mistaken view of the stage in historical development which England had reached in the early sixteenth century. Kautsky maintains that "In More's time capitalism was just beginning to gain the upper hand over the industry and agriculture of England. Its domination had not lasted long enough to effect a technical revolution. . . ."[9] It will be seen in Chapter I below that this description would probably apply better to the eighteenth century, better certainly to the end of the sixteenth century than to its beginning. Capitalism was yet a long way from *dominating* English society, but Kautsky's belief that it was doing so leads him to see the central conflict of the time as that between capitalism

---

9. Karl Kautsky, *Thomas More and His Utopia*, p. 205. On this book, see above, p. 157 and the dagger note on p. 162.

and the workers of England,[1] rather than between feudalism and capitalism.

Perhaps, as we all tend to do, Kautsky has transferred his own dominant interest in his own time into the life of the past. Whatever the reason for it, his idea that capitalism was dominant and feudalism completely broken[2] causes him to view princely absolutism as almost identical in interests with capital, the humanists as universally supporters of monarchy insofar as they had any political views, the English nobility as completely subservient to the Crown, the London citizens as the chief props of Tudor absolutism and the only rival of its power,[3] etc.

By claiming that the great landowners were at least temporarily helpless—as a result of the Wars of the Roses[4]—Kautsky tends, perhaps unconsciously, to consider the Tudor monarchy a great power in and of itself rather than a fulcrum for pressures, though occasionally he notes the rather feeble influence of various groups on government.[5]

Only one group is said to have had any substantial influence. "In More's time," Kautsky writes, "the citizens of London were a power for which the English kings had more respect than for the Church, the nobles, the peasants, and the country towns," the masters of London were "the actual masters of the country," and the "merchants possessed the greatest power in London."[6] When we add Kautsky's implication that More was the leading representative of the London merchants,[7] More appears almost as the uncrowned king of England.

Of course, Kautsky does not mean to imply just this. He notes that though "the middle classes could not be bribed or intimidated . . . their representatives could; while the king could have members of Parliament who displeased him executed for high treason." Also, he calls the London citizens "the decisive power in the realm *next to* [italics mine] the monarchy." And he does, finally, in a round-about way, suggest that the nobility had decisive power, saying that "in More's time the English nobility and clergy were the submissive servants of the monarchy, to which they imparted an absolute power such as it then possessed in no other country of Europe."[8] Aside from questions of its accuracy in detail, this statement is a paradox

---

1. Kautsky, pp. 168–69, 171 (reprinted on pp. 164–66 above).
2. Ibid., p. 119.
3. Ames refers successively to Kautsky, pp. 17; 99 (incorrect: should be pp. 62–63, 70); 115–16, 118; 123.
4. Ibid., p. 116.
5. Ibid., pp. 120–24.
6. Ibid., p. 121.
7. Ibid., pp. 140, 142.
8. The three quotations are from, respectively, Kautsky, pp. 124, 123, 118.

lodged at the very center of our problem. A class capable of impart-
ing absolute power cannot, in any logic, actually be feeble and servile. If the English nobility made the Crown more powerful than
London, then the nobles were the ruling class, even if not a very
strong one, and were as a group, in the last analysis, the masters
rather than the servants of monarchy.

However wrong or right Kautsky may be, he has been alone in
discussing such fundamental questions as a prelude to interpretation of *Utopia*, and the meaning of *Utopia* waits on our answer to
the question of the precise character of European, especially
English, society at the time the book was written. * * *

If it is held that the period of absolute monarchy has generally
been, almost to its end, feudal rather than capitalist, a number of
Kautsky's less sweeping generalizations also become suspect. Emphasis then shifts from merchant and humanist satisfaction with the
status quo to emphasis upon middle class discontent with monarchy
and sympathy with oppressed peasants and craftsmen. At least, this
seems the proper emphasis for the "advanced" elements in the middle class, and surely, at the time he wrote *Utopia*, More expressed
very advanced ideas which caused Kautsky to say: "We see how revolutionary *Utopia* was. . . ."[9]

It would be a mistake, however, to assume that Kautsky is crudely
inconsistent. He is far too conscious of the actual contradictory
nature of things for that, and it is difficult to suggest error in his
work without ignoring some telling correction of it. Nevertheless,
an attempt should be made to correct some of his interpretations—
partly to call his study forcefully to the attention of students of
More who may have missed it, and partly to warn them of the type
of theoretical weakness they may find in it. A few examples follow.

Though Kautsky recognizes that the London citizens were in
frequent opposition to the early Tudor Crown, he says that "scarcely
any class in the sixteenth century regarded the monarchy as more
necessary than did the merchants," and he says of capital that
"order was its most important vital element." Yet later he remarks
that "the vital principle of capitalism is free competition . . . and
therefore the abolition of caste distinctions."[1] Now it is certainly
true that mercantile capitalists needed many of the freedoms which
monarchial order established for them, and it is also true that the
essence of later, fully developed capitalism was free competition.
But to take only one side of this contradiction, then to ignore further contradictions within that side, and to draw from it the basic
political views of Thomas More—he was "an opponent of every

9. Ibid., p. 242.
1. The first two quotations are from Kautsky, p. 143, the third from p. 211.

popular movement and a champion of constitutional monarchy"[2]—is doubtful logic to say the least. It will be seen below that the more merchants loved order, the more they were devoted to and parasitic upon feudalism; that the lesser nobility were more devoted to the Crown than the merchants were; and that the merchants were more jealous of their own order of monopoly within the towns than of the king's order. As for More's politics, Kautsky repeats his opinion toward the end of his book and then partially corrects it: "It is characteristic of More that he could not imagine such a community [Utopia] without a prince. It is true the latter has nothing to do except to avoid coming under suspicion of striving for absolute power."[3] That is, Utopia's prince is not a prince in the Tudor sense, or in much of any other sense. Actually, he is elected by elected representatives of the people; the people themselves nominate him; and he may be deposed legally. If this may be called a species of bourgeois prince, it is so to the point of extinction. And there is, as a matter of fact, good reason to believe that the *princeps* of Utopia is a local city official, and that that republic has no monarch at all.[4]

Thus, it may be argued, the theoretical trend of Kautsky's thought drives him into presumable error. Other such interpretations will be discussed in appropriate places below.

Next to Kautsky's, the most valuable modern work on More is that by R. W. Chambers. Chambers, oddly enough, barely mentions Kautsky's book and substantially ignores everything it says, but his comments on *Utopia* are an implied refutation of Kautsky. Indeed, the two may be described as precise opposites, both in the form and content of their work. Kautsky sees More as a bourgeois, critical of rising capitalism, who could leap over an era to grasp the essentials of socialism. Chambers sees More as a bourgeois, critical of rising capitalism, who dreamed of reforming society in accord with the best elements of medieval thought and practice. Both approaches are based on substantial particles of truth, but it is the main thesis of this study that More was a bourgeois, critical of rising capitalism and especially of declining feudalism, who hoped to reform society along bourgeois-republican lines in the immediate future, and that to this aim his medieval and socialist ideas were subordinate. Kautsky sees the life and thought of More as contradictory in nature; Chambers sees them as a unity. The underlying social theories in Kautsky's work are clearly stated, but in Chambers' they are not. Kautsky's interest is primarily intellectual and social; Chambers' interest is mainly personal and spiritual. The one writes bald

2. Ibid., p. 206.
3. Ibid., p. 233.
4. In fact there is small reason to believe anything else (see above, p. 43 and n. 8).

historical exposition, the other charming informative essays and episodes. Kautsky has written a social interpretation of *Utopia*, and Chambers has created a kind of symphony in which the benign character of More is the theme. The reason for these differences is, of course, the fact that life made Kautsky a socialist and Chambers a conservative but tolerant medievalist.

Since Chambers' thought has been influenced by high church and liberal-capitalist English culture, it is not surprising that he tries to reconcile what may be called liberal and authoritarian, progressive and conservative elements in More's life and thought. The reconciliations made are quite plausible, for Chambers' book is scholarly and very skillfully written, and it is hard to resist the charm of his modesty, his generosity to opponents, and his fine idealism.

Chambers does not recognize any conflicts among More's ideas and attitudes, though he mentions many facts which, if made neighbors, fall to quarreling. His purposes, however, declared and implied, demand a harmony among the facts. What, precisely, are these purposes? His undeclared purpose seems to be to prove that More was conservative, medieval, in religion, politics, and economics. His declared purpose is to depict More for non-Catholic readers "not only as a martyr . . . but also as a great European statesman . . . [whose] farsighted outlook was neglected amid the selfish despotisms of his age . . . [and whose] words . . . acts and . . . sufferings were consistently, throughout life, based upon principles which have survived him."[5] It may be noted, incidentally, that these principles are nowhere in the book precisely described, but are only suggested by the goodness, kindness, and tolerance which the reader finds on each page.

Chambers sets himself a difficult task. It seems that he must prove that More was, in all ways and times, orthodox in his Catholicism, limited by the ideals of the past, yet spacious and prophetic in his social vision. If Chambers had openly faced certain contradictions in his task, and had made them a part of his hypothesis, his account of More would be at the same time less rigid and less fragmentary and would have in it more of the growth, flow, and struggle of real life. Erasmus said (and Chambers mentions this at the beginning of his book) that he felt incompetent to portray Thomas More's many-sided character.[6]

Most controversy concerning More has, however, centered on this question of his consistency. Liberal historians have found him an unfortunate example of that perennial phenomenon—the liberal in youth turned conservative with age—and Chambers has correctly

5. *Thomas More*, p. 15.
6. See pp. 144–45 above.

pointed out that this is nonsense, for More was a good thirty-eight years old when he wrote *Utopia*. But such historians are able to point out, in their turn, that More opposed religious coercion in *Utopia* and later, as chancellor, not only persecuted heretics but defended such persecution in theory. Such historians, being philosophical idealists, assume that views should never change, regardless of changing conditions: if one is against war, he should oppose all wars; if one is for tolerance, he should tolerate anyone and everything. Chambers, also a philosophical idealist, also believes that one should not change his views, and claims that More did not. It is probable, however, that More did change his views on religious tolerance gradually, after 1516, under the pressure of such events as the rise of Lutheranism, the knights' and peasants' wars in Germany—with the general decline of reformers' hopes in a period of sharpening social crisis. Chambers seeks to show that More was neither very liberal in *Utopia* concerning religion and politics nor bigoted and cruel in later years when he dealt with heretics. These two purposes lead him to some rather extraordinary evasions and confusions which merit special attention as extreme examples of the central weakness of a valuable study. The facts in this controversy seem clear: More did establish full toleration of all religions in Utopia, punishing only atheists; and he did, later, not only approve but also bring about the execution of heretics. Chambers, perhaps unconsciously, has blurred and obscured these facts to the point of giving precisely the opposite *impression*—that freedom of religion did not really exist in Utopia, and that More never harmed a heretic.[7]

That Chambers cannot successfully reconcile, in the person of More, even the best elements of feudal, capitalist, and socialist thought—and it must be admitted that More does express something of each in *Utopia* alone—should not blind us to the virtues of his work. Chambers makes some acute criticisms of those liberal historians who admire Henry VIII, and a whole generation of heartless pirate capitalists, because of their gifts to "progress" and "freedom." Certainly he was right, in part, in seeing More's social criticism as a medieval protest against a horrifying "New Order." But More was not a true feudal philosopher, such as we find today in Lin Yutang[8] or Gandhi. The New Order he opposed was not really new but a revival, an intensification, a harsh reorganization of the Old Order—just as fascism, in our day, is a spuriously "new" organization of moribund social forces. Thus it is seen that our basic criticism of Kautsky and Chambers is the same. From opposed points of view both see the

---

7. Ames discusses these confusions in an appendix to his book, pp. 179–81.
8. A Chinese writer, translator, and inventor whose literary works in both Chinese and English brought him great popularity and influence in the mid-20th century.

brutal aspects of rising capitalism as the object of More's critical thought. An attempt will be made in the following pages to show that More criticized decadent feudalism in the interests of the "best" aspects of rising capitalism, medieval and Renaissance.

J. H. HEXTER

The Roots of Utopia and All Evil[†]

We are better equipped to discover what those ends[1] are now that we know that bond labor, abolition of markets and money, and restriction of wants by enforced community of consumption are of a piece with the abolition of private property and profit and with the obligation to toil—indispensable motifs in the total pattern of More's best state of the commonwealth. A society where wants are tightly bound up and where the penal power of the state is made daily conspicuous by men in heavy gold chains[2]—this is no ideal society of Modern Socialism. Altogether missing from *Utopia* is that happy anarchist last chapter of modern socialism intended to justify all the struggle, all the suffering, all the constraint that we must undergo in order to reach it.[3] *Utopia* does not end in an eschatological dream.

[†] From *More's Utopia: The Biography of an Idea* (Princeton, N.J.: Princeton University Press, 1952), pp. 71–81 (Part 2, sect. 8). Reprinted by permission. Except where otherwise indicated, footnotes are by the editors—though for the most part the notes simply replace Hexter's page references to passages of *Utopia* with the corresponding page numbers in the present edition.
      Hexter (1910–1996), who ended his distinguished academic career as the John M. Olin Professor of the History of Freedom at Washington University in St. Louis, was the single most penetrating and influential writer on *Utopia* of the past half century, (1) making important contributions to our understanding of More's process of composition (see, e.g., p. 13, n. 5 above); (2) showing how the "Dialogue of Counsel" (Hexter's widely accepted term for the debate of Book I) marks a watershed moment in the development of social analysis, an advance deriving from More's "capacity to see past the symptoms to the sources of trouble, * * * his grasp of the intricacy and ramification of social structure and social action, * * * his skill in working out expedients to meet particular social problems" (*More's "Utopia,"* p. 64); and (3), in his analysis of Book II, arguing that the Utopian commonwealth was constructed as an elaborate system of institutions calculated to inhibit—nearly eradicate—the expression of fallen humanity's strong propensity to sin and, above all, to the foremost of the traditional Seven Deadly Sins, Pride. The success of the small book excerpted here led to Hexter's being made co-editor (with Edward Surtz, S.J.: see p. 202 below) of the massive edition of *Utopia* in the Yale *Complete Works of St. Thomas More*. In Hexter's 110-page section of the Yale introduction, he revisited the topics of his earlier treatment with even deeper acumen: any serious student of *Utopia* should at some point read and digest this second tour de force.
1. Referring to the final sentences of the book's preceding section: "What appear to be the economic institutions of Utopia—community of property, abolition of markets and money—are economic in form but not in purpose. Their strictly economic function is incidental. In More's eyes, as we shall see, they serve not economic but other and higher ends."
2. I.e., the chains borne by slaves and criminals in Utopia (p. 55 above).
3. As part of the movement to the final stage in the development of communism, there would be, Marx thought, a "withering away of the state."

More simply did not believe that all the evil men do can be ascribed to the economic arrangements of society, and that those evils and the very potentiality for evil will vanish when the economic arrangements are rectified and set on a proper footing. More believed no such thing because in his view of men and their affairs there was a strong and ineradicable streak of pessimism. More's pessimism was ineradicable because it was part and parcel of his Christian faith. He knew surely, as a profoundly Christian man he had to know, that the roots of evil run far too deep in men to be destroyed by a mere rearrangement of the economic organization of society. His residue of pessimism leads More to provide even "the best state of the commonwealth" with an elaborate complement of laws drastically limiting the scope given to individual human desires and to arm its government with extensive and permanent powers of coercion. Although he was convinced that the institutions of the society that he knew provided the occasions for the evils he saw, he did not—and as a profoundly orthodox Christian he could not—believe that the evils were totally ascribable to the institutions. His probings led him to believe that the roots of the evils of sixteenth century Europe, though nourished in the rich black earth of an acquisitive society, were moistened by the inexhaustible stream of sin.

Underlying the whole catalogue of evils of his time he finds one or another of several sins. Luxury, gluttony, envy, vanity, vainglory, lust, hypocrisy, debauchery, sloth, bad faith and the rest all find an easy vent in the Christendom he knew, whose institutions seemed to him as if contrived to activate human wickedness and anesthetize human decency. Yet More does not give equal attention to all the kinds of sin; the realm of evil is not a republic of equals. The Deadly Sins themselves are not on an even footing in the Utopian Discourse. Gluttony and Anger get short shrift, Envy is there only as a counterfoil to a deadlier sin,[4] and Lust, that whipping boy of our feeble latter-day Christianity, receives but a passing glance. The great triumvirate that rules the empire of evil, are Sloth, Greed, and Pride.

It is sloth that in More's day leads stout fellows able to work to enter into the idle bands of serving men; it is sloth that leads them to fill with drinking, gaming, and brawling the hours they ought to spend in honest toil.[5] It is sloth, the avoidance of labor, that the Utopians punish with bondage.[6] Yet although to More's mind idleness was among the most destructive cankers on the social body, although it preoccupied him as much as any other problem, he did not blame that idleness wholly on sloth. The lazy good-for-nothing

4. I.e., pride, the foremost of the Seven Deadly Sins of medieval tradition. (Hexter names all seven here.)
5. See pp. 17–19, 46 above.
6. See p. 53 above.

scum that the great leave in their wake is conjured into being by the great men themselves, who provide their followers with the means of debauchery and vice. And it is not sloth but a greater sin that leads the great men to foster the infection of idleness in the body of the commonwealth.

Even above sloth in the hierarchy of sin lie greed and pride. In dealing with these two paramount sins More's Christian faith stood him in good stead. It provided him with a basic insight into the underlying pattern of evil, a pattern somewhat obscured by our modern climate of opinion. For he did not believe that greed and pride were on a parity with each other as sources of the social ills of his day, or that they offered equal obstacles to the establishment of the Good Society; but at this point it requires special care to read More's meaning right. The best known passage of *Utopia*, the attack on enclosure in the Dialogue section, is directed against the "inordinate and insatiable covetousness" of landlords and engrossers.[7] Much of the Discourse section,[8] moreover, is taken up with variation after variation on a single theme; "The love of money is the root of all evil." Now the inordinate desire for riches is greed or avarice, and from this it would seem to follow almost as a syllogism that greed was what More discovered as a result of his social analysis to be the fount and origin of the sickness of his own society. Yet it is not so. Greed was a sin, revolting enough in More's eyes; but it is not a sufficiently attractive vice to stand alone. Men are impelled to it not by its charms, but, like other animals, by fear of want. *"Why,"* Hythloday asks, *"should anyone consider seeking superfluities, when he is certain that he will never lack anything? Indeed in all kinds of living things it is . . . fear of want that creates greed and rapacity."*[9] It is one of the perverse traits of the regime of private property, where each must make provision for and look after his own, that an amiable regard for his kin continually tempts man to the sin of avarice.[1]

But this sin, certain to beset a pecuniary society, is essentially a parasite on the insecurity inherent in that kind of society and has no roots of its own. It is sustained rather by the institutional roots of the property system itself. Even the rich, More suggests, realize this, and are "not ignorant how much better it were to lack no necessary thing than to abound with overmuch superfluity, to be rid out of innumerable cares and troubles, than to be *bound down* by great riches."[2] If avarice were the great danger to society the Utopian

---

7. Monopolists. See pp. 19–20 above.
8. I.e., Book II, which Hexter calls "The Discourse of Utopia."
9. Cf. p. 50 above. Hexter quotes *Utopia* from the Robinson translation (see p. 169, n. 8 above), modernizing the spelling. But whenever he finds Robinson's version inaccurate or (to a modern reader) unintelligible, he makes his own translation, placing it in italics.
1. See pp. 93–94 above.
2. See p. 96 above.

commonwealth could be instituted along lines far less rigorous and repressive than those More prescribes. But avarice is not all. Fear of want makes for greed in all living creatures, including man; in man alone greed has a second set of roots deeper in his nature even than fear. For men only of God's creatures are greedy out of "pride alone, which counts it a glorious thing to pass and excel others in the superfluous and vain ostentation of things."[3] Here, I think, lies the heart of the matter. Deep in the soul of the society of More's day, because it was deep in the soul of all men, was the monster Pride, distilling its terrible poison and dispatching it to all parts of the social body to corrupt, debilitate, and destroy them. Take but a single example: Why must the poor in Europe be "wearied from early in the morning to late in the evening with continual work like laboring and toiling beasts" leading a life "worse than the miserable and wretched condition of bondmen, which nevertheless is almost everywhere the life of workmen and artificers?"[4] Human beings are consigned to this outrageous slavery merely to support the enormous mass of the idle, and to perform the "vain and superfluous" work that serves "only for riotous superfluity and unhonest pleasure."[5] What feeds the unhonest pleasure that men derive from luxuries and vanities, or to use the phrase of a modern moralist, from conspicuous consumption and conspicuous waste? It is pride. Many men drudge out their lives making vain and needless things because other men "count themselves nobler for the smaller or finer thread of wool"[6] their garb is made of, because "they think the *value* of their own persons is thereby greatly increased. And therefore the honor, which in a coarse gown they dare not have looked for, they require, as it were of duty, for their finer gowns' sake. And if they be passed by without reverence, they take it angrily and disdainfully."[7] The same sickness of soul shows itself in "pride in vain and unprofitable honors." "For what natural or true pleasure doest thou take of another man's bare head or bowed knees? Will this ease the pain of thy knees or remedy the frenzy of thy head? In this image of counterfeit pleasure they be of a marvelous madness *who flatter and applaud themselves with the notion of their own nobility.*"[8] It is to support this prideful and conceited "opinion of nobility" that men must be treated like beasts of burden to keep idlers in luxury. The great mass of wastrels bearing down on Christendom are maintained to minister to the pride and vainglory of the great. Such are

3. See p. 50 above.
4. See p. 45 above.
5. See p. 47 above.
6. See p. 57 above.
7. See p. 62 above.
8. Ibid.

"the flock of stout bragging rushbucklers,"[9] "the great . . . train of idle and loitering servingmen," that "rich men, especially all landed men, which commonly be called gentlemen and noblemen,"[1] themselves fainéants, "carry about with them at their tails."[2] Such too are the armies, maintained by those paragons of pride, the princes of Europe, out of the blood and sweat of their subjects, to sustain their schemes of megalomaniac self-glorification.[3] Thus seeking in outward, vain, and wicked things an earthly worship which neither their achievement nor their inner virtue warrants, Christians lure their fellow men into the sin of sloth, or subject them to endless labor, or destroy their substance, their bodies, and their souls too, in futile wars; and over the waste and the misery, over the physical ruin and the spiritual, broods the monster sin of pride.

The Utopian Discourse then is based on a diagnosis of the ills of sixteenth century Christendom; it ascribes those ills to sin, and primarily to pride, and it prescribes remedies for that last most disastrous infection of man's soul designed to inhibit if not to eradicate it. For our understanding of the Utopian Discourse it is of the utmost importance that we recognize this to be its theme. Unless we recognize it, we cannot rescue More from the ideologically motivated scholars of the Left and the Right, both as anxious to capture him for their own as if he were a key constituency in a close Parliamentary election. According to the Rightist scholars, who have allowed their nostalgia for an imaginary medieval unity to impede their critical perceptions, More was one of the last medieval men. He was the staunch defender of Catholic solidarism represented in medieval order and liberties, in a stable, agrarian subsistence economy, in guild brotherhood, monastic brotherhood, and Christian brotherhood against the inchoate growth of modern universal otherhood, already embodied, or shortly to be embodied in nascent capitalism, the New Monarchy, Protestantism, and Machiavellianism.[4] On the other hand, the most recent exponent of the *Utopia* as an exemplification of dialectical materialism has seen More as a fine early example of the Middle Class Man whose social views are one and all colored by his antipathy to late medieval feudalism as represented in the enfeebled but still exploitative Church and in the predatory and decadent feudal aristocracy, making their final rally

9. Swashbucklers—swaggering ruffians. See p. 46 above.
1. See pp. 17 and 46 above.
2. Cf. p. 17 above. "Fainéants": idlers.
3. Cf. pp. 28–30 above.
4. "Chambers, passim; Campbell, passim. I borrow the concept of modern 'otherhood' from my friend Prof. Benjamin Nelson, *The Idea of Usury: From Tribal Brotherhood to Universal Otherhood*, The History of Ideas Series, 3 [Princeton: Princeton University Press, 1949]" [Hexter's note]. W. E. Campbell wrote *More's Utopia and His Social Teaching* (London: Eyre & Spottiswoode Publishers Ltd., 1930).

in the courts of equally predatory and decadent dynastic warrior princes.[5]

Both of these formulations—that of the Left and that of the Right—are subject to a number of weaknesses. They are both based on conceptions of economic development and social stratification in the sixteenth century and earlier more coherent than correct, and largely mythological in many respects. The Leftist scholars by regarding More's age from a particular twentieth century perspective, the Rightists by regarding it from what they fondly imagine to be a medieval perspective deprive both More's opinions and his age of the measure of internal cohesion that both in truth possess. But to document these criticisms adequately would require an inordinate amount of space.[6] For the moment it must suffice to point out that from Utopia and from the events of More's life, scholarly ideologues both of the Left and of the Right have been able to adduce a remarkable number of citations and facts to support their respective and totally irreconcilable views. Now this paradox is amenable to one of two possible explanations. The first would require us to assume that More's thought was so contradictory, disorderly, and illogical as to justify either of these interpretations or both, although in reason and common sense they are mutually contradictory. But the intellectual coherence and sureness of thought of the Utopian Discourse and the sense of clear purpose that it radiates seem to preclude this resolution of the paradox. The second possibility is that either point of view can be maintained only by an unconscious but unjustifiable underestimate of the weight of the citations and data offered in support of the opposite point of view, but that all the citations and data fall into a harmonious pattern if looked at in a third perspective.

The character of that third possible perspective I have tried to suggest: the Utopian Discourse is the production of a Christian humanist uniquely endowed with a statesman's eye and mind, a broad worldly experience, and a conscience of unusual sensitivity, who saw sin and especially the sin of pride as the cancer of the commonwealth. Now the social critic of any age is bound to direct his most vigorous attack at the centers of power in that age and reserve his sharpest shafts for the men possessing it. For however great the potentialities for evil may be in all men, real present social ills, the social critic's stock in trade, are immediately the consequence of

5. Ames, passim [Hexter's note].
6. "I have touched on two aspects of the general problem of sixteenth century society in two recent articles, 'The Education of the Aristocracy in the Renaissance,' *Journal of Modern History*, 22, 1950, pp. 1–20; and 'The Myth of the Middle Class in Tudor England,' *Explorations in Entrepreneurial History*, 2, 1949–1950, pp. 128–140" [Hexter's note]. Both articles became influential.

the acts and decisions of the men actually in a position to inflict their wills on the social body. In a pecuniary society enjoying a reasonable measure of internal security and order but subject to great disparities of wealth, the social critic is bound to attack the very rich, because in such a society, where direct violence does not bear all the sway, riches become a most important source of power. This does not necessarily imply that pride is wholly confined to rich and powerful men, although by their possession of and preoccupation with money and power, the two goods most highly prized by the worldly, they are sure to be especially vulnerable to that sin. It is more to the point, however, that the pride of the powerful is, by virtue of their power, socially efficacious, since it is armed with the puissance of command. It can get what it wickedly wants. In More's Europe— the illicit violence of lordship almost everywhere having been suppressed by the new monarchs—it was the pride of the rich that did the real wicked work in the world, the work of fraud, oppression, debauchery, waste, rapine, and death. So More's shafts find their target in the rich and the powerful—in the bourgeois usurer, the engrosser, the court minion, the mighty lord of lands and men, the princes of the earth, in the encloser and depopulator whether that encloser was a parvenu grazier-butcher still reeking of the blood of the City shambles[7] or a predacious noble of immaculate lineage or an ancient abbey rich in estates and poor in things of the spirit. These were his target not because together they form a homogeneous social class, for they do not, nor because they are all decadently medieval or all inchoately modern, for they are not all one or all the other, but because their riches and power sustained the empire of pride over the world that More knew and whose social ills he had traced to that center of evils.

Once we recognize that More's analysis of sixteenth century society led him to the conclusion that pride was the source of the greater part of its ills, the pattern of the Utopian commonwealth becomes clear, consistent, and intelligible. In its fundamental structure it is a great social instrument for the subjugation of pride. The pecuniary economy must be destroyed because money is the prime instrument through the use of which men seek to satisfy their yet insatiable pride. It is to keep pride down that all Utopians must eat in common messes, wear a common uniform habit, receive a common education, and rotate their dwelling places. In a society where no man is permitted to own the superfluities that are the marks of invidious distinction, no man will covet them. Above all idleness, the great emblem of pride in the society of More's time, a sure mark to elevate the aristocrat above the vulgar, is utterly destroyed by the common obligation

7. The butchers' market in the City of London.

of common daily toil. It is through no accident, through no back-wardness of the Tudor economy, that More makes the Utopian com-monwealth a land austere and rigorous beyond most of the imaginary societies elaborated by his later imitators. Had he cared only to con-sider man's material welfare, his creature comfort, it need not have been so. More was a logical man; he knew that to bind up pride on all sides it takes a strait prison, and he did not flinch from the conse-quences of his diagnosis. As he truly says this "kind of vice among the Utopians can have no place."[8]

Since More does not explicitly speak of pride very often in *Uto-pia*, my emphasis on its role in his social thought on both the criti-cal and constructive side may seem exaggerated. Let anyone who thinks this is so consider the words with which More draws Hyth-loday's peroration and the whole Discourse of the best state of a commonwealth to its conclusion: "I doubt not that the respect of every man's private commodity or else the authority of our Saviour Christ . . . would have brought all the world long ago into the laws of this weal public, if it were not that one only beast, the princess and mother of all mischief, Pride, doth withstand and let[9] it. She measureth not wealth and prosperity by her own commodities but by the miseries and incommodities of others; she would not by her good will be made a goddess if there were no wretches left *over whom she might, like a scornful lady, rule and triumph,* over whose miser-ies her felicity might shine, whose poverty she might vex, torment, and increase by gorgeously setting forth her riches. This hellhound creeps into men's hearts; and plucks them back from entering the right path of life, and is so deeply rooted in men's breasts that she cannot be plucked out."[1]

The disciplining of pride, then, is the foundation of the best state of the commonwealth. And more than that, it is pride itself that prevents actual realms from attaining to that best state.

8. See p. 50 above.
9. Prevent. "Commodity": advantage. "Weal public": commonwealth.
1. See p. 96 above.

C. S. LEWIS

[A Jolly Invention]†

* * * All seem to be agreed that * * * [*Utopia*] is a great book, but hardly any two agree as to its real significance: we approach it through a cloud of contradictory eulogies. In such a state of affairs a good, though not a certain, clue is the opinion of those who lived nearer the author's time than we. Our starting-point is that Erasmus speaks of it as if it were primarily a comic book; Tyndale despises it as 'poetry'; for Harpsfield it is a 'iollye inuention,' 'pleasantly' set forth;[1] More himself in later life classes it and the *Praise of Folly* together as books fitter to be burned than translated in an age prone to misconstruction; Thomas Wilson, fifty years later, mentions it for praise among 'feined narrations and wittie invented matters (as though they were true indeed)'.[2] This is not the language in which friend or enemy or author (when the author is so honest a man as More) refer to a serious philosophical treatise. It all sounds as if we had to do with a book whose real place is not in the history

---

† From C. S. Lewis, *English Literature in the Sixteenth Century Excluding Drama*, The Oxford History of English Literature, Vol. 3 (Oxford: Clarendon Press, 1954), pp. 167–71. Reprinted by permission of Oxford University Press. All footnotes are by the editors.
  Best known to the general reader as the author of *The Chronicles of Narnia*, the Belfast native Clive Staples Lewis (1898–1963) was, in his life as an Oxford and, later, Cambridge don, a brilliant and deeply learned scholar-critic of English medieval and Renaissance literature. For his role in the history of Utopian criticism, see p. 158 above.

1. Nicholas Harpsfield's biography of More was written a little over twenty years after his execution. For the passages Lewis refers to, see *The Life and Death of Sr Thomas Moore, Knight*, edited by E. V. Hitchcock (London: Published for the Early English Text Society by the Oxford University Press, 1963 [orig. publ. 1932]), pp. 102, 103. Lewis neglects to note that Harpsfield also says that *Utopia* is "singular and excellent, containing and prescribing a commonwealth far passing the commonwealths devised and instituted by * * * Plato and divers other" (p. 105). William Tyndale (1494?–1536) was the first translator of the Bible into English. More attacked him in several of his anti-Lutheran polemics, including the longest and most virulent of them, *The Confutation of Tyndale's Answer*. As for Erasmus, it is simply not true that he speaks of *Utopia* as if it were a merely comical book (see p. 152 above), and Lewis ignores the other best early "clues" to *Utopia*, the commendatory letters and poems that More's fellow humanists contributed to the first four editions. Though often alluding to the wit and irony of the book, these uniformly treat it as a fundamentally serious work of political thought.

2. In *The Art of Rhetoric* (first published 1553). Wilson adds that such narrations can "help well to set forward a cause," his point being that they can, like fables, be employed for serious purposes. See the edition by Peter E. Medine (University Park: The Pennsylvania State University Press, 1994), p. 222. In the *Confutation*, More wrote that "in these days in which men * * * misconstrue and take harm of [i.e., from] the very scripture of God, * * * if any man would now translate *Moria* [i.e., *The Praise of Folly*] into English, or some works either that I have myself written ere this * * * [,] I would not only * * * [Erasmus's] books but mine own also, help to burn them both with mine own hands, rather than folk should (though through their own fault) take any harm of them" (*CW* 8:179; spelling modernized). The fact that More, when reform turned into Reformation, was disturbed by the possible effects of his and Erasmus's earlier, reformist works scarcely implies that he regarded either *Utopia* or *The Praise of Folly* as an unserious book.

of political thought so much as in that of fiction and satire. It is, of course, possible that More's sixteenth-century readers, and More himself, were mistaken. But it is at least equally possible that the mistake lies with those modern readers who take the book *au grand sérieux*.[3] There is a cause specially predisposing them to error in such a matter. They live in a revolutionary age, an age in which modern weapons and the modern revolutionary technique have made it only too easy to produce in the real world states recognizably like those we invent on paper: writing Utopias is now a serious matter. In More's time, or Campanella's, or Bacon's,[4] there was no real hope or fear that the paper states could be 'drawn into practice': the man engaged in blowing such bubbles did not need to talk as if he were on his oath. And here we have to do with one who, as the Messenger told him in the *Dialogue*, 'used to look so sadly' when he jested that many were deceived.[5]

The *Utopia* has its serious, even its tragic, elements. It is, as its translator Robinson says, 'fruitful and profitable'. But it is not a consistently serious philosophical treatise, and all attempts to treat it as such break down sooner or later. The interpretation which breaks down soonest is the 'liberal' interpretation. There is nothing in the book on which the later More, the heretic-hunter, need have turned his back. There is no freedom of speech in Utopia.[6] There is nothing liberal in Utopia. From it, as from all other imaginary states, liberty is more successfully banished than the real world, even at its worst, allows. The very charm of these paper citizens is that they cannot in any way resist their author: every man is a dictator in his own book. It is not love of liberty that makes men write Utopias. Nor does the *Utopia* give any colour to Tyndale's view that More 'knew the truth' of Protestantism and forsook it: the religious orders of the Utopians and their very temples are modelled on the old religion. On the other hand, it is not a defence of that old order against current criticisms; it supports those criticisms by choosing an abbot as its specimen of the bad landlord, and making a friar its most contemptible character.[7] R. W. Chambers, with whom died so much that was sweetest and strongest in English scholarship, advanced a much more plausible view. According to him the Utopians represent the natural

---

3. With deadly seriousness (French).
4. Sir Francis Bacon wrote (though left unfinished at his death, in 1526) a scientific utopia, *The New Atlantis*. The most famous work of the Italian philosopher and theologian Tommaso Campanella (1568–1639) has always been *The City of the Sun*, a utopia that owes much to both More and Plato.
5. More on himself (in the voice of the other character in *A Dialogue Concerning Heresies*): "ye use . . . to look so sadly [i.e., seriously] when ye mean merrily, that many times men doubt whether ye speak in sport, when ye mean good earnest" (*CW* 6:68–69; spelling modernized).
6. An exaggeration. See, e.g., pp. 85–86 above.
7. See pp. 19 (abbot) and 26–27 (friar) above.

virtues working at their ideal best in isolation from the theological;
it will be remembered that they hold their Natural Religion only
provisionally 'onles any godlier be inspired into man from heuen.'[8]
Yet even this leaves some features unaccounted for. It is doubtful
whether More would have regarded euthanasia for incurables and
the assassination of hostile princes as things contained in the Law
of Nature. And it is very strange that he should make Hedonism the
philosophy of the Utopians. Epicurus was not regarded by most
Christians as the highest example of the natural light. The truth
surely is that as long as we take the *Utopia* for a philosophical treatise it will 'give' wherever we lean our weight. It is, to begin with, a
dialogue: and we cannot be certain which of the speakers, if any,
represents More's considered opinion. When Hythloday explains why
his philosophy would be useless in the courts of kings More replies
that there is 'another philosophy more ciuil'[9] and expounds this less
intransigent wisdom so sympathetically that we think we have caught
the very More at last; but when I have read Hythloday's retort I am
all at sea again. It is even very doubtful what More thought of communism as a practical proposal. We have already had to remind
ourselves, when considering Colet,[1] that the traditional admission
of communism as the law of uncorrupted Nature need carry with it
no consequences in the world of practical sociology. It is certain
that in the *Confutation* (1532)[2] More had come to include communism among the 'horrible heresies' of the Anabaptists and in the
Dialogue of Comfort he defends private riches. Those who think of
More as a 'lost leader' may discount these later utterances. Yet even
at the end of the *Utopia* he rejects the Utopian economics as a thing
'founded of no good reason'.[3] The magnificent rebuke of all existing
societies which precedes this may suggest that the rejection is
ironical. On the other hand, it may mean that the whole book is only
a satiric glass to reveal our own avarice by contrast and is not meant
to give us directly practical advice.

These puzzles may give the impression that the *Utopia* is a confused book: and if it were intended as a serious treatise it would be
very confused indeed. On my view, however, it appears confused
only so long as we are trying to get out of it what it never intended to
give. It becomes intelligible and delightful as soon as we take it for
what it is—a holiday work, a spontaneous overflow of intellectual
high spirits, a revel of debate, paradox, comedy and (above all) of

8. Lewis quotes from Robinson's translation. "Onles": unless. Cf. p. 66 above. For Chambers's view, see pp. 168–70 above.
9. See p. 33 above.
1. On Colet, see p. 152, n. 1 above.
2. I.e., *The Confutation of Tyndale's Answer.*
3. See p. 96 above.

invention, which starts many hares and kills none. It is written by More the translator of Lucian[4] and friend of Erasmus, not More the chancellor or the ascetic. Its place on our shelves is close to *Gulliver* and *Erewhon*, within reasonable distance of Rabelais, a long way from the *Republic* or *New Worlds for Old*.[5] The invention (the 'poetry' of which More was accused) is quite as important as the merits of the polity described, and different parts of that polity are on very different levels of seriousness.

Not to recognize this is to do More grave injustice. Thus the suggestion that the acquisitive impulse should be mortified by using gold for purposes of dishonour is infantile if we take it as a practical proposal. If gold in Utopia were plentiful enough to be so used, gold in Utopia would not be a precious metal. But if it is taken simply as satiric invention leading up to the story of the child and the ambassadors,[6] it is delicious. The slow beginning of the tale, luring us on from London to Bruges, from Bruges to Antwerp, and thence by reported speech to fabulous lands beyond the line, has no place in the history of political philosophy: in the history of prose fiction it has a very high place indeed. Hythloday himself, as we first see him, has something of the arresting quality of the Ancient Mariner. The dialogue is admirably managed. Mere conversation holds us contented for the first book and includes that analysis of the contemporary English situation which is the most serious and the most truly political part of the *Utopia*. In the second book More gives his imagination free rein. There is a thread of serious thought running through it, an abundance of daring suggestions, several back-handed blows at European institutions, and, finally, the magnificent peroration. But he does not keep our noses to the grindstone. He says many things for the fun of them, surrendering himself to the sheer pleasure of imagined geography, imagined language, and imagined institutions. That is what readers whose interests are rigidly political do not understand: but everyone who has ever made an imaginary map responds at once.

Tyndale's belief that More 'knew the truth and forsook it' is a crude form of the error which finds in the *Utopia* a liberalism inconsistent with More's later career. There is no inconsistency. More was from the first a very orthodox Papist, even an ascetic with a hankering for

---

4. For Lucian, see pp. 106–07 above.
5. A laudatory introduction to socialism by H. G. Wells (1908). Samuel Butler's romance *Erewhon* (1872) recounts a voyage to an imaginary country that, like the similar accounts in Swift's *Gulliver's Travels* (1726), satirizes the author's *own* country, England. The great French comic writer François Rabelais (1494?–1553) included an account of the utopian Abbey of Thélème—where the only rule is "Do what Thou Wilt"—in his sprawling *Gargantua and Pantagruel*.
6. See pp. 56–57 above; and, for a different way of interpreting those Utopian practices that cannot be taken as serious recommendations for reform, see Ames, pp. 179ff. above.

the monastic life. At the same time it is true that the *Utopia* stands apart from all his other works. Religiously and politically he was consistent: but this is not to say that he did not undergo a gradual and honourable change very like that which overtook Burke and Wordsworth and other friends of liberty as the Revolutionary age began to show its true features. The times altered; and things that would once have seemed to him permissible or even salutary audacities came to seem to him dangerous. That was why he would not then wish to see the *Utopia* translated. In the same way any of us might now make criticisms of democracy which we would not repeat in the hour of its danger. And from the literary point of view there is an even greater gulf between the *Utopia* and the works which followed. It is, to speak simply, beyond comparison better than they.

EDWARD L. SURTZ

From Humanism and Communism: The Background†

* * *

The predilection of many humanists for Plato must have encouraged a reëxamination of the accepted concepts of private property and communism. The communism of the guardians in the *Republic*, for whom Plato had prescribed that "none must possess any

---

† Reprinted by permission of the publishers from Edward L. Surtz, S.J., *The Pursuit of Pleasure: Philosophy, Education, and Communism in More's Utopia* (Cambridge, Mass.: Harvard University Press, 1957), chap. 14, pp. 161–74. © 1957 by the President and Fellows of Harvard College. Copyright © renewed 1985 by Howard J. Gray, S.J. Except where identified as Surtz's, footnotes are by the editors (though often drawn from Surtz's much heavier documentation).

Surtz (1909–1973), a Jesuit priest who exemplified the great tradition of scholarship in that order, published not one but two influential books on *Utopia* in 1957. (On the other—*The Praise of Wisdom*—see p. 306 below.) These books earned him the co-editorship, with J. H. Hexter, of the edition of *Utopia* (1965) in the Yale *Complete Works of St. Thomas More*; the huge commentary (i.e., set of explanatory notes to the text) that Surtz prepared for the edition remains the first place to look for information, especially background information, on any passage of More's book.

Both in the 1957 books and in the Yale edition (his share of the introduction as well as the commentary), Surtz brought massive learning to bear on the interpretation of *Utopia* by placing the ideas expressed in it into their contexts in the history of Western thought. The interpretation that he supported in this way is similar to Chambers's: *Utopia* is the work of "a zealous Catholic *reformer*" (*Praise of Pleasure*, p. 2) but not of a communist revolutionary. Some readers may, however, draw conclusions from Surtz's data not identical to his own. The strikingly pro-communist views of Erasmus (see pp. 209–12 below), whose views on many matters align closely with More's, are especially interesting in this connection. (For challenging arguments that More truly meant what he had Hythloday say, see the brilliant final segment [pp. cv–cxxiv] of Hexter's section of the Yale introduction, and Eric Nelson's article on "Greek nonsense" in *Utopia*, pp. 259–83 below.)

private property save the indispensable," is too well known to need description. Its foundation is the principle: "That city . . . is best ordered in which the greatest number use the expression 'mine' and 'not mine' of the same things in the same way."[1] In the *Laws*, it is necessary to remember, Plato retains the completely communistic state as an ideal, but reluctantly abandons it in a more sober moment, since "such a course is beyond the capacity of people with the birth, rearing and training we assume."[2] In *Politics*, Aristotle objects that Plato's attempt to produce uniformity is destructive of the state, which depends upon diversity of occupation, rank, etc. Common ownership, moreover, produces not harmony, but discord, for it generally leads to quarrels and litigations. It reduces the individual's interest in what is common, and waters down the force of family affection. This pithy summary of objections based on common sense and knowledge of normal human nature is to reappear in various form and phraseology throughout future centuries.[3]

To understand the relations of the Platonic and Aristotelian doctrine on communism to the Christian concept through the ages— and especially to the attitude of the Christian humanists at the time of the composition of the *Utopia*—it is essential to grasp clearly the practice of Christ and the early Christians. There can be no doubt that Christ Himself imposed upon His chosen band of apostles and disciples a strict and obligatory poverty and communism (Matt. x.9–10; Mark vi.8–9, x.21; Luke ix.57 58, x.4, xiv.33; John xii.6, xiii.29). But this common poverty was wholly voluntary, since a certain rich youth could refuse His gracious request to join this restricted group (Matt. xix.22; Mark x.22; Luke xviii.23), and was directed solely to the perfect fulfillment of an apostolic life of teaching and preaching. "It was not an attempt at a social revolution for the benefit of the 'proletarians' of Palestine."[4] In a word, the invitation to a life of communal poverty was *not* a *commandment*, but a *counsel*.[5]

In spite of frequent misinterpretation of the pertinent texts in the Acts (ii.44–45, iv.32–35),[6] the Christians in the church of Jerusalem did not practice a strict community of goods; they were free to retain their property or to sell it in order to give the proceeds to the poor.

---

1. *Republic* 3.416D, 5.462C. For the former, see p. 102 above.
2. *Laws* 5.740A. The *Laws*, Plato's last dialogue, is his other major work of political theory.
3. Aristotle's critique of the *Republic*, which is echoed in *Utopia* (p. 37 above), is found in *Politics* 2.1–2.
4. M.-B. Schwalm, "Communisme," *Dict. de théol. cath.*, III, 578 [Surtz's note].
5. The distinction between a counsel and a commandment was taken for granted among Christians in the Middle Ages and the Renaissance. Even * * * [Chaucer's] Wife of Bath says of St. Paul's advice on virginity: "conseillyng is no comandement" (*Prol.*, line 67) [Surtz's note].
6. For the latter passage, see pp. 105–06 above.

As for the Fathers of the Church,[7] they in their genuine writings praise the voluntary communism among the monks, but condemn the heretics wishing to make it compulsory and universal; they assert the right of the individual to private property, but oblige the rich to the alleviation of the needs of the poor.

Of special importance are the texts on the common life in Gratian's *Decretum.*[8] Gratian gives as an example of the natural law "the common possession of all things," and later reiterates that "by the natural law all things are common."[9] The right of private property arises from custom or positive human enactment. As St. Augustine maintains in his commentary on St. John, even the Church holds its goods, not by divine right, but by human right. The spurious epistle of Clement[1] is quoted in its entirety in the *Decretum.* This epistle gives six reasons, ranging from the natural law and Plato's authority to texts in the Acts, to prove that all things ought to be common to all men, and explains that it was "through iniquity" that private ownership entered the world.[2] The glosses on the assertions on communism in the *Decretum* are extremely interesting for their sense of the purely theoretical nature of the discussion and for their defense of the existing system of private property. There was agreement among the Scholastics,[3] however, that if Adam had not sinned, things would have remained common. There was also agreement on salient points in regard to the justice of private property.

The doctrine of Aquinas[4] in its baldest form is the following. Private ownership is not against the natural law, for it is a necessary addition made to the natural law by human reason. As a right, it belongs, not strictly to positive human law, but to the *ius gentium* (Law of Nations), which, in the words of Drostan Maclaren, "lies as an intermediary between natural law and human positive law" and which "consists of precepts derived from the primary precepts of the natural law in the same way as conclusions are derived from their premises; without the *ius gentium* it would be impossible for man to live peacefully in society."[5] Private property is best because man takes more care of his own than of the community's possessions, less confusion results, and greater order is effected since altercations are fewer. Goods, however, remain common at least in respect to *use,*

---

7. The theologians of the early Christian centuries.
8. A collection of canon law—ecclesiastical law of the Catholic Church—compiled in the 12th century. Little is known about the Bolognese compiler, Gratian.
9. On the natural law, see pp. 49, n. 7, and 137, n. 8 above. "Positive" law (next sentence) is, by contrast, *enacted* law—statutory law.
1. Clement of Alexandria (2nd century C.E.) was a Greek theologian.
2. St. Ambrose takes the same view of the origin of private property: see p. 109 above.
3. Theologians of the later Middle Ages.
4. The supreme Scholastic, St. Thomas Aquinas (1225?–1274).
5. Drostan Maclaren, *Private Property and the Natural Law* (Oxford: Blackfriars, 1948), pp. 12–13.

insofar as the owner must be ready to share his goods with others in time of need. Aquinas views the common life of the early church in Jerusalem as only a temporary expedient for a particular church. The Utopians, of course, claim that communism begets greater care of common property, perfect order, and no lawsuits.[6]

Following the lead of earlier Scholastics, Duns Scotus[7] tries to reconcile the texts of Gratian, Augustine, and Clement by developing the theory that in the state of innocence all things would have been common by a precept of the law of nature or of God, but in the state of fallen nature private property is a just right which is founded, not on the natural law (since it had determined human nature to common ownership), nor on divine positive law, but on human positive law. The natural or divine precept of community of possessions was revoked after the fall for the sake of greater peace and order and for the protection of the weaker members of society. Private property is natural, therefore, in the sense that it rests upon the general principle that a community or a commonwealth must have peace. * * * Thus, private property, according to Scotus, is not a simple and absolute necessity; but, in view of the weakness and acquisitiveness of most men, the system is most suitable for peaceful existence. From such statements it is clear that, except for a different approach and terminology, Scotus is in substantial agreement with Aquinas for all *practical* purposes—and so is almost every Scholastic.

In summary, one may say that the Schoolmen[8] were ardent defenders of the theoretical right of private property. Strict communism on an extensive popular level, according to both Thomists and Scotists, was impracticable in existing conditions, whatever might have been the rule before the fall of man. * * *

This rapid survey of the medieval background would hardly be complete without a word on * * * [a] group in the Netherlands, the Brethren of the Common Life, the educators and inspirers of many northern humanists, including Erasmus. During their first days, the Brethren were attacked for presuming to lead the common life without religious vows taken in an order or congregation. In reply to these enemies, Gerard Zerbolt of Zutphen (1367–1398) wrote a treatise on the common life, entitled *The Manner of Life for a Society of Devout Men (De Modo Vivendi Devotorum Hominum Simul Commorancium)*, in which he collected all the pertinent arguments: Christ's advice to the rich young man (Matt. xix), the apostolic church in Jerusalem (Acts ii, iv), the recommendation of Fathers and Doctors

---

6. Surtz cites passages that come on pp. 36 and 95 above.
7. The great 13th-century philosopher-theologian John Duns of Scotland ("Scotus"). He was scorned by humanists, whose view of his highly technical theology is forever enshrined in the common noun *dunce*, which derived from their mockery of him.
8. I.e., the Scholastics.

of the Church, communism in the state of original innocence, the authority of pagan philosophers like Pythagoras and Seneca, the nature of men as social and mutually helpful animals, etc. Erasmus may have formed some of his ideas from the reading of Zerbolt's treatise or from conversation with the Brethren about the common life.

English literature before *Utopia* offers interesting side lights on the whole question of communism. In the second half of the fourteenth century, the author of *Piers Plowman*[9] denounces the friars for teaching communism to the people in spite of God's command not to covet one's neighbor's goods. Reginald Pecock in the middle of the fifteenth century tries to prove to the Lollards[1] that the practice of the common life in the church of Jerusalem was a matter of counsel, not of precept. Early in the sixteenth century, Alexander Barclay, following Locher,[2] speaks of the original golden age in which all things were common. A petition in the middle of the sixteenth century gives as a reason for putting an end to the original communism of the Church the fact that the idle and slothful need an incentive to work, namely, private ownership and profit.

What are the views of More's humanistic friends and acquaintances in respect to communism and private property? The views of John Colet,[3] who exerted great influence on Erasmus and More, should prove interesting and revealing. Before the coming of Christ, the majority of fallen mankind lived, not according to revelation, but according to *"the law of nature:*—not the law of simple, holy, and inviolate nature (for that state of innocence was in paradise alone), but of a defiled and corrupted nature." It was this law, under the aspect of the law of nations, which "brought in ideas of *meum* and *tuum*—of property, that is to say, and deprivation; ideas clean contrary to a good and unsophisticated nature: for that would have a community in all things."[4] Colet, therefore, seems to hold that man's real nature is man's nature in the state of original justice, which inclined him toward common possession of all things. This natural inclination to communism remains, even though private property is now best in view of the weaknesses or evil propensities which afflict human nature at present. If Colet in the quotation given above really means to identify the natural law (even though it now is the "law of a corrupter nature") with the law of nations (which is "resorted to by

9. William Langland's long religious allegory in verse, which includes much social criticism.
1. Followers of the 14th-century religious reformer John Wycliffe. Bishop Reginald Pecock wrote *The Repressor of Over-Much Blaming of the Clergy.*
2. Barclay's allegorical poem *The Ship of Fools* followed, in this particular, a Latin poem by the German humanist Jakob Locher.
3. For Colet, see p. 152, n. 1 above.
4. The two quotations are from J. H. Lupton, *A Life of John Colet* (London: George Bell and Sons, 1887), p. 134. The second one is Lupton quoting Colet's *Exposition of St. Paul's Epistle to the Romans.* "*Meum* and *tuum*": mine and yours (Latin).

nations all over the world")—the two are usually distinguished—he disagrees with Scotus in making the natural law, and not positive human enactment, the source of rights of property. But he does concur with Scotus in emphasizing communism for the state of original justice.

The question is: does Colet advocate Christian communism? It is impossible to give a categorical reply: One must use the distinction between three states: the first, original justice (*status iustitiae originalis*), the second, fallen nature (*status naturae lapsae*), and the third, nature fallen and restored (*status naturae lapsae et reparatae*). The last is that of the regenerated Christian in the state of grace. Needless to say, Colet holds communism to be the best system for the state of original justice. For the state of fallen nature, private ownership is the inevitable order. As for the state of nature fallen and restored (but not restored to the complete simplicity and integrity of the state of original justice, since mortality and concupiscence remain in the regenerated man), Colet would probably say that for perfect followers of Christ communism is the ideal but that practically private property, animated by a spirit of generosity and self-sacrifice toward the poor and needy, is best for this state; for, though a redeemed nature is restored to justice, it remains, in certain respects, a fallen nature, and therefore a nature subject to weakness and defect. For this reason, Lupton can rightly maintain that the *Utopia* echoes the teaching of Colet who "expressed approval, though briefly and guardedly, of a Christian communism."[5]

Another English humanist, Thomas Elyot,[6] believes that in the beginning the people "had all things in common, and equality in degree and condition," but that now "the best and most sure governance is by one king or prince, which ruleth only for the weal of his people to him subject." He apparently can conceive of a communistic state only as a "communalty" without order and without distinction of superior and inferior. He insists that *respublica* should be translated *public weal*, not *common weal*. The persons who think that it is called the *common weal* because "every thing should be to all men in common, without discrepance of any estate or condition," are led to this opinion "more by sensuality than by any good reason or inclination to humanity."[7] Elyot has no more than these few words to say on communism.

* * *

5. Ibid.
6. Sir Thomas Elyot (ca. 1490–1546) was a friend of More's; the passages Surtz quotes in this paragraph are from his well-known educational treatise, *The Governor*. See the edition by S. E. Lehmberg (New York: Dutton, 1962), pp. 103–04, 7, 1.
7. Cf. "More"'s remarks to Hythloday on p. 37 above.

The opinion of Guillaume Budé, if one is to judge from his letter to Thomas Lupset first prefixed to the Paris edition (1517) of *Utopia*,[8] is less conservative. The island of Utopia, according to Budé, "is said, . . . by what must be owned to be a singular good fortune, to have adopted Christian usages both in public and in private; to have imbibed the wisdom thereto belonging; and to have kept it undefiled to this very day." * * * There is a certain ambiguity about this statement. In Budé's view, did the Utopians have Christian rites and wisdom only after the coming of Christianity? Certainly the phrase "to have kept it undefiled to this very day" has little significance if it applies merely to the slightly more than a decade which has elapsed since Hythloday's arrival in Utopia. The phrase must apply rather to the rites and wisdom of the Utopians, curiously similar to those of the Christians, prevalent before the missionary endeavors of Hythloday. Later on, Budé marvels that avarice and covetousness have failed to penetrate Utopia "for so many ages" (*tot seculis*), a phrase which indicates that the Utopians had Christian practices and wisdom before the introduction of Christianity. Budé's comparison thus gains immensely in strength: pagan Utopia, unlike the Christian West, has clung tenaciously to "three divine institutions": (1) "the absolute equality, or . . . the civil communication of all things good and bad among fellow-citizens"; (2) "a settled and unwavering love of peace and quietness"; and (3) "a contempt for gold and silver." One may well speculate whether Budé designedly used the term *divine* instead of *Christian*. If he did, it would mean that such were God's plans for man from the very creation and that the Utopians have recaptured and preserved these three ideals independently of the preaching of Christ's gospel, which, of course, reëstablishes and perfects God's original designs. The three institutions are directed against crying evils of contemporary Europe: the first, against the great inequality of rich and poor, nobles and commons, among Christian peoples; the second, against the uninterrupted wars of Christian princes; and the third, against the greed for wealth which was corrupting Christian countries. If Europeans had as firm convictions on these points as the Utopians, there would be an end to all fraud, deception, avarice, pride, and litigation. Hence, Budé cries out: "Would that great Heaven in its goodness had dealt so kindly with the countries which keep, and would not part with, the appellation [i.e., Christian] they bear, derived from His most holy name!"

Christ, Budé writes, was the founder and dispenser of all possessions (Matt. xxviii.18; I Cor. xv.24–27, etc.). What disposition did He make of property? As far as His followers were concerned, He

established among them "a Pythagorean communion and love"
(*Pythagoricam communionem et charitatem*), a reference to the
early Christians in Jerusalem where they held "all things in common" (Acts ii.44, iv.32). Budé seems to believe that these Christians
not merely shared all their goods but actually practised a loving
communism such as prevailed among the Utopians. For Christ
showed what a heavy sanction He laid on His law by making an
impressive example of the case of Ananias, whom He condemned
to death for violation of the law of communion (*ob temeratam com-
munionis legem*).[9] Evidently Budé holds that Ananias was not punished for telling a serious falsehood (as exegetes generally hold), but
for violation of the communism of the church in Jerusalem. Nevertheless, he does not make even an academic plea for the adoption of
communism, but draws out of Christ's law a more immediate and
practical lesson for Christians: the abolition of the thousand and
one unedifying litigations about property in both the civil and the
ecclesiastical courts. Instead of making the noble law of love and
communion, enunciated by Pythagoras and proclaimed by Christ,
the guiding principle of their lives, Christians have lowered themselves to the ignoble norms and increasing tyranny of the civil and
canon laws.

In summary of Budé's view, one may say that theoretically he sees
a mutual sharing of all things, if not strict communism itself, as the
ideal state for contemporary Europeans as it was for the earliest
Christians and as it is now for the Utopians, who are Christian in
all but name. Practically, he descends to a concrete and particular
application of the law of love and communion: he wants the simple
precepts of Christ set forth in the gospel to displace the intricate
and specious laws of church and state on property and possession.

Christ and Pythagoras and Plato are often linked together as religious teachers in the minds and works of many humanists, just as
they are in Budé's letter. In the introduction to his *Adages*,[1] Erasmus
declares that, if one examines thoroughly the saying of Pythagoras
on the community of all things among friends, one will find therein
the whole of human happiness in a nutshell.[2] Plato did nothing else
than advocate this community and friendship among the founders
of his republic. If he had been successful in his plea, war, envy, and
fraud would have departed forthwith from the city; and, to be brief,
the whole mass of human plagues would have left once for all. Erasmus continues: "What else than this did Christ, the head of our
religion, do? In fact, He gave to the world only a single command-

9. See p. 106 above.
1. On the *Adages*, see p. 77, n. 4 above.
2. See CWE 31:15.

ment, that of charity, teaching that the whole of the law and the prophets depended upon it. Or what else does charity urge upon men but that all things must be common to all men?" Erasmus then reinforces his point with an appeal to the doctrine of the mystical body of Christ.

This espousal of Christian communism by Erasmus is continued in the commentary on the very first of his *Adages*: "Friends have all things in common" (*Amicorum communia omnia*). He points out the use of this proverb by Aristotle and Plato. Plato, for example, realizes that the citizens of the best and happiest commonwealth, like friends, must have all things in common and must not utter the word *mine* and *not mine*. Yet it is wonderful to mark what displeasure Christians show toward this communism in Plato, in fact, what violent criticism they launch against it, although nothing has ever been said by a pagan philosopher more in accordance with the mind of Christ. Even Aristotle, who moderates Plato's communistic thought by assigning ownership and goods to definite private persons, wishes all things to be in common under the aspect of free and unhampered *use*. Gellius is Erasmus' authority for the statement that Pythagoras not only was the author of the saying on the community of all things among friends, but also introduced among his followers a communism of life and resources, "such as Christ wished to exist among all Christians."[3] Whoever had been initiated into the company of Pythagoras' disciples, put into the common stock whatever he possessed in the way of money and household. In the second of his *Adages*, however, Erasmus observes that communism is not to be carried to the extent of giving things equally to old and young, learned and ignorant, stupid and wise, but goods are to be distributed in accordance with everyone's office, dignity, etc.

The *Praise of Folly* even makes humorous use of this famous axiom of Pythagoras. Folly singles out "certain Pythagoreans, in whose eyes all things are common—to such a degree, in fact, that whatever they light upon that is lying around loose they carry off with a tranquil spirit, as if it passed to them by inheritance."[4] * * *

Erasmus thus seems to have had a settled conviction that Christ had wished communism—not merely the communism of use or alms, but the communism of joint ownership—to be the proper state for His followers. Here is yet another point of conflict between the humanistic Erasmus and the Aristotelian Schoolmen. The author of the *Adages* does not spare the latter in his denunciation of their amalgamation of the doctrines of Aristotle and Christ, which

3. CWE 31:30. Aulus Gellius (2nd century c.e.) was the author of a sprawling Latin miscellany, *Attic Nights*. Erasmus refers to Book 1, chap. 9.
4. Surtz quotes from the sprightly translation of *The Praise of Folly* by Hoyt Hopewell Hudson (New York: The Modern Library, 1941), p. 69.

to him are as incompatible as fire and water. Here are his indignant words:

> We have reached such a point that the whole of Aristotle is accepted in the heart of Christian theology, in fact, accepted to such an extent that his authority is almost more sacred than that of Christ. For, if he says anything that is little in keeping with our Christian life, it is permissible to twist its meaning by a clever interpretation; but the man who dares even slightly oppose his oracular utterances, is downed [and silenced] on the spot. From Aristotle we have learned that the happiness of man is imperfect without the addition of goods of body and fortune. From Aristotle we have learned that the commonwealth in which all things are common cannot flourish. We keep trying to amalgamate the principles of Aristotle with the doctrine of Christ, that is, to mix water and fire.[5]

The whole implication of this passage is that for the Christian philosopher Aristotle's criticism of Plato's communism should be invalid. Christians should follow, not Aristotle's condemnation of joint ownership and his defense of private property, but Christ's doctrine which enjoins communism for the entire Christian community, not merely for monks and friars. In spite of his strong words in the *Adages*, however, Erasmus strangely has little to say on the practices of the early church in Jerusalem in his notes on the crucial texts in the Acts of the Apostles, either in his New Testament or in his paraphrase of the Acts.

In the preceding citations, Christ's law of love and community is linked to that of Pythagoras and Plato. On another occasion Erasmus found a bond between Christ and the Spartan Lycurgus.[6] In his *Apophthegms* Erasmus writes:

> It was customary [among the Lacedaemonians] to use the slaves of neighbors, if anyone had need, as one's own. The same held for dogs and horses, unless their master had occasion to use them. What is more, in the country, if anyone needed anything, he opened the doors and took away from its possessor what was necessary for his present task; he merely marked the place from which he had taken anything and then went his way. In the midst of customs of this kind, where could insatiable avarice find a place? where the rapacity of men who appropriate other people's property as their own? where the arrogance springing from riches? where the cruelty of robbers who cut the throat of an unknown and innocent

---

5. From Erasmus's long essay on the proverb *"Dulce bellum inexpertis"* (War is sweet, to those who have not tried it), in his *Adages*: see CWE 35:419.
6. The legendary lawgiver of ancient Sparta. (Cf. Utopus.)

traveler for a few pennies? Would you not say that this was a genuinely Christian custom if they had obtained Christ, instead of Lycurgus, as a maker of laws?[7]

Here, it is true, is found a communism of use, rather than of ownership, a concept which is more in the Aristotelian tradition, but it is a use carried so far that it amounts, for all practical purposes, to a communism of ownership.

Erasmus' whole concept of the strict communism which should prevail in Christendom must have received a severe jolt in the early years of the Reformation. Except on a purely theoretical basis, he seems hardly to have conceived of Christian communism on a large scale. If it had come peacefully and gradually, Erasmus would have welcomed the transformation and change. The violent espousal of total communism, as on the part of some Anabaptists,[8] was quite another matter. Erasmus admits that for some time in the apostolic period at the origins of the early Church a community of all goods prevailed, but not even at that time among all Christians. For, with the spread of the gospel far and wide, communism could not be preserved, for the reason that it would have ended in revolt. He seems to be referring to distressing disagreements and conflicts, from which even the primitive church in Jerusalem had suffered in a small way: "Now in those days, as the number of the disciples was increasing, there arose a murmuring among the Hellenists against the Hebrews that their widows were being neglected in the daily ministration" (Acts vi.1). His final decision is expressed thus: "More in accord with harmony is the following policy: the ownership of goods and the right of administration should be in the hands of lawful proprietors, but the use of these goods should be made common by charity."[9] Face to face with hard reality, even the scholarly idealist has to admit that the sane judgment of Aristotle and Aquinas, after all is said and done, is the best: private ownership with common use inspired by Christian love.

The author of *Utopia*, too, in the heat of conflict indirectly asserts against the Anabaptists the right of private property. One of the worst charges he can launch against Tyndale is that the latter has added to his own heresies those of the Anabaptists, who say "that there ought to be no rulers at all in Christendom, neither spiritual nor temporal, and that no man should have anything proper of his

---

7. Surtz's translation from Erasmus's *Apophthegmata* (a collection of ancient aphorisms, with Erasmus's commentaries on them).
8. A name applied to various radical Protestant sects that denied the validity of infant baptism (the name means "re-baptizer") and also held other views shocking to most of their contemporaries.
9. Surtz's translation from Erasmus's exposition of Psalm 84 (in the Latin Vulgate Bible, Psalm 83).

own, but that all lands and all goods ought by God's law to be all men's in common, and that all women ought to be common of all men."[1] Did More, in a way similar to Erasmus, suffer a change of opinion in regard to Christ's view of communism?

NORTHROP FRYE

From Varieties of Literary Utopias†

There are two social conceptions which can be expressed only in terms of myth. One is the social contract, which presents an account of the origins of society. The other is the utopia, which presents an imaginative vision of the *telos* or end at which social life aims. These two myths both begin in an analysis of the present, the society that confronts the mythmaker, and they project this analysis in time or space. The contract projects it into the past, the utopia into the future or some distant place. * * *

The utopia is a *speculative* myth; it is designed to contain or provide a vision for one's social ideas, not to be a theory connecting social facts together. There have been one or two attempts to take utopian constructions literally by trying to set them up as actual communities, but the histories of these communities make melancholy reading. Life imitates literature up to a point, but hardly up to that point. The utopian writer looks at his own society first and tries to see what, for his purposes, its significant elements are. The utopia itself shows what society would be like if those elements were fully developed. Plato looked at his society and saw its structure as a hierarchy of priests, warriors, artisans, and servants— much the same structure that inspired the caste system of India. The *Republic* shows what a society would be like in which such a hierarchy functioned on the principle of justice, that is, each man doing his own work.[1] More, thinking within a Christian framework

---

1. *The Confutation of Tyndale's Answer,* CW 8:664; spelling modernized.

† Reprinted by permission of *Dædalus,* the Journal of the American Academy of Arts and Sciences, from an issue titled "Utopia": 94.2 (spring 1965): 323–47. © 1965 by the American Academy of Arts and Sciences. Used by permission of MIT Press Journals. Except for the one identified as Frye's, all notes are by the editors.
    The Canadian literary theorist and critic Northrop Frye (1912–1991), best known for *Anatomy of Criticism* (1957)—an enormously influential attempt to develop an objective and fully comprehensive theory of literature and criticism anchored in the archetypal constants of the human imagination—was one of the great taxonomists (classifiers) of literature. Bringing profound intelligence and encyclopedic knowledge to this task, Frye illuminated at once the various literary species he overviewed and individual works within them.

1. Frye does not make the usual distinction between works of political theory that discuss the ideal form of a polity (here the *Republic* is the prototype) and utopian fiction (with More's book as prototype), in which an alternative commonwealth is described as if it actually exists.

of ideas, assumed that the significant elements of society were
the natural virtues, justice, temperance, fortitude, prudence. The
Utopia itself, in its second or constructive book, shows what a society would be like in which the natural virtues were allowed to assume
their natural forms. Bacon, on the other hand, anticipates Marx by
assuming that the most significant of social factors is technological
productivity, and his *New Atlantis*[2] constructs accordingly.

The procedure of constructing a utopia produces two literary qualities which are typical, almost invariable, in the genre. In the first
place, the behavior of society is described *ritually*. A ritual is a significant social act, and the utopia-writer is concerned only with the
typical actions which are significant of those social elements he is
stressing. In utopian stories a frequent device is for someone, generally a first-person narrator, to enter the utopia and be shown around
it by a sort of Intourist[3] guide. The story is made up largely of a
Socratic dialogue between guide and narrator, in which the narrator asks questions or thinks up objections and the guide answers
them. One gets a little weary, in reading a series of such stories, of
what seems a pervading smugness of tone. As a rule the guide is
completely identified with his society and seldom admits to any
discrepancy between the reality and the appearance of what he is
describing. But we recognize that this is inevitable given the conventions employed. In the second place, rituals are apparently irrational
acts which become *rational* when their significance is explained. In
such utopias the guide explains the structure of the society and
thereby the significance of the behavior being observed. Hence, the
behavior of society is presented as rationally motivated. It is a common objection to utopias that they present human nature as governed more by reason than it is or can be. But this rational emphasis,
again, is the result of using certain literary conventions. The utopian
romance does not present society as governed by reason; it presents it
as governed by ritual habit, or prescribed social behavior, which is
explained rationally.

Every society, of course, imposes a good deal of prescribed social
behavior on its citizens, much of it being followed unconsciously,
anything completely accepted by convention and custom having in
it a large automatic element. But even automatic ritual habits are
explicable, and so every society can be seen or described to some
extent as a product of conscious design. The symbol of conscious
design in society is the city, with its abstract pattern of streets and
buildings, and with the complex economic cycle of production, dis-

2. On Bacon's scientific utopia, see p. 199, n. 4 above.
3. Before its privatization in 1992, Intourist was the government-run travel agency of the
Soviet Union, strictly controlling what tourists saw and heard.

tribution, and consumption that it sets up. The utopia is primarily a vision of the orderly city and of a city-dominated society. Plato's Republic is a city-state, Athenian in culture and Spartan in discipline. It was inevitable that the utopia, as a literary genre, should be revived at the time of the Renaissance, the period in which the medieval social order was breaking down again into city-state units or nations governed from a capital city. Again, the utopia, in its typical form, contrasts, implicitly or explicitly, the writer's own society with the more desirable one he describes. The desirable society, or the utopia proper, is essentially the writer's own society with its unconscious ritual habits transposed into their conscious equivalents. The contrast in value between the two societies implies a satire on the writer's own society, and the basis for the satire is the unconsciousness or inconsistency in the social behavior he observes around him. More's *Utopia* begins with a satire on the chaos of sixteenth-century life in England and presents the Utopia itself as a contrast to it. Thus the typical utopia contains, if only by implication, a satire on the *anarchy* inherent in the writer's own society, and the utopia form flourishes best when anarchy seems most a social threat. Since More, utopias have appeared regularly but sporadically in literature, with a great increase around the close of the nineteenth century. This later vogue clearly had much to do with the distrust and dismay aroused by extreme laissez-faire versions of capitalism, which were thought of as manifestations of anarchy.

Most utopia-writers follow either More (and Plato) in stressing the legal structure of their societies, or Bacon in stressing its technological power. The former type of utopia is closer to actual social and political theory; the latter overlaps with what is now called science fiction. Naturally, since the Industrial Revolution a serious utopia can hardly avoid introducing technological themes. And because technology is progressive, getting to the utopia has tended increasingly to be a journey in time rather than space, a vision of the future and not of a society located in some isolated spot on the globe (or outside it: journeys to the moon are a very old form of fiction, and some of them are utopian). The growth of science and technology brings with it a prodigious increase in the legal complications of existence. As soon as medical science identifies the source of a contagious disease in a germ, laws of quarantine go into effect; as soon as technology produces the automobile, an immense amount of legal apparatus is imported into life, and thousands of non-criminal citizens become involved in fines and police-court actions. This means a corresponding increase in the amount of ritual habit necessary to life, and a new ritual habit must be conscious, and so constraining, before it becomes automatic or unconscious. Science and technology, especially the latter, introduce into society the conception of directed social change, change with logical consequences attached to it. These consequences turn on[4] the increase of ritual habit. And as long as ritual habit can still be seen as an imminent possibility, as something we may or may not acquire, there can be an emotional attitude toward it either of acceptance or repugnance. The direction of social change may be thought of as exhilarating, as in most theories of progress, or as horrible, as in pessimistic or apprehensive social theories. Or it may be thought that whether the direction of change is good or bad will depend on the attitude society takes toward it. If the attitude is active and resolute, it may be good; if helpless and ignorant, bad.

A certain amount of claustrophobia enters this argument when it is realized, as it is from about 1850 on, that technology tends to unify the whole world. The conception of an *isolated* utopia like that of More or Plato or Bacon gradually evaporates in the face of this fact. Out of this situation come two kinds of utopian romance: the straight utopia, which visualizes a world-state assumed to be ideal, or at least ideal in comparison with what we have, and the utopian satire or parody, which presents the same kind of social goal in terms of slavery, tyranny, or anarchy. Examples of the former in the literature of the last century include Bellamy's *Looking Backward*, Morris' *News from Nowhere*, and H. G. Wells' *A Modern Utopia*. Wells is one of the few writers who have constructed both serious and satirical utopias. Examples of the utopian satire include Zamiatin's *We*, Aldous Huxley's *Brave New World*, and George Orwell's *1984*. There are other types of utopian satire which we shall mention in a moment, but this particular kind is a product of modern technological society, its growing sense that the whole world is destined to the same social fate with no place to hide, and its increasing realization that technology moves toward the control not merely of nature but of the operations of the mind. We may note that what is a serious utopia to its author, and to many of its readers, could be read as a satire by a reader whose emotional attitudes were different. *Looking Backward* had, in its day, a stimulating and emancipating influence on the social thinking of the time in a way that very few books in the history of literature have ever had. Yet most of us today would tend to read it as a sinister blueprint of tyranny, with its industrial "army," its stentorian propaganda delivered over the "telephone" to the homes of its citizens, and the like.

The nineteenth-century utopia had a close connection with the growth of socialist political thought and shared its tendency to think in global terms. When Engels attacked "utopian" socialism and con-

---

4. I.e., hinge upon, depend on.

trasted it with his own "scientific" kind, his scientific socialism was utopian in the sense in which we are using that term, but what he rejected under the category of "utopian" was the tendency to think in terms of a delimited socialist society, a place of refuge like the phalansteries of Fourier.[5] For Engels, as for Marxist thinkers generally, there was a world-wide historical process going in a certain direction; and humanity had the choice either of seizing and directing this process in a revolutionary act or of drifting into greater anarchy or slavery. The goal, a classless society in which the state had withered away, was utopian; the means adopted to reach this goal were "scientific" and anti-utopian, dismissing the possibility of setting up *a* utopia within a pre-socialist world.

We are concerned here with utopian literature, not with social attitudes; but literature is rooted in the social attitudes of its time. In the literature of the democracies today we notice that utopian satire is very prominent (for example, William Golding's *Lord of the Flies*), but that there is something of a paralysis of utopian thought and imagination. We can hardly understand this unless we realize the extent to which it is the result of a repudiation of Communism. In the United States particularly the attitude toward a definite social ideal as a planned goal is anti-utopian: such an ideal, it is widely felt, can produce in practice only some form of totalitarian state. And whereas the Communist program calls for a revolutionary seizure of the machinery of production, there is a strong popular feeling in the democracies that the utopian goal can be reached only by allowing the machinery of production to function by itself, as an automatic and continuous process. Further, it is often felt that such an automatic process tends to decentralize authority and break down monopolies of political power. This combination of an anti-utopian attitude toward centralized planning and a utopian attitude toward the economic process naturally creates some inconsistencies. When I was recently in Houston, I was told that Houston had no zoning laws: that indicates a strongly anti-utopian sentiment in Houston, yet Houston was building sewers, highways, clover-leaf intersections, and shopping centers in the most uninhibited utopian way.

There is however something of a donkey's carrot in attaching utopian feelings to a machinery of production largely concerned with consumer goods. We can see this if we look at some of the utopian romances of the last century. The technological utopia has one literary disadvantage: its predictions are likely to fall short of what comes true, so that what the writer saw in the glow of vision we see only as

---

5. The French socialist and philosopher Charles Fourier (1772–1837) proposed utopian communities called phalanxes, centered in "phalanstères": large buildings to house the 1600–1800 members of the community and most of their activities. A number of phalanxes were actually established in 19th-century America.

a crude version of ordinary life. Thus Edgar Allan Poe has people crossing the Atlantic in balloons at a hundred miles an hour one thousand years after his own time.[6] I could describe the way I get to work in the morning, because it is a form of ritual habit, in the idiom of a utopia, riding on a subway, guiding myself by street signs, and the like, showing how the element of social design conditions my behavior at every point. It might sound utopian if I had written it as a prophecy a century ago, or now to a native of a New Guinea jungle, but it would hardly do so to my present readers. Similarly with the prediction of the radio (called, as noted above, the telephone, which had been invented) in Bellamy's *Looking Backward* (1888). A slightly earlier romance, said to be the original of Bellamy's book, is *The Diothas*, by John MacNie (1883).[7] It predicts a general use of a horseless carriage, with a speed of twenty miles an hour (faster downhill). One passage shows very clearly how something common-place to us could be part of a utopian romance in 1883:

> "You see the white line running along the centre of the road," resumed Utis. "The rule of the road requires that line to be kept on the left, except when passing a vehicle in front. Then the line may be crossed, provided the way on that side is clear."

But while technology has advanced far beyond the wildest utopian dreams even of the last century, the essential quality of human life has hardly improved to the point that it could be called utopian. The real strength and importance of the utopian imagination, both for literature and for life, if it has any at all, must lie elsewhere.

The popular view of the utopia, and the one which in practice is accepted by many if not most utopia-writers, is that a utopia is an ideal or flawless state, not only logically consistent in its structure but permitting as much freedom and happiness for its inhabitants as is possible to human life. Considered as a final or definitive social ideal, the utopia is a static society; and most utopias have built-in safeguards against radical alteration of the structure. This feature gives it a somewhat forbidding quality to a reader not yet committed to it. An imaginary dialogue between a utopia-writer and such a reader might begin somewhat as follows: Reader: "I can see that this society might work, but I wouldn't want to live in it." Writer: "What you mean is that you don't want your present ritual habits disturbed. My utopia would feel different from the inside, where the ritual hab-its would be customary and so carry with them a sense of freedom rather than constraint." Reader: "Maybe so, but my sense of freedom

---

6. In Poe's story "Mellonta Tauta."
7. I owe my knowledge of *The Diothas*, and much else in this paper, to the admirable col-lection *The Quest for Utopia, An Anthology of Imaginary Societies* by Glenn Negley and J. Max Patrick (New York: Schuman, 1952) [Frye's note].

right now is derived from *not* being involved in your society. If I were, I'd either feel constraint or I'd be too unconscious to be living a fully human life at all." If this argument went on, some compromise might be reached: the writer might realize that freedom really depends on a sense of constraint, and the reader might realize that a utopia should not be read simply as a description of a most perfect state, even if the author believes it to be one. Utopian thought is imaginative, with its roots in literature, and the literary imagination is less concerned with achieving ends than with visualizing possibilities.

There are many reasons why an encouragement of utopian thinking would be of considerable benefit to us. An example would be an attempt to see what the social results of automation might be, or might be made to be; and surely some speculation along this line is almost essential to self-preservation. Again, the intellectual separation of the "two cultures"[8] is said to be a problem of our time, but this separation is inevitable, it is going steadily to increase, not decrease, and it cannot possibly be cured by having humanists read more popular science or scientists read more poetry. The real problem is not the humanist's ignorance of science or vice versa, but the ignorance of both humanist and scientist about the society of which they are both citizens. The quality of an intellectual's social imagination is the quality of his maturity as a thinker, whatever his brilliance in his own line. In the year that George Orwell published *1984*,[9] two other books appeared in the utopian tradition, one by a humanist, Robert Graves' *Watch the North Wind Rise*, the other by a social scientist, B. F. Skinner's *Walden Two*. Neither book was intended very seriously: they reflect the current view that utopian thinking is not serious. It is all the more significant that both books show the infantilism of specialists who see society merely as an extension of their own speciality. The Graves book is about the revival of mother goddess cults in Crete, and its preoccupation with the more lugubrious superstitions of the past makes it almost a caricature of the pedantry of humanism. Skinner's book shows how to develop children's will power by hanging lollipops around their necks and giving them rewards for not eating them: its Philistine vulgarity makes it a caricature of the pedantry of social science. The utopia, the effort at social imagination, is an area in which specialized disciples can meet and interpenetrate with a mutual respect for each other, concerned with clarifying their common social context.

8. The phrase was popularized by C. P. Snow's Cambridge lecture "The Two Cultures" (1959). In it, Snow, a physicist who became a novelist, lamented the communications breakdown between scientists and humanists.
9. Though completed in 1948, *1984* (officially titled *Nineteen Eighty-Four*) was published in 1949. Of the two books Frye goes on to say were published the same year as Orwell's, only Graves's was: Skinner's had appeared in 1948.

The word "imaginative" refers to hypothetical constructions, like those of literature or mathematics. The word "imaginary" refers to something that does not exist. Doubtless many writers of utopias think of their state as something that does not exist but which they wish did exist; hence their intention as writers is descriptive rather than constructive. But we cannot possibly discuss the utopia as a literary genre on this negatively existential basis. We have to see it as a species of the constructive literary imagination, and we should expect to find that the more penetrating the utopian writer's mind is, the more clearly he understands that he is communicating a vision to his readers, not sharing a power or fantasy dream with them.

* * *

ELIZABETH McCUTCHEON

From Denying the Contrary:
More's Use of Litotes in the *Utopia*†

Thomas More's talk of a "neglectam simplicitatem" of language and style in his "libellum", his little book,[1] says a great deal about the apparently impromptu and effortless effect he wanted, and implies what it seems to deny: a rhetorical sophistication we are exploring in increasing detail. Two articles, in particular, have surveyed major areas of More's Latin style. In the one, R. Monsuez looks at the language and grammar of the *Utopia* in relationship to classical Latin texts and the ideals of the humanists. In the second, Father Surtz, drawing specifically upon Erasmus' *De copia,* studies More from the point of view of Renaissance rhetoric, and finds a style shaped as a whole by More's awareness of his audience, other Christian humanists, and his form, a dialogue.[2] Because of these studies it is now

---

† Reprinted with permission of the Amici Thomae Mori from *Moreana* no. 31–32 (November 1971), 107–21. Except where otherwise indicated, footnotes are the author's (sometimes pruned due to space limitations). At several points McCutcheon inserts, in brackets, English translations of phrases she quotes in Latin. The editors have expanded this practice.

    In what is probably the single most frequently cited article on *Utopia*, McCutcheon here combines the close-reading techniques of 20th-century literary criticism with a knowledge of the classical rhetorical tradition (in its Renaissance form) to create a revelatory study of a key aspect of the relation between style and meaning in More's book.

1. See More's prefatory letter to Peter Giles in *Utopia, The Complete Works of St. Thomas More,* eds. Edward Surtz and J. H. Hexter, IV (New Haven: Yale Univ. Press, 1965), 38/13 and 38/3. Subsequent citations from the *Utopia* are from this, the Yale edition, unless otherwise specified. ["*Neglectam simplicitatem*": casual simplicity (cf. p. 5 above); editors' note.]

2. R. Monsuez, "Le Latin de Thomas More dans 'Utopia'," *Annales publiées par la Faculté des Lettres et Sciences Humaines de Toulouse,* Nouvelle Série, Tome II, Fasc. I (Janvier, 1966), *Caliban* 3, 35–78; Edward Surtz, "Aspects of More's Latin Style in *Utopia*," *Studies in the Renaissance,* 14 (1967), 93–109. As Father Surtz writes, "Detailed and painstaking studies need to be made of every element of style . . .", p. 107.

both possible and necessary to look still more closely at the foreground of More's text. By isolating a single rhetorical turn of thought and phrase—in this instance, litotes, "in which a thing is affirmed by stating the negative of its opposite",[3]—and fine variations in its use, we can catch hold of what is in fact a far more intricate and subtle verbal structure and a denser, more distinctively literary texture, than the narrator of the *Utopia* was always willing to admit, except by indirection.

The most immediate and obvious fact about litotes in the *Utopia* is how often More uses it; I count over one hundred and forty examples in the one hundred Latin pages of the Yale text.[4] It is hard, at first, to know how much to make of this. Litotes was a common figure in the Renaissance, and the Tudor rhetorician, sensitive to the state of his own language, and anxious to enrich it, tended at times to dismiss it rather casually. As Hoskins says, "But why should I give examples of the most usual phrases in the English tongue? As, we say *not the wisest man that ever I saw*, for *a man of small wisdom.*"[5] From this point of view, then, perhaps all we can surely say is that More is concerned with a functional and idiomatic, even colloquial, prose, rather than an ornate one; litotes, whether in Latin or English, is not, usually, the showiest of figures.

A closer look at More's text, however, suggests that these litotes cannot be seen simply in the light of a period style at its most ordinary or habitual, that they are, rather, a major element in the fine brushwork of the *Utopia*. The repetition, which allows us to think of litotes as part of More's technique and style to begin with, is too various, too purposeful.

             ☆   ☆   ☆

As More uses litotes again and again, continuously affirming something by denying its opposite, the figure becomes, ultimately, a paradigm of the structure and method of the book as a whole, echoing, often in the briefest of syntactical units, the larger, paradoxical and double vision which will discover the best state of the commonwealth in an island called Noplace. The more immediate purpose and effects of litotes can rarely be apprehended in a single term, however. ☆ ☆ ☆ Inevitably one rhetorical effect merges more or less imperceptibly

---

3. I have deliberately used a common handbook definition here; see William Flint Thrall and Addison Hibbard, *A Handbook to Literature,* rev. and enlarged C. Hugh Holman (New York: The Odyssey Press, 1960), "Litotes," p. 263. Richard A. Lanham, *A Handlist of Rhetorical Terms: A Guide for Students of English Literature* (Berkeley: Univ. of California Press, 1968), is also useful. *The Encyclopedia of Poetry and Poetics,* ed. Alex Preminger et al. (Princeton, N.J.: Princeton University Press, 1965), includes a working bibliography.
4. R. Monsuez, "Le Latin de Thomas More dans 'Utopia'," also comments on its frequency in a brief discussion of litotes, p. 48. ☆ ☆ ☆
5. John Hoskins, *Directions for Speech and Style,* ed. Hoyt Hudson (Princeton: Princeton Univ. Press, 1935), p. 35.

with another, sometimes changing before our eyes, because litotes is not a static figure. The understatement and the mental movement inherent in a process of negation allow for a multiple effect which it becomes exceedingly difficult to generalize about. * * *

* * *

Irony of some sort is, of course, inseparable from the understatement and process of denied denial in litotes. * * * When * * * Raphael compares the justice (so-called) of other nations with that of the Utopians, and asks how it can possibly be just that the nobleman, the banker, or anyone whose work "non sit Reipublicae magnopere necessarium" (238/24–25) [is "not very essential to the commonwealth" (239/32)][6] lives in magnificence, while the common man lives less well than the beasts of burden, the ironic understatement is painfully intensive. * * *

Irony is itself sometimes subsumed in a more complex effect which is satiric in force, a result of the alternatives which litotes as a figure requires. The denied negations do, in fact, frequently comment indirectly, but nevertheless pointedly, on aspects of life elsewhere. * * * While, then, the speaker seems to be looking at some new world when he says, for instance, that the Polylerites are not unwisely governed, the words he denies come closer to home. Again, the virtuous and loving behavior of those "haud sane pauci" (224/20–21)[7] in Utopia who pursue hard work for the well-being of others obliquely points to the very few in the known world who would dream of doing such a thing. Thus that general and ironic "awareness of contradiction between the two worlds" which Father Surtz speaks of in his introduction to the *Utopia* (clii) is made much more precise by way of litotic contrasts like these.

* * *

Still other effects are inherent in litotes, as More uses them. Ambiguity is one, for reasons both logical and psychological. The Renaissance was well aware of the logical complications and ambiguities which result when something is affirmed by negating the contrary. Litotes and ten other figures (an important group in the *Utopia*, including antithesis, irony, paradox and paralipsis[8]) can be specifically related to that topic of invention[9] called opposites, of which

---

6. Cf. p. 94 above [editors' note].
7. Literally, "not very few" (cf. p. 88 above) [editors' note].
8. A rhetorical figure in which a speaker or writer claims to be omitting something while actually *not* omitting it; usually introduced via set phrases such as *not to mention, to say nothing of, far be it from me to mention* [editors' note].
9. The rhetorical term for the process of finding materials for a composition. *Topics* of invention are standard subject-matter categories (such as "opposites") that are useful in that process [editors' note].

there were thought to be four sorts in all: contraries, relatives, priva-
tives, and contradictories. To affirm one contradictory is to deny the
other, but litotes based on the first three categories may well be
ambiguous. Though immediate contraries (faith/unbelief, for example) have no species between, so that "one or the other must be
affirmed",[1] mediate contraries do have a mediate or middle ground
between the two extremes. "Not white" is the seemingly inevitable
text-book example; as Thomas Wilson says, "if a cloth be not white,
it is no reason to call it blacke. For it may bee blewe, greene, redd,
russett. . . ."[2] Relatives (Isidore cites "few" and "many") and priva-
tives (sight and blindness, for example, for which a mediate could be
an eye inflammation, according to Isidore)[3] can also be ambiguous.
On these grounds such common litotes as "non pessime" (48/28,
52/1, 80/16), "non exigvi" (46/8, 214/22), "haud pauca" (54/2, 244/14),
"haud pauci" (218/9, 224/20–21), "nec pauci" (222/14), "haud multi"
(158/5), "haud saepe" (188/25), "non saepe" (184/29), or "haud semel"
(212/6)[4] are logically ambiguous. We may, at first, think of their opposites, just as we do with white-black, yet all have one or more species
between. "Non pessime", for instance, has to move from *worst* through
rather bad and *bad* even before it can move towards *good, quite good*,
or *the best*, if it does; "haud pauci" may mean *more than a few, some,*
or *many,* and "haud semel" [not once] is even more open ended.

A second kind of ambiguity arises from the psychological pecu-
liarity of negating a negation. As Jespersen has observed, ". . . it
should be noted that the double negative always modifies the idea,
for the result of the whole expression is somewhat different from
the simple idea expressed positively." He calls attention to the same
phenomenon which led Puttenham to call litotes the "Moderator",
though he interprets it differently, when he adds that "*not uncommon*
is weaker than *common,* . . . the psychological reason being that the
detour through the two mutually destroying negatives weakens the
mental energy of the hearer and implies on the part of the speaker
a certain hesitation absent from the blunt, outspoken *common* . . ."[5]
In fact, since litotes as a rhetorical and literary technique not
only moderates but intensifies, so that, as John Smith points out,

1. Sister Miriam Joseph, *Rhetoric in Shakespeare's Time: Literary Theory of Renaissance
   Europe* (1947; rpt. New York: Harcourt, 1962), p. 322.
2. Thomas Wilson, *The Rule of Reason; Conteining the Art of Logike* [1551] (London,
   1567), fol. 52ᵛ, as cited in Sister Miriam Joseph, *Rhetoric in Shakespeare's Time,* p. 322.
3. Isidore of Seville (7th–8th centuries C.E.) was an encyclopedic transmitter of classical
   learning to the Middle Ages [editors' note].
4. In order, "not the worst," "no slight," "not a few" (three forms), "not many," "not often"
   (two forms), "not [just] once" [editors' note].
5. Otto Jespersen, *Negation in English and Other Languages,* in *Selected Writings of Otto
   Jespersen* (1917; rpt. London: George Allen & Unwin Ltd., n.d.), p. 63. Cf. Ch. 24 in his
   The Philosophy of Grammar (1924; rpt. Allen & Unwin, 1948). [George Puttenham
   calls litotes "the Moderator" in *The Arte of English Poesie* (1589; rpt. Menston, UK:
   Scolar Press, 1968), p. 153; editors' note.]

". . . *sometimes a word is put down with a sign of negation, when as much is signified as if we had spoken affirmatively, if not more*,"[6] it may be either stronger or weaker. But it is ambiguous. We can and must depend upon the context, of course, but even so we do have to hesitate and decide to what extent a particular litotes is moderating, to what extent emphasizing, or better, attempt to hold two apparently contradictory but equally real effects in our minds at the same time. I do not think, pace Jespersen, that this necessarily "weakens the mental energy of the hearer". More probably it arouses it, requiring us to linger over the construction and its context—hence its particular effectiveness as a figure of emphasis. But we are required to undergo a complex mental action; if something is, for example, *not uncommon,* to pursue Jespersen's example, we move from a *common* which isn't quite stated to the *uncommon* which is, and then, because that is denied, back towards *common* again. But we do not usually know quite where to stop, a process we can visualize this way:

$$[\text{COMMON}] \longrightarrow \text{UNCOMMON}$$
$$\text{BUT}$$
$$\text{"NOT UNCOMMON"}$$
$$? \longleftarrow\text{-----}\underline{\qquad} \quad \therefore$$

It is just this sort of ambiguous area which a recent cartoon exploits.[7] A husband and wife are standing in front of what should be a welcome mat. But this mat reads, "not unwelcome", to the chagrin of the wife, who says, "'*See what I mean? You're never sure just where you stand with them*'".

In a larger sense we're never quite sure where we stand in the *Utopia,* either. It is, of course, a commonplace to talk about ambiguity in the *Utopia.* But on the smallest syntactical level ambiguity does exist of a sort which can never be altogether resolved, and probably was not meant to be. For this ambiguity vivifies the text, arouses its readers, and agitates its points, however casually they appear to be made, so that they neither evaporate nor solidify. We are constantly, though obliquely, teased by the many litotes already cited, not least those institutions "non pessime" ["not the worst"] (52/1) which Raphael found in the new world, or persona More's "haud pauca" (244/14) ["not a few"] in his concluding speech. Curiously, perhaps consciously, this last "haud pauca" contradicts the implications of another "haud pauca" early in Book I (54/2), which More uses in apparent and ironic antithesis to the positive "multa" (54/1) earlier in

6. John Smith, *The Mystery of Rhetorick Unveil'd* (London, 1688), sig. *a*4.
7. *The New Yorker,* February 6, 1971, p. 36.

the sentence. Here More observes that [although] Raphael did, of course, find many ["multa"] customs which were ill-advised in those new countries, "so he rehearsed not a few points from which our own cities, nations, races, and kingdoms may take example for the correction of their errors" (55/2-4).[8]

We can sense inherent ambiguities and the potential spread of meaning in a given litotes from still another point of view by looking at various translations of the "non exigvi momenti negocia" (46/8) ["matters of no small importance"] of More's first sentence. Ralph Robinson, thinking of litotes as an emphatic and intensifying device, doubles the idea in a positive sense; it becomes "weightye matters, and of greate importaunce". Gilbert Burnet, however, preserves the litotic implications, though slightly modifying the meaning, when he renders the litotes as "some Differences of no small Consequence". Closer to our period, H. V. S. Ogden, who chiefly hears the moderating possibilities, turns the phrase into "some differences". In an attempt to reconcile the moderating impulse and the emphatic one, Paul Turner writes of "a rather serious difference of opinion".[9] The Yale translation settles for simple emphasis: "certain weighty matters" (47/10). Burnet alone has left some of the ambiguities unresolved; all the other translators have, in a sense, made our minds up for us. But what we gain in clarity we lose elsewhere. The alternatives, and therefore any possible irony, disappear, as does the ambiguity, and with that, the tension and movement of mind, so that nuances of meaning are also dissolved. In short, this litotes becomes far less significant, both in what it says and the way it says it, as an anticipation of the *Utopia* to come. For the phrase More writes certainly calls attention, however obliquely, to the kind of issue being argued about in the known world. He does not, admittedly, spell out the details of what was a massive commercial problem,[1] but he certainly says enough to reinforce our sense of the power and splendor and pride which activates almost all states (except, as we shall discover, Utopia). Indeed, "negocia" itself has commercial overtones which are very unlike the word[s] Raphael will later use for what he thinks of as the public welfare: "salutem publicam" (104/8). By beginning, then, with "non exigvi momenti negocia" More is able to raise, for just a moment, a question to which much of the subsequent discussion returns: what sorts of state matters are trifling? And what sorts are not? But, what-

8. Cf. p. 13 above [editors' note].
9. Ralph Robynson, trans. (1551) in *The Utopia of Sir Thomas More*, ed. J. H. Lupton (Oxford: Clarendon Press, 1895), p. 21; Gilbert Burnet, trans., *Utopia: Written in Latin by Sir Thomas More, Chancellor of England: Translated into English* (London, 1684), p. 1; H. V. S. Ogden, ed. and trans., *Utopia*, by Sir Thomas More (New York: Appleton-Century-Crofts, 1949), p. 1; Paul Turner, trans., *Utopia*, by Thomas More (Harmondsworth, Middlesex, Eng.: Penguin Books Ltd., 1965), p. 37.
1. In this connection see the note to 46/8, 295 in the Yale *Utopia*.

ever else it does, this first "non" foreshadows the processes of negation and opposites which typify so much of the *Utopia.*

Like all other negatives, only more so, because now the negative is
itself negated, litotes speak of a habit of mind, a tendency to see more
than one side to a question. Intellectual, judicial, and persuasive,
they ask us to weigh and consider alternatives which the writer has
himself considered. So each litotes does, then, link writer with
reader, who tries to repeat, as best he can, the mental and judicial
processes the figure so economically and often ambiguously encloses.
As Puttenham says, litotes is a "sensable figure", one which *"alter[s]
and affect[s] the minde by alteration of sense".*[2] The persuasive bias of
Renaissance rhetoric is implicit here. Where a modern writer in the
ironic mode, like Herman Melville or Henry James, will use this sort
of negation to reveal hesitations, qualifications, uncertainties and
ambiguous complications in the consciousness of the narrator or a
major character in his fiction, More's fiction, though no less ironic,
uses litotes, primarily, to affect and alter *our* minds. Yet it is also true
that the alternatives were More's to begin with, so that litotes makes
us simultaneously much more aware of his mind in action and certain divisions in it; it reinforces our sense of More himself as one
who, indeed, saw more than one side of a question.[3]

From this point of view, even such a seemingly conventional litotes
as "haud dubie" (62/25, 86/16, 96/32, 236/3) or a more emphatic
"Neque dubium est" (216/27–28) or a "non dubito" (242/16) ["doubtless"; "There's no doubt"; "I don't doubt"] implies a process of mental
assessment on the part of the speaker. It suggests, as "to be sure" or
"certainly" cannot, that someone has weighed the possibilities and
reached a decision—hence its usefulness as a persuasive figure. The
same effect is multiplied in one of More's favorite litotic constructions, which, unlike most, does spell out (but qualify) its alternatives:
some combination of a negative with *minus* or *minus quam.* Like the
"nec minus salutaris quam festiuus" of the title page ["no less beneficial than entertaining"], or the several *non minus . . . quam* ["no
less . . . than"] litotes in the passage describing the Utopian way with
gold, these constructions seem to ask us to weigh or try to balance
different ideas or values, almost as if we were asked to find the balance point on a moving see-saw. The ideas are grammatically "equal",
yet, often, the figure is weighted on one side; there is, in other words,
a kind of dynamic emphasis which requires that we hold the two
elements both together and apart. It can startle, or it can result in

2. Puttenham, *The Arte of English Poesie,* p. 148.
3. An intensive example of a reading on these lines is David Bevington, "The Dialogue in
    Utopia: Two Sides to the Question," *S.P.* [*Studies in Philology*], 58 (1961), 496–509.
    Compare and contrast with this J. H. Hexter, *More's Utopia: The Biography of an Idea*
    (1952; rpt. Torchbook ed., New York: Harper, 1965).

ironic or satiric incongruities: things which shouldn't be "equal" are, but things which should be, too often aren't. Raphael's description of the robber, who is in no less danger "if merely condemned for theft" than "if he were convicted of murder as well" (75/8–9)[4] is an instance of the first sort; his description of the Utopian way of providing for its citizens, an instance of the second: "Then take into account the fact that there is no less provision for those who are now helpless but once worked than for those who are still working" (239/22–25).[5] But most litotes in *Utopia* do not, in fact, spell out the alternative in this way. With litotes like "non pessime" or "haud pauca" ["not the worst" or "not a few"] it is almost as if we saw one side of a metaphysical see-saw. So the mind is stimulated or teased into the sort of action described earlier, having, often, to construct the opposite which is denied and hold on to contraries which it weighs, each against the other. And once again, though in a more oblique way, we discover a weighting, a persuasive action which often favors Utopian attitudes, however negatively they may appear to be described. As More says, in a fine piece of understatement, which also reveals an awareness of just how complex this sort of question is, Raphael found nations "non pessime institutas" ["not the worst governed"] (52/1).[6] But with this we come * * * to Peacham's point; litotes does, indeed, "praise or dispraise, and that in a modest forme and manner".[7] In the *Utopia*, more precisely, it praises and dispraises, often almost simultaneously, since to deny something about Utopia is to affirm it, indirectly, of the world as we know it.

More ended his book with a famous wish. My own present hope is a more modest one—that somehow litotes be more systematically retained in translations of *Utopia*, which have, usually, made at best tepid attempts to preserve it, often converting a litotic construction to a simple positive. Obviously, syntactical patterns are difficult to turn from one language to another, and negatives are trickier still. But when, for example, More's final "haud pauca" (244/14) ["not a few"] becomes "many" (245/17), or the frequent litotic descriptions of the Polylerites and the Utopians, which comment *via diversa*[8] on the way of this world, are transformed into straightforward descriptions, we lose the emphasis and the understatement, the irony and possible satire, and the ambiguity of the original. The complicated action of More's mind is coarsened, his meaning blurred, the energy and tension of a muscular prose relaxed. On a larger

4. Cf. p. 22 above [editors' note].
5. Cf. p. 94 above [editors' note].
6. Cf. p. 12 above [editors' note].
7. [Henry]Peacham, *The Garden of Eloqvence* [London, 1593], p. 151.
8. In an oblique manner. The phrase is from a letter (*CWE* 3:111–39) in which Erasmus defends *The Praise of Folly*—which, he says, though it employs the indirect method of satire, is in intention just as serious as any of his other works [editors' note].

scale, we lose the cumulative effect of a device much repeated, and we have, too often, only one side of what is at least a two-sided vision inherent in every denial of the contrary. In More's hands, litotes was, in fact, a superlative tool for both the exceedingly polite gentleman, the fictional More, and the passionate visionary who had seen Utopia. Avoiding controversy, it constantly calls attention, without seeming to do so, to the purpose and values behind the countless delightful details with which More created both dialogue and discourse; it truly is a figure of and for the mind. Intensive yet understated, emphatic, often drily ironic, sometimes humorous or wry, concealing tremendous energy in its apparent ease and frequent brevity, litotes is not the least of the rhetorical figures in the vision and satire we call *Utopia*.

ALISTAIR FOX

[An Intricate, Intimate Compromise][†]

* * *

The circumstances were right for More to entertain his eutopian[1] fantasy when he sat down to write *Utopia* in 1515. His imagination had been excited by the discoveries of Cabot and Vespucci in the New World and the explorations of the Portuguese around the Cape of Good Hope to the East; his legal career in the City was advancing as well as he could wish; the momentum of Erasmian reform was approaching its height; and he had the stimulating company on the Flanders mission of Cuthbert Tunstal, Busleiden and Peter Giles, humanists with interests and ambitions similar to his own. The eutopian quality of the book can be seen in the extent to which More created the Utopians in his own image. They share his contempt for material ostentation, as attested by their simple monastic garb and their debasing use of gold for chamber pots and slaves' fetters, and of

---

† Reprinted with permission, from *Thomas More: History and Providence* (New Haven and London: Yale University Press, 1983), chap. 2, "The Morean Synthesis: *Utopia*," pp. 53–69. Except where otherwise indicated, footnotes are by the editors. To save space, Fox's bibliographical footnotes have been pruned, and his occasional quotations of More's Latin have been omitted. Fox quotes *Utopia* from the Yale edition (CW 4), but references have been changed to the corresponding pages in the present edition.

Fox's book—greatly facilitated by the massive Yale edition of More's *Works* (then two-thirds complete)—immediately became an influential survey of More's *oeuvre*, setting individual works into the contexts of others as well as into an overarching psychobiographical account of More as a deeply conflicted personality. An English professor, Fox reads *Utopia* much as if it were a novel, focusing especially on the character of its narrators and their relation to the author.

1. As *utopia* means "noplace," *eutopia* (also from Greek) means "good place." One of the prefatory poems in the early editions of *Utopia* employs the pun, and More himself was doubtless aware of it.

jewels for children's toys. They, too, believe that the secret of a happy life consists in the cultivation of the mind[2] and achieve the same kind of communal domestic order for which More strove in his own household. Specifically, he projected into the eutopians his own fondness for gardens, his liking for music, his delight in fools, and his receptivity towards foreign guests. Even the monkey to be seen in Holbein's sketch of the family group finds his way into the action, having ripped up Hythlodaeus' copy of Theophrastus during the voyage.[3]

Once the degree of whimsy in this self-projection is grasped, some of the book's thematic problems become more comprehensible, particularly those which arise from the Utopians' epicurean philosophy. This derives in part from Vespucci's description in *Mundus Novus* of people who 'live according to nature, and may be called Epicureans rather than Stoics', but also from More's own engagement with the problem that had interested him in Lucian's *Cynicus*:[4] whether the enjoyment of temporal things is compatible with virtue, a thing indifferent, or repugnant, the ascetic way being better. Observing (like Menippus) the inconsistency in even the sternest ascetics who, while imposing a life of labour, vigils and general discomfort on one nevertheless exhort that same person to relieve the privations of others, the Utopians focus the issue into a combined proposition-question:

> either a joyous life, that is, a pleasurable life, is evil, in which case not only ought you to help no one to it, but as far as you can, should take it away from everyone as being harmful and deadly, or else, if you not only are permitted but are obliged to win it for others as being good, why should you not do so first of all for yourself, to whom you should show no less favour than to others?[5]

More then allows them a privilege he would never have allowed himself in real life: to explore the implications of an assumption that virtue and pleasure *are* compatible. After having Hythlodaeus utter a discreet disclaimer against it, he gives a serious and coherent praise of pleasure.[6]

Utopian hedonism is founded on much the same religious beliefs as those More was still asserting as the basis of salvation at the end of his career: 'Those principles are as follows: that the soul is immortal

---

2. See p. 48 above.
3. See pp. 67–69 above.
4. More had translated this work. For Vespucci on the Epicureanism of the Native Americans, see p. 120 above.
5. Cf. pp. 60–61 above.
6. Fox notes that he is echoing the title of Edward Surtz's study *The Praise of Pleasure* (see p. 202 above). "Discreet disclaimer": see p. 59 above.

and born for happiness through the beneficence of God, and that our virtues and good deeds are destined to be rewarded after this life, and our misdeeds punished.'[7] These beliefs make the Utopians Christians *de facto*, if not in name, because, as More asserted later, pagans who accepted the end of salvation implicitly professed Christ, who was the means.[8] One should not, therefore, make too much of their paganism to explain away More's excursus into theoretical hedonism. It cannot be seriously argued that the Utopians' view embodies merely the findings of blind reason unilluminated by faith, for the Utopians themselves, acknowledging that reason alone is inadequate for the investigation of happiness, realize that the very legitimacy of their ethic depends upon religious principles,[9] and accept the necessary co-operation of reason and faith just as fervently as More did later in *A Dialogue Concerning Heresies*.[1] As far as their morality was concerned, More allowed the Utopians to live as he would have liked to have been able to live, but could not. Nothing would have pleased him more than to have been able to be a married priest, or to have gratified his five senses with the harmless pleasures that grace, for example, Utopian meals; but although desire inclined him towards them, other forces in his personality caused him to withhold the assent of his will to them.

Much the same is true of the common ownership upon which Utopian polity rests. More could have it both ways: he could explore the implications of a communal way of living without necessarily proposing it, however much he may have felt emotionally or intellectually inclined towards it, as one suspects he was. Hythlodaeus' summation of the general advantage of the Utopian way of life betrays the reason for its attractiveness to More; although no man owns anything, all are rich: 'For what can be richer than to live with a happy and tranquil mind, free from anxiety?'[2] In effect, the Utopians' repudiation of private property is a remedy against the same Fortuna against whom More had railed in the *Verses for the Book of Fortune*.[3] Once again, he allows them to live according to a synthesis he could only imagine: a fusion of the religious and secular lives. As Budé and Beatus Rhenanus recognized, and Giles indicated in his marginal glosses, the Utopians have adopted 'the customs and true wisdom of Christianity for public and private life',[4] consisting of 1) the equality of all

---

7. Cf. p. 60 above.
8. *A Treatise upon the Passion* CW 13, p. 43 [Fox's note].
9. See pp. 59–60 above.
1. CW 6, p. 131/19–32 [Fox's note].
2. Cf. p. 94 above.
3. A lengthy poem More wrote in early adulthood.
4. Cf. Bude's letter, p. 138 above. Beatus Rhenanus supervised the printing of the 1518 editions of *Utopia* and supplied a commendatory letter for them.

things among citizens, 2) love of peace and quiet, and 3) contempt for gold and silver. In short, they import all the virtues of monastic life into political and social affairs, and when More in a famous daydream indulged the fantasy that he was their king, it was in a 'Franciscan frock' that he saw himself, 'crowned with a diadem of wheat . . . carrying a handful of wheat as my sacred scepter'.[5] The complex collocation of associations in these images suggests that More enviously viewed the Utopians as successful Carthusian (Franciscan if you like) mercers, the governing of whom would allow him to bring the cloister into the court, where he already knew he might be headed.[6]

A large part of book 2, then, describes the happy place of More's dream; but that reflects only one aspect of the titular paradox. As happy as eutopia is, it is also 'nusquama', nowhere, and 'udepotia',[7] a land that will never be. To complicate the matter further, Utopia was conceived from the outset as being in an ambiguous relation with England: the more the two countries appear to be opposed, the more they turn out to be similar—the obvious differences paradoxically serve to underline the more significant parallels.

At one level, particularly with respect to geographical details, Utopia and England share a shadowy identity. Utopia is an island separated from the continent by a channel, Amaurotum, its capital city, together with the tidal river Anydrus, and the magnificently arched stone bridge across it, resemble London and the Thames, as the marginal glosses make clear,[8] and the houses reflect those evolved in England in their disposition, their handsome flint facings, and their glass windows (even if their flat roofs and occasional oil-smeared linen window-screens are calculated to blur the image slightly). The stage is thus set up for the Utopian illusion to dissolve into the reality of England and Europe, as it does—at the very point where Hythlodaeus asserts the most extreme degree of contrast between the two.

This occurs in the description of the Utopians' mistrust of treaties, and of their military affairs. They never make treaties with any nation, Hythlodaeus says, 'because in those parts of the world treaties and alliances between kings are not observed with much good

5. *St. Thomas More: Selected Letters*, edited by Elizabeth Frances Rogers (New Haven and London: Yale University Press, 1972), p. 85.
6. "See G. R. Elton, 'Thomas More, Councillor', in *St. Thomas More: Action and Contemplation*, ed. R. S. Sylvester (New Haven: Yale University Press, 1972), pp. 87–122" [Fox's note]. "Carthusian": an allusion to the claim in William Roper's biography of More that he had, in early adulthood, lived for four years with the Carthusian monks [editors' note].
7. See p. 138 above.
8. "Just like the Thames in England"; "Here too [i.e., the bridge] London is just like Amaurotum."

faith.' He then draws a savagely satiric contrast with Europe, meaning the exact opposite of what he says:

> In Europe, however, and especially in those parts where the
> faith and religion of Christ prevails, the majesty of treaties is
> everywhere holy and inviolable, partly through the justice and
> goodness of kings, partly through the reverence and fear of the
> Sovereign Pontiffs.[9]

This ironic inversion is not simply rhetorical, but serves to focus
the reader's attention on the presence in the antipodean world of
something that makes the rationally ideal polity of the Utopians
somewhat of a lie, if not an irrelevancy—the ineradicable sinful-
ness of human nature.

Utopia gradually turns out to be no more and no less removed
from Europe in a social and moral sense than it is in a geographical
one. As an island it resembles England, but it also differs in that its
tapering ends give it the appearance of a 'renascent' moon. The
emblem suggests at one level that Utopia figures forth the renovated
polity that an optimistic humanist might envision for England in the
context of the contemporary historical 'Renaissance'. But beneath
the seductive appearance of the Utopians' simplified, rationalized
laws and mores is the human perversity that makes their existence
necessary: the lust that wrecks their ideal of the inviolability and
permanence of marriage and leads them to permit an extremely liberal policy of divorce, the recalcitrance of hardened criminals which
forces them to slaughter repeated offenders with a savagery equal to
that in Europe, and the anger which, in their warfare, induces them
to duplicate some of the most fiendish practices devised by human
nature: vengeful reprisals, rewards for assassination, the hiring of
mercenaries, the fostering of treason, discord, and rival claims to
the throne of the enemy, and the surrounding of soldiers on the
battlefield by their wives and children. The Utopians even have their
own heretics, notably after the introduction of Christianity.[1]

As well as being frustrated in their reformist idealism by the sin-
fulness of human nature, the Utopians also experience a paradox in
the nature of things: that rational action can give rise to unreasonable consequences. Their most determined efforts to fulfill the most
laudable of intentions often meet with failure.

The most striking example of this is the war they fight on behalf
of the Nephelogetes against the Alaopolitans. Ironically, this grew
out of their willingness to fulfill what More would later describe
as God's behest, in which 'he byndeth euery man to the helpe and
defence of his good and harmless neyghbour / agaynst the malyce

9. Cf. p. 76 above.
1. See p. 85 above.

and cruelty of the wronge doer', according to the text of Ecclesiastes 17.[2] On these grounds, the Utopians went to the assistance of
the Nephelogetes, who claimed that they had suffered injustice at
the hands of the Alaopolitans under the pretext of law. The outcome
was catastrophically tragic:

> whether right or wrong, it was avenged by a fierce war. Into this
> war the neighboring nations brought their energies and
> resources to assist the power and to intensify the rancor of both
> sides. Most flourishing nations were either shaken to their
> foundations or grievously afflicted. The troubles upon troubles
> that arose were ended only by the enslavement and surrender of
> the Alaopolitans. Since the Utopians were not fighting in their
> own interest, they yielded them into the power of the Nephelo-
> getes, a people who, when the Alaopolitans were prosperous,
> were not in the least comparable to them.[3]

More recognized, just as acutely as he had in * * * [his] English
poems, that what men experience is often very different from anything they intend, desire, seek or foresee.

Utopia is full of comparable instances of tragic paradox; for example, the suffocating constraints on individual liberty required to effec-
tuate the Utopians' attempt to secure more liberty and leisure for all,
or the moral injustice of the rational justice by which they regulate
numbers in their families and colonies.[4] Through imaginatively regis-
tering this vitiation of Utopian reformist aspirations, the reader is
eventually brought to the same recognition that More had expressed
in his earlier English poems: that in this temporal world men are
always deprived of some portion of their will, however rationally or
virtuously they try to act. Utopia thus contains an inbuilt ambiguity;
it represents to a large extent what More wished for, even while he
saw that if it could be, which it never would, the human situation
would remain essentially unchanged in its character and function.

Once More had finished describing his imaginary commonwealth,
he could have left the work as it was—a self-contained speaking
picture; instead, he chose to surround it with an elaborately developed dialogue concerning the question of whether or not a wise
man should enter a king's service.

By late 1516 More was about to join Henry VIII's Court himself.
Book I was contrived to dramatize the nature of the choice before

---

2. A Dialogue Concerning Heresies, CW 6:415. More actually cites Ecclesiasticus 17.12,
which he paraphrases as "god hath gyuen euery man charge of his neyghbour to kepe
hym frome harme." Ecclesiasticus (or Sirach), not to be confused with Ecclesiastes, is
a book accepted as canonical by Catholics but not by most Protestants.
3. Cf. pp. 77–78 above.
4. See p. 49 above.

him (or, possibly, already recently behind him) in terms that anticipate the frustration of Utopian eutopianism in book 2. Both books
lead the reader into experiencing parallel cruces bearing closely upon
what More might expect to achieve, or not achieve, in office, and
what he was doing in accepting it. To gain this end, he created a dispute between two new characters: Raphael Hythlodaeus, the embit-
tered idealistic reformer, and Morus, a fictional version of himself.

The precise relation between Hythlodaeus and Morus to More
has been the subject of much inconclusive scholarly debate. Opinions range from assumptions that More is Hythlodaeus, through
Chambers' belief that More is Morus, to Hexter's gymnastic argument that More was Hythlodaeus when he wrote book 2, but Morus
by the time he wrote book 1.[5] Viewing *Utopia* in the context of More's
earlier works enables one to see that Hythlodaeus and Morus are
both More, but in a far more complicated way than has been suggested of late.[6]

There are, in fact, two Hythlodaeuses, who resemble the two Mores
reflected in the English and Latin poems. The Hythlodaeus who
enthusiastically extols the example of the Utopian commonwealth
might have written the epigrams on the accession of Henry VIII;[7]
the Hythlodaeus who lacerates European perversity and declares
his willingness to abandon it to its own satanic devices, in book 1,
could easily have written the *Verses for the Book of Fortune*. Hythlodaeus' reformist impulse and his pessimism are both sides of the
same Morean coin, and in him More contemplated the meaning of
the conflict within his earlier self. Both impulses, he saw, were inadequate. Hythlodaeus' attitude towards reform is flawed because he
believes in the necessity for absolute, radical change; he cannot
comprehend the possibility of allowing to remain in existence a state
that contains good and bad together; hence he is not satisfied merely
with applying remedies that relieve symptoms of disease, but looks
for the means of a complete cure. This attitude leads him wilfully to
misread the meaning of his own exemplum by overestimating the
extent to which Utopian communism has eliminated Pride. His peroration, which Hexter has convincingly argued was written at the
same time as book 1,[8] commits, metaphorically speaking, a form of
euthanasia in the way it desperately frees Utopian polity from the

5. J. H. Hexter, *More's "Utopia": The Biography of an Idea* (New York: Harper Torchbooks,
   1965; orig. publ. 1952), pp. 99–155. R. W. Chambers, *Thomas More* (London: Jonathan Cape, 1938; orig. publ. 1935), p. 155. On these books, see dagger notes on pp. 167
   and 190.
6. "As by David M. Bevington, 'The Dialogue in *Utopia*: Two Sides to the Question', *Studies in Philology*, 58 (1961), pp. 496–509; and W. J. Barnes, 'Irony and the English
   Apprehension of Renewal', *Queen's Quarterly*, 73 (1966), pp. 357–76" [Fox's note].
7. About which More was extremely positive: for his epigrams on the occasion, see *CW*
   1:97–117.
8. See *CW* 4:xx–xxi.

human ills More had taken pains to depict in it—just as the Utopians themselves free their incurably sick from the ills of the body.
His summation is full of images of deracination and pruning whose
very forcefulness serves to beg the question:

> In Utopia all greed for money was entirely removed with the use
> of money. What a mass of troubles was then cut away! What a
> crop of crimes was then pulled up by the roots! Who does not
> know that fraud, theft, rapine, quarrels, disorders, brawls, sedi-
> tions, murders, treasons, poisonings, which are avenged rather
> than restrained by daily executions, die out with the destruction
> of money? Who does not know that fear, anxiety, worries, toils,
> and sleepless nights will also perish at the same time as money?[9]

Hythlodaeus cannot imagine that his questions are anything more
than rhetorical, whereas the whole exemplum has served to emphasize that they are. He distorts the truth by reading into Utopia what
he needs to be able to do in order to save himself from despair, but
More has made it impossible for the reader to do likewise, even
while inviting him to do so.

Just as Hythlodaeus' expectations are unrealistic, his reaction to
their imagined frustration by European reality is out of all proportion in the degree of its pessimism. When Peter Giles suggests that
his wide experience would make him an invaluable royal councillor
if he were to enter some king's service, he denounces such a course
of action as 'servitude'. The distinction Giles tries to draw between
'servitude' and 'service' has no meaning for him. In the same way
that he wanted to see Utopian polity as more perfected than it really
was, he wants to see European polity as more hopelessly vitiated
than it really is. The most striking example of this occurs when he
recounts his experience in the household of Cardinal Morton.

This inset story anticipates the mode and meaning of the larger
Utopian exemplum by subverting the view it is ostensibly meant to
illustrate. Hythlodaeus recounts the episode to prove his contention
that people are so jealous of everyone else's ideas, so self-opinionated,
and so full of proud, absurd and obstinate prejudices that he would
not be listened to in a king's council if he were to suggest any wise
policy. He was once sitting at Morton's table, he says, when an English
lawyer's boasting over the stern measures taken to punish thieves
provoked him into anatomizing the social and economic causes of
thievery and proposing remedies for them. When Morton asked him
to declare why he objected to capital punishment for theft, Hythlodaeus proposed as an alternative the example of the Polylerites, who
punish crime more conveniently and humanely with slavery. He then

9. Cf. p. 95 above.

describes the array of different reactions his proposal received: the lawyer patronizingly dismissed it out of hand; a jester treated it face-tiously by using the occasion to propose a mock remedy for friars; and a friar aborts the whole proceeding by becoming indignantly outraged at the fool's affront to his vanity, eventually forcing the Cardinal to direct the conversation another way and then wind up the party. Hythlodaeus thinks the occasion justifies his determina-tion to remain out of public service; however, he failed to appreciate the most important response he elicited—that of Morton himself.

Morton, significantly, is already *in* public office, and that the high-est in the land under the king: Lord Chancellor of England. Without seeming to acknowledge that fact, Hythlodaeus praises him in the highest terms as 'a man who deserved respect as much for his pru-dence and virtue as for his authority', and as being 'greatly experi-enced in the law'.[1] Morton has developed extraordinary natural gifts of remarkable intellect and a phenomenal memory further by 'learn-ing and practice,' with the result that 'the king placed the greatest confidence in his advice, and the commonwealth seemed much to depend upon him'. Although Hythlodaeus conceals any recognition of it, Morton is thus an example of a man with his own kind of tal-ents who has decided to follow the advice of Morus and Giles, and his reaction to Hythlodaeus will inevitably be more crucial to the ultimate significance of the exemplum than that of any of the other characters present.

Hythlodaeus was so paranoically indignant at the behaviour of the lawyer, jester and friar that he fails to see that Morton's response confutes him. Morton was genuinely interested in his anatomy of England's ills, and was keen to hear his objection to capital punish-ment for theft. When Hythlodaeus proposed the Polylerite system of penal servitude, far from dismissing it out of hand, Morton not only suggests an accommodation of the system to English circumstances, but contemplates its possible extension to cover vagrants as well. In short, he reacts with exactly the same kind of judicious receptivity that the Utopians themselves show towards any new possibility.

Not surprisingly, Morus sees a meaning in the exemplum directly opposite to that which Hythlodaeus intends, and urges his own viewpoint even more strongly:

> Even now, nevertheless, I cannot change my mind but must needs think that, if you could persuade yourself not to shun the courts of kings, you could do the greatest good to the com-mon weal by your advice. The latter is the most important part of your duty as it is the duty of every good man.[2]

1. Cf. p. 16 above.
2. Cf. p. 27 above.

Such service is no longer described merely as being 'convenient', but as a positive responsibility; however, Morus' refusal to acclaim spontaneously the self-evident rightness of Hythlodaeus' conclusion drives the latter to deny even more vehemently any possible merit in the alternative course being suggested to him.

The most perturbing irony in book 1 is that however wrong Hythlodaeus is in some respects, he is nonetheless ultimately right. At the very moment More seems unequivocally to have destroyed Hythlodaeus' credibility by putting his objectivity in doubt, he permits Hythlodaeus' main point to challenge all that has been established against it. This occurs in the climactic clash of views after Hythlodaeus has imagined himself proposing the laws of the Achorians and Macarians in the French king's council. When he suggests that his advice would fall on deaf ears, Morus voices the objection that might occur to anyone moved by pragmatic common sense: '"Deaf indeed, without doubt", I agreed, "and, by heaven, I am not surprised. Neither, to tell the truth, do I think that such ideas should be thrust on people, or such advice given, as you are positive will never be listened to."' Developing Menippus' sceptical conclusion in Lucian's *Necromantia*,[3] More goes on to assert, with a blend of idealistic cynicism, that there is another kind of practical philosophy, which amounts to acting one's part in the play at hand, observing the decorum of the piece so as not to turn it into a tragicomedy. This saves one from having to abandon the ship in a storm when one cannot control the winds, and allows that which cannot be turned to good to be made as little bad as possible: '"For it is impossible that all should be well unless all men were good, a situation which I do not expect for a great many years to come"'.[4] Since More chose to act according to this pragmatic philosophy for the next 16 years, it comes as a shock to find that Hythlodaeus' repudiation of it is not refuted. If this advice were to be followed, he replies, almost everything Christ himself taught would need to be dissembled, when he forbad such dissembling '"to the extent that what He had whispered in the ears of His disciples He commanded to be preached openly from the housetops"'. To do otherwise is to accommodate Christ's teaching to men's morals like a rule of soft lead, which is merely to allow men to be bad in greater comfort. All that the indirect approach achieves, he continues, is to force one openly to 'approve the worst counsels and subscribe to the most ruinous decrees', since at Court one cannot keep one's opinion to

---

3. More had translated this work (which is also known as *Menippus*). At the end of the dialogue, the Cynic Menippus says that, when he visited Hades to consult the shade of Tiresias, the seer advised him to give up abstruse philosophy and focus on making good use of the present.

4. Cf. pp. 33–34 above.

oneself without being considered a traitor. The result is either a loss of personal integrity, or else a willing connivance in the wickedness and folly of others. Although More chose to follow Morus' advice for the time being, he foresaw the truth of Hythlodaeus' claims as much as his own future experience would tragically confirm them.

Book 1, by forcing the reader to recognize this moral crux, anticipates the frustration of his idealism that he will experience in book 2, and thus serves to make his sense of the absolute insolubility of the human dilemma more complete; there is, More shows, no way of escaping the experience of it. The problem is far larger than either Hythlodaeus or Morus thinks. Hythlodaeus' response is inadequate because it renders him impotent in a way that perverts the public responsibility that every man is enjoined to fulfil. His insights are just, but his actions are not justified. To be right he has to be wrong, and as his name implies, he is a faithless angel[5] whose pessimism amounts to an indictment of the human situation which God, in his wisdom, has instituted. Morus' response, on the other hand, is vitiated because it requires a man to compromise himself by winking at tainted deeds.

Once the presence of this crux has been felt, the function of book 1 becomes clear. It has been constructed to force its readers into a state of intellectual helplessness so as to make them all the more eager for Hythlodaeus to make good his claim that communal living can yet put all things right. When the Utopian exemplum fails to justify the full extent of Hythlodaeus' confidence in communal living as a radical cure-all, the reader's perplexity is compounded because book 1 has made desperately necessary the proof of its success. The two books taken together drive the reader into the same corner, from which he cannot move without either choosing some form of self-deception, or else acknowledging his helplessness as a human being to determine the shape and condition of his existence entirely according to his own wishes. But at the very point where book 2 seems about to deprive the reader of any sure support, it presents evidence of a true remedy, of which Hythlodaeus' eutopian remedy turns out to have been a parody: the religious response of the Utopians.

The essential feature of Utopian religion is that it is not definitive, and resides in a responsive condition of mind rather than an elaborate and arbitrary dogma. Its main principles were instituted by Utopus, the founder of Utopia, who allowed for a range of beliefs and provided for the possibility of wise doubting: 'On religion he did not venture rashly to dogmatize. He was uncertain whether God did not desire a varied and manifold worship and therefore did not inspire different people with different views'.[6] The Utopians must,

---

5. Cf. (and contrast) p. 5, n. 4 above.
6. Cf. p. 86 above.

however, accept two fundamental tenets: that the world is governed by providence, not chance, and that the soul is immortal and will receive rewards and punishments after this life. To believe otherwise is to degenerate from the dignity of human nature. In practice, they let their faith instruct their reason, so that they are capable of modifying the rational rigour of their hedonistic philosophy to allow for the justified existence of their ascetic religious order as well as that whose members prefer to marry and enjoy honest pleasures:

> The Utopians regard these men as the saner but the first-named as the holier. If the latter based upon arguments from reason their preference of celibacy to matrimony and of a hard life to a comfortable one, they would laugh them to scorn. Now, however, since they say they are prompted by religion, they look up to and reverence them. For there is nothing about which they are more careful than not lightly to dogmatize on any point of religion.[7]

At the level of their religious response to life, as against their strictly rational one, the Utopians are prepared, as here, to accept the experience of paradox. Correspondingly, they become far more flexible and responsive to the leadings of the providence they believe in. Even more crucially, in their common prayers, the account of which is strategically placed by More at the climactic point of the whole work, they profess willingness to contemplate the possibility that all their assumptions may, after all, be false. After acknowledging God as the author of all blessings and returning him thanks, particularly for having been placed in the happiest commonwealth and given the truest form of religion, each individual reaffirms his readiness to follow wherever God might lead him:

> If he errs in these matters or if there is anything better and more approved by God than that commonwealth or that religion, he prays that He will, of His goodness, bring him to the knowledge of it, for he is ready to follow in whatever path He may lead him. But if this form of a commonwealth be the best and his religion the truest, he prays that then He may give him steadfastness and bring all other mortals to the same way of living and the same opinion of God—unless there be something in this variety of religions which delights His inscrutable will.[8]

Their prayers manifest immediate faith and hope arising out of mediate doubt, as reflected in the accumulation of conditional clauses and qualifications. In repudiating absolute certitude, the Utopians show themselves prepared to respond to the providence of each emergent occasion, without presuming to fix a form and limit

7. Cf. p. 89 above.
8. Cf. p. 93 above.

to the purpose of the Almighty, and in so doing, they diverge from Hythlodaeus, whose inability to accept the providential nature of actual human experience amounts to a form of despair.

By choosing to opt for the political role of Morus, More must have believed he was affirming the same faith as the Utopians. His trust in providence was revealed in his readiness to commit himself to action, not in any confidence that his chosen course was definitively the best. On the contrary, he knew from the outset that his political career was fraught with moral dangers, but he knew equally that Hythlodaeus' way was even more perilous because it ended in a negation of human responsibility, both temporal and spiritual. More chose action because he realized that there was no solution in trying to escape from the continuous experience of the human dilemma: a frightened withdrawal from one peril could merely land one in another. But as he was later to declare in *A Dialogue of Comfort against Tribulation*, the danger of falling into a further peril should not prevent one from escaping from the immediate, Hythlodaean one:

> if the ship were in danger of falling into Scylla, the fear of fall-ing into Charybdis on the other side shall never let[9] any wise master thereof to draw him from Scylla toward Charybdis first in all that ever he may. But when he hath him once so far away from Scylla that he seeth him safe out of that danger, then will he begin to take good heed to keep him well from the other.[1]

More's career after *Utopia* shows his efforts to know when to avoid Hythlodaeus' Scylla, by being Morus, and to realize the time when, to save himself from falling into Morus' Charybdis, he had to choose to be Hythlodaeus. Rather than being the helpless victim of his contrary impulses, More, by 1516, had concluded that to avoid the dangers of either one, he needed to be prepared to enact both as the time required. He believed that one must be in a perpetual state of responsiveness, just as he had shown the Utopians ulti-mately prepared to be. As he advised John Batmanson in his *Letter to a Monk* of 1519–20, one should

> live in trembling, and though hopeful, still [be] very fearful not only of the possibility of falling in the future, according to the saying 'He who stands, let him take heed lest he fall,' but also of the possibility of having fallen in the past, yes, even at the very moment you thought you were advancing the most.[2]

*   *   *

9. Prevent. Scylla and Charybdis were the equally fearsome dangers—devouring monster and whirlpool—that Odysseus had to steer between in *Odyssey* 12.
1. *CW* 12:48; spelling modernized by the editors.
2. *Selected Letters*, p. 140. "He who stands . . . ": 1 Corinthians 10.12.

DOMINIC BAKER-SMITH

From Words and Deeds[†]

Raphael's peroration,[1] by which he brings his criticism of European society to its searing climax, introduces the final section of *Utopia*. Its unremittingly hostile tone has the effect of leaving the reader ill at ease about the driving forces of human society, and at this point Morus,[2] whose uncertain response wins some sympathy from the reader, brings the narrative to what may seem an indecisive close. In any literal reading of *Utopia*, one that assumes its admonitory or prescriptive intent, the conclusion can seem to be little more than a convenient device for closing the discourse in an Antwerp garden, rounding off the fiction which frames the real content rather like the frill around a cake. If, on the other hand, the book is taken as a complex rhetorical performance, one which aims to involve the reader in its own heuristic experience, then this final section is of the utmost importance in opening out the argument well beyond the confines of Antwerp.

If we accept Hexter's conjectural sequence of composition,[3] the inference is that this closing section represents the last part to be completed, after More had worked backwards from his original account of a society free of the divisive pressures of ownership to present in Book I a debate over wider issues of political engagement. The evolution of the work might be summarized as a shift in emphasis from the literal theme, *de nova insula Utopia*, to the implicit theme, *de optimo reipublicae statu*,[4] and this shift involves

---

† Reprinted with permission, from Dominic Baker-Smith, *More's "Utopia"* (Toronto: University of Toronto Press in association with the Renaissance Society of America, 2000; orig. publ. 1991), chap. 8, pp. 201–27. Except where otherwise indicated, footnotes are the author's (though they have been pruned here and there). Baker-Smith quotes *Utopia* from the Yale edition (*CW* 4), but all page references are to the corresponding passages in the present edition.

    Baker-Smith's book (of which this is the culminating chapter), written in lucid prose and exhibiting an admirable combination of learning and critical acumen, synthesizes previous scholarship and criticism to argue that More's aim was to change the way we *think about* politics and society rather than to advocate a particular course of action: "we are made aware of issues and possibilities, but not of positive recommendations" (p. 248 below).

1. I.e., the concluding pages of his long speech on Utopia: "Now I have described to you as accurately as I could the structure of that commonwealth * * *" (pp. 93ff. above) [editor's note].
2. The form that More's name takes in the Latin of *Utopia* [editor's note].
3. First Book II (with an opening similar to that of the present Book I), then Book I, and finally Hythloday's peroration and the character More's concluding remarks as narrator. For Hexter's arguments, see *CW* 4:xv–xxiii. Last of all, of course, More added the prefatory letter to Giles [editor's note].
4. The two parts of the full title of *Utopia*: *De optimo reipublicae statu deque nova insula Utopia* ("Concerning the Best State of a Commonwealth and the New Island of Utopia") [editor's note].

the introduction of dialogue and thus of competing perspectives. Through the friction of these divergent views, which lends dramatic form to the clash between ideal politics and a recalcitrant world, the discussion takes on an increasingly epistemological character. How far can the ideal be known, *known* not simply as an object of intellectual contemplation but as an operative principle? It was in the light of this debate, with its characteristically Platonic overtones, that More added to Raphael's account of Utopia the peroration and conclusion which appear to leave us all too literally nowhere—Raphael castigating a society built on pride, and Morus apprehensively keeping his reservations to himself as he leads his discomfortable guest into supper.

The anger which sounds in Raphael's outburst has much in common with the earlier attack on enclosures of Book I; but now, with his description of Utopia behind us, we are better able to seize on the point that money is the means by which a natural community is corrupted into an artificial system, one controlled by the rich for their own benefit. * * *

* * *

* * * In fact the preoccupations which surface in Raphael's peroration support the idea that More composed it immediately after the Morton episode. The earlier discussion is provoked by the common lawyer who laments the ineffectivenss of capital punishment in checking crime; now, as Raphael anatomizes the inequities of the non-Utopian world, he claims that a whole catalogue of crimes against property, the person, or the state, 'which are avenged rather than curbed (*refrenata*) by daily executions', would disappear overnight if money were to be abolished. * * *

The paradox of money, therefore, is that it was devised to ensure access to the necessities of life but has actually worked to prevent the majority from obtaining them.[5] It is the recognition that prompts Raphael to his most radical statement: the one thing which supports the retention of money against the counsels of good sense, and even of Christ himself, is pride, the chief and progenitor of all plagues (p. 96 above). Pride is the serpent from hell which twines itself around the hearts of men and prevents them from adopting a better mode of life; it is concerned less with simple self-interest than with the assertion of ascendancy over others. Whatever form it may take, its essential motive is the urge to dominate, *libido dominandi*.

5. The force of More's irony is best conveyed by Robinson's translation, 'So easily might men get their living, if that same worthy princess Lady Money did not alone stop up the way between us and our living, which, a God's name, was very excellently devised and invented, that by her the way thereto should be opened' (*Utopia* [Everyman's Library, 1985], p. 133). [Cf. pp. 95–96 above; editor's note.]

If there is an Augustinian ring about Raphael's peroration at this juncture it is because both *Utopia* and *The City of God* are concerned with the diagnosis of social decline, and both—directly or indirectly—echo the diagnosis in Plato's *Republic*. To Augustine Rome is the type of the *civitas terrena*, the city of this world, 'dominated by the lust for domination'. In contrast there is the city of God where 'rulers and ruled serve one another in love'.[6] Raphael associates this lust for domination with money, since money is a mobile asset which easily separates value from production and opens the way to inequitable distribution and the triumph of avarice. Plato had warned of the effects of the pursuit for wealth, but the most sustained attack on money as a means of social decline in classical literature is probably that in More's favourite historian, Sallust, one which is echoed by Augustine in his analysis of the secular city. In fact Sallust himself, in his history of Catiline's conspiracy, appears to adopt the pathology of the sick state just as Plato had outlined it in Books VIII and IX of the *Republic*: avarice, the besetting sin of oligarchy, is exposed as the radical cause of social decline.[7] * * *

When More devised an imaginary state without money he was aligning it with the schemes of those who, ever since Plato, had seen the control of avarice as a necessary step in ensuring the ascendancy of reason over appetite and public order over private advantage. Otherwise the prestige attached to wealth opens the way for pride to domineer and generates the false values by which display and consumption oust virtue as the basis for nobility. In such an analysis money is sharply divisive, it separates citizen from citizen and status from worth. The Utopians' decision to do without it frees them from the haemorrhage of ambition and factional strife which weakens other states. It is true that individual crimes do occur and there is a penal system to deal with the consequences, but in a very real way Utopian institutions seem to be free of the effects of social sin. There is no reason why this island commonwealth should not go on forever.

So Raphael ends his long narration, and the reader is once again in Antwerp. After the imaginary excursion we find ourselves looking back at the island through the limited gaze of our primary narrator, Morus. The effect of this is to distance us abruptly from Raphael's vision as Morus shares with us his misgivings about the

6. *The City of God*, XIV, 28. There is a similarity here between the unanimity of the heavenly city and that of Plato's 'first best' society in *Laws*, 739c–d. [Baker-Smith quotes (with small changes here as elsewhere) from *Concerning the City of God against the Pagans*, translated by Henry Bettenson, introduction by John O'Meara (Harmondsworth, Middlesex: Penguin Books, 1984); editor's note.]

7. Sallust (86–35 B.C.E.), *Catiline* 10–12. "More's favourite historian": in truth, More seems to have been as fond of another Roman historian—Tacitus (b. 56 or 57 C.E.; d. after 117)—as of Sallust [editor's note].

islanders' ways. Coming so suddenly after Raphael's vehement attack on established society and his triumphant conclusion in favour of the Utopian alternative, the reservations of our fellow listener are disconcerting. In the brief closing section Morus leads us through three distinct steps: the first is his almost impatient response to the Utopian experience, and that is distinctly negative; he then confides in us his discreet handling of his prickly guest; finally, in a sentence that returns us to the present tense, he appears to hesitate and reopen the issue. In spite of its brevity it is a conclusion of some complexity.

Morus admits that 'not a few' of the customs and laws described by Raphael struck him as absurd, but since these include the Utopians' social customs, their methods of waging war, their religious ceremonies and the founding principle of the state—'their common life and subsistence without any exchange of money'—his dismissal seems pretty comprehensive. Morus then elaborates on his rejection of their moneyless community of goods with a sentence which has become a major skirmishing point in the interpretation of *Utopia*, 'This latter alone overthrows all the nobility, magnificence, splendour, and majesty which are, in general esteem, the true glories and adornments of a commonwealth' (pp. 96–97).[8] At this junction it may seem that the discrepancy between Raphael's point of view and that of Morus is such that irony offers the only way out. 'Nobilitas, magnificentia, splendor, maiestas' are just the terms, resonant with heraldic pomp, that are invariably used to sustain the official image of power; Columbus, in a passage that has its Brobdingnagian overtones, relates how the 'governoure' that he met on Cuba was surprised to learn that he was subject to another, 'And muche more, when the interpretour towlde hym of the glorye, magnificence, pompes, great powre, and furnymentes of warre of oure kynges'.[9] The crucial phrase used by More, 'ut publica est opinio'—literally, 'according to the commonly received opinion'—puts squarely before the reader the problematic term *opinio*, the equivalent of Plato's δόξᾱ, a mental state based on surmise which is lighter than ignorance but darker than the clear vision of the philosopher (*Republic*, 478c). So that even if Morus's deferential use of royal titles in the opening sentence of the book can be taken as an optional irony,

8. To Hexter (*More's Utopia*, p. 34) the passage offers a 'frivolous' response to Raphael's argument; to Brendan Bradshaw ('More on Utopia', *Historical Journal*, 24 (1981), 25) it is 'an indication of More's serious reservations about the ideal system'. [For J. H. Hexter's *More's "Utopia": The Biography of an Idea*, see the dagger note on p. 190; editor's note.]
9. *The First Three English Books of America* (Birmingham, 1885), ed. E. Arber, p. 78. ["Brobdingnagian overtones": i.e., the passage puts one in mind of Gulliver's chauvinistic account (in Part 2, chap. 3, of *Gulliver's Travels*) of English politics, warfare, etc., which seem despicably petty to his auditors, the gigantic Brobdingnagians; editor's note.]

here after the imaginative flight of our journey to Utopia the ironical potential is hard to miss. A major aim of the whole exercise has been to weaken our comfortable hold on conventional terms and to teach us to weigh them with a new caution. * * *

Yet to deny wholly the relevance of such qualities to the well-being of the commonwealth is to take a very negative view of their meaning. * * * If we hesitate over Morus's words here it is because we can recognize a positive sense to nobility, magnificence, splendour, or majesty which can make them valid qualities within a political community. The point, surely, is that they are all irrational terms, evocative rather than definitive, which point towards an ideal order so as to elevate the status of existing political power. Their function is, in other words, patently rhetorical, designed to invest the actual with the allure of the possible, distracting us in the process from the discrepancy between them. For Plato knowledge (ἐπιϐτήμη) is the prerogative of the philosopher who has made his way out of the cave and perceived unchanging truth. So the rational state, founded on this secure knowledge, can only exist when philosophers have access to power and can transform the possible into the actual.

Until that happens states will have to survive on opinion, and opinion is the stuff of rhetoric, subject to the persuasive arts of language; and unless philosophers have power, terms like 'nobility', 'magnificence', 'splendour' and 'majesty' will continue to have the appeal of persuasive definition. There is a clear link between this crucial sentence and the earlier clash between Raphael and Morus over that *philosophia civilior* which 'adapts itself to the drama in hand' (p. 33): while Raphael relies on the self-evident power of truth, as we must assume Plato's philosopher would do, Morus advocates the flexible approach of the rhetorician who applies his persuasive art to the limited scope of the possible. At both points we are made aware of the uneasy relation between absolute values and political expediency.

The confiding manner in which Morus tells us of his efforts to avoid vexing Raphael is itself a good illustration of the *philosophia civilior* in operation, and it has the effect of distancing us from the figure who only moments before had held our entire attention. Morus is unsure about Raphael's capacity to take criticism and so he falls back on the elementary rhetorical tactic of praise, leading him into supper with the promise that these things will be discussed more fully on another occasion. Of course, this has the effect of presenting the reader with an invitation to take them up, but it also qualifies our attitude to Raphael, placing him back in the ranks of ordinary humanity. There is a distinct irony in the patronizing courtesy which his host feels it advisable to extend to this ardent advocate of flexibility who cannot brook contradiction. The reader may even recall the rather different stance shown by that wily practitioner of the counsellors' art, Cardinal Morton, when confronted by Raphael's unsettling proposals, but Raphael has evidently forgotten. This modification of our attitude prepares us for Morus's final remarks on Raphael and his island:

> though in other respects he is a man of the most undoubted learning as well as of the greatest knowledge of human affairs, I cannot agree with all that he said. But I readily admit that there are very many features in the Utopian commonwealth which it is easier for me to wish for in our countries than to have any hope of seeing realized. (p. 97)

This concluding statement, a single sentence in the Latin, represents something of a volte-face by which Raphael's own credentials—those which initially prompted the suggestion that he should serve a prince—are reaffirmed, 'he is a man of unquestioned learning and highly experienced in the ways of the world', but, at the same time, Morus's own comprehensive dismissal of Utopian practices is modified and he now declares that there are many things which he would like to see imitated elsewhere. Then, much as at an earlier stage in Book I he had voiced the sceptical view that all things would not go well until all men were good—a condition unlikely to be realized for some time (p. 34)—so here too he is far from sanguine, and the wistful tone of his final statement is sharpened by two subjunctive verbs, *optarim* and *sperarim*, which conjure up a whole range of human aspiration only to leave it hovering in an uncertain state of potentiality. Thus the book ends, returning us to the present tense and to the perplexities of opinion.

One question which hovers persistently in the background of the discussion in *Utopia* is the status of rhetoric. There is inevitably some ambiguity about an art which aims to mediate between the intellectual order and the world of practical action, and Plato—in common with Raphael—has misgivings about the process by which truth is accommodated to the capacity of the auditor. Rhetoric is concerned with probabilities, and its function is to influence opinion rather than demonstrate knowledge. But *Utopia* is itself a work of considerable rhetorical subtlety. From the outset the reader is subjected to a series of voices which collude in setting up a fiction that masquerades as reality but then proceed to pull the argument in contrary directions. As a result no single reading of the work emerges which can exhaust the capacity of More's design to provoke meaning. We may leave the text with a preferred interpretation but that is our own responsibility—it does not allow us to close the issue with complete assurance.

Dialogue was an instinctive mode of writing for More, one that cohered naturally with his aptitude for adopting roles and examining an issue from competing perspectives. From his translation of the *Life of John Picus* in 1505 to the composition of *A Dialogue of Comfort* in 1534[1] More used such a tactic to face major issues in life, and many have linked *Utopia* to his uncertainty over entering royal service. Perhaps that uncertainty has been overestimated, and in any case if he wrote *Utopia* simply to clarify his own priorities then the history of conflicting interpretations suggests that he was not very successful. But the dialogue form, by holding conflicting or rival views in balance, could stimulate heightened awareness of an issue. This refusal to force a conclusion, so very contrary to Plato's idea of the dialectical process as leading to assured knowledge, is typical of the rhetorical tradition which with its sceptical views about the reach of human reason prefers to stick to the level of probabilities. Cicero's impartial handling of different philosophical views in his dialogues can be seen as a consequence of his recognition of the part played by irrational forces in human life, a perception encouraged by the orator's need to direct these forces. So the humanist tradition, with its indebtedness to Cicero, derived from his handling of the dialogue the practice of viewing an issue from alternate sides, 'in utramque partem'.[2] Petrarch's *Secretum* with its 'dialogue' between the author's *persona* and the figure of St Augustine as the voice of conscience, represents an early revival, and the dialogue was firmly established in the civic humanism of Leonardo Bruni at the beginning of the fifteenth century.[3]

A major source of disagreement over the nature and purpose of *Utopia* arises from the haste with which its readers opt for one voice rather than another, deciding for instance that the final words of Morus are silly and insincere, or that they represent a perfectly reasonable response to Raphael's inflexible idealism. But, as the previous chapters have shown, no one can be said to emerge from the Antwerp episode with his reputation unqualified. The very opening device, More's letter to Gillis,[4] has its part in this, since one major effect is to undercut the figure of the author which might otherwise unbalance the dialogue. From the start of the letter to the end of Book II the reader is continuously subjected to rhetorical controls which complicate response and work against any easy identification with a single view. Once Morus has introduced himself and alerted

1. More's translation of a Latin biography of the Florentine philosopher Giovanni Pico della Mirandola (1463–1494), whom he greatly admired, was one of his early works (though usually dated about 1510). *A Dialogue of Comfort against Tribulation* was one of his final works, written while he was imprisoned in the Tower of London [editor's note].
2. On both sides; for and against [editor's note].
3. See David Marsh, *The Quattrocento Dialogue* (Cambridge, Mass., 1980), ch. 1 for a useful account.
4. Pieter Gillis, whose name is Anglicized in most editions of *Utopia* as Peter Giles [editor's note].

us to the problematic location of Utopia, an island which many hope to evangelize but which none can actually place, we are drawn into the debate between two representatives of civic administration, the Under-Sheriff of London and the Secretary to the Council of Antwerp, and a Platonic voyager who has glimpsed a rational society. The contrast may too easily seem to be between insipid compromise and prophetic intensity. The attraction that Raphael undoubtedly possesses for the reader lies in his rejection of compromise, a habit which marks not only his intellectual stance but equally the independence of his wandering life; but his refusal to participate in conventional politics and his rejection of society as the reader knows it do have a distancing effect. By contrast, when Morus sounds a note of reserve at the conclusion, he does so in an aside to the reader which is persuasive even if it lacks radical panache: 'there are very many features in the Utopian Commonwealth which it is easier for me to wish for in our countries than to have any hope of seeing realised'. It is one thing to be excited by the concept of a just and happy society but quite another to find means of implementing it. Thus, while Raphael occupies the centre of our attention both for his passionate intensity and for the fact that he does most of the talking, Morus's contribution should not be underestimated; he holds his own in the dispute over counselling in Book I, just as he reserves his position over the feasibility of Utopian practices of Book II; the first of these, his argument for a more practical philosophy (*philosophia civilior*) is voiced with an urgency that matches his opponent, while in the second his concluding words substantially modify our response to the Utopian experience. We may find Raphael's voice more enthralling but that is not a particularly reliable criterion in the circumstances and Morus's doubts have their nagging validity. So, from the disorienting effect of the prefatory letter to Gillis until the ambiguous close of the book, the reader is faced by a series of conflicting voices; even the earnest commentator projected by the marginal notes only adds to the uncertainty.[5]

As a result it is highly unwise to rely on either protagonist as a straightforward exponent of the author's ideas; we are made aware of issues and possibilities, but not of positive recommendations. It is this characteristic that marks *Utopia* as a work of fiction rather than a tract, and it is one which is never far removed from the use of dialogue. * * * More sharpened up his Greek on Lucian[6] and * * * this had implications for his reading of Plato. To the Renaissance Plato was important not only as the philosopher of a higher spiritual real-

5. See Dana G. McKinnon, 'The marginal glosses in More's *Utopia*: the character of the commentator', *Renaissance Papers* (Durham, NC, 1970), 11–19.
6. On Lucian, see p. 106–07 above [editor's note].

ity, a feature dramatized in the upward pointing gesture of Raphael's portrait in the Stanza della Segnatura,[7] but as an exponent of dialogue—and this would be emphasized by approaching him through the playful, sceptical dialogues of Lucian. More, confronted by the absentee Plato of *A True Story*,[8] would have been intrigued by the ambiguities which mark the conclusion of the political debate in the *Republic* at the end of Book IX. If, as has already been suggested, *Utopia* was provoked by the idea of an ideal republic 'which . . . exists in words alone and nowhere on earth', a suggestion supported by Peter Gillis's verses,[9] then More must have been particularly struck by the way Socrates leaves open the political obligations of the philosopher:

> Well, said I, perhaps there is a pattern of it laid up in heaven for him who wishes to contemplate it and so beholding to constitute himself its citizen. But it makes no difference whether it exists now or ever will come into being. The politics of this city only will be his and of none other. (592b)[1]

Both Plato and More, having delivered an account of an ideal commonwealth, end with what might appear to be a theoretical fudge. At the point in the *Republic* when the philosopher-king is first introduced (473a), Socrates had raised a very basic question, 'Is it possible for anything to be realised in deed as it is spoken in word, or is it the nature of things that action should partake of exact truth less than speech?' The whole point of that freak the philosopher-king, the type of Utopus, is that he will make words match with deeds. But in the meanwhile what happens?

The sombre conclusion of Book IX is that the ideal city will perhaps only exist in words and never in deeds: barring some inconceivable intervention it will remain a pattern laid up in heaven for contemplation by the elect. Or, to put it another way, the *Republic* is not proffered as the blueprint for a realizable project but as a stimulus to private reflection and individual action.[2] So far as Morus and

---

7. One of four rooms in the Palace of the Vatican adorned with frescoes by Raphael and his workshop [editor's note].
8. In Lucian's *True Story* (a parody of lying travelers' tales) he visits the Islands of the Blest (the classical paradise of departed worthies), where he finds all the famous Greeks except Plato, who is reported to be living in his imaginary republic [editor's note].
9. Earlier in his book (pp. 79–80), Baker-Smith had discussed the connection between the acknowledgment in *Republic* 9:592a that the Republic exists only in words, and a prefatory poem in the early editions of *Utopia* (the poem, ostensibly by the Utopian poet laureate, Anemolius, is possibly—not certainly—the work of Gillis). In it, the personified Utopia claims to be a rival, even a superior, to the Republic, since what Plato sketched in words, "I alone have exhibited in men and resources and laws of surpassing excellence" (CW 4:21) [editor's note].
1. Quoting *The Republic*, translated by Paul Shorey, 2 vols., Loeb Classical Library (Cambridge, Mass.: Harvard University Press, 1935) [editor's note].
2. 'Plato seems on the whole reconciled to leaving the just state as an ideal, whereas he wants individuals actually to improve by reading the *Republic* and using it as an ideal

Gillis are concerned, or the reader for that matter, Utopia may offer a working model of a true commonwealth far more vivid in its realization than Plato's abstract proposals, but it still only exists in words. That is to say, the manner of transferring words into deeds is far from clear: they are still mentally citizens of the city of their birth, even if their complacency has been shaken, while Raphael has contemplated the pattern and made himself its citizen, 'The politics of this city only will be his and of none other'. No wonder More and Gillis have lost track of him by the time they write their prefatory letters; having made himself a citizen of the ideal he should, like Lucian's Plato, rapidly become invisible.

If we leave the internal dialogue aside for the moment, we can see that *Utopia* contributes to a wider dialogue initiated by the *Republic*. One work which can be seen as a direct response to the Socratic ambiguities of Book IX is St Augustine's *The City of God*, on which More lectured at St Lawrence Jewry in 1501. According to Stapleton, who presumably reported a family tradition, these lectures had concentrated not on the theological dimension but on 'the standpoint of history and philosophy',[3] and this suggests that they treated Augustine in terms of the tradition *de republica* and its preoccupation with the availability of the ideal as a political option. As Stapleton remarks, the earlier books of *The City of God* are almost wholly concerned with history and philosophy since Augustine's aim is to cut away myth and expose the rise of imperial Rome as the brutal process it had been. His two cities, the city of the world and the city of God, can be seen as an adaptation of the two cities mentioned by Socrates, the city into which the philosopher is born and that into which he can enter—mentally—by contemplation. * * *

* * * In one sardonic chapter (II, 20) Augustine offers a picture of the debased Roman commonwealth which makes it no more than a frame for private interest: 'it doth belong to our care that everyone might have the means to increase his wealth, to nourish the expense of his continual riot, and wherewithal the greater might still keep under the meaner.'[4] The cumulative effect of Augustine's tirade against private wealth begins to sound very like Raphael's exposure of the conspiracy of the rich. This negative image of Roman society becomes in *The City of God* the model for the *civitas terrena*, the secular city whose institutions perpetuate the transmission of injustice from generation to generation. As Plato had recognized, the

---

to which to conform themselves' (Annas, *An Introduction to Plato's Republic* (Oxford, 1981), p. 187). For a similar view see also H. D. Rankin, *Plato and the Individual* (London, 1964), p. 138.

3. Thomas Stapleton, *The Life and Illustrious Martyrdom of Sir Thomas More*, translated by Philip E. Hallett, edited by E. E. Reynolds (London: Burns & Oates, 1966), pp. 7–8. Stapleton's biography appeared in 1588 [editor's note].

4. I.e., lesser; those of lower socioeconomic status [editor's note].

only hope for reform is to break the sequence by some kind of ideological rift, to wipe clean the slate (*Republic*, 501a).

But is such reform feasible? * * * for Augustine there can be no
such thing as a just state: 'there can be no true justice except in that
commonwealth whose founder and governor is Christ, if it is acceptable to call that a commonwealth since we cannot deny that it is a
people's estate' (II, 21). When, as he promises, he returns to the issue
at a later point (XIX, 21) it is to reinforce this claim on theological
grounds by arguing that the absence of moral justice in the individual, the consequence of original sin, condemns the state to political
injustice. So the just state * * * will only exist when its predestined
members are drawn together in the *civitas Dei* at the end of time.

Meanwhile we live in the midst of time, looking backwards to a lost
innocence or forward to an inconceivable millennium, haunted by
the memory of a perfection we cannot hope to emulate. Such issues
would have been acutely evident to More at the outset of his public
career as he prepared his lectures on *The City of God* and, again, on
the eve of his admission to the royal council while he prepared his
dialogue 'de optimo reipublicae statu' in Antwerp and London. Far
from being a concentration of thought brought about by the prospect
of royal service, the dualism represented by Morus and Raphael
had been clearly formulated for him at least since *The Life of John
Picus*.[5] This dualism is seen at its starkest in the heated exchange in
Book I over the compatibility of philosophy with princes: according
to Raphael this is out of the question, while Morus urges his *philosophia civilior*, his adaptable mode of counselling which operates dis-
creetly and indirectly, 'thus what you cannot turn to good, you may
at least make less bad. For it is impossible to make all institutions
good unless you make all men good, and that I don't expect to see for
a long time to come' (p. 34). The crux here lies in that remark about
the standards that may be expected of human beings, at least as we
know them. Human nature cannot be changed without a reform of
institutions, but institutions cannot be reformed unless human
nature changes. The implication is that we must either look outside
the current situation altogether to some transforming intervention,
or we settle for an imperfect world and try to make the best of it.

This is more or less how things stand at the conclusion, Raphael
an intransigent witness to the absolute and Morus privately sceptical
about the prospects for change. Such a tantalizing juxtaposition of
prophetic intensity and practical compromise is conventional enough
in the tradition of the dialogue, especially as humanism had developed

---

5. As Baker-Smith had noted earlier in his book (p. 17), the *Life* "raises fundamental
questions about the relation between public business and reflective solitude" [editor's
note].

it from Ciceronian and Lucianic models, since both of these tend to thrust the interpretive responsibility on to the reader. * * *

The perspectives held out to us in *Utopia* might be characterized rather loosely as Augustinian and Platonic. Morus is resistant to Raphael's enthusiasm because he bases his judgements on life as he has perceived it in daily experience. In one sense this echoes Aristotle's critique of Plato, which explicitly enters the discussion under the issue of private property;[6] but the assumption which governs Morus's whole attitude is summarized in that sentence, 'For it is impossible to make all institutions good unless you make all men good, and that I don't expect to see for a long time to come'. Seen in such terms the prospects for the earthly city hold out little prospect of change; the initiative lies with individual moral reform, but even that must be set against the pressure of custom. Hence the modest goal proposed: 'what you cannot turn to good, you may at least make less bad'. But Raphael's perspective stresses the effect of what we have already referred to as 'social sin', in other words custom, the very target of Christ's preaching. It is custom, as Erasmus had pointed out in the 'Dulce bellum inexpertis',[7] which makes vile things acceptable and distorts natural response, so it is particularly interesting that Raphael sees in community of property as practised by the Utopians the chief way to puncture the membrane of familiar practice which inhibits our entry into a new social order. Where Morus expects little variation in the pattern of human behaviour, Raphael looks to a transformation of consciousness stimulated by a change in social institutions. So far as justice is concerned, Morus expects it in a world to come—though a little on the way will be welcome—but Raphael appears to see no good reason why it should not be available sooner, if only the inheritance of social sin can be shaken off.

Morus's position, then, can be termed conservative since it posits nothing that will radically disturb the existing order this side of the Judgement, and so he feels able to participate in the political world on its current terms. Raphael's revulsion from the tepid compromises of ordinary life, by contrast, has all the signs of being the obverse, a kind of chiliastic enthusiasm. Augustine had no patience with the chiliasts, or millenarians, and brushed them aside in *The City of God* with scant sympathy (XX, 7), but chiliasm remained a recurrent temptation to the reforming mind, as Thomas More was well aware. The critical distinction between such modest policies of social amelioration as Morus might accept and the radical changes

---

6. See p. 37, n. 6 above [editor's note].
7. "War is sweet, to those who have not tried it" (Latin). An ancient proverb, here cited as the title of Erasmus's famous essay on it in his *Adages* (IV.i.1)—a huge collection of proverbs, with commentaries on them. Some of the commentaries, like the one referred to here, are quite substantial essays [editor's note].

demanded by Raphael lies in their different assessments of original sin and its social effects. How far was an escape from, or at least a lightening of, this burden possible? Those Christians who had hoped for such alleviation as might allow a new quality of life had to argue from some providential ordering of events, and this normally meant declaring the imminent dawn of a new age, the prelude to Christ's second coming. The most pervasive formulation of such an apocalyptic scheme was that of Joachim of Fiore.[8] * * * Joachim proposed a trinitarian pattern in history, starting with an era or *status* of the Father from creation to the advent of Christ, an era of the Son which still persists, and an impending era of the Spirit when mankind would live in ordered communities and follow a quasi-monastic regimen comparable to that of the Utopians.[9]

We do not have to suppose that Thomas More had Joachim's ideas specifically in mind when he devised Utopia, but contemporary manifestations of Joachist influence do offer an intriguing perspective on the newly found island. There is the current of Franciscan speculation, for a start, which combined Joachist ideas with the ideal of apostolic poverty in order to get behind the system of property ownership and recover a lost innocence. A more localized but representative episode, one which would certainly have engaged Thomas More's attention, is the remarkable period of Savonarola's domination in Florence between 1494 and 1497.[1] The striking thing about this radical exercise in social *renovatio* is that it combines an apocalyptic reading of history—which makes Florence the centre for a movement of world reform—with a careful emphasis on the quality of political life. The ordinances imposed by the new republic aimed to curb self-love and promote the common good; severe penalties were directed against any attempt to concentrate power. The inclusion of leading intellectuals among Savonarola's intimate supporters, the *piagnoni*, a development which influenced Giovanni Pico, More's 'Erle of Myrandula', resulted in a fusion of Plato and Christ that would have been fully acceptable to Raphael.[2] * * *

There is no necessity to go further into the fertile but bizarre effects of Joachist prophecy between the 1490s and the date of

8. An apocalyptic interpreter of Scriptural prophecy, the Italian Joachim (ca. 1135–1202) was an enormously popular and influential but also, after his death, controversial figure [editor's note].
9. See F. Seibt, 'Liber Figurarum XII and the classical ideal of *Utopia*', in Ann Williams, (ed.) *Prophecy and Millenarianism: Essays in Honour of Marjorie Reeves* (London, 1980), pp. 259–72.
1. The Dominican friar Girolamo Savonarola, an extraordinarily compelling preacher, led Florence for three years of puritanical theocratic democracy [editor's note].
2. The fullest account is Donald Weinstein, *Savonarola and Florence* (Princeton, NJ, 1970), ch. 2, and the Joachist background is treated in Marjorie Reeves, *Joachim of Fiore and the Prophetic Future* (London, 1976), pp. 83–95. Pico della Mirandola had studied the works of Joachim.

Utopia, except to note their relevance to the discovery of the New World. Columbus, it seems, saw his travels within a Joachist scheme for the unification of mankind, and a similar vision lingered with his successors, above all with the Franciscans who saw in the New World an opportunity to recover the simplicity of the apostolic age. In such a perspective the discovery of new lands, inhabited by natives who showed a startling innocence of those practices which oppressed European man with the burden of social sin, could be recognized as an important sign of the approach of the last days. If Thomas More could ironically invent a theologian who had petitioned to be sent to Utopia as bishop to further the conversion of the natives, this is not so far removed from the dreams of those who set out to proselytize the Indians in order to unite the human race under the Holy Roman Emperor and the church. Above all, the Americas seemed to be peopled by apt subjects for a Platonic experiment.[3]

* * *

The point celebrated by Anemolius in his prefatory verses—that Utopia outshines Plato's republic since it expresses in concrete form what Plato leaves in words[4]—no doubt has its ironical reference to Socrates' city of words, but on a more mundane level it expresses a real feature of More's text, the way in which the reader instinctively tests Utopian institutions by the standards of actual experience. Few works of fantasy are so successful in teasing us into speculation on the practicability of their arrangements, and there is no reason to doubt that this is an intentional effect, prodding us into constant acts of comparison between the ideal model proposed and our own social environment. No doubt the rise of individualism has intervened in our modern response to the character of Utopian institutions, and the islanders' way of life may strike us as oppressive in a way that it would not have done to More's contemporaries; but there can be little disagreement about the desirability of that kind of rational justice which is the ultimate result of Utopus's planned experiment. In fact the fascination of More's work lies in the way it makes the ideal seem almost tangible, so very near to potential realization. Perhaps the most effective element in this is the way in which the issue of property is made central, so that the whole scheme rises or falls by that single standard; if such a radical gesture of rational order can be effected in society then all the other issues may be

---

3. On the American background, in addition to John Leddy Phelan, *The Millennial Kingdom of the Franciscans in the New World* (Berkeley, 1956; ch. 6, n. 59), see F. Chiappelli et al. (ed.) *First Images of America* (Berkeley, Los Angeles, and London, 1976), vol. 1 (especially the articles by J. H. Elliott, Antonello Gerbi, John W. O'Malley), and H. C. Porter, *The Inconstant Savage* (London, 1979).
4. See p. 249, n. 9 above [editors' note].

taken for granted. And, as we have seen, this symbolic issue of common property has had a powerful resonance in Christian history as a means of remedying, at least in part, the effects of the fall.[5] The result is that *Utopia* combines in a highly convincing way reform of institutions with reform of moral attitudes: the reader is left with the feeling that if one could be achieved then the realization of the other might not be far behind. Even in the twentieth century, as the Marxist style of communism slides into discredit, there is an attractiveness about Raphael's ideal since it locks together a reordering of the social milieu with a reordering of the human spirit. If only the experiment could be made look at what would follow: that, at least, is Raphael's vision and it is one which many readers have found compelling. And not the least compelling thing is that it is held by an individual, against the odds. This lends it a touch of the heroic.

Raphael's appeal is to the reasonableness of his audience; what he offers is a means to satisfy the perennial instinct to sociability. If we can accept that the community of property which he describes will entail a transformation of mind then it is irresistible, but even if we do accept it we are left at a loss as to how it can be initiated. The achievements of Utopus are lost in antiquity and there is no mention of how the Abraxans, as they originally were, reacted at being turned into Utopians. What is omitted from Raphael's account is that crucial phase of re-education which must be the consequence of radical change, the phase when in Plato's terms the slate is wiped clean. Exactly what this might entail is suggested in a rather ominous passage of the *Republic*: once the philosophers have achieved power, 'All the inhabitants over the age of ten . . . they will send out into the fields, and they will take over the children, remove them from the manners and habits of their parents, and bring them up in their own customs and laws which will be such as we have described' (541a). It is, of course, a procedure that has recommended itself to later revolutionaries, perhaps most notoriously to the Khmer Rouge in their restructuring of Cambodia. The common link between such totalitarian courses and the apparently benign intentions of Socrates or Utopus is precisely the need to break free from the fetters of the past. These fetters, in sociological terms the inherited conglomerate, bind society in the care of custom, and it is custom, *consuetudo*, which is the main butt of the satirical programme generated by Erasmus and More, a programme which extends beyond the simple exposure of folly to raise the issue of social sin, the injustice endemic in the fabric of society. The Lucianic perspective that More adopted

5. See pp. 252–53 above, and, earlier in Baker-Smith's book, pp. 143–44. On Christian communism, see also pp. 105–06, 109–11, 202-13 above [editor's note].

in his early collaboration with Erasmus[6] enabled him to mock the official gestures of a society obsessed with public performance; it equally enabled him to seize on Plato's dream of a society liberated from the tyranny of ideology. The only snag was that such liberation depended on another kind of tyranny for its realization.

Since More was obviously alert to this issue it may be no accident that the only detailed account we are given of Utopian agricultural practice describes the remarkable scheme ('mirabilis artificium') used to hatch chicks:

> The hens do not brood over the eggs, but the farmers, by keeping a great number of them at a uniform heat, bring them to life and hatch them. As soon as they come out of the shell, the chicks follow and acknowledge humans as their mothers! (p. 40)

The system of parental substitution has its echo of Plato's scheme for wiping the slate clean, and while it may seem forced to compare the Utopians to their chicks, the fact remains that they, too, have been programmed. The initiative of Utopus has set in motion a political mechanism which removes so far as is possible the moral challenge of individualism. It is necessary to be cautious here, since the existence of legal punishments in Utopia argues for the possibility of individual relapse. But Utopian life is designed both to remove opportunities for vice and to provide a constant pressure to right doing which is typified by their hierarchy of pleasure as well as the constant presence of observing eyes. In theory a Utopian could move in total contentment from the cradle to the grave, leading a life in conformity with the highest demands of rationality, without so much as one positive act of will. Such an arrangement appears to aim at the state of Adam in Eden before the fall, and it is interesting to compare John Milton's dismissal of what he terms 'a fugitive and cloistered virtue, unexercised and unbreathed', in the *Areopagitica* where he argues for the necessity of trial for 'the wayfaring Christian':

> Assuredly we bring not innocence into the world, we bring impurity much rather: that which purifies us is triall, and triall is by what is contrary. That virtue therefore which is but a youngling in the contemplation of evil, and knows not the utmost that vice promises to her followers, and rejects it, is but a blank virtue, not a pure; her whiteness is but an excrementall whiteness.[7]

Here, for a moment at least, Milton could be said to voice the Augustinian view with its emphasis on the fallen nature of human history: moments of moral order may be achieved by individual

---

6. On Erasmus and More as students of Lucian, see p. 107 above [editor's note].
7. *The Works of John Milton* (New York, 1931–8), vol. 4, p. 311.

struggle, but in so far as they are socially induced they only result in 'a blank vertue'.

For Augustine the virtuous community, the city of God, will only be recognized at the end of time and any millenarian dream of identifying it here and now can only be a dangerous illusion.[8] And set against the robust imagery of spiritual warfare evoked by Milton the rational calculus of Utopian morality offers little scope for self-transcendence. Only the Buthrescae, a mirror image of Catholic religious orders, who undertake the harshest physical tasks and bind themselves to celibacy, offer some conception of a virtue based on post-mortem expectations. But how far do Utopians have 'selves' to transcend? Milton's attack on 'cloistered virtue' is an attack on any attempt to remove the moral focus from the individual to the social order, and yet monasticism represented to More one of the few viable attempts to release the individual from the negative influence of social custom by establishing an alternative community. In its purest realization, rare enough perhaps in More's assessment, the monastic ideal aimed to harmonize personal effort with a supportive environment to achieve transformation of the self. But entry was inevitably a personal initiative, and the real problem lay in extending it to society as a whole; only Joachim of Fiore's visionary third age held much hope of achieving that. And yet the speculations of Plato and the reports from the Indies gave the prospect a tantalizing novelty. The result is the compelling tension of attitudes which controls the close of *Utopia*—Raphael committed to his remote island commonwealth and Morus locked in a world where the best that can be hoped for is that things may get a little less bad. One speaker is preoccupied with the possibility of collective change and the other is wryly convinced of its remoteness 'unless you make all men good'. It is not the least of the paradoxes in this paradoxical book that Raphael should express so forcefully the evil consequences of pride, that serpent in the individual heart, which is to Morus the chief obstacle to the reconstruction of society.

How far, then, is *Utopia* a book that intends reform? At one level it is clear that various proposals point out of the text to the conditions of Tudor England, and beyond. The most obvious case would be the debate between Raphael and the lawyer at Morton's house over capital punishment for theft. Here, we may suppose, More is engaging with contemporary legal discussion.[9] Such features have their historical interest. But what gives *Utopia* its lasting literary force, its status as a classic, is its juxtaposition of fundamental

---

8. The relevant passages of *The City of God* are XX, chs 7 and 8.
9. For a contemporary echo see Thomas Starkey, *A Dialogue between Pole and Lupset*, ed. T. F. Meyer (London, 1989), p. 80.

human perceptions. More, like Erasmus, used satire as a stimulus
to reform; what is not so clear is how much practical effect they
expected their writings to have. In spite of the optimism of some of
his later interpreters, there seems little to support the idea that
More was more sanguine than his own *persona*, Morus. But there is
a point at which satire passes beyond remedial projection to express
an attitude towards experience. The ironical stance which is so
characteristic of More, and which is so effectively presented by the
contrast between Raphael and Morus, is by no means that of a
sceptic. By remaining alert to the nature of the dialogue, and resist-
ing any inclination to close the debate, we are brought to a fuller
recognition of the problematic relation between collective and individual values. Satire for More is the starting point for a deeper
challenge to customary attitudes, one that can be compared to an
exercise in intellectual ascesis.

It should not be a matter for surprise that readers have differed so
much in their response to *Utopia*, or that a single reader's attitudes
can fluctuate, since the function of the book is not to establish a
preferred viewpoint but to convey through its literary form a complex interplay of ideas which lie at the very roots of Western political
discussion. From the reader's point of view Raphael, the austere
Platonist, and Morus, the cautious Augustinian, need each other;
their respective arguments formulate a conflict in human experience which, it seems, cannot easily be resolved. If it is the case that
More devised *Nusquama*[1] as a response to Socrates' ambiguous
remarks about the philosopher's true city, then it is significant that
he chose a literary response rather than a philosophical one. After
the lectures on *The City of God* it would not have been surprising if
he had offered a treatise on 'the best state of a commonwealth',
instead he decided to attempt a fiction, and when we look at the end
of *Utopia* it is not difficult to see why. It has been argued that there
would be no fiction in an ideal world: story is a consequence of our
exile from Eden.[2] It mirrors a state in which aspiration and performance are at odds, just as we find them in the Antwerp garden at
the close of the book. The fact that the two speakers remain at odds,
that there is no closure, is an important part of More's narrative
conception since it forces on us a comprehensively human perspective, poised unremittingly between the polarities of Utopian idealism and pragmatic accommodation. It is doubly ironic, therefore,
that *Utopia* has so often been denied literary status and handled as
a bare proposal for social engineering, as though its literary features

---

1. "Noplace." On this Latin equivalent of "*Utopia*," see p. 5, n. 1 [editor's note].
2. See Michael Edwards, *Towards a Christian Poetic* (London, 1984), pp. 72–3, 'a happy
   people has no history; it also has no story'. This certainly seems to be the case in Utopia.

were little more than a frivolous irrelevance. The real power of More's work, and the only explanation of its enduring fascination, lies in the way the political debate is passed on unresolved to the reader as a metaphor of our quest for self-understanding.

ERIC NELSON

From Greek Nonsense in More's *Utopia*[†]

I

At the end of Sir Thomas More's *Utopia*, the character 'More' rejects Raphael Hythloday's suggestion that the Utopians have achieved the *optimus reipublicae status* ('the best state of a commonwealth'):

> When Raphael had finished his story, I was left thinking that not a few of the laws and customs he had described as existing among the Utopians were really absurd. These included their methods of waging war, their religious practices, as well as other customs of theirs; but my chief objection was to the basis of their whole system, that is, their communal living and their moneyless economy.[1]

This passage represents a pivotal moment in More's text. At issue is whether 'More' the character should be identified in this instance with More the author, and whether in consequence we are meant to take the Utopian example as the true 'best state of a commonwealth'[2]

---

† Reprinted with permission, from *The Historical Journal* 44 (2001), 899–917. Except where otherwise indicated, footnotes are by the author. Quotations from Greek, Latin, and Italian have been omitted in the notes (and sometimes in the text), and the notes have also been pruned in other ways, including by converting brief citations to *Utopia* (and occasionally other works) into parenthetical references in the text. Nelson cites *Utopia* in the Cambridge edition (1995), but all the page references have been changed to the corresponding ones in the present edition. Nelson's article, lightly revised, was later incorporated as Chapter 1 in his 2004 book, *The Greek Tradition in Republican Thought* (Cambridge University Press). The earlier version, being self-contained, is more suitable to the present volume.

   Nelson completed his doctorate at Cambridge under the great historian of political thought Quentin Skinner. Like Skinner, whose influential work on *Utopia* he extends and partly contradicts, Nelson interprets More's book by viewing its ideas in their contexts in Greek, Roman, and Renaissance political theory. He may or may not succeed in convincing the reader that Utopia is indeed More's ideal commonwealth, but his treatment is learned and subtle, and it reflects great credit on both master and pupil in the Skinner-Nelson relationship.

1. Thomas More, *Utopia*, ed. George M. Logan, Robert M. Adams, and Clarence H. Miller (Cambridge, 1995), p. 247 [p. 96 above]. All quotations from *Utopia* in Latin and English are taken from this edition (hereafter cited as 'More'). On occasion I have modified the translation for accuracy's sake; where this is done, it is duly noted. [To save space, these records have been omitted; editor's note.]

2. The phrase 'de optimo reipublicae statu' is found in Cicero, *De legibus* 1.15. In this passage, Atticus explicitly compares Cicero's enterprise to what 'was done by your beloved Plato'. See Cicero, *De re publica, De legibus*, ed. and trans. C. W. Keyes

or as part of a rhetorical exercise.[3] There is much to be said for both positions, but we should at least begin by noticing that, within the economy of the text, 'More's' rejection of the Utopian system as 'absurd' is precisely the result the reader is led to expect. Every time Raphael outlines the sort of Utopian advice he would give if he were a councillor, his interlocutor dismisses it as absurd or out of place, and adds that such advice would be greeted with derision by his fellow Europeans. In Book I, Hythloday observes that, if he gave his sort of advice in court, he would be 'either kicked out forthwith, or made into a laughing stock' (cf. p. 28 above), and More readily agrees. Later, when Raphael asks 'More' whether men would greet his proposals with deaf ears, 'More' replies 'with completely deaf ears, doubtless' because Hythloday's stance is 'outlandish' (p. 33). A frustrated Hythloday is forced to insist that his advice should not be rejected as 'outlandish to the point of folly' and his ideas as 'outlandish and absurd' simply because they run counter to 'corrupt custom' (p. 34). None the less, he knows full well that they will be, and the reader is not surprised when 'More' ends up rejecting Hythloday's advice as nonsensical and contrary to *publica opinio*.

But 'nonsense' is not an innocent idea in *Utopia*, and, while many scholars have stressed More's indebtedness to the Lucianic tradition of *serio ludere* ('playing seriously'), the fact that 'nonsense' constitutes a structuring force in the text has gone largely undiscussed. More's network of Greek puns do not simply entertain; they organize. Hythloday is a distributor (δαίων) of nonsense (ὕθλος),[4] and almost everything he describes from his travels has a name coined from Greek words connoting 'nonsense' or 'non-existence' (a quality which renders things nonsensical): the Polylerites are people of much (πολύ) nonsense (λῆρος); the Achorians are people without a country (ἀχώριοι); Utopia is 'no place' (οὔτοπος)—a pun on 'happy place' (εὔτοπος)—and the title of its governor is Ademus, an official 'without people' (ἄδημος); the river Anyder is without water (ἀνύδωρ), and runs through Amaurot, the unknown city (ἀμαυρός).[5] As we have seen, however, the content of Hythloday's account is 'nonsense' *from a particular point of view*, namely that of 'More' and those whom he

(Cambridge, MA, 1928). The classic Greek discussion of the distinction between the 'best possible political community' and those communities which actually exist is found in Book II of Aristotle's *Politics* (1260b27).

3. Especially after perusing Baker-Smith's chapter (pp. 241–59 above), the reader may feel that these are not the only two possibilities [editor's note].

4. See Nigel Wilson, 'The name Hythlodaeus', *Moreana*, 29 (1992), p. 33. Some scholars have wanted to derive 'daeus' from δαίος, meaning 'hostile' or 'wretched', but also (very occasionally) 'knowing' or 'cunning'. This interpretation draws strength from the fact that νέμω, not δαίω, is the regular Greek verb meaning 'to distribute'; however, I tend to prefer the first alternative.

5. For an account of More's toponymy, see James Romm, 'More's strategy of naming in the *Utopia*', *Sixteenth Century Journal*, 22 (1991), pp. 173–83. * * * Ultimately, however, we should be wary of agonizing over these names to the point where we miss the joke.

represents. But the name 'More' is the most significant pun of all: *Utopia*'s readers would remember Erasmus's dedication to More in *The praise of folly* (*Moriae encomium*), in which he attributes the inspiration for his panegyric to 'your family name of More (*Mori cognomen tibi*), which is as similar to the word for Folly (*Moriae vocabulum*), as you yourself are far from that quality',[6] and concludes by exclaiming 'farewell, most learned More, and zealously defend your Folly (*Moria*)' (p. 70). More subsequently made frequent use of this pun,[7] and his readers would certainly have recorded that Hythloday's advice is dismissed as nonsense by a *moros*.[8]

So More's word-play leaves us as witnesses to a dialogue between a speaker of nonsense and a fool, and it is our task to determine who the true *stultus* is. A possible way out of the impasse is to recall two facts. First, the title of More's tract, *De optimo reipublicae statu deque nova insula Utopia*, indicates his agreement with Hythloday's claim that Utopia constitutes the *optima forma reipublicae*.[9] And second, Hythloday is not the first speaker of ὕθλος in the Western tradition: Socrates receives this epithet in a famous passage in the *Republic*,[1] and the conceit that Socratic and Platonic advice will always be laughed at by those still in 'the cave' (i.e. Europe) is, as we shall see, one of the structuring elements in *Utopia*, as it was in *The praise of folly*. In the confrontation between 'More' and Hythloday we have a clash between a man trapped in the cave and one who has seen the sun. But for More, a founding member of the group of 'baby Greeks' (*Graeculi*) Erasmus so jovially satirizes, this confrontation is dramatized as a battle between Greece and Rome—between the values of the Roman republican tradition and those of a rival commonwealth theory based on Greek ethics. *Utopia* suggests that, when seen from a Roman perspective, Greek advice looks like 'nonsense'. But, for More, that 'nonsense' yields the *optimus reipublicae status*.

---

6. Clarence H. Miller, ed., *Opera omnia Desiderii Erasmi Roterodami*, IX (Amsterdam, 1979), p. 68. All translations from Erasmus's Latin are my own.
7. See Richard Marius, *Thomas More* (London, 1999), p. 88. One prominent example is More's 1515 *Letter to Dorp* (Daniel Kinney, ed., *The complete works of St. Thomas More*, XV (New Haven, 1986)), where he comments that Erasmus dedicated *The praise of folly* to 'my patronage'. * * *
8. Dominic Baker-Smith notes parenthetically that the name Morus 'implies a family relationship to Folly', but neglects to identify the implications of this fact for interpreting More's text. See Dominic Baker-Smith, *More's Utopia* (New York, 1991), p. 52.
9. Nelson omitted this sentence when he revised the article as a chapter of his book, perhaps because he recognized that the conjunction (*que* = and) joining the two parts of More's title leaves the relation between "the new island of Utopia" and "the best state of a commonwealth" (cf. p. 5 above) studiously ambiguous [editor's note].
1. In Book I, Thrasymachus characterizes Socrates's thoughts on justice as ridiculous, and exclaims 'I won't accept it if you speak such nonsense as that' (336d). English translations from Plato are taken from Edith Hamilton and Huntington Cairns, eds., *Plato: the collected dialogues, including the letters* (Princeton, 1989). In this case, however, I have substituted my own translation for Shorey's less literal one.

II

The political structure of the island of Utopia, with its governors,[2] senates, and assemblies, would surely have reminded More's readers of the standard 'mixed constitution' recommended by Polybius, and authorized in Renaissance Europe by the stability of the Venetian regime.[3] But republicanism in the Renaissance was far more than a set of claims about political structures: it was an ethical position.[4] Accordingly, in order to locate *Utopia* as precisely as possible within the intellectual landscape of the period, it becomes essential to identify the ethical framework of Utopian republicanism. In this respect, the most striking fact about More's text is its comprehensive rejection of the civic ideology Quentin Skinner has dubbed 'neo-Roman'. Synthesized out of the *Codex* of Justinian and the works of Cicero, Sallust, Livy, and Tacitus, this intellectual tradition provided the framework for the republicanism of the Italian city-states, and later made prominent appearances during the English Civil War and Interregnum.[5] On this Roman view, liberty is a status of non-domination, to be contrasted with slavery; it is both a good in itself and a necessary condition for human achievement. Liberty encourages virtue, which in turn yields justice. The concept of *iustitia* at issue here is authoritatively defined in the Roman *Digest* as the 'constant and perpetual aim of giving each person *ius suum*',[6] and is characterized by Cicero in *De officiis* 1.7 as an imperative to do no harm, and to respect private property.[7] Dedication to justice thus

2. There is no 'governor' (*princeps*) of Utopia as a whole; rather, each city's *phylarchs* (who represent thirty households each) elect that city's governor. See More, p. 43.
3. The Venetian constitution was thought to owe its durability to its mixture of monarchy (the Doge—the elected head of government), aristocracy (the Senate), and democracy (the Great Council). Polybius (2nd century B.C.E.), a Greek historian of the rise of Rome, was one of the very greatest historical and political thinkers of the ancient West [editor's note].
4. This claim has been most recently disputed (unsuccessfully I think) in the case of English republicanism by Arihiro Fukuda in his otherwise excellent *Sovereignty and the sword: Harrington, Hobbes, and mixed government in the English Civil Wars* (Oxford, 1997). See Jonathan Scott's incisive review in *English Historical Review*, 115 (2000), pp. 660–2.
5. See Quentin Skinner, *The foundations of modern political thought*, 1 (*The Renaissance*) (Cambridge, 1978); idem, 'Machiavelli's *Discorsi* and the pre-humanist origins of republican ideas', in Gisela Buck, Quentin Skinner, and Maurizio Viroli, eds., *Machiavelli and republicanism* (Cambridge, 1990); idem, 'Political Philosophy', in Charles B. Schmitt, Quentin Skinner, Eckhard Kessler, and Jill Kraye, eds., *The Cambridge history of Renaissance philosophy* (Cambridge, 1988); idem, *Liberty before liberalism* (Cambridge, 1998).
6. *Digest* 1.1.10. See also *Institutes* 1.1.1. ["*Ius suum*": his due; what rightfully belongs to him (or her). The *Digest* was the great compilation of Roman law. The *Institutes* (published, like the *Digest*, in the sixth century C.E.) was an elementary textbook of law; editor's note.]
7. For Ciceronian and Stoic views on property, see Julia Annas, 'Cicero on Stoic moral philosophy and private property', in Miriam Griffith, Jonathan Barnes, eds., *Philosophia togata I: essays on philosophy and Roman society* (Oxford, 1989), pp. 151–73. For the neo-Roman exaltation of wealth and money-making, see James Hankins, 'Humanism and modern political thought', in Jill Kraye, ed., *The Cambridge companion to Renaissance humanism* (Cambridge, 1996), pp. 126–7.

understood allows the cultivation of the common good (*commune bonum*), which produces concord (*concordia*) and peace (*pax*), and enables the *civitas* to seek *gloria*, its highest good.[8] Finally, implicit in all of this is that individuals should reject *otium* and embrace *negotium* (the *vita activa*), performing their *officia* to their friends and family, promoting the *gloria* of their *civitas* or *patria*, and securing *honor* for themselves.[9] In short, neo-Roman authors embrace republican government because they regard living in a free state as the only means of achieving virtue, and identify active civic participation as the only defence against enslavement.

In his important study of *Utopia*, George Logan argues that More's dialogue should be seen as an attempt to muster Greek 'city-state theory' to defend the 'traditional humanist' or neo-Stoic programme.[1] Now that Skinner and others have excavated that traditional, neo-Roman story more effectively, however, we can recognize that this is not the case. More was not criticizing the practices of contemporary republican theory from within the neo-Roman framework, but rather using the description of Utopia to reject that framework altogether. Machiavelli, who was writing the *Discorsi* as More was writing *Utopia*, furnishes an instructive comparison. Although Machiavelli's republican theory is utterly subversive across the spectrum, it none the less continues to inhabit the basic categories set out above. Machiavelli may turn the conventional content of *virtus* upside down, but his *virtù* still remains an instrument for the acquisition of *gloria* and *grandezza*. He still praises the *vivere libero*,[2] and insists that the central mission of a republic and a free people is actively *mantenere lo stato*—to avoid *servitù* (p. 126). He notoriously suggests that Christianity is antagonistic to a civic life dedicated to *gloria*, but leaves no doubt that glory wins the day and remains

---

8. Jacob Burckhardt long ago commented on the fundamentally Roman character of the Renaissance preoccupation with glory. In the chapter on 'Glory' in his great study of Renaissance culture, he writes that 'the Roman authors, who were now zealously studied, are filled and saturated with the concept of fame, and . . . their subject itself—the universal empire of Rome—stood as a permanent ideal before the minds of Italians'. See Jacob Burckhardt, *The civilization of the Renaissance in Italy*, trans. S. G. C. Middlemore, with an introduction by Peter Burke (London, 1990), p. 104. See also Markku Peltonen, *Classical humanism and republicanism in English political thought: 1570–1640* (Cambridge, 1995), p. 34ff, and Skinner, 'Political philosophy', p. 413ff.

9. For a helpful analysis of Roman ideology, see A. A. Long, 'Cicero's politics in *De officiis*', in André Laks, Malcolm Schofield, eds., *Justice and generosity: studies in social and political philosophy: proceedings of the sixth Symposium Hellenisticum* (Cambridge, 1995), pp. 213–40.° ° ° ["*Otium*": leisure, the opposite of *negotium* (business, the active life). "*Officia*": duties. "*Civitas*": state, commonwealth. "*Patria*": fatherland; editor's note.]

1. George M. Logan, *The meaning of More's 'Utopia'* (Princeton, 1983), p. 111. [In point of fact, I argued nothing as general as that More mustered Greek theory to defend the "neo-Stoic programme," but only that he employed the analytic methods of Greek theory to support the Stoic (and, frequently, humanist) claim that if one analyzes political choices with sufficient depth, morality and expediency will never be found to be at odds; editor's note.]

2. Niccolò Machiavelli, *Discorsi sopra la prima deca di Tito Livio*, ed. Giorgio Inglese, introduzione di Gennaro Sasso (Milano, 1984), p. 68.

intact as the goal of civil association (p. 298). In short, the subversiveness of Machiavelli lies in his radical reappraisal of the traditional neo-Roman categories.

More's text, as we shall see, mounts an attack on these categories and asserts a different, fundamentally Greek ethical framework for political life. As Montesquieu observed acutely in *De l'esprit des lois*, More 'wanted to govern all states with the simplicity of a Greek city'.[3] This is not to repeat the familiar and obvious claim that Plato plays a significant role in *Utopia* and furnishes the source for Utopian communism. It is rather to stress that, for More, the abolition of private property was not the means to Roman *iustitia* and, thence, to Roman *gloria*, but rather part of an entirely separate schema— one that is essentially Greek and sharply divergent from *Romanitas*.[4] This Greek view (accessible from either Plato or Aristotle) does not particularly emphasize freedom as a value, and, to the extent that it does, it invariably has in mind the state of living according to one's nature.[5] It assumes that the purpose of civic life (and indeed the purpose of human life) is not glory, but happiness, defined as the human fulfillment achieved completely through contemplation. But most important for our purposes, it also exhibits a sharply contrasting theory of justice. Justice (δικαιοσύνη), on this Greek view, is not a matter of giving each person *ius suum* in the Roman sense,[6] but is rather an arrangement of elements that accords with nature. In the case of the state, justice is instantiated by the rule of reason in the persons of the most excellent men; it results in a social existence

---

3. XXIX.19. See Montesquieu, *De l'esprit des lois*, ed. Victor Goldschmidt, II (Paris, 1979), p. 308. [The French Enlightenment thinker Charles de Secondat, Baron de Montesquieu, published *The Spirit of the Laws* in 1748; editor's note.]

4. In one sense, therefore, this essay constitutes a partial response to the claim advanced by Paul Rahe that Skinner's 'neo-Romanism' is a misleading historical category, since no significant differences exist between Greek and Roman political philosophy. This essay will try to make the case that More and his circle perceived the differences only too well, and self-consciously mounted a Greek critique of Rome. See Paul Rahe, 'Situating Machiavelli', in James Hankins, ed., *Renaissance civic humanism: reappraisals and reflections* (Cambridge, 2000), pp. 270–308.

5. See, for example, Plato, *Gorgias* 467a–468e, *Republic* 431a (IV), 515c (VII), and *Laws* 860d (IX); see also Aristotle, *Ethics* 1110b (III.1), 1138b9 (V.11). Aristotle argues in *Politics* 1283a (III.7) that, while wealthy men and free men 'are indispensable for a state's existence' (because a state cannot consist entirely of poor men or of slaves), 'justice and civic virtue are indispensable for its good administration' and are, thus, of greater value (since the state aims at the good life). This tepid endorsement, however, does not approach the Roman and neo-Roman glorification of *libertas* (nor that of the broader Athenian political culture which Aristotle was criticizing). Skinner discusses this issue in 'The republican ideal of political liberty', in Buck, Skinner, and Viroli, eds., *Machiavelli and republicanism*, p. 296. All references to Aristotle's *Ethics* are found in Aristotle, *Nicomachean ethics*, ed. and trans. H. Rackham (Cambridge, MA, 1926).

6. In *Republic* I, Plato begins from Simonides's view that 'it is just to give each person those things which are owed to him' (331e), but then interprets it in a revolutionary, holistic sense. For Plato, a person's 'due' is his natural place within a rationally balanced, organic whole. As a result, Plato prefers to speak of justice as the natural ordering of elements—not, as in the Roman tradition, the protection of private property and the prevention of bodily harm.

which teaches citizens virtue. This view of justice as a natural balance among elements in turn leads to a completely anti-Roman endorsement of property regulations.[7] If property is allowed to flow freely among citizens, both Plato and Aristotle reason, extremes of wealth and poverty will inevitably develop. The resulting rich and poor will both be corrupted by their condition: the rich will become effeminate, luxurious, and slothful, while the poor will lose their public spirit.[8] These corrupt souls will no longer defer to the rule of the best men, an 'unjust' regime will develop, and virtue will be undermined.[9]

This 'Greek view', as I have set it out, is clearly a minimal and composite summary, designed to highlight a certain orientation shared by Plato and Aristotle. In presenting it, I do not intend to minimize the extent to which medieval, Renaissance, and early modern thinkers posited deep divisions between Plato and Aristotle, nor, indeed, to suggest that the works of Plato and Aristotle alone constitute 'Greek thought' (any more than the works of Cicero, Sallust, Livy, and Tacitus constitute 'Roman thought').[1] The intention is, rather, to emphasize that authors who took Plato or Aristotle for their model could (and often did) emerge with a substantially different kind of republican theory. In particular, they might, for the reasons set out above, come to base their republican frameworks either on the abolition of private property or on some mechanism designed to secure its egalitarian distribution—two proposals wholly anathema to the neo-Roman view, which rejects any political interference in property dis-

---

7. It is true that, in the subset of particular justice which Aristotle calls 'distributive', we have a forerunner of the Roman standard of giving each person *ius suum*. But Aristotle makes clear that his theory of justice, like Plato's, is intimately connected to a claim about nature. For Aristotle, distributive justice in the political sense concerns giving each person the role for which his nature suits him. Aristotle argues that all citizens *qua* rational human beings have sufficient virtue to participate in governance, but that it is just (i.e. natural) that the best men be given political offices. Likewise, in Book I of the *Politics* we learn that there are natural slaves, and that it is just to go to war in order to put these unfortunates in their proper (i.e. natural) place. In Aristotle's worldview, a state is in a natural condition only when it is governed according to justice— that is, when reason and virtue rule in the persons of the wisest and best men. * * *
8. See, for example, *Republic* 421d–422a (IV), *Laws* 729a (V), 742e–743c (V), 744d–745b (V), and *Politics* 1295b4–1296a22 (IV.9). * * *
9. Aristotle argues that a state exhibiting extreme disparities in wealth may have one of two degenerate destinies: either it will become an 'unmixed oligarchy', or the poor might revolt and establish 'extreme democracy' (*Politics* 1295b39 (IV.9)). Both resulting situations will soon develop into tyranny. Indeed, in cases where one citizen or a very small number of citizens possess inordinate wealth, Aristotle goes so far as to recommend ostracism as a pre-emptive measure (1284b15–43 (III.13)). See also *Republic* 550c–553a (VIII).
1. Plato and Aristotle are singled out in this article because they constituted by far the most important sources for Greek ethical and political theory in Renaissance and early-modern Europe—not because these two authors reflected the mainstream of Greek political philosophy. Indeed, Josiah Ober does well to remind us that Plato and Aristotle were critics, rather than purveyors of mainstream political ideas and values. See Josiah Ober, *Political dissent in democratic Athens: intellectual critics of popular rule* (Princeton, 1998). * * *

tribution as a violation of its principle of justice.[2] Indeed, it is precisely on this issue of property distribution that several significant Renaissance and early modern thinkers *did* insist on the compatibility of Plato and Aristotle. Erasmus, for example, observed that, while Plato advocated a society without private property, Aristotle had simply 'tempered' this view a bit by arguing that 'ownership and title should be in the hands of certain individuals, but that, in every other respect, all things should be held in common, in accordance with the proverb [i.e. that 'among friends all things are common property'] for the sake of utility, virtue, and civil society.'[3] Likewise, James Harrington, who listed More among his favorite philosophers and whose *Oceana* bears the mark of *Utopia*,[4] would later insist that Plato's *Laws* and Aristotle's *Politics* were of one mind in endorsing agrarian laws.[5]

More's attraction to this Greek value system, and his antipathy to its neo-Roman counterpart, were as much cultural as theoretical, and, in order to understand them, we have to reconstruct a particular aspect of his intellectual context: his association with the Erasmian circle. These Oxford–London humanists, whom Erasmus befriended during his periods of residence in England (the longest of which lasted from 1509 to 1514), became the first Englishmen to dedicate themselves to the study of Greek, and to make a polemical point of preferring Greece to Rome.[6] Members of this Graecophile coterie (whom More dubbed *Graecistes*)[7] included William Grocyn (More's tutor and the first lecturer in Greek at Oxford), John Colet (founder of St Paul's school, and author of the Platonizing Oxford lectures on Paul's Epistle to the Romans), Thomas Linacre (the doctor-turned-priest who helped introduce Erasmus to Greek studies), William Lily (author of a pioneering Latin grammar, and More's partner in translating Greek epigrams into Latin elegiacs), Richard Pace (a diplomat and Greek scholar) and, of course, More himself.[8] From 1514 to 1520, the general period of *Utopia*'s preparation and publication, this circle's advocacy of Greek culture took on a new intensity, as several of its members were called upon to defend Erasmus's controversial project of using the Greek New Testament to correct the Vulgate. * * *

---

2. In Robert Nozick's vocabulary, we have here a quarrel between a 'historical' theory of justice and a 'patterned', or 'end-result' theory. See Robert Nozick, *Anarchy, state, and utopia* (New York, 1974), pp. 153–5. * * *

3. M. L. van Poll-van de Lisdonk, M. Mann Phillips, and Chr. Robinson, eds., *Opera omnia Desiderii Erasmi Roterodami*, XX (Amsterdam, 1993), p. 84.

4. J. G. A. Pocock, ed., *The political works of James Harrington* (Cambridge, 1977), p. 395.

5. Ibid., pp. 166, 234–5, 382, 412, 460. * * *

6. Marius, *Thomas More*, p. 72; *Complete works*, XV, p. lxxxi.

7. See, for example, More's *Letter to Dorp* (1515) in Kinney, ed., *Complete works*, XV, p. 96.

8. Other associates included Richard Croke, Richard Foxe, William Latimer, Thomas Lupset, Cuthbert Tunstall, and Christopher Urswick. Peter C. Bietenholz and Thomas B. Deutscher, eds., *Contemporaries of Erasmus*, I (Toronto, 1986), p. 327.

Erasmus's English defenders adopted a posture that was * * *
overtly polemical. In the 1517 treatise *De fructu qui ex doctrina
percipitur* (On the benefit of a liberal education), Richard Pace provides a representative statement of what emerged as the Erasmian
party line:

> Whatever seems to have originated with the Romans, for exam-
> ple, in rhetoric and history, was all taken from the Greeks as if
> it were a loan. For Demosthenes and Isocrates produced Cicero,
> as great as he was in the art of oratory (Quintillian acknowl-
> edges this). In philosophy, indeed, Cicero called Plato and Aris-
> totle the most learned of the Greeks, and he calls one of them
> 'divine' and the other 'most wise'. But philosophy among the
> Romans was so feeble that nothing could seem more stupid to
> learned ears than to compare Roman philosophers to the
> Greeks. And I include Cicero in this group, if he'll forgive me
> for saying so.[9]

More evidently shared Pace's sentiments and polemical style. In his
1519 letter to the monk John Batmanson, he declares that the superiority of Greek culture is clear from 'those arts they call liberal,
along with philosophy, in which subjects the Romans wrote next to
nothing', and offers similar observations in his *Letter to Oxford* and
in his * * * [*Letter to Dorp*] (1515).[1] In short, for More and his
circle, an impassioned defence of the Erasmian project and the new
Greek learning carried with it a corresponding attack on Rome in
general, and on Roman philosophy in particular.[2]

But More was not undiscriminating in his affection for Greek
philosophy. He evinced the same marked preference for Plato over
Aristotle shared by almost all of the Oxford–London humanists.[3]
This circle was deeply influenced by the writings of Giovanni Pico
della Mirandola, the notorious syncretist,[4] whom the Erasmians

---

9. Richard Pace, *De fructu qui ex doctrina percipitur*, ed. and trans. Frank Manley, Richard S. Sylvester (New York, 1967), p. 128. The translation is my own. For an excellent
   discussion of Pace's *œuvre*, see Catherine M. Curtis's unpublished doctoral thesis,
   Richard Pace on pedagogy, counsel, and satire (University of Cambridge, 1996).
1. Kinney, ed., *Complete works*, XV, p. 220. * * *
2. Needless to say, the attacks on Rome that we find in the writings of the Erasmian circle
   are polemical and, as a result, hyperbolic in character. An appreciation of the central
   role these comments play in the presentation of the Erasmian case does not entail taking them at face value. Indeed, to do so would be deeply mistaken. Erasmus himself
   annotated Cicero's *De officiis* and prepared an edition of Seneca, whom he admired.
3. More did not, however, reject Aristotle along with scholasticism. He tried all his life to
   rescue Aristotle from the schoolmen, and to arrive at a temperate assessment of the
   philosopher's merit. * * * See Kinney, ed., *Complete works*, XV, p. 100ff.
4. Pico tangled with Ficino over the latter's attack on Averroës in the *Theologia platonica*,
   sought wisdom from occult, Arabic, and kabbalistic sources (a fact which More notably
   glosses over in his translation of the *Life*), and argued for the compatibility of Plato and
   Aristotle (for example, in *De ente et uno*). Kristeller suggested the term 'syncretist',
   rather than 'eclectic' to designate Pico's approach in order to differentiate it from that
   of the ancient eclectics (i.e. Pico never suggested that all great philosophers were in

admired for his thoroughly Platonic renunciation of the *vita activa*. In More's *Life of John Picus* (1510), for example, the protagonist appears as a man whose mind was 'evermore on high cleued fast in contemplation & in thenserching of natures cownceill', unable to 'let down hit selfe to the consideration and ouerseing of these base abiecte and vile erthly trifles'.[5] Likewise, in a 1492 letter which More admired enough to translate, Pico insists to an interlocutor that he prefers 'the rest and peace of my mynde' to 'all your kingis palacis, all your commune besines, all your glory' (the phrase 'all your glory' is, incidentally, More's own addition).[6]

But perhaps even more important than Pico to the Erasmian circle was Marsilio Ficino, author of the first complete Latin translation of Plato's dialogues. Colet corresponded with Ficino during a visit to Italy (1492–5),[7] and Erasmus drew heavily on the Florentine's work (especially the 1469 *Commentarium in Convivium, De amore*) in his *Enchiridion militis christiani*.[8] Indeed, although More was accomplished in Greek, it is probable that he too consulted Ficino's translations. To take only one example, Ficino's *argumentum*[9] for the *Republic* summarizes Plato's theory that cities made up of rich and poor are not one city, but two, and describes the philosopher's novel approach to this problem:

> Whence he arrived step by step at his mystery, that everything should certainly be held in common. Some would not have less, nor truly others more. And it is from the former circumstance [i.e. some having less] that jealousies, lies, thefts are born, while extravagance, pride, and sloth are born from the latter circumstance [i.e. some having more].[1]

This is not at all far from Hythloday's insistence that Platonic communism would eliminate theft, frauds and a host of other crimes and seditions (More, p. 95), along with pride and jealousy (p. 96). And, as we shall see, Ficino's characterization of Platonic 'justice'

---

fundamental agreement). See Paul Oskar Kristeller, 'Introduction' to Pico's *Oration on the dignity of man* in Ernst Cassirer, Paul Oskar Kristeller, and John Herman Randall, Jr, eds., *The Renaissance philosophy of man* (Chicago, 1948), p. 220. See also Kristeller, *Eight philosophers of the Italian Renaissance* (Stanford, 1964). [See also p. 247, n. 1 above; editor's note.]

5. Anthony S. G. Edwards, Katherine Gardiner Rodgers, and Clarence H. Miller, eds., *The complete works of St. Thomas More*, I (New Haven, 1997), p. 68. More's text is a free translation of the biography written by Pico's nephew, Gianfrancesco.

6. Ibid., p. 86. This passage appears in the letter to Andrea Corneo which More translates and appends to his *Life*. * * *

7. John B. Gleason, *John Colet* (Berkeley, 1989), pp. 47–52.

8. I.e., Erasmus's very popular *Handbook of a Christian Soldier* (1503) draws (though by no means exclusively) on Ficino's most famous work, *On Love*, a collection of fictitious orations purporting to be a commentary on Plato's great dialogue on love, the *Symposium* [editor's note].

9. Abstract [editor's note].

1. Marsilio Ficino, *Platonis opera* (Florence, 1517), p. 232. * * *

as 'the order and health of the society' (*civitatis ordo atque salus*) is very much the view of justice we encounter in *Utopia*.

But the text which most nearly anticipates More's Platonic reassessment of *Romanitas* is certainly Erasmus's *The praise of folly*. In Logan's phrase, Erasmus's encomium represents a sort of hall of mirrors in which the personification of Folly hails herself as the determining force in human affairs, and as the source of all blessings—leaving it to the reader to recall that some of what Folly praises *is* folly to praise. Many of the issues raised by Folly are picked up again in *Utopia* (often in precisely the same terms, as in the case of the 'problem of counsel' and the Utopian rejection of hunting), but the correspondence between the approaches to Greek theory in the two texts is perhaps the most striking. Throughout Erasmus's mock panegyric, Folly insists that her gift of *stultitia* [folly] is what allows human beings to lead happy lives: in a foolish world, only fools are happy. Accordingly, she argues that the Greek philosophers led unpleasant, impractical lives because they did not accept her gift; they chose wisdom instead. Folly first addresses the subject in chapter twenty-four, attacking both Greeks and Romans, but reserving her worst venom for Socrates (on whom she unleashes every Aristophanic weapon in her arsenal):

> As evidence of how useless philosophers are when it comes to the practices of real life take Socrates himself, dubbed the one wise man by Apollo's oracle, but chosen with little wisdom, since when he tried to do something in public life, he had to give up amidst the hearty laughter of all men . . . For while he philosophized about clouds and ideal forms, measured the feet of a flea, and wondered at the voice of a midge, he learned nothing at all relevant to civic life.[2]

Folly expands on this theme considerably, lamenting that philosophers are not foolish enough to be able to perform the essential *officia* of Roman ethics:

> He [a philosopher] is not at all able to be of any use to himself, to his country, or to his own family, because he is ignorant of public business, and entirely out of touch with popular opinion and the practices of the masses. From which cause he unavoidably incurs hatred, without question due to the great gulf between normal life and minds like his. For what happens among mortals that is not full of folly, done by fools, among fools? (p. 100)

Erasmus's implication is devastating: in a bitterly ironic paraphrase of Callicles's argument in the *Gorgias* (484d), Folly argues that

---

2. Erasmus, *Opera omnia*, IX, p. 98.

philosophers live unhappy lives and are laughed at and scorned
because their wisdom prevents them from being viable in a world of
fools (Erasmus's μῶροι). Philosophy is incompatible with *popularis
opinio* (recall that 'More' condemns Hythloday's advice because it
is contrary to *publica opinio*). And although Folly mentions Cicero
briefly in her list of useless philosophers,[3] the passages quoted above
along with Folly's suggestion that these philosophers lack *decorum*[4]
reveal that Folly is engaged in a Ciceronian critique of Greek
philosophy—precisely the sort of critique 'More' offers in *Utopia*.

Folly, we should recall, does not claim credit for the content of
Greek philosophy, but, rather, for what occurs when Greek philosophers attempt to act in the 'real world' of fools. And what happens in
The praise of folly when someone tries to give Platonic advice in that
real world? An important passage from chapter sixty-six provides the
answer:

> And so what is likely to come to pass for those men is, I believe,
> what happens in Plato's myth to those who are chained in a cave
> and wonder at the shadows of things, and also to that escapee
> who returns to the cave and announces that he has seen the
> true things and that those men are much mistaken who believe
> that nothing else exists besides the wretched shadows. And
> indeed this wise man commiserates and deplores the insanity of
> those men who are gripped by such a great error. But those men
> laugh at him as if he were deranged, and throw him out.[5]

The *miserae umbrae* [wretched shadows] which beguile the captives,
it turns out, are nothing other than the ethics of Roman republican
theory.

In chapter twenty-seven, Folly asks 'what state ever adopted the
laws of Plato or Aristotle, or the teachings of Socrates?'[6] None, she
replies, because they are all too busy chasing Roman *gloria*. She proceeds to identify two sets of martyrs to the Roman *patria* as her aco-
lytes, and launches into a brutal satire of the Roman *vita activa*,
claiming it as an instance of folly. Cicero's famous dictum in Book II
of the *De officiis* that *summa et perfecta gloria* depends on 'the affection, the confidence, and the mingled esteem of the people'[7] is surely
Erasmus's target:

---

3. Ibid.
4. Ibid., p. 100. ["*Decorum*": propriety, of actions or words; an important concept in classical ethical and rhetorical theory. See p. 33, n. 8 above; editor's note.]
5. Ibid., p. 190. Recall that Hythloday predicted he would be 'thrown out' (*eiciendum*) for
   the same reason (More, p. 28). [Folly refers to the Myth of the Cave in the *Republic*
   (514a–521b); editor's note.]
6. Erasmus, *Opera omnia*, IX, p. 102.
7. Cicero, *De officiis*, ed. and trans. Walter Miller (Cambridge, MA, 1997), p. 198.
   ["*Summa et perfecta gloria*": the highest and perfect glory; editor's note.]

Besides, what was it that prevailed upon the Decii, so that they offered themselves of their own free will to the gods of the underworld? What dragged Q. Curtius into the chasm, if not vain glory, the sweetest Siren, but one denounced passionately by those wise men of yours? What could be more foolish, they ask, than for a man seeking office to flatter the mob, to purchase support with gifts, to pursue the applause of all the fools, to be pleased with their acclamations, to be carried about in triumph as if he were some image to be gazed at by the people, and to stand in the forum cast in bronze. Add to these things adopted names and family-names. Add divine honors bestowed on little men, and even the most wicked tyrants being transformed into gods in public ceremonies . . . This is the folly which spawns states; dominions are established by it, as are magistracies, civil religion, councils, and law courts. Nor is human life anything other than some game of folly.[8]

Folly could hardly be more clear: in case we were unsure which kind of *inanis gloria* we were talking about, Folly makes sure we know it is the sort of *gloria* for which men organize *civitates* and *imperia*, *consilia* and *magistratus*—that is, the institutions of *Romanitas*.

In the Erasmian framework, Platonic philosophy is thought ridiculous by those living amidst the ethical categories of Roman theory—what Folly later calls the 'middle, quasi-natural affections' such as love of country and family, when valued for themselves and not as manifestations of the *summum bonum*.[9] The Platonism Erasmus opposes to *Romanitas* is deeply metaphysical, drawn, as we have seen, from Ficino and from the broader context of the Greek revival in England. Erasmus uses Folly to demonstrate that the Roman *vita activa* is incompatible with an interior life lived on correct, Platonic terms. None the less, Erasmus does not hesitate to identify the social and political implications of his Platonism. In the *Adagia*, he explains Plato's use of the proverb 'friends have everything in common' by stating that 'through this passage [Plato] tries to demonstrate that the happiest state of a commonwealth consists in the common ownership of all things'.[1] 'If it were only possible for mortals to be persuaded of this', Erasmus muses, 'in that very instant

---

8. Erasmus, *Opera omnia*, IX, p. 102. A similar passage appears in *Enchiridion* (O'Malley, ed., *The collected works of Erasmus*, LXVI, p. 27); the Decii and Curtius are discussed in identical terms in the *Ciceronianus* (O'Malley, ed., *The collected works of Erasmus*, XXVIII, trans. and ed. Betty I. Knott (Toronto, 1986), p. 385). See also Augustine, *City of God* IV.20.

9. Erasmus, *Opera omnia*, IX, p. 191. ["*Summum bonum*": the supreme good; editor's note.]

1. Erasmus, *Opera omnia*, XX, p. 84. David Wootton adduces this passage in his excellent discussion of Erasmus's 'proto-Utopianism'. See Wootton, 'Friendship portrayed: A new account of *Utopia*', *History Workshop Journal*, 45 (1998), pp. 25–47. See also Wootton, 'Introduction', to Thomas More, *Utopia, with Erasmus's the sileni of Alcibiades*, ed. and trans. David Wootton (Indianapolis, 1999), p. 8.

war, envy and fraud would depart from their midst'.[2] However, Erasmus was under no illusions: 'But it is exceedingly strange that this community of possessions advocated by Plato should so displease Christians that they attack it with stones, since nothing ever said by a pagan philosopher is more similar to the judgment of Christ'.[3] In 1519, three years after the initial publication of *Utopia*, More would offer an extended discussion of precisely this theme:

> God showed great foresight when he instituted that all things should be held in common; Christ showed as much when he tried to recall mortals again to what is common from what is private. For he perceived that the corrupt nature of mortals cannot cherish what is private without injury to the community, as experience shows in all aspects of life. For not only does everyone love his own plot of land or his own money, not only does everyone cherish his own family or his own set of colleagues, but to the extent that we call anything our own it absorbs our affections and diverts them from the service of the common good.[4]

More's solution to this problem, like Plato's, was Utopia, the land without private property where the entire community was one large family (More, p. 54). In composing a Platonic account of the *felicissimus reipublicae status*[5] which could stand up to the neo-Roman tradition, More was taking up the task Erasmus had begun. The Utopians, we should recall, also put up statues of their great men in the market-place (p. 74). But their great men are of a very different sort, and their statues are put up for very different reasons.

III

The dichotomy between Greece and Rome is made explicit from the very outset of More's text. Hythloday is first introduced as a 'stranger', much like the 'strangers' who serve as Platonic alter-egos in the *Sophist*, the *Statesman*, and the *Laws*. Giles then explains to 'More' that Hythloday has not sailed around (*navigavit*) like Palinurus,[6] the unfortunate watchman of Roman epic, but rather like the Greek Ulysses, or 'even more' like Plato. The allusion is most likely to the account of Plato's travels found in Cicero's *De finibus*

---

2. Erasmus, *Opera omnia*, XX, p. 61. * * *
3. Ibid., p. 84. Recall Hythloday's observation that Jesus's doctrines would seem strange (*aliena*) among contemporary Christians (More, p. 34), and his comment that 'I have no doubt that every man's perception of where his true interest lies, along with the authority of Christ our Saviour . . . , would long ago have brought the whole world to adopt the laws of this commonwealth . . .' (p. 96) [substituting the Cambridge translation for Nelson's quotation of the Latin; editor's note].
4. Kinney, ed., *Complete works*, XV, p. 279. [*Letter to a monk*; editor's note.]
5. The happiest state of a commonwealth [editor's note].
6. See p. 11, n. 6 above [editor's note].

and Diogenes's *Lives*,[7] and later presented as the *Navigatio Platonis* in Ficino's text.[8] Both Ulysses and Plato surveyed the manners of different societies (Homer introduces Odysseus as the man who 'saw the cities of many men, and knew their minds'),[9] but Hythloday, like Plato, has studied them as a philosopher. Giles then tells 'More' that, while Hythloday is not ignorant of Latin, he is extremely learned in Greek (p. 11). In fact, Giles reports, Hythloday has studied Greek instead of Latin because his main interest is philosophy, and 'he recognized that, on that subject, nothing very valuable exists in Latin except certain works of Seneca and Cicero'. More himself makes a similar statement in his *Letter to Oxford*: 'For in philosophy, apart from those works which Cicero and Seneca left behind, the schools of the Latins have nothing to offer that is not either Greek or translated from Greek.'[1] But when Hythloday recommends books to the Utopians, he goes even further. He states clearly that 'we thought that, except for the historians and poets, there was nothing in Latin that they would value' (p. 67). This more extreme iteration, as we have seen, anticipates a passage from More's *Letter to a monk*. On that occasion, More argues that 'speakers of Latin write practically nothing' in 'those arts they call liberal, along with philosophy'.[2] Accordingly, Hythloday gives the Utopians most of Plato's works, and some of Aristotle's—none of Cicero's or Seneca's—and continues by noting that the Utopian language is related to Greek. This opposition between Greece and Rome works itself out through the same sort of clash between ethical systems that we located in *The praise of folly*.

Thomas White's study of More's use of Plato in *Utopia* identifies a wide range of Platonic references in the text, and this present analysis will not attempt to reinvent the wheel.[3] Rather, it will hope to assess how More structures the Utopian story around the essentially Greek value system we have identified, and opposes it to *Romanitas*. In this respect, it is best to begin at the beginning. Book I occupies itself with the 'problem of counsel', a standard humanist topic which inevitably relates to the quarrel between *otium* and *negotium* to which we have already alluded. This theme is announced unmistakably by

7. Cicero, *De finibus* V.87 (see Cicero, *De finibus bonorum et malorum* [*On the supreme good and evil*; editor's note], ed. and trans. H. Rackham (Cambridge, MA, 1967), p. 490); Diogenes, *Lives* III.6 (see Diogenes Laertius, *Lives of eminent philosophers*, ed. and trans. R. D. Hicks, vol. 1 (Cambridge, MA, 1966), p. 281).
8. Ficino, 'Militia et Navigatio Platonis Trina'. ["The Three Military Expeditions and Sea Voyages of Plato"; editor's note.]
9. Homer, *The Odyssey*, ed. W. B. Stanford, I (London, 1958), 1.3. * * *
1. See Kinney, ed., *Complete works*, XV, p. 143. I have modified Kinney's translation here.
2. Kinney, ed., *Complete works*, XV, p. 220. * * *
3. Thomas White, 'Pride and the public good: Thomas More's use of Plato in *Utopia*', *Journal of the History of Philosophy*, 20 (1982), pp. 329–354. See also Surtz's discussion of Plato in Surtz and Hexter, eds., *Complete works*, IV, p. clviff, and Baker-Smith, 'Uses of Plato by Erasmus and More', in Anna Baldwin and Sarah Hutton, eds., *Platonism and the English imagination* (Cambridge, 1994), pp. 86–99.

all the prefatory letters which various humanists appended to the
1517 and 1518 editions of the text. Erasmus's letter (first included in
1518) raises the issue in the guise of a standard *captatio benevolen-
tiae*, an attempt to earn the good-will of the reader by pointing out
what a busy man the author is, and under what harried conditions
the work was produced. But, as a preface to *Utopia*, this is more
than a *topos*.

> Apart from the cares of a married man and the responsibilities
> of his household, apart from his official post and floods of legal
> cases, he [More] is distracted by so many and such important
> matters of state business (*tantisque regni negotiis*) that you
> would marvel he finds any free time (*otium*) at all for books.
> (p. 141 above)

Guillaume Budé follows suit, and observes that reading about the
mores and *instituta* of the Utopians made him disdainful of his *negotium* and his obsession with *industria oeconomica* (p. 135 above). It
is, however, More's own letter which frames the issue most explicitly:

> Well, little as it was, that task [of writing *Utopia*] was rendered
> almost impossible by my many other obligations (*negotia mea*).
> Most of my day is given to the law—pleading some cases, hear-
> ing others, arbitrating others and deciding still others; this
> man is visited for the sake of duty (*officii causa*), that man for
> the sake of business (*negotii*); and so almost all day I'm out
> dealing with other people, and the rest of the day I give over to
> my household; and then for myself—that is, my studies—
> there's nothing left. (p. 6)

The reader is being prepared for a humanist showdown between
the Roman values of *officia* and *negotium* and the Greek *vita
contemplativa*.

In Book I, as Skinner has shown conclusively, the figure of 'More'
becomes the *porte-parole* for the Ciceronian *vita activa*, and coun-
ters Hythloday's defence of *otium* with virtual quotations from the
De officiis.[4] What is remarkable about *Utopia*, however, is not simply that Hythloday defends *otium*, but *why* he does. In response to
'More's' insistence that he should become a councillor, Hythloday

---

4. Quentin Skinner, 'Sir Thomas More's *Utopia* and the language of Renaissance humanism', in Anthony Pagden, ed., *The languages of political theory in early-modern Europe*
(Cambridge, 1987), esp. pp. 132–5. Baker-Smith largely follows Skinner in his analysis
of Book I (Baker-Smith, 'Uses of Plato by Erasmus and More', pp. 98–102). He
rightly emphasizes the self-conscious Platonism of those who defended the *vita contemplativa*
against the Ciceronian *vita activa*, but neglects to locate that Platonist commitment
within the context of a wider ethical and political theory, or to acknowledge the explicit
critique of *Romanitas*. As a result, he concludes (incorrectly, I believe) that 'More' is an
Augustinian critic of Plato (p. 225), and that *Utopia* represents a confrontation between
Platonism and Augustinianism. ["*Porte-parole*": mouthpiece; editor's note.]

argues (clearly echoing Erasmus's Folly) that Latinized Europeans will not accept Greek advice. Hythloday understands that 'More' and his ilk will find Utopian advice absurd (just as, he notes, Dionysius of Syracuse found Plato's absurd) (p. 28) because they have been imbued with Roman views on justice and the ends of civic life— two positions that Hythloday spends the whole of *Utopia* attacking from a Greek perspective. He asks, 'what if I told them the kind of thing that Plato imagines in his republic, or that the Utopians actually practise in theirs', and answers that, no matter how superior, 'here they [the practices] would seem alien' (p. 34). His views are only confirmed when 'More' champions a 'philosophia civilior' (one more suited to the *vivere civile*) over what he dismisses as Hythloday's 'philosophia scholastica' (where *scholastica* is clearly another 'nonsense' word) (p. 33). Hythloday is forced to conclude that, in attempting to advise Europeans 'deeply immersed as they are and infected with false values from boyhood on' (p. 28) and languishing in the grasp of *stultitia* (another nod to Erasmus) (p. 35), he would simply end up acquiring the disease he was trying to cure (p. 34).

'More' begins with the Ciceronian claim that, in becoming a councillor, Hythloday would advance his own interests as well as those of his family and friends[5] (p. 14; see *De officiis* 1.5), and proceeds to offer the standard humanist observation that a 'philosophic nature' is suited to advise princes (pp. 14–15) (a view, 'More' tells Hythloday, that is shared by 'your Plato')[6]—and, later, that it is every good man's *officium* to do so. Hythloday replies that he would not part with his precious *otium* (his ability 'to live as he likes', a privilege Cicero rejects as un-civic)[7] on that account, since courtiers are incredulous and defensive when 'a man should suggest something he has read of in other ages or seen in practice elsewhere' (part of his constant insistence that his advice would be ill-received by Europeans) (p. 15). When 'More' retorts that he should not be so impatient to 'pluck up bad ideas by the root', but should rather aim to make the

---

5. This argument [actually put forward by Giles, not 'More'; editor's note] is also advanced by Callicles during his exchange with Socrates in *Gorgias* 483b–486d—a discussion which largely mirrors the debate between 'More' and Hythloday in Book I.

6. P. 27. This is a particularly significant detail, since Hythloday has not yet referred to Plato directly. Here, without being told, 'More' reveals his awareness that Hythloday is ventriloquizing Plato.

7. P. 14. See Cicero, *De officiis* 1.70. Interestingly, this is an aspect of the debate More stresses repeatedly in his *Life of John Picus*. * * * More writes of Pico that 'liberte a boue all thing he loued to which both his owne naturall affection & the study of philosophy enclined him' (*Complete works*, I, p. 69), and in the letter to Corneo we read that philosophers 'love liberte; they can not bere the prowde maners of estates [i.e., noblemen; editor's note]: they can not serve' (p. 85). The first clause of this second passage is More's own interpolation * * *. Baker-Smith provides an illuminating account of the similarities between the letter and Book I of *Utopia*, although he does not stress the theme of 'liberte' in the earlier work. See Baker-Smith, 'Uses of Plato by Erasmus and More', esp. pp. 18–20, 99.

regime as good as possible, Hythloday replies that such conduct
would simply force him to imitate the degeneracy of the multitude.
He illustrates his point by taking an image out of the *Republic*:

> This is why Plato in a very fine comparison declares that wise
> men are right in keeping away from public business. They see
> the people swarming through the streets and getting soaked
> with rain; they cannot persuade them to go indoors and get out
> of the wet. If they go out themselves, they know they will do no
> good, but only get drenched with the others. So they stay indoors
> and are content to keep at least themselves dry, since they can-
> not remedy the folly of others (*alienae stultitiae*). (p. 35)

The analogy to which Hythloday refers is found at the end of a
passage in Book VI—one which surely must have been in More's
thoughts when he composed this debate. Earlier in the passage,
Plato writes as follows:

> [The enlightened few realize] that no one can do anything
> sound, so to speak, concerning the business of cities, nor is
> there an ally with whose aid the champion of justice could
> escape destruction, but, rather, that he would be as a man who
> has fallen among wild beasts, unwilling to share their misdeeds
> and unable to hold out against the savagery of all, and that he
> would thus, before he could in any way benefit his friends or the
> state, come to an untimely end, useless to himself and others—
> for all these reasons I say the philosopher remains quiet, minds
> his own affair. (*Republic* 496c)

In its emphasis on the inability of a philosopher to help his friends,
himself, or the state by entering public service in a commonwealth
not ruled by philosophers (and its rejection of 'More's' sort of collu-
sion as 'sharing the misdeeds' of the rulers), this passage encapsu-
lates the debate between 'More' and Hythloday—and reveals it to
be a debate between Cicero and Plato, between Rome and Greece.[8]

Moreover, Plato's portrayal of the philosopher as a 'champion of
justice' in the midst of those who argue over the 'shadows of justice'
(*Republic* 517d) frames the extensive discussion of *iustitia* in Book I
and its distinctive treatment in Book II. In the midst of the debate on
negotium, Hythloday recounts how he participated in a discussion on
the punishment for theft at the court of Cardinal Morton, More's

---

8. Brendan Bradshaw provides an excellent account of the relationship between the
   'More'/Hythloday debate and *Republic* VI, although he neglects to comment on 'More's'
   Ciceronianism, or to emphasize that More imports an extremely specific thought from
   his source (i.e. that the advice of philosophers will seem like nonsense to those in the
   cave) which has implications for our overall view of *Utopia*. Bradshaw also concludes
   that 'More' is the victor in the debate. See Brendan Bradshaw, 'More on Utopia', in *The
   Historical Journal*, 24 (1981), pp. 1–27.

patron and the only European in *Utopia* who appreciates Greek advice. Hythloday repeats his argument that the practice of hanging thieves is unjust and ineffective, and offers two principal reasons. First, the punishment is disproportionate; second, 'it would be much better to enable every man to earn his own living, instead of being driven to the awful necessity of stealing and then dying for it' (p. 17).

This second objection is fleshed out extensively and develops into an attack on Roman 'iustitia' (giving each person *ius suum*) and a defence of Greek δικαιοσύνη.[9] In the Platonic framework, as we have seen, 'justice' indicates an arrangement of elements that accords with nature; it relies on σωφροσύνη, or 'balance', which produces 'harmony' and prevents the corruption of the established order; the arrangement of the whole, when just and balanced, reflects itself on to the souls of the citizens and moulds their characters. Justice is, indeed, in Ficino's phrase,[1] the *civitatis ordo atque salus*, and just institutions are essential for the cultivation of virtue. Logan notices More's focus on 'institutions' or 'root-causes', but attributes it mistakenly to a 'scholastic' strain in his thought.[2] There is no trace of the scholastic idiom in *Utopia*; we find no references to *ius naturale, lex naturalis, iurisdictio, dominium, imperium, universitas*, or any of the other standard scholastic vocabulary (which, lest we forget, both Erasmus and More ridicule mercilessly).[3] On the contrary, More has Hythloday articulate a fundamentally Greek, holistic concept of justice which he proceeds to oppose to the more narrow, ad hoc Roman notion. Nor should we be surprised that it is Cardinal Morton's fool who comes to Hythloday's aid when he has finished speaking—and that More chooses the uncommon word *morio* to designate the fool so that he can pun on μόριον, 'councillor' (p. 25).[4]

It quickly becomes apparent that Hythloday's 'justice' does not consist in giving each person what belongs to him (and punishing those who take what is another's by *ius*), but in producing a natural and harmonious institutional arrangement:

> Restrict the right of the rich to buy up anything and everything, and then to exercise a kind of monopoly. Let fewer people be

9. Thomas White tries to connect More's 'justice' to Aristotelian distributive justice and, more broadly, to ideas about the 'common good'. While helpful, however, his analysis ignores the most basic, holistic sense in which More intends the term—and, thus, the explicit critique of Roman *ius*. See Thomas White, 'Aristotle and *Utopia*', *Renaissance Quarterly*, 29 (1976), p. 657.
1. See pp. 268–69 above [editor's note].
2. Logan, *The meaning of More's 'Utopia'*, p. 79.
3. For an analysis of the scholastic idiom during the sixteenth century, see Annabel Brett, *Liberty, right and nature: individual rights in later scholastic thought* (Cambridge, 1997), and Richard Tuck, *Natural rights theories: their origin and development* (Cambridge, 1979), esp. ch. 2.
4. For an instance of the word being used in this way, see Aristotle, *Politics* 1282a37 (III.6). * * *

brought up in idleness. Let agriculture be restored, and the wool-manufacture revived as an honest trade, so there will be useful work for the idle throng . . . Certainly unless you cure these evils it is futile to boast of your justice (*iustitia*) in punishing theft. Your policy may look superficially like justice, but in reality it is neither just nor expedient. If you allow young folk to be abominably brought up and their characters corrupted little by little, from childhood; and if then you punish them as grownups for committing the crimes to which their training has consistently inclined them, what else is this, I ask, but first making them thieves and then punishing them for it? (pp. 20–21)

Hythloday endorses the Platonic notion that justice as an arrangement of the soul is produced and reinforced by justice in the arrangement of the state. The justice 'they' boast of in punishing theft is Roman *iustitia*—applying a punishment for a crime that has been committed. But Hythloday argues that this *iustitia* is hollow; he later says that he finds 'no trace' of justice in the 'justice of the nations' (p. 94). When souls are unjust (that is, not balanced according to nature) education (which we should recall is *part* of the institutional arrangement, as well as, more broadly, a result of it) is to blame. Accordingly, Hythloday praises the practice of the Polylerites (those people of 'much nonsense'), who force thieves to make restitution (a practice reminiscent of the one Plato endorses in the *Laws*)[5] and insist that the purpose of punishment is educative. Plato had written that 'the purpose of the penalty is not to cancel the crime—what is once done can never be made undone—but to bring the criminal . . . to complete renunciation of such criminality, or at least to recovery in great part from the dreadful state' (934a-b), and Hythloday extols the Polylerite custom in similar terms: 'It is clear how mild and practical they are, for the aim of the punishment is to destroy vices and save men. The men are treated so that they necessarily become good, and they have the rest of their lives to make up for the damage done' (p. 24).

This notion of justice as δικαιοσύνη, in turn, becomes the essential justification for Utopian communism as praised by Hythloday in Book I, and then described in Book II. The Utopians agree with Plato that, in a just society, 'no one can ever be reduced to poverty or forced to beg' (p. 53; cf. *Laws* 936c), and, therefore, they have abolished private property.[6] Hythloday shares their view, and argues that a society based on private property cannot be just:

---

5. *Laws* 857a (IX).
6. Hexter and others have stressed, however, that while Plato's communism in the *Republic* may be restricted to the class of guardians, More's is generalized. See Surtz and Hexter, eds., *Complete works*, IV, pp. lxxxvii, cixff. None the less, More leaves no doubt that he views the abolition of private property as a Platonic measure.

But as a matter of fact, my dear More [*mi More*—note the pun], to tell you what I really think, wherever you have private property, and money is the measure of all things, it is hardly ever possible for a commonwealth to be just or prosperous—unless you think justice can exist where all the best things (*optima*) are held by the worst citizens (*pessimi*), or suppose happiness can be found where the good things of life are divided among the very few, where even those few are always uneasy. (p. 35)

This passage introduces three interconnected claims about why private property produces injustice, all dependent on the Greek tradition. The first has to do with rulership. Hythloday and the Utopians—like Plato—take it as axiomatic that justice requires the rule of the better over the baser: in a Platonic universe, there are those naturally suited to rule (Hythloday uses the image of shepherds who rule for the good of their flock, recalling Plato's treatment of rulership in the *Republic* and the *Statesman*),[7] just as there are those who are suited by nature to soldiering, or weaving, or any other τέχνη (art). This Platonic claim about just rulership represents the point of contact between *Utopia* and the humanist tradition of equating *virtus* with *vera nobilitas*.[8] Articulated in a series of important fifteenth-century treatises (such as Buonaccorso's *Controversia de nobilitate*, and Poggio Bracciolini's *De nobilitate*), this trope developed in opposition to the scholastic tradition of equating *nobilitas* with *longae divitiae* (that is, long-established wealth), and its attendant *splendor* and *magnificentia* (Skinner, p. 137). Taking aim at the schoolmen, humanists declared (citing a variety of classical authorities) that true worth was not determined by pomp and pedigree, but by personal virtue.

Because the contrary position is rooted in scholastic sources (and because the phrase itself derives from Juvenal, Horace, and Cicero), the temptation is to see the ideology behind *virtus vera nobilitas* as essentially Roman. But we should recall that the notion is as Platonic as it is Ciceronian (Cicero, after all, took the concept from Plato),[9] and that the scholastic defence of *longae divitiae* was itself a bowdlerization of Aristotle's claim in *Politics* IV that 'nobility means ancient wealth and virtue (ἀρετή)'.[1] Aristotle's statement relies on a discussion in Book III, in which he argues that the well-born and

---

7. More, p. 32. See, for example, *Republic* 345c, and *Statesman* 261d.
8. Skinner discusses this issue from a different point of view ('Sir Thomas More's *Utopia*', pp. 135–47). ["*Virtus*": virtue. "*Vera nobilitas*": true nobility; editor's note.]
9. See *De officiis* 2.20. Skinner points out that Poggio made this connection. See Skinner, 'Political philosophy', p. 423.
1. *Politics* 1294a21 (IV.6). [For the version of this article that appears in his book, Nelson added a few sentences on the precise context of Aristotle's statement: see *The Greek Tradition in Republican Thought*, p. 43; editor's note.]

wealthy should rule because manual labourers 'cannot practise the pursuits in which goodness is exercised' (1278a21). He does not deny that *virtus* constitutes *vera nobilitas*: he simply asserts that the *banausoi*[2] are rendered incapable of achieving virtue by the material conditions of their lives. And while it is certainly true that Aristotle (not unlike Cicero)[3] offers a qualified defence of *magnificentia* in *Ethics* 1122a (IV.2), he argues explicitly in *Politics* IV that rule by the 'middle class' is best, because both extreme wealth and extreme poverty corrupt (1295a39–1296a22). Thus, as Jacob Burckhardt observed almost 150 years ago,[4] it was entirely possible to defend the equation of *virtus* with *vera nobilitas* from an Aristotelian perspective. * * * Ultimately, both Aristotle and Plato agree that the just polity is one in which the most virtuous men rule.

More, in turn, uses the *virtus vera nobilitas* trope to assert the connection between rulership and δικαιοσύνη, and to insist that the abolition of private property is necessary for that connection to be realized. In Utopia, Hythloday tells us, 'virtuti pretium sit'— virtue has its reward (p. 35). The Utopians, indeed, find it downright bizarre that 'a dunderhead who has no more brains than a post, and who is as vicious as he is foolish, should command a great many wise and good men, simply because he happens to have a big pile of gold coins' (p. 57). In a society of private property, however, where 'money is the measure of all things' and the wealth goes to the *pessimi*, the worst citizens will tend to rule, thus producing an unjust arrangement by definition (that is, rule by the appetitive over the rational—which Hythloday, following Plato, calls contrary to 'nature') (p. 60). Hythloday rejects the claim that simple legislation will prevent public offices 'which ought to go to the wise' (p. 36) from going to the wealthy, and identifies such usurpations as the inevitable result of private property. But because all their property is held in common, the Utopians are able to favour the most excellent members of society—those who should rule by nature.[5] In domestic matters (in conformity with both

2. *"Banausoi"*: in classical Greek, a characteristically derogatory term for manual laborers [editor's note].
3. Cicero, *De officiis* 2.16–17. It is worth noting that Cicero cites Aristotle as his source for a temperate assessment of *magnificentia*.
4. 'From a theoretical point of view, when the appeal was made to antiquity, the conception of nobility could be both justified and condemned from Aristotle alone.' See Burckhardt, *The civilization of the Renaissance in Italy*, p. 231.
5. More emphasizes this aspect of Utopian political thought in a letter to Erasmus dated 31 October 1516. Professing himself to be gratified that men such as Giles and Busleyden approve of his treatise, he writes, 'in this commonwealth of mine the ruling class would be completely made up of such men as are distinguished for learning and virtue. No matter how powerful those men are in their present governments—and, true, they are very powerful—still they have some high and mighty clowns as their equals, if not their superiors, in authority and influence' (*St. Thomas More: Selected Letters*, edited by Elizabeth Frances Rogers [New Haven and London: Yale University Press, 1961], p. 80) [substituting Rogers's translation for Nelson's quotation of More's Latin; editor's note].

Platonic and Aristotelian doctrine),[6] 'wives act as servants to their husbands, children to their parents, and generally the younger to their elders' (p. 50), while government is reserved for those who 'from childhood have given evidence of excellent character, unusual intelligence, and a mind inclined to the liberal arts' (p. 58). This small Platonic elite is excused from labour, and left to cultivate itself for future service to the *respublica* (p. 47).

Hythloday later adds to this first argument by claiming that the unnatural rulership brought about by private property topples the institutional arrangement of the state by causing it to lose sight of its own nature. In Greek thought, the state aims at αὐτάρκεια (self-sufficiency), and, for Plato, justice is above all the natural ordering of the elements which are necessary to produce this quality. In the *Republic*, when Socrates builds *Kallipolis* from scratch, self-sufficiency dictates that the very first, most essential members of the society are the farmers, the builders, the weavers, and other craftsmen.[7] However, in a society of private property, Hythloday argues, this natural priority is subverted:

> Now isn't this an unjust and ungrateful commonwealth? It lavishes rich rewards on so-called gentry, goldsmiths and the rest of that crew, who don't work at all or are mere parasites, purveyors of empty pleasures. And yet it makes no proper provision for the welfare of farmers and colliers, labourers, carters, and carpenters, without whom the commonwealth would simply cease to exist . . . Before, it appeared to be unjust that people who deserve most from the commonwealth should receive least. But now, by promulgating law, they have transmuted this perversion into justice. (pp. 94–95)

Private property and the warped rulership that accompanies it undermine the connection between justice and self-sufficiency—they subvert the natural ordering of the essential elements which compose the state.

But above all, as we have come to expect, Hythloday argues that communism is essential for justice because private property and its accompanying institutions corrupt the souls of citizens. In Platonic thought, no one emerges unscathed from this process: in the *Republic*, Socrates argues that wealth brings 'luxury' and 'idleness' (422a), while poverty makes the poor unable to discharge their natural functions, denying them happiness. Likewise, Hythloday observes that wealth makes the rich 'rapacious, wicked, and useless' (p. 36), and, as for the poor, 'bitter necessity, then, forces them to think that they must look out for themselves, rather than for the people' (p. 94)—and,

6. See *Republic* 412c (III), *Politics* 1254b (I).
7. See *Republic* 370d (II). ["*Kallipolis*": Plato's name for his ideal republic; editor's note.]

as we have seen, turns them into criminals. Utopian communism prevents all of this, Hythloday argues, and ensures that the citizens are brought up with 'sound principles' which 'their education and the good institutions of their republic both reinforce' (p. 82)—that is, the Utopians preserve justice in its true, Greek sense.[8]

It only remains to point out that, for Hythloday and the Utopians, the purpose of justice is to produce happiness (Greek εὐδαιμονία)— the quality which they agree with the Greeks in identifying as the end of human and civic life. *Felicitas* is among the most ubiquitous words in More's text, and is often explicitly opposed to forms of *gloria*.[9] The Polylerites, for example, have a system of justice which has allowed them to 'live in a useful rather than splendid manner, more happy than renowned or famous . . . they are hardly known by name to anyone but their immediate neighbours' (p. 23). Anonymity is not, to say the least, a pillar of the Roman value system; but the Polylerites aim for happiness, not glory, so it does not disturb them.

This is even more true of the Utopians, who have understood that happiness (*felicitas*) cannot be achieved without justice—and that justice requires the abolition of private property (p. 35). Only if goods are held in common can mortals live happily (*feliciter*) (p. 36), which explains, for Hythloday, why the Utopians live more happily than Europeans—indeed more happily than any other commonwealth (p. 66). Again, at the end of Book II, Hythloday claims that, as a result of their 'structures of life', the Utopians live 'the most happily' (*felicissime*), and he contrasts this 'happiness of the Utopian republic' to the wretchedness of all societies built around private property. As for glory, the Utopians (again echoing Erasmus's Folly) despise the *gloria* won in battle (p. 77),[1] and, when they are forced to fight, they have no thought of *laus* (praise) or *fama* (fame) (p. 79). Rather, in direct opposition to Cicero's injunction in the *De officiis* (1.41), they make unrepentant use of *fraus* (fraud) and overwhelming *vis* (force) in order to end their wars as quickly as possible: they traffic in assassinations, bribes, seditions, mercenaries, and various other instruments of *ars et dolus* (skill and cunning) in order

8. We are now in a position to dispute Hexter's claim that, for More, 'equality is justice' (Surtz and Hexter, eds., *Complete works*, IV, p. cxxiii). We should say rather that the abolition of private property (and the level social order it creates) is *necessary* for justice. Justice itself is the rational ordering of all elements which contribute to self-sufficiency. Athanasios Moulakis endorses Hexter's position, see 'Pride and the meaning of *Utopia*', *History of Political Thought*, 11 (1990), p. 247.
9. Thomas White, among others, observes that happiness is the aim of Utopian life in his study of More's Aristotelianism. The hope here is to build on that common observation by noticing that, in this respect, More is challenging the traditional values of *Romanitas*, and, thus, of the republican tradition as understood in his lifetime. See White, 'Aristotle and *Utopia*', p. 640. See also similar comments in Logan, *The meaning of More's 'Utopia'*, p. 185.
1. See, for example, Erasmus, *Opera omnia*, IX, p. 96.

to carry the day (pp. 78–83).[2] They endorse these practices, not (as Machiavelli does in *Il Principe*) because they believe that *vis* and *fraus* will ultimately secure them *gloria*, but because glory is not the point of their actions. In their ethical system, the 'first concern' is to identify the nature of 'human happiness', and then pursue 'true happiness' (*vera felicitas*) as the primary goal of human life (pp. 59–60). It is in this context that the Utopians intervene in the debate between *otium* and *negotium* (a debate which, we should recall, is waged in terms of *felicitas* in Book I):[3]

> The structure of their republic is dedicated above all to this objective: that, as far as public needs permit, all citizens should be free to withdraw as much time as possible from the service of the body and devote themselves to the freedom and culture of the mind. For in that, they think, lies the happiness of life (*vitae felicitas*). (p. 48)

With this connection between justice, happiness, and the *vita contemplativa* established, our story comes full circle.

---

2. Thus, More takes Plato's case for 'happiness' to its logical conclusion in a way that Plato never did. See Surtz on the un-Platonic military practices of the Utopians (Surtz and Hexter, eds., *Complete works*, IV, p. clix). The classic work on the Erasmian and Utopian rejection of military glory remains Robert P. Adams, *The better part of valor: More, Erasmus, Colet, and Vives, on Humanism, war and peace, 1496–1535* (Seattle, 1962). Adams's analysis, however, is coloured by his argument that the Erasmian political programme was almost exclusively 'neo-Stoic'.
3. See, for example, Giles's claim that being a counselor would make More 'happier' (*felicior*). More, p. 14. [Nelson means "Hythloday," not "More"; editor's note.]

Utopia's Modern Progeny

In the centuries following its publication, More's book became the eponymous representative of a new literary genre, the utopia: an account of a voyage to an imaginary country that embodies the author's social and political ideals. (These works are massively surveyed in Frank E. and Fritzie P. Manuel's *Utopian Thought in the Western World*; see "Suggestions for Further Reading.") From as early as the seventeenth century, a prominent subgenre was the *scientific* utopia (Sir Francis Bacon's unfinished *New Atlantis*, published in 1627, is the prototypical English example), in which science and its accompanying technological advances supply the foundations of the perfected society.

As Northrop Frye says (see p. 213 above), "The utopian writer looks at his own society first and tries to see what, for his purposes, its significant elements are. The utopia itself shows what society would be like if those elements were fully developed." In the twentieth century, as it became clear that the scientific and technological advancements that increasingly determined the shape of society did not always lead to improvements in human life (and might irremediably foul the human nest), and as the world experienced the results—ranging from stultifying sameness to mass horrors—of ideologically driven and technologically facilitated social engineering, the most influential new works in the tradition initiated by More became not utopias but "anti-utopias" (or "dystopias"): books such as Aldous Huxley's *Brave New World* (1932) and George Orwell's *Nineteen Eighty-Four* (written in 1948 and published the following year) that depicted societies in which the full development of the most significant elements in the author's own society have produced nightmarish places. Some of the same technologies that engendered dystopian anxieties also, of course, made possible a powerful new form for these fictions, the dystopian movie: three particularly striking and influential examples are *Blade Runner* (1982), *The Terminator* (1984), and *Terminator 2* (1991).

In addition to the focus on technology, modern works—whether utopian or dystopian—in the tradition inaugurated by More's book typically differ from their predecessors in a second, related respect: as the possibility of finding an unknown part of the world to situate the alternative society became vanishingly small (and as superpowers rather than isolated islands became the focus of attention), authors increasingly tended to set their works in the near or distant future rather than in some obscure part of the globe, or else situated them in outer space: on the moon or another planet (or *its* moon), perhaps orbiting another sun. In both these developments—its reliance on fantasized (but in some cases all too plausible) scientific and technological break-throughs and on displacement to the future and/or off-planet—fiction in the utopian tradition merged (as in both of the works excerpted be-low) with *science* fiction.

ALDOUS HUXLEY

From Brave New World[†]

[Huxley's sardonic novel *Brave New World* grew out of the author's reali-zation that most of the technical procedures for bringing utopia out of the realm of fantasy and into the world of practical reality either already existed or would soon exist. Taking Henry Ford and his newly developed assembly-line procedures as patterns for the new age, he moved his ac-tion some six hundred years into the future and assumed (as More had also done) that the people of the new society would have to be engi-neered to fit its new conditions. As Huxley foresaw it, though, the engi-neering of people would have to be done biologically as well as socially. His brave new world managers begin by controlling the different genetic endowments of the embryos and then conditioning them within arti-ficial glass wombs, by means of specifically tailored environments, to develop the various classes and qualities of creature that society needs.

The novel opens with a group of new students being shown through the main London Hatchery and Conditioning Center. The offensive Director and an even more offensive subordinate patiently explain the appalling perfection of the machinery for producing and condi-tioning embryos. But of course conditioning does not stop when the pseudo-persons have been decanted from their bottles at the end of the assembly line. They have to be shaped to the exact measures of docility and unimaginative self-satisfaction that represent the soci-ety's ideal; they have to be shaped and reshaped for the rest of their existence. Potential problems like parental affection, romantic love, and individual anxieties have to be conditioned out of the population. Total promiscuity, addiction to a stupefying drug called "soma," orga-nized games, and mindless entertainments are among the approved activities of this completely "successful," completely self-satisfied community. Though it resembles both fascism and communism, the basic character of the brave new world is managerial—bureaucratic. It isn't cheap and grungy, like George Orwell's sullen anti-utopia,

---

Nineteen Eighty-Four. Everything in Huxley's fictional world glitters, and everything works, to the satisfaction of the inhabitants; indeed, the fact that they are perfectly comfortable with their strictly cir- cumscribed selves and lives becomes before long the most infuriating thing about them.]

Chapter I

A squat grey building of only thirty-four stories. Over the main entrance the words, CENTRAL LONDON HATCHERY AND CONDITION- ING CENTRE, and, in a shield, the World State's motto, COMMUNITY, IDENTITY, STABILITY.

The enormous room on the ground floor faced towards the north. Cold for all the summer beyond the panes, for all the tropical heat of the room itself, a harsh thin light glared through the windows, hun- grily seeking some draped lay figure, some pallid shape of academic goose-flesh, but finding only the glass and nickel and bleakly shin- ing porcelain of a laboratory. Wintriness responded to wintriness. The overalls of the workers were white, their hands gloved with a pale corpse-coloured rubber. The light was frozen, dead, a ghost. Only from the yellow barrels of the microscopes did it borrow a certain rich and living substance, lying along the polished tubes like butter, streak after luscious streak in long recession down the work tables.

'And this,' said the Director opening the door, 'is the Fertilizing Room.'

Bent over their instruments, three hundred Fertilizers were plunged, as the Director of Hatcheries and Conditioning entered the room, in the scarcely breathing silence, the absent-minded, solilo- quizing hum or whistle, of absorbed concentration. A troop of newly arrived students, very young, pink and callow, followed nervously, rather abjectly, at the Director's heels. Each of them carried a note- book, in which, whenever the great man spoke, he desperately scrib- bled. Straight from the horse's mouth. It was a rare privilege. The D. H. C. for Central London always made a point of personally con- ducting his new students round the various departments.

'Just to give you a general idea,' he would explain to them. For of course some sort of general idea they must have, if they were to do their work intelligently—though as little of one, if they were to be good and happy members of society, as possible. For particulars, as every one knows, make for virtue and happiness; generalities are intellectually necessary evils. Not philosophers but fret-sawyers[1] and stamp collectors compose the backbone of society.

---

1. Craftsmen who saw fretwork—ornamental woodwork.

'To-morrow,' he would add, smiling at them with a slightly menacing geniality, 'you'll be settling down to serious work. You won't have time for generalities. Meanwhile . . .'

Meanwhile, it was a privilege. Straight from the horse's mouth into the note-book. The boys scribbled like mad.

Tall and rather thin but upright, the Director advanced into the room. He had a long chin and big, rather prominent teeth, just covered, when he was not talking, by his full, floridly curved lips. Old, young? Thirty? fifty? fifty-five? It was hard to say. And anyhow the question didn't arise; in this year of stability, A.F. 632,[2] it didn't occur to you to ask it.

'I shall begin at the beginning,' said the D. H. C., and the more zealous students recorded his intention in their note-books: *Begin at the beginning*. 'These,' he waved his hand, 'are the incubators.' And opening an insulated door he showed them racks upon racks of numbered test-tubes. 'The week's supply of ova. Kept,' he explained, 'at blood heat; whereas the male gametes,' and here he opened another door, 'they have to be kept at thirty-five instead of thirty-seven.[3] Full blood heat sterilizes.' Rams wrapped in thermogene[4] beget no lambs.

Still leaning against the incubators he gave them, while the pencils scurried illegibly across the pages, a brief description of the modern fertilizing process; spoke first, of course, of its surgical introduction—'the operation undergone voluntarily for the good of Society, not to mention the fact that it carries a bonus amounting to six months' salary'; continued with some account of the technique for preserving the excised ovary alive and actively developing; passed on to a consideration of optimum temperature, salinity, viscosity; referred to the liquor in which the detached and ripened eggs were kept; and, leading his charges to the work tables, actually showed them how this liquor was drawn off from the test-tubes; how it was let out drop by drop onto the specially warmed slides of the microscopes; how the eggs which it contained were inspected for abnormalities, counted and transferred to a porous receptacle; how (and he now took them to watch the operation) this receptacle was immersed in a warm bouillon containing free-swimming spermatozoa—at a minimum concentration of one hundred thousand per cubic centimetre, he insisted; and how, after ten minutes, the container was lifted out of the liquor and its contents re-examined; how, if any of the eggs remained unfertilized, it was again immersed, and, if necessary, yet again; how the fertilized ova

2. A.F. (After Ford) 1 is 1908, the year in which the first Model T rolled off Henry Ford's assembly line. So A.F. 632 is 2540 C.E.
3. I.e., sperm is stored at 35°C—two degrees less than normal body temperature.
4. A brand name of medicated cotton wool; an insulator.

went back to the incubators; where the Alphas and Betas remained until definitely bottled; while the Gammas, Deltas and Epsilons were brought out again, after only thirty-six hours, to undergo Bokanovsky's Process.[5]

'Bokanovsky's Process,' repeated the Director, and the students underlined the words in their little note-books.

One egg, one embryo, one adult—normality. But a bokanovskified egg will bud, will proliferate, will divide. From eight to ninety-six buds, and every bud will grow into a perfectly formed embryo, and every embryo into a full-sized adult. Making ninety-six human beings grow where only one grew before. Progress.

'Essentially,' the D.H.C. concluded, 'bokanovskification consists of a series of arrests of development. We check the normal growth and, paradoxically enough, the egg responds by budding.'

Responds by budding. The pencils were busy.

He pointed. On a very slowly moving band a rack-full of test-tubes was entering a large metal box, another rack-full was emerging. Machinery faintly purred. It took eight minutes for the tubes to go through, he told them. Eight minutes of hard X-rays being about as much as an egg can stand. A few died; of the rest, the least susceptible divided into two; most put out four buds; some eight; all were returned to the incubators, where the buds began to develop; then, after two days, were suddenly chilled, chilled and checked. Two, four, eight, the buds in their turn budded; and having budded were dosed almost to death with alcohol; consequently burgeoned again and having budded—bud out of bud out of bud were thereafter— further arrest being generally fatal—left to develop in peace. By which time the original egg was in a fair way to becoming anything from eight to ninety-six embryos—a prodigious improvement, you will agree, on nature. Identical twins—but not in piddling twos and threes as in the old viviparous days, when an egg would sometimes accidentally divide; actually by dozens, by scores at a time.

'Scores,' the Director repeated and flung out his arms, as though he were distributing largesse. 'Scores.'

But one of the students was fool enough to ask where the advantage lay.

'My good boy!' The Director wheeled sharply round on him. 'Can't you see? Can't you *see?*' He raised a hand; his expression was solemn. 'Bokanovsky's Process is one of the major instruments of social stability!'

Major instruments of social stability.

---

5. Products of the hatchery are classified by intelligence, from Alpha (superior) to Epsilon (minimal). Bokanovsky (an imaginary person) is the author of an artificial process for cloning (as we now call it) embryos.

Standard men and women; in uniform batches. The whole of a small factory staffed with the products of a single bokanovskified egg.

'Ninety-six identical twins working ninety-six identical machines!' The voice was almost tremulous with enthusiasm. 'You really know where you are. For the first time in history.' He quoted the planetary motto. 'Community, Identity, Stability.' Grand words. 'If we could bokanovskify indefinitely the whole problem would be solved.'

Solved by standard Gammas, unvarying Deltas, uniform Epsilons. Millions of identical twins. The principle of mass production at last applied to biology.

'But, alas,' the Director shook his head, 'we *can't* bokanovskify indefinitely.'

Ninety-six seemed to be the limit; seventy-two a good average. From the same ovary and with gametes of the same male to manufacture as many batches of identical twins as possible—that was the best (sadly a second best) that they could do. And even that was difficult.

'For in nature it takes thirty years for two hundred eggs to reach maturity. But our business is to stabilize the population at this moment, here and now. Dribbling out twins over a quarter of a century—what would be the use of that?'

Obviously, no use at all. But Podsnap's Technique[6] had immensely accelerated the process of ripening. They could make sure of at least a hundred and fifty mature eggs within two years. Fertilize and bokanovskify—in other words, multiply by seventy-two—and you get an average of nearly eleven thousand brothers and sisters in a hundred and fifty batches of identical twins, all within two years of the same age.

'And in exceptional cases we can make one ovary yield us over fifteen thousand adult individuals.'

Beckoning to a fair-haired, ruddy young man who happened to be passing at the moment, 'Mr. Foster,' he called. The ruddy young man approached. 'Can you tell us the record for a single ovary, Mr. Foster?'

'Sixteen thousand and twelve in this Centre,' Mr. Foster replied without hesitation. He spoke very quickly, had a vivacious blue eye, and took an evident pleasure in quoting figures. 'Sixteen thousand and twelve; in one hundred and eighty-nine batches of identicals. But of course they've done much better,' he rattled on, 'in some of the tropical Centres. Singapore has often produced over sixteen

---

6. Podsnap's Technique, though mentioned only once in passing, is important. In Dickens's novel *Our Mutual Friend*, Mr. Podsnap is the epitome of self-satisfaction and self-importance.

thousand five hundred; and Mombasa[7] has actually touched the seventeen thousand mark. But then they have unfair advantages. You should see the way a negro ovary responds to pituitary! It's quite astonishing, when you're used to working with European material. Still,' he added, with a laugh (but the light of combat was in his eyes and the lift of his chin was challenging), 'still, we mean to beat them if we can. I'm working on a wonderful Delta-Minus ovary at this moment. Only just eighteen months old. Over twelve thousand seven hundred children already, either decanted or in embryo. And still going strong. We'll beat them yet.'

'That's the spirit I like!' cried the Director, and clapped Mr. Foster on the shoulder. 'Come along with us and give these boys the benefit of your expert knowledge.'

Mr. Foster smiled modestly. 'With pleasure.' They went.

In the Bottling Room all was harmonious bustle and ordered activity. Flaps of fresh sow's peritoneum[8] ready cut to the proper size came shooting up in little lifts from the Organ Store in the sub-basement. Whizz and then, click! the lift-hatches flew open; the Bottle-Liner had only to reach out a hand, take the flap, insert, smooth-down, and before the lined bottle had had time to travel out of reach along the endless band, whizz, click! another flap of peritoneum had shot up from the depths, ready to be slipped into yet another bottle, the next of that slow interminable procession on the band.

Next to the Liners stood the Matriculators. The procession advanced; one by one the eggs were transferred from their test-tubes to the larger containers; deftly the peritoneal lining was slit, the morula[9] dropped into place, the saline solution poured in . . . and already the bottle had passed, and it was the turn of the labellers. Heredity, date of fertilization, membership of Bokanovsky Group— details were transferred from test-tube to bottle. No longer anonymous, but named, identified, the procession marched slowly on; on through an opening in the wall, slowly on into the Social Predestination Room.

'Eighty-eight cubic metres of card-index,' said Mr. Foster with relish, as they entered.

'Containing all the relevant information,' added the Director.

'Brought up to date every morning.'

'And co-ordinated every afternoon.'

'On the basis of which they make their calculations.'

'So many individuals, of such and such quality,' said Mr. Foster.

'Distributed in such and such quantities.'

---

7. A city in Kenya.
8. The membrane enclosing the viscera.
9. The mass of the embryo at an early stage of segmentation. It resembles a mulberry (*morum* is Latin for "mulberry").

'The optimum Decanting Rate at any given moment.'

'Unforeseen wastages promptly made good.'

'Promptly,' repeated Mr. Foster. 'If you knew the amount of over-time I had to put in after the last Japanese earthquake!' He laughed good-humouredly and shook his head.

'The Predestinators send in their figures to the Fertilizers.'

'Who give them the embryos they ask for.'

'And the bottles come in here to be predestined in detail.'

'After which they are sent down to the Embryo Store.'

'Where we now proceed ourselves.'

And opening a door Mr. Foster led the way down a staircase into the basement.

The temperature was still tropical. They descended into a thickening twilight. Two doors and a passage with a double turn insured the cellar against any possible infiltration of the day.

'Embryos are like photograph film,' said Mr. Foster waggishly, as he pushed open the second door. 'They can only stand red light.'

And in effect the sultry darkness into which the students now followed him was visible and crimson, like the darkness of closed eyes on a summer's afternoon. The bulging flanks of row on receding row and tier above tier of bottles glinted with innumerable rubies, and among the rubies moved the dim red spectres of men and women with purple eyes and all the symptoms of lupus.[1] The hum and rattle of machinery faintly stirred the air.

'Give them a few figures, Mr. Foster,' said the Director, who was tired of talking.

Mr. Foster was only too happy to give them a few figures.

Two hundred and twenty metres long, two hundred wide, ten high. He pointed upwards. Like chickens drinking, the students lifted their eyes towards the distant ceiling.

Three tiers of racks: ground-floor level, first gallery, second gallery.

The spidery steelwork of gallery above gallery faded away in all directions into the dark. Near them three red ghosts were busily unloading demijohns from a moving staircase.

The escalator from the Social Predestination Room.

Each bottle could be placed on one of fifteen racks, each rack, though you couldn't see it, was a conveyor traveling at the rate of thirty-three and a third centimetres an hour. Two hundred and sixty-seven days at eight metres a day. Two thousand one hundred and thirty-six metres in all. One circuit of the cellar at ground level, one on the first gallery, half on the second, and on the two hundred

---

1. Reddened skin is one symptom of the tubercular disease lupus vulgaris.

and sixty-seventh morning, daylight in the Decanting Room. Independent existence—so called.

'But in the interval,' Mr. Foster concluded, 'we've managed to do a lot to them. Oh, a very great deal.' His laugh was knowing and triumphant.

'That's the spirit I like,' said the Director once more. 'Let's walk round. You tell them everything, Mr. Foster.'

Mr. Foster duly told them.

Told them of the growing embryo on its bed of peritoneum. Made them taste the rich blood-surrogate on which it fed. Explained why it had to be stimulated with placentin and thyroxin.[2] Told them of the *corpus luteum*[3] extract. Showed them the jets through which at every twelfth metre from zero to 2040 it was automatically injected. Spoke of those gradually increasing doses of pituitary administered during the final ninety-six metres of their course. Described the artificial maternal circulation installed in every bottle at Metre 112; showed them the reservoir of blood-surrogate, the centrifugal pump that kept the liquid moving over the placenta and drove it through the synthetic lung and waste-product filter. Referred to the embryo's troublesome tendency to anæmia, to the massive doses of hog's stomach extract and fœtal foal's liver with which, in consequence, it had to be supplied.

Showed them the simple mechanism by means of which, during the last two metres out of every eight, all the embryos were simultaneously shaken into familiarity with movement. Hinted at the gravity of the so-called 'trauma of decanting,' and enumerated the precautions taken to minimize, by a suitable training of the bottled embryo, that dangerous shock. Told them of the tests for sex carried out in the neighbourhood of metre 200. Explained the system of labelling—a T for the males, a circle for the females and for those who were destined to become freemartins[4] a question mark, black on a white ground.

'For of course,' said Mr. Foster, 'in the vast majority of cases, fertility is merely a nuisance. One fertile ovary in twelve hundred—that would really be quite sufficient for our purposes. But we want to have a good choice. And of course one must always leave an enormous margin of safety. So we allow as many as thirty per cent of the female embryos to develop normally. The others get a dose of male sex-hormone every twenty-four metres for the rest of the course. Result:

2. Or thyroxine, a hormone produced by the thyroid gland; it regulates growth and development. "Placentin": evidently a placenta extract. The technology is of course fictional.
3. A yellowish body developed in the ovary after the discharge of an ovum; it secretes progesterone.
4. A term borrowed from animal husbandry. Freemartins are female calves (rarely, lambs) masculinized and rendered sterile in the womb, apparently from the action of male hormones there.

they're decanted as freemartins—structurally quite normal (except,' he had to admit, 'that they *do* have the slightest tendency to grow beards), but sterile. Guaranteed sterile. Which brings us at last,' continued Mr. Foster, 'out of the realm of mere slavish imitation of nature into the much more interesting world of human invention.'

He rubbed his hands. For of course, they didn't content themselves with merely hatching out embryos: any cow could do that.

'We also predestine and condition. We decant our babies as socialized human beings, as Alphas or Epsilons, as future sewage workers or future . . .' He was going to say 'future World Controllers,' but correcting himself, said 'future Directors of Hatcheries' instead.

The D.H.C. acknowledged the compliment with a smile.

They were passing Metre 320 on Rack 11. A young Beta-Minus mechanic was busy with screw-driver and spanner on the blood-surrogate pump of a passing bottle. The hum of the electric motor deepened by fractions of a tone as he turned the nuts. Down, down . . . A final twist, a glance at the revolution counter, and he was done. He moved two paces down the line and began the same process on the next pump.

'Reducing the number of revolutions per minute,' Mr. Foster explained. 'The surrogate goes round slower; therefore passes through the lung at longer intervals; therefore gives the embryo less oxygen. Nothing like oxygen-shortage for keeping an embryo below par.' Again he rubbed his hands.

'But why do you want to keep the embryo below par?' asked an ingenuous student.

'Ass!' said the Director, breaking a long silence. 'Hasn't it occurred to you that an Epsilon embryo must have an Epsilon environment as well as an Epsilon heredity?'

It evidently hadn't occurred to him. He was covered with confusion.

'The lower the caste,' said Mr. Foster, 'the shorter the oxygen.' The first organ affected was the brain. After that the skeleton. At seventy percent of normal oxygen you got dwarfs. At less than seventy, eyeless monsters.

'Who are no use at all,' concluded Mr. Foster.

Whereas (his voice became confidential and eager), if they could discover a technique for shortening the period of maturation, what a triumph, what a benefaction to Society!

'Consider the horse.'

They considered it.

Mature at six; the elephant at ten. While at thirteen a man is not yet sexually mature; and is only fully grown at twenty. Hence, of course, that fruit of delayed development, the human intelligence.

'But in Epsilons,' said Mr. Foster very justly, 'we don't need human intelligence.'

Didn't need and didn't get it. But though the Epsilon mind was mature at ten, the Epsilon body was not fit to work till eighteen. Long years of superfluous and wasted immaturity. If the physical development could be speeded up till it was as quick, say, as a cow's, what an enormous saving to the Community!

'Enormous!' murmured the students. Mr. Foster's enthusiasm was infectious.

He became rather technical; spoke of the abnormal endocrine co-ordination which made men grow so slowly; postulated a germinal mutation to account for it. Could the effects of this germinal mutation be undone? Could the individual Epsilon embryo be made to revert, by a suitable technique, to the normality of dogs and cows? That was the problem. And it was all but solved.

Pilkington, at Mombasa, had produced individuals who were sexually mature at four and full grown at six and a half. A scientific triumph. But socially useless. Six-year-old men and women were too stupid to do even Epsilon work. And the process was an all-or-nothing one; either you failed to modify at all, or else you modified the whole way. They were still trying to find the ideal compromise between adults of twenty and adults of six. So far without success. Mr. Foster sighed and shook his head.

Their wanderings through the crimson twilight had brought them to the neighbourhood of Metre 170 on Rack 9. From this point onwards Rack 9 was enclosed and the bottles performed the remainder of their journey in a kind of tunnel, interrupted here and there by openings two or three metres wide.

'Heat conditioning,' said Mr. Foster.

Hot tunnels alternated with cool tunnels. Coolness was wedded to discomfort in the form of hard X-rays. By the time they were decanted the embryos had a horror of cold. They were predestined to emigrate to the tropics, to be miners and acetate silk spinners and steel workers. Later on their minds would be made to endorse the judgment of their bodies. 'We condition them to thrive on heat,' concluded Mr. Foster. 'Our colleagues upstairs will teach them to love it.'

'And that,' put in the Director sententiously, 'that is the secret of happiness and virtue—liking what you've *got* to do. All conditioning aims at that: making people like their unescapable social destiny.'

In a gap between two tunnels, a nurse was delicately probing with a long fine syringe into the gelatinous contents of a passing bottle. The students and their guides stood watching her for a few moments in silence.

'Well, Lenina,' said Mr. Foster, when at last she withdrew the syringe and straightened herself up.

The girl turned with a start. One could see that, for all the lupus and the purple eyes, she was uncommonly pretty.

'Henry!' Her smile flashed redly at him—a row of coral teeth.

'Charming, charming,' murmured the Director, and, giving her two or three little pats, received in exchange a rather deferential smile for himself.

'What are you giving them?' asked Mr. Foster, making his tone very professional.

'Oh, the usual typhoid and sleeping sickness.'

'Tropical workers start being inoculated at metre 150,' Mr. Foster explained to the students. 'The embryos still have gills. We immunize the fish against the future man's diseases.'[5] Then, turning back to Lenina, 'Ten to five on the roof this afternoon,' he said, 'as usual.'[6]

'Charming,' said the Director once more, and, with a final pat, moved away after the others.

On Rack 10 rows of next generation's chemical workers were being trained in the toleration of lead, caustic soda, tar, chlorine. The first of a batch of two hundred and fifty embryonic rocket-plane engineers was just passing the eleven hundredth metre mark on Rack 3. A special mechanism kept their containers in constant rotation. 'To improve their sense of balance,' Mr. Foster explained. 'Doing repairs on the outside of a rocket in mid air is a ticklish job. We slacken off the circulation when they're right way up, so that they're half starved, and double the flow of surrogate when they're upside down. They learn to associate topsy-turvydom with well-being; in fact, they're only truly happy when they're standing on their heads.

'And now,' Mr. Foster went on, 'I'd like to show you some very interesting conditioning for Alpha-Plus Intellectuals. We have a big batch of them on Rack 5. First Gallery level,' he called to two boys who had started to go down to the ground floor.

'They're round about metre 900,' he explained. 'You can't really do any useful intellectual conditioning till the fœtuses have lost their tails.[7] Follow me.'

But the Director had looked at his watch. 'Ten to three,' he said. 'No time for the intellectual embryos, I'm afraid. We must go up to the Nurseries before the children have finished their afternoon sleep.'

Mr. Foster was disappointed. 'At least one glance at the Decanting Room,' he pleaded.

'Very well, then.' The Director smiled indulgently. 'Just one glance.'

---

5. Smart Mr. Foster to the contrary, human embryos don't ever have functional gills and aren't properly fish.
6. The Director and Henry share in Lenina's favors; in *Brave New World*, casual copulation is the required morality.
7. Human fetuses have visible tails, which they lose about eight weeks after conception.

URSULA K. LE GUIN

From The Left Hand of Darkness†

[If anti-utopianism is the characteristic modern development of the literary tradition that began with More's book, utopian idealism is, though chastened, not dead. In a series of highly acclaimed science fiction novels, Ursula K. Le Guin depicts a series of future societies on planets scattered across our end of the Milky Way, colonized by the original humanoid species (from the planet Hain—thus the books are known collectively as the Hainish novels) and loosely united (long after the colonizations and much evolutionary diversification) in the Ekumen or League of All Worlds—a federation made possible by light-speed travel and instantaneous communication via a useful sort of super-typewriter called the ansible, on which as words are keyboarded they simultaneously appear on a target ansible on another planet. Le Guin's many and varied societies (her planets tend to harbor multiple societies, often quite diverse) are, for the most part, far from utopian, and many of them are quite *dy*stopian. Yet there are distinctly utopian elements in the thought experiments she conducts on some of her worlds—explicitly on the harsh moon, Anarres, of a rather earth-like planet in *The Dispossessed: An Ambiguous Utopia* (1974). In the other most celebrated Hainish novel—*The Left Hand of Darkness* (1969), set on the dispiritingly cold planet Gethen ("Winter")—there are various nations, none of them utopian but all of them embodying the results of a bold genetic experiment by the Hains: the Gethenians are androgynous; neither men nor women, they are simply human beings. Like most mammals (though unlike standard-issue human beings) they are not continuously sexual, but *become* sexual for a monthly estrus (what the Gethenians call "kemmer" and we, speaking of our dogs and cats, call "heat"); depending on circumstances, an individual comes into kemmer as either male or female. Le Guin brilliantly works out the implications of this extraordinary premise, in a way that gives us a remarkable outside perspective on our sexuality and its hazards, and also leaves us thinking that a human society of simply *human* beings, free of sex for most of the time, might, at least arguably, *be* to some extent utopian.

In narrative technique, *The Left Hand of Darkness* is a classic utopia: a report on the alternative society by an outside visitor. The visitor is Genly Ai, emissary of the Ekumen, come to Gethen (which has long ago lost contact with the other Hainish worlds) to observe, and, if all goes well, to proffer membership in the Ekumen. The excerpts here are the part of Ai's report that formally describes Gethenian sexuality, and a passage of the novel's final chapter when the starship that has

---

† From pp. 89–96 (chap. 7) and 278–79 (chap. 20) of *The Left Hand of Darkness* by Ursula K. Le Guin, copyright © 1969 by Ursula K. Le Guin. Used by permission of Ace Books, an imprint of The Berkley Publishing Group, a division of Penguin Group (USA) Inc. All footnotes are by the editor.

orbited the planet for the three-year duration of Ai's mission descends
to the surface, and the emissary—and we—having grown accustomed
to the Gethenians, suddenly see standard-issue human beings in a
new way.]

Chapter 7

The Question of Sex

*From field notes of Ong Tot Oppong, Investigator, of the first Eku-
menical landing party on Gethen/Winter, Cycle 93 E.Y. 1448.*[1]

1448 day 81. It seems likely that they were an experiment. The
thought is unpleasant. But now that there is evidence to indicate that
the Terran Colony was an experiment, the planting of one Hainish
Normal group on a world with its own proto-hominid autochthones,[2]
the possibility cannot be ignored. Human genetic manipulation was
certainly practiced by the Colonizers; nothing else explains the hilfs
of S or the degenerate winged hominids of Rokanan; will anything
else explain Gethenian sexual physiology? Accident, possibly; natural
selection, hardly. Their ambisexuality has little or no adaptive value.

Why pick so harsh a world for an experiment? No answer. Tinibossol thinks the Colony was introduced during a major Interglacial.
Conditions may have been fairly mild for their first 40 or 50,000
years here. By the time the ice was advancing again, the Hainish
Withdrawal was complete and the Colonists were on their own, an
experiment abandoned.

I theorize about the origins of Gethenian sexual physiology. What
do I actually know about it? Otie Nim's communication from the
Orgoreyn region has cleared up some of my earlier misconceptions.
Let me set down all I know, and after that my theories; first things
first.

The sexual cycle averages 26 to 28 days (they tend to speak of it as
26 days, approximating it to the lunar cycle). For 21 or 22 days the
individual is *somer*, sexually inactive, latent. On about the 18th day
hormonal changes are initiated by the pituitary control and on the
22nd or 23rd day the individual enters *kemmer*, estrus. In this first
phase of kemmer (Karh.[3] *secher*) he remains completely androgy-

---

1. The Ekumen's initial investigation of a newly discovered inhabited world is conducted
by an incognito team. Ai's "report" here incorporates field notes from a member of the
team for Gethen. That Le Guin's father (Alfred Kroeber) was a distinguished anthro-
pologist and her mother (Theodora Kroeber Quinn) a psychologist and writer is the
opposite of surprising.
2. I.e., evidence indicates that human beings on Earth originated as a Hainish colony
among indigenous primates. "Autochthones": indigenes. The etymology is "of the soil
itself" (Greek).
3. I.e., the language of the Gethenian nation Karhide.

nous. Gender, and potency, are not attained in isolation. A Gethenian in first-phase kemmer, if kept alone or with others not in kemmer, remains incapable of coitus. Yet the sexual impulse is tremendously strong in this phase, controlling the entire personality, subjecting all other drives to its imperative. When the individual finds a partner in kemmer, hormonal secretion is further stimulated (most importantly by touch—secretion? scent?) until in one partner either a male or female hormonal dominance is established. The genitals engorge or shrink accordingly, foreplay intensifies, and the partner, triggered by the change, takes on the other sexual role (? without exception? If there are exceptions, resulting in kemmerpartners of the same sex, they are so rare as to be ignored). This second phase of kemmer (Karh. *thorharmen*), the mutual process of establishing sexuality and potency, apparently occurs within a timespan of two to twenty hours. If one of the partners is already in full kemmer, the phase for the newer partner is liable to be quite short; if the two are entering kemmer together, it is likely to take longer. Normal individuals have no predisposition to either sexual role in kemmer; they do not know whether they will be the male or the female, and have no choice in the matter. (Otie Nim wrote that in the Orgoreyn region the use of hormone derivatives to establish a preferred sexuality is quite common; I haven't seen this done in rural Karhide.) Once the sex is determined it cannot change during the kemmerperiod. The culminant phase of kemmer (Karh. *thokemmer*) lasts from two to five days, during which sexual drive and capacity are at maximum. It ends fairly abruptly, and if conception has not taken place, the individual returns to the somer phase within a few hours (note: Otie Nim thinks this "fourth phase" is the equivalent of the menstrual cycle) and the cycle begins anew. If the individual was in the female role and was impregnated, hormonal activity of course continues, and for the 8.4-month gestation period and the 6- to 8-month lactation period this individual remains female. The male sexual organs remain retracted (as they are in somer), the breasts enlarge somewhat, and the pelvic girdle widens. With the cessation of lactation the female re-enters somer and becomes once more a perfect androgyne. No physiological habit is established, and the mother of several children may be the father of several more.

Social observations: very superficial as yet; I have been moving about too much to make coherent social observations.

Kemmer is not always played by pairs. Pairing seems to be the commonest custom, but in the kemmerhouses of towns and cities groups may form and intercourse take place promiscuously among the males and females of the group. The furthest extreme from this practice is the custom of *vowing kemmering* (Karh. *oskyommer*), which is to all intents and purposes monogamous marriage. It has no legal status, but socially and ethically is an ancient and vigorous

institution. The whole structure of the Karhidish Clan-Hearths
and Domains is indubitably based upon the institution of monogamous marriage. I am not sure of divorce rules in general; here in
Osnoriner there is divorce, but no remarriage after either divorce or
the partner's death: one can only vow kemmering once.

Descent of course is reckoned, all over Gethen, from the mother,
the "parent in the flesh" (Karh. *amha*).

Incest is permitted, with various restrictions, between siblings,
even the full siblings of a vowed-kemmering pair. Siblings are not
however allowed to vow kemmering, nor keep kemmering after the
birth of a child to one of the pair. Incest between generations is
strictly forbidden (in Karhide/Orgoreyn; but is said to be permitted
among the tribesmen of Perunter, the Antarctic Continent. This
may be slander.).

What else have I learned for certain? That seems to sum it up.

There is one feature of this anomalous arrangement that might
have adaptive value. Since coitus takes place only during the period
of fertility, the chance of conception is high, as with all mammals
that have an estrous cycle. In harsh conditions where infant mortality is great, a race survival value may be indicated. At present neither infant mortality nor the birthrate runs high in the civilized
areas of Gethen. Tinibossol estimates a population of not over 100
million on the three continents, and considers it to have been stable
for at least a millennium. Ritual and ethical abstention and the use
of contraceptive drugs seem to have played the major part in maintaining this stability.

There are aspects of ambisexuality which we have only glimpsed
or guessed at, and which we may never grasp entirely. The kemmer
phenomenon fascinates all of us Investigators, of course. It fascinates us, but it rules the Gethenians, dominates them. The structure
of their societies, the management of their industry, agriculture,
commerce, the size of their settlements, the subjects of their stories,
everything is shaped to fit the somer-kemmer cycle. Everybody has
his holiday once a month; no one, whatever his position, is obliged or
forced to work when in kemmer. No one is barred from the kemmer-
house, however poor or strange. Everything gives way before the
recurring torment and festivity of passion. This is easy for us to
understand. What is very hard for us to understand is that, four-
fifths of the time, these people are not sexually motivated at all. Room
is made for sex, plenty of room; but a room, as it were, apart. The
society of Gethen, in its daily functioning and in its continuity, is
without sex.

Consider: Anyone can turn his hand to anything. This sounds
very simple, but its psychological effects are incalculable. The fact
that everyone between seventeen and thirty-five or so is liable to be

(as Nim put it) "tied down to childbearing," implies that no one is quite so thoroughly "tied down" here as women, elsewhere, are likely to be—psychologically or physically. Burden and privilege are shared out pretty equally; everybody has the same risk to run or choice to make. Therefore nobody here is quite so free as a free male anywhere else.

Consider: A child has no psycho-sexual relationship to his mother and father. There is no myth of Oedipus on Winter.

Consider: There is no unconsenting sex, no rape. As with most mammals other than man, coitus can be performed only by mutual invitation and consent; otherwise it is not possible. Seduction certainly is possible, but it must have to be awfully well timed.

Consider: There is no division of humanity into strong and weak halves, protective/protected, dominant/submissive, owner/chattel, active/passive. In fact the whole tendency to dualism that pervades human thinking may be found to be lessened, or changed, on Winter.

The following must go into my finished Directives: When you meet a Gethenian you cannot and must not do what a bisexual naturally does, which is to cast him in the role of Man or Woman, while adopting towards him a corresponding role dependent on your expectations of the patterned or possible interactions between persons of the same or the opposite sex. Our entire pattern of socio-sexual interaction is nonexistent here. They cannot play the game. They do not see one another as men or women. This is almost impossible for our imagination to accept. What is the first question we ask about a newborn baby?

Yet you cannot think of a Gethenian as "it." They are not neuters. They are potentials, or integrals. Lacking the Karhidish "human pronoun" used for persons in somer, I must say "he," for the same reasons as we used the masculine pronoun in referring to a transcendent god: it is less defined, less specific, than the neuter or the feminine. But the very use of the pronoun in my thoughts leads me continually to forget that the Karhider I am with is not a man, but a manwoman.

The First Mobile, if one is sent, must be warned that unless he is very self-assured, or senile, his pride will suffer. A man wants his virility regarded, a woman wants her femininity appreciated, however indirect and subtle the indications of regard and appreciation. On Winter they will not exist. One is respected and judged only as a human being. It is an appalling experience.

Back to my theory. Contemplating the motives for such an experiment, if such it was, and trying perhaps to exculpate our Hainish ancestors from the guilt of barbarism, of treating lives as things, I have made some guesses as to what they might have been after.

The somer-kemmer cycle strikes us as degrading, a return to the estrous cycle of the lower mammals, a subjection of human beings to the mechanical imperative of rut. It is possible that the experimenters wished to see whether human beings lacking continuous sexual potentiality would remain intelligent and capable of culture.

On the other hand, the limitation of the sexual drive to a discontinuous time-segment, and the "equalizing" of it in androgyny, must prevent, to a large extent, both the exploitation and the frustration of the drive. There must be sexual frustration (though society provides as well as it can against it; so long as the social unit is large enough that more than one person will be in kemmer at one time, sexual fulfillment is fairly certain), but at least it cannot build up; it is over when kemmer is over. Fine; thus they are spared much waste and madness; but what is left, in somer? What is there to sublimate? What would a society of eunuchs achieve? —But of course they are not eunuchs, in somer, but rather more comparable to preadolescents: not castrate, but latent.

Another guess concerning the hypothetical experiment's object: The elimination of war. Did the Ancient Hainish postulate that continuous sexual capacity and organized social aggression, neither of which are attributes of any mammal but man, are cause and effect? Or, like Tumass Song Angot, did they consider war to be a purely masculine displacement-activity, a vast Rape, and therefore in their experiment eliminate the masculinity that rapes and the femininity that is raped? God knows. The fact is that Gethenians, though highly competitive (as proved by the elaborate social channels provided for competition for prestige, etc.) seem not to be very aggressive; at least they apparently have never yet had what one could call a war. They kill one another readily by ones and twos; seldom by tens or twenties; never by hundreds or thousands. Why?

It may turn out to have nothing to do with their androgyne psychology. There are not very many of them, after all. And there is the climate. The weather of Winter is so relentless, so near the limit of tolerability even to them with all their cold-adaptations, that perhaps they use up their fighting spirit fighting the cold. The marginal peoples, the races that just get by, are rarely the warriors. And in the end, the dominant factor in Gethenian life is not sex or any other human thing: it is their environment, their cold world. Here man has a crueler enemy even than himself.

I am a woman of peaceful Chiffewar, and no expert on the attractions of violence or the nature of war. Someone else will have to think this out. But I really don't see how anyone could put much stock in victory or glory after he had spent a winter on Winter, and seen the face of the Ice.

From *Chapter 20*

[*A Star Descends*]

On the screens, coming in, the crew must have seen the terminator[4] lying clear across the Great Continent along the border, from Guthen Bay to the Gulf of Charisune, and the peaks of the Kargav still in sunlight, a chain of stars; for it was twilight when we, looking up, saw the one star descending.

She came down in a roar and glory, and steam went roaring up white as her stabilizers went down in the great lake of water and mud created by the retro; down underneath the bog there was permafrost like granite, and she came to rest balanced neatly, and sat cooling over the quickly refreezing lake, a great, delicate fish balanced on its tail, dark silver in the twilight of Winter.

Beside me Faxe of Otherhord spoke for the first time since the sound and splendor of the ship's descent. "I'm glad I have lived to see this," he said. So Estraven[5] had said when he looked at the Ice, at death; so he should have said this night. To get away from the bitter regret that beset me I started to walk forward over the snow towards the ship. She was frosted already by the interhull coolants, and as I approached the high port slid open and the exitway was extruded, a graceful curve down onto the ice. The first off was Lang Heo Hew, unchanged, of course, precisely as I had last seen her, three years ago in my life and a couple of weeks in hers.[6] She looked at me, and at Faxe, and at the others of the escort who had followed me, and stopped at the foot of the ramp. She said solemnly in Karhidish, "I have come in friendship." To her eyes we were all aliens. I let Faxe greet her first.

He indicated me to her, and she came and took my right hand in the fashion of my people, looking into my face. "Oh, Genly," she said, "I didn't know you!" It was strange to hear a woman's voice, after so long. The others came out of the ship, on my advice: evidence of any mistrust at this point would humiliate the Karhidish escort, impugning their shifgrethor.[7] Out they came, and met the Karhiders with a beautiful courtesy. But they all looked strange to me, men and women, well as I knew them. Their voices sounded strange: too deep, too shrill. They were like a troupe of great, strange animals, of two different species: great apes with intelligent eyes, all of them in rut, in kemmer. . . . They took my hand, touched me, held me. * * *

4. The line of separation between daylight and darkness on a planet or moon.
5. Estraven, prime minister of Karhide, had suffered disgrace and finally death to protect Genly Ai from the skepticism and cynical manipulation of other Gethenian politicians. He and Ai had made a seemingly impossible journey across a huge glacial expanse, the "Gobrin Ice."
6. The starship's crew had been in suspended animation during Ai's mission.
7. I.e., causing a loss of face.

Suggestions for Further Reading

Editions

The modern edition of More's writings (other than his personal letters) is the monumental *Complete Works of St. Thomas More*, 15 vols. (New Haven and London: Yale University Press, 1963–97). Elizabeth F. Rogers edited *The Correspondence of Sir Thomas More* (Princeton, N.J.: Princeton University Press, 1947)—without translations of the Latin letters—and, for the Modernized Series of the Yale edition, *St. Thomas More: Selected Letters* (1961—with the Latin letters in English translation). *Utopia*, ed. Edward Surtz, S.J., and J. H. Hexter, is vol. 4 (1965) of the *Complete Works*. A full critical edition, it includes an original-spelling version of the Latin text, a translation of it on facing pages, a lengthy introduction, and a massive interpretive commentary, which provides detailed background information on every passage of More's book. Better for many purposes is the other, later standard edition, the "Cambridge *Utopia*": *Utopia: Latin Text and English Translation*, ed. George M. Logan, Robert M. Adams, and Clarence H. Miller (Cambridge: Cambridge University Press, 1995), which includes a version of the Latin text with standardized modern spelling and punctuation, a version of the Adams translation somewhat different from that in the present volume, an introduction, and a compact commentary.

Biographies

The earliest biography of More is the attractive brief *Life of Sir Thomas More* by his son-in-law William Roper: there is an excellent modern-spelling edition in *Two Early Tudor Lives*, ed. Richard S. Sylvester and Davis P. Harding (New Haven and London: Yale University Press, 1962). Roper's *Life* and two other sixteenth-century biographies—by Nicholas Harpsfield and Thomas Stapleton—are central (though not always reliable) sources for later biographers. The most influential modern biography has been R. W. Chambers's *Thomas More* (London: Jonathan Cape, 1935). Humane and highly readable, Chambers's book is (inevitably) somewhat dated and is doubtless too uniformly laudatory. The portrayal of More in Robert

Bolt's play *A Man for All Seasons* (1960) was based on Chambers; and the hugely successful movie version of the play (1966)—which won six Oscars, including Best Actor and Best Picture—is primarily responsible for More's enormous and almost entirely favorable reputation in today's general culture. In sharp contrast to Chambers's book, Richard Marius's *Thomas More* (New York: Knopf, 1984)—the most influential biography of the last several decades and by far the most controversial one—is a revisionist work, portraying More as a highly conflicted and in some ways unattractive figure. The other full-scale recent biography, Peter Ackroyd's *Life of Thomas More* (London: Chatto & Windus, 1988), which views More as fighting a rearguard action for the positive values of late medieval Catholic culture, is better balanced though less invigorating. The major Tudor historian John Guy's *Thomas More* (London: Arnold, 2000) provides an excellent brief introduction to More and a salutary discussion of the fact that the limitations of the source materials render some questions about him incapable of definitive answer. Guy's *A Daughter's Love: Thomas and Margaret More* (London: Fourth Estate, 2008) views More's life from the special angle of a double biography of the man and his favorite child. The chapter on More in Stephen Greenblatt's seminal "New Historicist" work *Renaissance Self-Fashioning: From More to Shakespeare* (Chicago and London: University of Chicago Press, 2005; orig. publ. 1980), pp. 11–73, is a rich, brilliant, and intensely readable psychobiographical study. *The Cambridge Companion to Thomas More*, ed. George M. Logan (Cambridge: Cambridge University Press, 2011), contains a dozen new essays surveying More's life and writings.

Criticism

Much valuable criticism of *Utopia* can be found in the *other* parts of the works excerpted in the Criticism section of the present edition. There are important treatments of *Utopia* in the biographies by Chambers and Marius and in Greenblatt's chapter on More in *Renaissance Self-Fashioning* (for all three, see above). J. H. Hexter's section of the introduction to the Yale *Utopia* (above) expands the treatment in his *More's "Utopia": The Biography of an Idea* (p. 190 above) and constitutes the single most powerful study of *Utopia*. Edward Surtz, S.J., *The Praise of Wisdom: A Commentary on the Religious and Moral Problems and Backgrounds of St. Thomas More's "Utopia"* (Chicago: Loyola University Press, 1957), is a companion volume to his *The Praise of Pleasure* (p. 202 above) and, like it, includes a wealth of valuable contextual information. Robert P. Adams, *The Better Part of Valor: More, Erasmus, Colet, and Vives, on Humanism, War, and Peace, 1496–1535* (Seattle: University of

Washington Press, 1962), situates *Utopia* in the context of Erasmian pacifism. Quentin Skinner has written three superbly learned and lucid treatments of *Utopia* in the context of classical and Renaissance political thought: *The Foundations of Modern Political Thought*, 2 vols. (1978), 1:213–21, 255–62; "Sir Thomas More's *Utopia* and the virtue of true nobility," in *Visions of Politics*, 3 vols. (2001; original form of essay publ. 1987), 2:213–44; *The Cambridge History of Renaissance Philosophy*, ed. Charles B. Schmitt et al. (1988), chap. 12, "Political Philosophy," especially pp. 448–51 (all are published by Cambridge University Press). George M. Logan, *The Meaning of More's "Utopia"* (Princeton, N.J.: Princeton University Press, 1983), also focuses on the connections between *Utopia* and classical and Renaissance political thought. Elizabeth McCutcheon, *My Dear Peter: The "Ars Poetica" and Hermeneutics for More's "Utopia"* (Angers: Moreana, 1983), shows (like her article on More's use of litotes; p. 220 above) how much More's book yields to close stylistic analysis. Clarence H. Miller, "Style and Meaning in *Utopia*: Hythloday's Sentences and Diction," in *Acta Conventus Neo-Latini Hafniensis*, ed. Rhoda Schnur et al. (Binghamton, N.Y.: Medieval and Renaissance Texts and Studies, 1994), pp. 675–83, demonstrates the *variation* of style in Hythloday's speeches, and its import. Richard Halpern, *The Poetics of Primitive Accumulation: English Renaissance Culture and the Genealogy of Capital* (Ithaca and London: Cornell University Press, 1991), pp. 136–75, offers a sophisticated Marxist reading of More's book. Eric Nelson, *The Greek Tradition in Republican Thought* (Cambridge: Cambridge University Press, 2004), includes, on pp. 19–48, a slightly revised version of the article reprinted herein, and puts that study into a larger context. Dominic Baker-Smith (p. 241 above) revisits *Utopia* in an essay in *The Cambridge Companion to Thomas More* (above).

A number of influential articles on *Utopia*, including McCutcheon's study of More's litotes, are reprinted in *Essential Articles for the Study of Thomas More*, ed. R. S. Sylvester and G. P. Marc'hadour (Hamden, Conn.: Archon Books, 1977). Sylvester's own well-known article " 'Si Hythlodaeo Credimus': Vision and Revision in Thomas More's *Utopia*" (orig. publ. 1968) is also included; a somewhat similar treatment of the book, arguing that More's primary purpose is to point out the shortcomings of both Hythloday and Utopia, forms part of Harry Berger Jr.'s "The Renaissance Imagination: Second World and Green World," *The Centennial Review* 9 (1965), 36–77. There is an excellent collection of extracts from books (and a few articles) edited by William Nelson: *Twentieth Century Interpretations of "Utopia"* (Englewood Cliffs, N.J.: Prentice-Hall, 1968). Many articles on *Utopia* have appeared in the journal *Moreana*, which, in addition to publishing articles on More, reviews scholarship on him and serves as a clearing house for More studies worldwide. An online collection of *Moreana* articles on *Utopia* is included in the remarkably rich and valuable website of the Center for Thomas More Studies (www.thomasmorestudies.org), located at the University of Dallas under the directorship of Gerard B. Wegemer. All but one of the articles (an essay by R. S. Sylvester) in this collection, plus a few from other journals, are also available online through Luminarium: Anthology of English Literature (www.luminarium.org/renlit/tmore.htm). Both collections include George M. Logan, "Interpreting *Utopia*: Ten Recent Studies and the Modern Critical Traditions," *Moreana* 31 (1994), 203–58, which overviews modern criticism and is a good place to start on it.

Literary Relations

Utopia draws on a wide range of classical Greek and Roman works. These are handily available in the volumes of the Loeb Classical Library, which include, on facing pages, the original text and an English translation. In the case of Aristotle's *Politics*, the edition by Ernest Barker (Oxford: Clarendon Press, 1948) should also be mentioned. A brief list of the most useful books on utopia may begin with Frank E. and Fritzie P. Manuel's massive survey, *Utopian Thought in the Western World* (Cambridge, Mass.: The Belknap Press of Harvard University Press, 1979). A second huge, comprehensive work is *Utopia: The Search for the Ideal Society in the Western World*, ed. Roland Schaer, Gregory Claeys, and Lyman Tower Sargent (New York and Oxford: The New York Public Library/Oxford University Press, 2000), which includes, along with essays on numerous aspects of utopianism, many fascinating illustrations, and valuable selective bibliographies of utopian and dystopian books and films, and of studies of utopia. Sargent has also produced a compact overview of the field: *Utopianism: A Very Short Introduction* (Oxford: Oxford University Press, 2010). On the modern phase of the utopian tradition, see Krishan Kumar, *Utopia and Anti-Utopia in Modern Times* (Oxford: Basil Blackwell, 1987), and, specifically on the connection with science fiction, Tom Moylan, *Demand the Impossible: Science Fiction and the Utopian Imagination* (London: Methuen, 1986). Chad Walsh, *From Utopia to Nightmare* (New York and Evanston, Ind.: Harper & Row, 1962), is a good, though now rather dated, study of the modern dystopia. The scholarly journal *Utopian Studies* publishes articles and book reviews on a wide range of topics in the field. Collections of utopian writings include *Famous Utopias of the Renaissance*, ed. Frederic R. White (Chicago: Packard, 1946); Frank E. and Fritzie P. Manuel, ed. and trans., *French Utopias: An Anthology of Ideal Societies* (New York: The Free Press, 1966); and two broadly ranging anthologies: *The Faber Book of Utopias*, ed. John Carey (London: Faber and Faber, 1999), and *The Utopia Reader*, ed. Gregory Claeys and Lyman Tower Sargent (New York and London: New York University Press, 1999).

A list of particularly noteworthy utopian and dystopian fictions in the centuries since the publication of *Utopia* would include the following: François Rabelais, the account of the Abbey of Thélème in *Gargantua* (1534); Johann Valentin Andreae, *Christianopolis* (1619); Tommaso Campanella, *The City of the Sun* (1623); Francis Bacon, *The New Atlantis* (1627); James Harrington, *The Commonwealth of Oceana* (1656); Daniel Defoe, *Robinson Crusoe* (1719); Jonathan Swift, *Gulliver's Travels* (1726); Nathaniel Hawthorne, *The Blithedale Romance* (1852); Samuel Butler, *Erewhon* (1872); Edward Bellamy, *Looking Backward* (1888); Theodor Hertzka, *Freeland* (1890); William Morris, *News from Nowhere* (1890); H. G. Wells, *The Time Machine* (1895), *A Modern Utopia* (1904–05), and *The Shape of Things to Come* (1933); Charlotte Perkins Gilman, *Herland* (1915); Karel Čapek, *R. U. R. (Rossum's Universal Robots)* (1921); Evgeny Zamiatin, *We* (1924); Aldous Huxley, *Brave New World* (1932) and *Island* (1962); James Hilton, *Lost Horizon* (1933); Austin T. Wright, *Islandia* (1942); George Orwell, *Animal Farm* (1945) and *Nineteen Eighty-Four* (1949); B. F. Skinner, *Walden Two* (1948); Ray Bradbury, *Fahrenheit 451* (1953); Arthur C. Clarke, *Childhood's End* (1953); William Golding, *Lord of the Flies* (1954); Ayn Rand, *Atlas Shrugged* (1957); Anthony Burgess, *A Clockwork Orange* (1962); Robert H. Rimmer, *The Harrad Experiment* (1966); Ursula K. Le Guin, *The Left Hand of Darkness* (1969), *The Dispossessed: An Ambiguous Utopia* (1974), and *Always Coming Home* (1985); Doris Lessing, *Canopus in Argos* (a 5-volume series: 1979–83); Margaret Atwood, *The Handmaid's Tale* (1985); P. D. James, *The Children of Men* (1992); Toni Morrison, *Paradise* (1998).

Bibliographies

There are two recent book-length bibliographies of More studies: Michael D. Wentworth, *The Essential Sir Thomas More: An Annotated Bibliography of Major Modern Sources* (New York: G. K. Hall, 1995); Albert J. Geritz, *Thomas More: An Annotated Bibliography of Criticism, 1935–1997* (Westport, Conn., and London: Greenwood Press, 1998). There is also an online bibliography by Romuald Lakowski, devoted to *Utopia* alone and covering the period ca. 1890–1995 (www.chass.utoronto.ca/emls/01-2/lakomore.html). The journal *English Literary Renaissance* periodically reviews More scholarship in its "Recent Studies" series: see *ELR* 9 (1979), 442–58; 22 (1992), 112–40; and 35 (2005), 123–55. For selective (but extensive) bibliographies of utopias and utopian studies, see above, *Utopia: The Search for the Ideal Society in the Western World.* There is also a wide-ranging online bibliography of Utopian Writing, 1516–1798, by Richard Serjeantson and Clare Jackson (www. trin.cam.ac.uk/rws1001/utopia/bibliog.html).

Index†

† "Suggestions for Further Reading" is not indexed; "Criticism" is indexed lightly.